11/24

$15,—

OLD BREED GENERAL

OLD BREED GENERAL

HOW MARINE CORPS GENERAL WILLIAM H. RUPERTUS BROKE THE BACK OF THE JAPANESE IN WORLD WAR II FROM GUADALCANAL TO PELELIU

AMY RUPERTUS PEACOCK AND DON BROWN

STACKPOLE
BOOKS

Guilford, Connecticut
Blue Ridge Summit, Pennsylvania

STACKPOLE BOOKS

An imprint of Globe Pequot, the trade division of
The Rowman & Littlefield Publishing Group, Inc.
4501 Forbes Blvd., Ste. 200
Lanham, MD 20706
www.rowman.com

Distributed by NATIONAL BOOK NETWORK

British Library Cataloguing in Publication Information available

Library of Congress Cataloging-in-Publication Data
Names: Peacock, Amy Rupertus, 1970– author. | Brown, Don, 1960– author.
Title: Old breed general : how Marine Corps General William H. Rupertus broke the back of the
    Japanese in World War II from Guadalcanal to Peleliu / Amy Rupertus Peacock and Don Brown.
Other titles: How Marine Corps General William H. Rupertus broke the back of the Japanese in
    World War II from Guadalcanal to Peleliu
Description: Guilford, Connecticut : Stackpole Books, [2021] | Includes bibliographical references.
    | Summary: "This book is the biography of Marine General William Rupertus, who led his troops
    in a series of blistering battles in the Pacific that paved the way for the ultimate American victory
    there. This is an American story of love, loss, shock, horror, tragedy, and triumph that focuses on
    Rupertus and the 1st Marine Division in World War II"— Provided by publisher.
Identifiers: LCCN 2021027493 (print) | LCCN 2021027494 (ebook) | ISBN
    9780811770347 (cloth) | ISBN 9780811770354 (epub)
Subjects: LCSH: Rupertus, W. H. (William Henry), 1889–1945 | United States. Marine Corps.
    Marine Division, 1st—History—20th century. | Generals—United States—Biography. | United
    States. Marine Corps—Biography. | Marines—United States—Biography. | World War,
    1939–1945—Campaigns—Pacific Area. | World War, 1939–1945—Regimental histories—
    United States.
Classification: LCC D769.37 1st .R87 2021 (print) | LCC D769.37 1st
    (ebook) | DDC 355.0092 [B]—dc23
LC record available at https://lccn.loc.gov/2021027493
LC ebook record available at https://lccn.loc.gov/2021027494

♾™ The paper used in this publication meets the minimum requirements of American National
Standard for Information Sciences—Permanence of Paper for Printed Library Materials, ANSI/
NISO Z39.48-1992.

To Patrick Hill Rupertus
Captain, United States Marine Corps
August 18, 1939–March 6, 1991

My Rifle

The Creed of a United States Marine
By Major General William H. Rupertus, USMC
Published March 13, 1942, in *Marine Corps Chevron*

This is my rifle. There are many like it, but this one is mine.
My rifle is my best friend. It is my life. I must master it as
I must master my life.
My rifle, without me, is useless. Without my rifle, I am useless. I must
fire my rifle true. I must shoot straighter than my enemy who is trying
to kill me. I must shoot him before he shoots me. I will . . .
My rifle and myself know that what counts in war is not the rounds
we fire, the noise of our burst, nor the smoke we make. We know
that it is the hits that count. We will hit . . .
My rifle is human, even as I, because it is my life. Thus, I will learn it as a
brother. I will learn its weaknesses, its strength, its parts, its accessories, its
sights and its barrel. I will ever guard it against the ravages of weather and
damage as I will ever guard my legs, my arms, my eyes, and my heart against
damage. I will keep my rifle clean and ready, even as I am clean and ready.
We will become part of each other. We will . . .
Before God, I swear this creed. My rifle and myself are the
defenders of my country. We are the masters of our enemy.
We are the saviors of my life.
So be it, until victory is America's and there is no enemy, but peace!

Contents

Contents

Introduction

HE LED AMERICA'S FIRST GROUND VICTORY AGAINST THE JAPANESE IN THE Pacific, at Tulagi Island; commanded the 1st Marine Division in the Pacific War longer than any other general; commanded the United States' first amphibious attack in World War II; personally escorted the First Lady of the United States on her wartime trip to Melbourne, Australia; wrote the famed Marine Corps "Rifleman's Creed"; and had a destroyer, the USS *Rupertus*, DD-851, named in his honor.

Yet no biographical account has been written about Major General William Rupertus and his time as one of America's great wartime commanders in the Pacific—until now.

This book features a "literary nonfiction" style. Dialogue is provided throughout to supplement the great historical points telling the general's story commanding the famed 1st Marine Division, known as "the Old Breed."

Although dialogue ties this story together in an action-packed manner, we also include direct quotations from General Rupertus's wartime diary, showing his notes contemporaneously with the events. Rupertus's journal and his personal war correspondence provide our most accurate and authentic information source, never before publicly revealed until the publication of this book.

Rupertus commanded four great victories in World War II, including (1) the first American victory at Tulagi, (2) the final major land battle at Guadalcanal, (3) the Battle of Cape Gloucester, and (4) the Battle of Peleliu.

To our knowledge, until this book's publication, no other book has ever given significant details on the Battle of Tulagi Island, which is surprising, because Tulagi was America's first ground war victory against the Japanese in the Pacific.

One notation should be made concerning Guadalcanal's final major land battle and the island's bloodiest battle, called the "Battle for Henderson Field," which was featured partially in HBO's miniseries *The Pacific*, highlighting the heroic exploits of Medal of Honor winner Sergeant John Basilone.

Several histories recount this battle, which lasted over three days, from October 23 to October 25, 1942. All historical accounts agree on one essential point: Major General Alexander Vandegrift, then the commander of the 1st Marine Division, before later becoming commandant of the Marine Corps in 1944, left Guadalcanal on October 23 with Commandant Holcomb to fly to New Caledonia for talks with Admiral Halsey.

Before Vandegrift left, he brought his assistant division commander, Brigadier General Rupertus, to Guadalcanal from nearby Tulagi to assume command in his absence. On this point, all historical accounts agree.

Because some biographies were written six decades after the fact, along with oral histories that suffer from fading memories, recollections can differ. One work, published in 2002, sixty years after the battle, correctly placed General Rupertus in command of ground forces when Vandegrift left for New Caledonia. But that author suggests that before Vandegrift left, Rupertus became afflicted with dengue fever, a mosquito-borne virus, and therefore could not carry out his command duties during the battle.

While it is true that Rupertus, like so many Marines on Guadalcanal, suffered at times from mosquito-borne dengue fever, the most accurate historical evidence shows Rupertus remained in command during the Battle for Henderson Field. This fact is revealed in another fine book that we recommend, *No Bended Knee: The Battle for Guadalcanal*, an autobiographical account written by General Merrill Twining, who at Guadalcanal was a lieutenant colonel and served as Vandegrift's operations officer during the battle.

As operations officer, Twining took direct orders from the commanding general and relayed those orders to subordinates in the field like Lieutenant Colonels Chesty Puller, Herman Hanneken, and others. In the best position of any Marine to know who was in command, because he took orders directly from the commander, Twining shows Rupertus actively in command during the Battle for Henderson Field, in Vandegrift's absence.

In addition to Twining's fine autobiography, Rupertus's command of the battle is supported not only by official US Marine Corps and Navy records but also in the extensive, authoritative work titled *Pearl Harbor to Guadalcanal: History of U.S. Marine Corps Operations in World War II, Volume I*, by Lieutenant Colonel Frank O. Hough, USMCR, Major Verle E. Ludwig, USMC, and Henry I. Shaw Jr.

Beyond all that, General Rupertus, in his wartime diary, which he kept each day of battle, corroborates Twining's account. The war diary shows details of Rupertus commanding the battle, leaving no doubt about the active chain of command during the fight. Rupertus's detailed diary keeps exact timelines of the events and commands surrounding the battle, and it aligns with the record of events by Twining and official USMC records.

On October 27, 1942, once the battle ended, Rupertus returned to Tulagi to recover from dengue fever, as recorded in his battle diary and 1st Marine Division Record of Events. Before that, he remained in command for the Battle for Henderson Field. Based on the best historical evidence, any contradictory account marks a mistake in recollection. In fairness, no other authors have had access to General Rupertus's war diary, and so excerpts from the diary have not been publicly revealed until publication of this book.

Before World War II, Rupertus served with the China Marines during two stints in the 1920s and 1930s, where he witnessed the brutal Japanese bombing and slaughter of two hundred thousand Chinese military and civilians in Shanghai in 1937. Rupertus knew the Japanese enemy as well as (if not better than) any senior officer in the American military.

Our historical research for this work is based on numerous official US Navy and Marine Corps records and other archival sources recounting the Marines' invasion of the Solomon Islands, Cape Gloucester, and Peleliu, as well as the Rupertus family's extensive private collection. That collection includes not only the general's war diary and personal writings revealing his account of the war but also numerous letters, photographs, notes, and articles from wartime leaders such as MacArthur, Nimitz, Vandegrift, and Eleanor Roosevelt.

A final important note: During the war, phrases such as "Japs" and other terms that are now considered derogatory were commonly used in the heated passion of the era. The inclusion of those terms in this book is not meant to slur our Japanese friends and allies, who today stand with the United States, but rather to reflect the historical authenticity of those times.

We hope you will find this story enjoyable, and we especially hope we have done justice to the general and the great men serving under his command.

Semper Fi.

—Amy Rupertus Peacock and Don Brown

Prologue

WAR FEVER.

Like a great tsunami flooding a vulnerable beach, a red-hot dose of angry war fever flowed through America's veins at the beginning of 1942.

Images of the American fleet smoldering at Pearl Harbor, with 2,300 Americans killed in one fell swoop, ignited a fire throughout the country that would not be extinguished.

Following Pearl Harbor, another unforgettable image emerged: Americans standing in lines. All over the country, long lines snaked hundreds of yards in front of military recruiting stations. The lines formed at dawn in the days following Pearl Harbor, with thousands of young men all around the country, many standing in the cold, anxious to take vengeance on Japan.

Like no other time in American history, Americans primed themselves for war. But war fever exceeded America's ability to prosecute a war.

January 1, 1942.

Three weeks had passed since Pearl Harbor. In the rumored words of the great Japanese admiral Isoroku Yamamoto, the man who orchestrated the attack, Japan had "awakened a sleeping giant."

On this New Year's Day, with the nation at war, the US government banned new car sales, mustering steel to produce ships, tanks, and other military weapons.

Despite America's industrial potential, a decade of unpreparedness left the United States far behind her adversaries in Berlin and Tokyo.

And while Congress declared war on Japan, Germany, and Italy the day after Pearl Harbor, President Franklin Roosevelt's two-front strategy, in practical application, would devolve into first winning the war in Europe and then later finishing off Japan.

The US Army's greatest fighting generals—Dwight Eisenhower, George S. Patton Jr., Matthew Ridgway, Mark Clark, and Omar Bradley—were all dispatched to Europe, with one exception. Roosevelt ordered the great Douglas MacArthur to the Pacific to establish the army's Pacific Military Command in the Philippines.

But for MacArthur, America's Pacific campaign quickly turned disastrous.

As the Japanese tightened the noose around American and Filipino forces, President Roosevelt ordered MacArthur to flee from the Philippines.

The American military's immediate goals in the Pacific devolved into (1) stop the bleeding, (2) save General MacArthur, and (3) mount a counteroffensive against the Japanese.

On March 11, 1942, with the help of the US Navy, MacArthur and his party escaped on four US Navy PT boats, slicing through the rough waters of the Philippine Sea, playing hide-and-seek with the Imperial Japanese Navy, which controlled all the waters around the Philippine Islands with its naval blockade. MacArthur's capture or death would mean a major symbolic and tactical victory for Japan. That could not happen.

The responsibility of extricating MacArthur fell on Navy Lieutenant (JG) John D. Bulkeley, who commanded a small, fast-moving PT boat flotilla. With MacArthur and his family aboard, Bulkeley's boats dodged Japanese warships and submarines. They zigzagged through rough, dangerous waters, navigating from Corregidor to the southern tip of the Philippines to Mindanao, which remained under Allied control.

At Mindanao, MacArthur and his family and staff boarded a B-17 bound for Australia. On March 21, MacArthur arrived in Melbourne, where, having been run off by the Japs, he made his immortal "I shall return" speech to the people of the Philippines.

On April 9, 1942, with MacArthur secluded in Australia, Major General Edward King, defying MacArthur's orders, surrendered more than seventy-five thousand US and Filipino forces to the Japanese. Bataan marked the most significant American defeat in World War II and the largest troop surrender in American military history, triggering the brutal Bataan Death March.

From Pearl Harbor to the American surrender at Bataan, the Pacific situation worsened. Aside from Doolittle's symbolic victory in the airstrike against Tokyo, which killed about fifty Japanese on April 18, the Pacific war heavily favored the Japanese. In early 1942, the Japanese sliced through large swathes of the Pacific. The Japanese were dominating, and America needed a win.

With MacArthur sidelined in the Philippines, the US Navy and Marine Corps, led by Admiral Chester Nimitz as commander-in-chief of the Pacific Theater, would prosecute the bulk of the Pacific War until the army finished the job in Europe.

The disastrous military situation in the Pacific weighed upon the US Marine Corps' senior officers, including Brigadier General William H. Rupertus. Soon Rupertus would take command of the 1st Marine Division in the Pacific. But first, the division would have to be formed and made ready for battle.

As 1941 turned to 1942, Rupertus possessed a significant advantage over most officers in the US military. He had twice seen the Japanese, up close and personal.

During Rupertus's time in China, Chiang Kai-shek had unified his nationalist forces to try and suppress the Communist rebellion. At the same time, the Japanese showed increasing belligerency within China.

Rupertus's first tour to Peking, from 1929 to 1932, ended with greater personal hardship than any military encounter with America's future enemy. In Peking, Rupertus lost his first wife and two children to scarlet fever. Rupertus nearly died himself from the fever and remained quarantined in a Peking hospital as the Marine Corps shipped his family's bodies back to America for burial.

In the spring of 1937, as America struggled through the last years of the Great Depression, the Marine Corps again sent Rupertus to China, this time to Shanghai. Now a lieutenant colonel, Rupertus would return to the 4th Marines to command the Marine detachment guarding American interests in the International Settlement. Like his earlier tour in Peking, the Shanghai

4th Marines officers of the Peking Legation. (USMC PHOTO)

tour started as an accompanied tour, as Marine officers were allowed to bring their wives and families.

From April 20, 1937, when they arrived in China aboard USS *President Polk*, Shanghai proved to be an enchanting duty station through the rest of the spring and summer, at least for "Sleepy," Rupertus's second wife. The city offered unmatched oriental beauty and cultural richness.

Yes, the Japanese had invaded Manchuria six years earlier, in 1931, and still maintained an occupation force there. But Manchuria stood a long way from Shanghai, and though in 1932 the Japanese bombed Chapei, a suburb of Shanghai, killing one thousand civilians, Lieutenant Colonel Rupertus hoped that Japanese belligerency had ended.

But on August 13, 1937, Japanese tanks, artillery, and infantrymen rolled into Shanghai to begin one of the bloodiest occupations in world history. All American dependents, including Sleepy, were ordered to evacuate. But Rupertus and his China Marines stayed behind to guard the American sector of the International Settlement, where, from the front lines, they witnessed incredible Japanese savagery.

Americans paid little attention to China until October 1937, when on October 4 *Life* published a black-and-white photograph showing a Chinese

On the USS *Polk* with fellow Marine friends, the Masters and Krulaks.

Photo by H. S. Wong taken on "Bloody Saturday." Shanghai, China, August 28, 1937.

baby in the bombed-out remnants of the South Shanghai railway station. The unidentified baby sat alone on the tracks, crying. The child's mother lay dead nearby, killed by bombs dropped on the city by Japan. The photograph became known as "Bloody Saturday," and by the end of October 1937, in an era long before the internet, 136 million people worldwide had seen the photo.

The photo ignited outrage against Japan, but it marked only a small example of the carnage witnessed by Rupertus and his men every single day in Shanghai.

During three months in 1937, from August 13 to November 26, the Japanese slaughtered 200,000 Chinese in Shanghai alone. At the time the world's sixth-largest city, an international trade center before the attack, it was reduced to a massive ruin.

For perspective, this massive military slaughter in the late summer and early fall of 1937 came four years before Japan attacked Pearl Harbor. In one city alone, Shanghai, Japan killed half the number of people (200,000) that America would later lose (405,000) over four years in World War II. Historians estimate that more than twelve million, possibly up to twenty million, Chinese died at the hands of the brutal Japanese.

Four years after Shanghai, in late 1941 and into 1942, Japan turned its full military might against the United States. After Pearl Harbor, and after the Philippines' fall and Allied naval defeats at the Battle of Java Sea, the Japanese were winning the war in the Pacific.

Now William Rupertus received a new assignment: not to China, but to the South Pacific, to eventually command the 1st Marine Division, which he would command longer than any other general in the war, and defeat the Japanese in the hot, muggy, mosquito-ridden, malaria-infested islands north of Australia.

First, however, his new assignment in March 1942 was to help his friend General Alexander Vandegrift form and train the 1st Marine Division before leading them in the Pacific. They would soon be in the Pacific by June and in battle by August.

Rupertus and his Marines would stand as a fighting wall between the Japanese advance and the Australian mainland, where General MacArthur and his staff had retreated to avoid capture.

The consequences were dire. Rupertus knew Japanese capabilities. He knew that he and his Marines must defeat them on the ground in the South Pacific islands to win the war.

American victory or American defeat in the Pacific hung in the balance.

Old Breed General tells an immortal story of love, tragedy, family, and honor, encapsulating the true American spirit of William Rupertus, the kind of spirit that made America the greatest superpower in world history.

Chapter 1

The South Pacific
US Naval Task Force (Task Force TARE)
Course 360 Degrees (Course Due North)
On Approach to the Solomon Islands (40 Miles SW of Guadalcanal)
August 6, 1942
2200 Hours

They moved seamlessly through the ocean, cutting a course to the north, through the dark waters of the South Pacific. There were eighty of them altogether, a massive American naval armada that somehow had avoided destruction at Pearl Harbor. They steamed on a secret mission, with the fate of the war—and of the world—in the balance.

Visibility remained poor across the sea. If they could have seen through the clouds above, for many of them, tonight would mark the last night they would view the heavens displayed in their glory above the Earth.

These were the men of the 1st Marine Division. If the troop transport ships carrying them were lucky enough to avoid being torpedoed by a Japanese submarine lurking below the surface, tomorrow they would face the Japanese army's fury.

Of course, the Japs would also get their version of hell, US Marine Corps style. Only one thing remained certain: Some would never come home.

On board the lead transport ship, the USS *Neville*, the Marines ordered to the tip of the American spear twisted in their racks. A few got some shut-eye. Many could not sleep. These Marines would be the first Americans to fire weapons against the Japanese in America's island-hopping campaign to retake the South Pacific.

Tomorrow would mark D-Day of "Operation Watchtower," launching America's invasion of the Solomon Islands.

So far the Japanese had dominated the US Army on the ground. The army's stunning defeat in the Philippines, driving General MacArthur's retreat to Australia, marked one of America's greatest military defeats.

Since Pearl Harbor, Japan had conquered the Philippines, Thailand, Malaysia, Singapore, the Dutch East Indies, Wake Island, and New Britain.

The Japanese were flushed with victory, as Allied losses mounted. The losses had to end, or America could lose the war.

In the command spaces aboard the *Neville*, Brigadier General William Rupertus, 1st Marine Division assistant commander and the man leading the first wave into battle, replayed the battle plans in his mind. His naval task force, code-named "Squadron Yoke," would steam north through the South Pacific, north of Australia, on a course just west of Guadalcanal.

Sometime around 2230 hours local time, the ships of Squadron Yoke and its sister task force, "Squadron X-Ray," would execute a course correction in the water to the northeast. From there they would steam past the east end of Guadalcanal, destined for a sunrise attack against three islands north of Guadalcanal: Tulagi, Gavutu, and Florida. Like angry hornets swarming a hive, Japanese infantry infested those islands with military airfields capable of sinking the invasion fleet.

America had called on Rupertus and his Marines to reverse the ground war in the Pacific, break the Japs' backs, and push them back to Tokyo. That began in the Solomon Islands, with the large airfield being built by the Japanese on Guadalcanal as their target. But before attacking Guadalcanal, they first had to attack and neutralize Tulagi and Gavutu.

For these Marines, their war started at sunrise. America needed victory on the ground. It started with them. They all knew it.

Rupertus, the second-highest-ranking Marine in the entire task force, served under the 1st Marine Division commander, Major General Alexander Vandegrift. Rupertus and Vandegrift had spent the spring in New River, North Carolina, assembling the newly formed 1st Marine Division and training them to fight.

As they planned for the Pacific, Vandegrift tabbed Rupertus to command the Marines' first offensive against Japan on Tulagi and Gavutu Islands before launching against Guadalcanal. Over 1,300 miles to the south, behind the ships' churning propellers, across the dark waters of the Coral Sea, General Douglas MacArthur, holed up in his headquarters in Brisbane, awaited news from the naval/Marine task force.

Above and beyond Vandegrift, Nimitz, and MacArthur, the entire senior American military command, including President Roosevelt, would be watching the Marines' performance.

The American strategy for conquering the Pacific would start with Tulagi, the former British colonial capital in the Solomon Islands, and then quickly pivot to Guadalcanal.

Solomons Island, Maryland, April 1942. Review of the 1st Marine Division's amphibious training with Brigadier General DeValle, Secretary of the Navy Frank Knox, Marine Commandant Holcomb, and Brigadier General Rupertus. (USMC PHOTO)

General Rupertus with Secretary Knox. (USMC PHOTO)

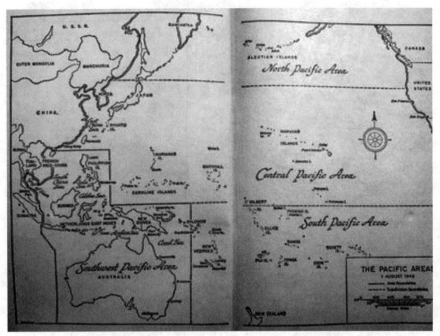

Map from *Once a Marine: The Memoirs of General A. A. Vandegrift* by Robert Asprey.

From there, after defeating the Japanese in the western Solomons, the 1st Marine Division would cross the ocean in navy ships, moving north and west, attacking island after island, tightening the noose around Japan's neck and moving closer to the enemy before the final, bloody invasion of the Japanese homeland.

But first America needed victory against the Japs somewhere on the ground.

The Marine Corps chose Bill Rupertus, fifty-two years old, fit with blue eyes, a square jaw, and the wrinkles of a warrior, to spearhead the first attack. But why Rupertus? Why not someone else?

Perhaps his broad experience? Perhaps his service in World War I and Haiti in the Banana Wars? Perhaps because he authored the famed "Rifleman's Creed" right after Pearl Harbor, recited by every Marine in boot camp and memorized by all Marines going into battle?

Perhaps because of his time with the China Marines in Peking from 1928 to 1931, when he lost his wife and two children to scarlet fever, and then Shanghai in 1937 and 1938, which gave him an up-close-and-personal look at the Japanese enemy.

He never forgot his time in Shanghai, where, day after day, his Marines guarded their three-and-a-half-mile-long sector while watching the Chinese and Japanese battle before their eyes. They stood firm along the barriers but were ordered to hold fire.

They witnessed death and destruction, were taunted by Japanese soldiers, and were under constant stray gunfire. Rupertus and his men saw brave volunteers from the Shanghai Municipal Force scurrying into the streets to remove the bodies and connect missing families during lulls in the bombing.

No matter the reason for being selected, Rupertus and his men were ready.

As war drums thumped in the distance, growing louder by the moment across the waters, and as the task force closed in on the Solomons, thoughts of family surfaced.

The thing about going into battle, or even sailing through enemy waters where a single torpedo could take out an entire ship, is that you never know

Rupertus and officers of the 4th Marines, International Settlement, Shanghai, China, August 1937.

Rupertus and his wife, Sleepy, with Marine officers and wives, survey damage after the Japanese bombing of Shanghai.

Damaged buildings in Shanghai.

whether you will see your family again. Sleepy, his second wife and more than twenty years his junior, exuded energy, beauty, and charm. She became his life's love, stayed beside him through thick and thin, and restored him from the doldrums after his first family died.

Alice Hill Rupertus, known as "Sleepy" Rupertus.

Major Rupertus.

Alice Hill had earned the nickname "Sleepy" as a child and also as an adult, as her eyes could captivate and mesmerize a man into a "sleepy" trance in a palpitating instant. And she affected Rupertus that way, even now, separated by eight thousand miles and on the other side of the world.

Rupertus checked his watch. By now it was mid-morning back in Washington. He could see her, in his mind, sitting at home with her sisters, her shiny dark brown hair bouncing on her shoulders, her fair skin like a princess, her blue eyes like sparkling sapphires in the sun.

After he lost his first son and daughter, Sleepy gave him an unexpected new excitement for life when, on August 18, 1939, Patrick Hill Rupertus was born.

Rupertus holding his son, Patrick Hill Rupertus, in September 1939.

Little Patrick, an irrepressible energy ball, would be three years old on August 18. Rupertus had already lost one family. He couldn't bear never seeing Sleepy and Patrick again.

But he could not entertain those thoughts. The task before his Marines required focus on the mission alone. He checked his watch again. Ten hours to go. Ten hours to the beginning of bloodshed.

Ten hours until the beginning of victory.

Chapter 2

The South Pacific
Japanese Garrison
Tulagi Island (Solomon Islands)
August 6, 1942
2215 Hours

Commander Masaaki Suzuki looked out from his bunker, out over the ocean, out into the night. This close to the water, the warm nighttime breeze carried humidity from the tropical jungle. The lapping waves against the sand created a false serenity, about to be turned upside-down.

They were out there, the Americans. He knew it in his gut. Sooner or later, they would come. But when they came, he would be ready. And so would his men. The Solomons, starting with Tulagi, would not be lost for Japan.

In January 1942, Imperial Japanese Navy warplanes commenced bombing Tulagi around the clock, attacking the seat of the British government in the Solomons. Once the heart of the British Solomon Islands protectorate, Tulagi housed the British governor's mansion on the southeast side of the island, with a golf course and cricket field. The British had begun evacuating people in the spring.

On May 2, British intelligence discovered the Japanese planned to assault Tulagi. The following day, May 3, Japanese forces landed on Tulagi, unopposed, with a critical strategic mission: take over the Tulagi harbor and build airstrips on Guadalcanal for Japanese air forces.

With the defeat suffered by the Imperial Japanese Navy at the Battle of the Coral Sea and later at Midway, Japan lost four hundred carrier-based aircraft. These islands became more important than ever—strategic air bases to attack the US Navy and a staging area for the eventual invasion against Australia.

Lieutenant Commander Suzuki, who commanded all Japanese military forces on Tulagi, understood Tulagi's strategic importance. In taking command of Tulagi, Suzuki controlled a tropical strip of a humid, mosquito-infested jungle island, two miles long and a half mile wide. Hot, oppressive, windy, often under gray overcast skies during the day, Tulagi stood as a Pacific hellhole with one of the best harbors, to be held by Japan at all costs.

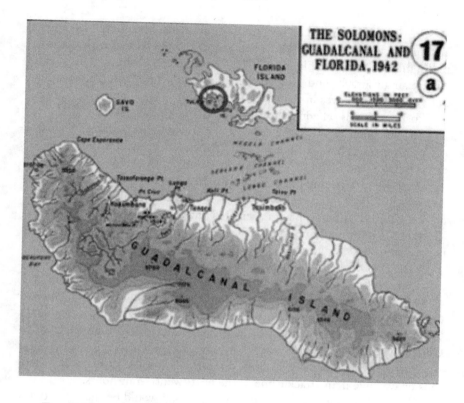

For the Japanese, controlling these islands gave them forward military airpower projection, needed now more than ever, after the US Navy sank four Japanese aircraft carriers at the Battle of Midway, June 4–7, 1942.

Until Japanese shipbuilders rebuilt those lost carriers, the emperor needed island-based airstrips throughout the Pacific. From here, the emperor's air forces could launch airstrikes against the American navy in the region and support Japanese invasion forces headed south to Australia.

Suzuki's men were ready for the task. They would fight to the death.

The crack forces under Suzuki's command were the Japanese equivalent of the US Marines. They had formed the unit in the city of Kure (thus bearing the name 3rd Kure SNLF, for Special Naval Land Forces), in the Hiroshima Prefecture, and home to the Kure Naval Base, Japan's largest naval port. The SNLF, known as "Rikusentai," like their US Marine adversaries, were trained to hit the beaches, hold the islands, and help build military airfields on the islands.

Suzuki arrived on Tulagi on July 15 by seaplane. He relieved Lieutenant Yoshimoto, who at age fifty-three had grown too old to deal with the inhumane, mosquito-infested living conditions on Tulagi. Yoshimoto also feared American air attacks and ordered the Rikusentai to excavate bunkers, dugouts, caverns, and caves in the island's lower end.

Yoshimoto was scheduled to leave the island on August 8.

The sheltered bunkers and caves could provide a formidable defense to the coming aerial bombardment by the Americans. But Suzuki redrew the entire out-of-date island defense plan devised by Yoshimoto.

As a military commander, Suzuki worried about numbers. The American invasion force could be larger than the Japanese defense force stationed on the island. His battle plan anticipated this disadvantage. So he ordered Warrant Officer Fukumoto to take the 4th Platoon and establish a defensive perimeter around the governmental wharf area.

Warrant Officer Takeo Ideka and his men stood guard at headquarters.

Warrant Officer Tsurusaburo Shigeta commanded the platoon and covered the sector between the old governor's residence and Sasapi. Warrant Officer Yoshiharu Muranika and his men defended the hospital area. Petty Officer Third Class Harubumi Ishada, with 2nd Squad, 2nd Platoon, guarded Chinatown.

Another thirty-eight men were dispatched to Guadalcanal Island and thus unavailable if an attack came in the next twenty-four hours.

The deadliest Japanese units defending Tulagi would be the 1st and 4th Platoons and a thirty-six-man platoon serving as a floater unit, meaning they could move to anywhere on the island at a moment's notice.

Also, the machine gun company of the Kure SNLF provided tremendous firepower. If the Americans showed up, they would face a death trap. Suzuki instructed Lieutenant Mitsuwa, whose men on Gavutu Island carried 13- and 25-millimeter machine guns, to fire at will when the Americans approached. Preferably, his warplanes would locate the invasion fleet and sink them before they arrived. But if not, he would kill them all. Everyone. From the highest-ranking American general to the lowest-ranking private. They would fight to the last man. His men would die serving the emperor.

Chapter 3

The South Pacific
US Naval Task Force (Task Force TARE)
Bridge, USS *Neville* (APA-9)
Course 360 Degrees (Course Due North)
On Approach to the Solomon Islands (40 Miles SW of Guadalcanal)
August 6, 1942
2233 Hours

Captain Carlos A. Bailey, commanding officer of USS *Neville*, checked the circular clock mounted on the gray bulkhead. Two minutes to course correction.

On *Neville*'s bridge, the night crew moved about with a silent, solemn purpose, steering the five-hundred-foot troop carrier through the calm waters of the South Pacific. Tonight's conditions proved more bearable than the rougher seas they had encountered as they steamed from Wellington on July 22.

Tonight the cloud cover had not yet broken, which prevents good visibility. In most cases, a mariner at night preferred calm seas and clear skies. But that cut both ways. While clear skies made nighttime navigation easier, if the skies remained clear in the morning, the task force would become an easy target for Japanese warplanes.

Bailey had served on active duty for thirty-one years since his graduation from the Naval Academy in 1911. He served on numerous warships in his career, as commanding officer of the USS *McKee*, USS *Hopkins*, and USS *Sturtevant* from July 1921 until December 1923.

The fifty-five-year-old Massachusetts native had served on eight different warships before taking command of the *Neville* in May 1941. A highly experienced naval officer, with extensive combat experience on battleships and cruisers, now commanding a troop transport ship seemed odd.

Wouldn't command of the USS *North Carolina*, the battleship protecting the entire task force, have made more sense?

Then it hit him.

Commanding a troop transport like the *Neville* now was one of the most important missions of the war. Below decks, the assistant division commander of the entire 1st Marine Division, Brigadier General William Rupertus, waited, along with the 1,150 Marines aboard who would spearhead America's initial ground offensive against the Japanese. Success depended on the general and his men arriving at their launch point on time. The navy chose one of its best sea captains to get the job done.

In some ways, Bailey and General Rupertus came from the same ilk. Both were over fifty. Both had given their lives to the military—Bailey to the navy and Rupertus to the Marines. Both had been eligible for retirement a decade earlier. Bailey would be sixty in less than five years. Yet, with their careers now in the twilight, they were called to save their best for last.

One significant difference separated them. Rupertus now had a star pinned on his collar. For Bailey, his dreams of becoming a rear admiral hung by a thread, fading with each passing day.

No matter. As a professional naval officer, Bailey embraced the ideal of duty, and that victory must always overshadow personal advancement. His duty tonight placed him upon a historical precipice, at a crucial hour for the United States. This moment stood as something few officers in naval history would ever experience.

Bailey looked out through the waters at the dark silhouettes of the other American warships surrounding his position.

The four troop transports, including the *Neville*, steamed north through the ocean, at the center of a concentric circle of warships, all guarding them from every direction. *Neville* steamed ahead of the four other ships in the transport group for "Task Force Yoke." At 507 feet in length and with a 56-foot beam, the lightly armed *Neville* bore four 50-caliber machine guns and several 40- and 20-millimeter anti-aircraft guns. At best, left alone, she could fend off a close-in strafing attack by enemy fighter planes. But she would become a sitting duck in the water against heavier naval armor—enemy battleships, cruisers, destroyers, and submarines. If she sank, she would sink fast, without enough lifeboats for the Marines below.

The American warships surrounding the *Neville*, armed with depth charges, torpedoes, and active sonar capabilities, provided maximum naval firepower to protect the Marine Division.

Bailey preferred his own firepower on board to protect his ship and attack the enemy. With Japanese submarines, destroyer escorts were sometimes fool's gold. Jap subs could pop up at any time and place.

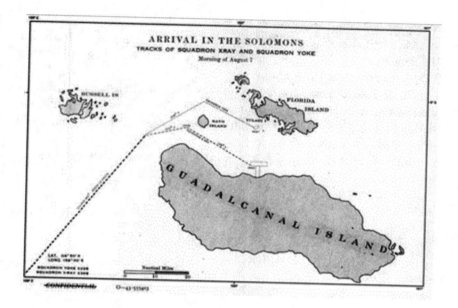

One torpedo from a sub slipping through the screen would spell disaster for thousands of Marines. Japanese aircraft could also drop deadly torpedoes, and the Japs had a seaplane base on Tanambogo and Gavutu, just east of Tulagi.

So far, *Neville's* sonar room reported no contact with enemy subs. Prayers answered for now. Bailey glanced at the navigation chart as they approached the course correction point.

They were now forty nautical miles southwest of Guadalcanal. "Task Force X-Ray," the second naval task force, which carried General Vandegrift, who would lead the main assault on Guadalcanal, steamed behind them, about one hour to their rear.

Bailey glanced at the clock again: 2234 hours, local.

"Helmsman. Stand by for course correction to zero-four-zero degrees."

"Aye, Captain. Standing by for course correction to zero-four-zero degrees."

Bailey waited another thirty seconds as the second hand swept from the nine o'clock position to the twelve position.

2235 hours, local.

"Helmsman. Make your course zero-four-zero degrees. Steady as she goes."

"Aye, sir. Making my course zero-four-zero degrees."

Moments later, Bailey felt his ship turning in the water, to the starboard. He glanced at the clock again. The next course change would come just after 0300, about three and a half hours from now.

Down below, America's finest fighting force, lead elements of the 1st Marine Division, crammed like sardines in a tight can in the ship's small berthing spaces, tried to rest. The Marines would need all the rest they could get. And so would his crew.

Bailey headed down to the captain's quarters for some shut-eye.

Chapter 4

IJN Japanese Navy Surveillance Aircraft
The South Pacific
25 Nautical Miles West of Savo Island
Altitude 500 Feet
August 6, 1942
2300 Hours

The long-range reconnaissance seaplane, which the American pilots had nicknamed the "Mavis," the largest and most used seaplane in the Imperial Japanese Navy, flew from its forward base on Tanambogo Island, off Tulagi's east coast. With two pontoons for water landings, and four Mitsubishi Kinsei 43 engines sitting atop a 130-foot wingspan, the large plane carried three crew members. It also carried 1,700-pound torpedoes, each with enough firepower to sink or damage any ship in the US Navy.

The plane's reconnaissance capabilities were stellar. With a 2,500-mile range, the Mavis could stay aloft for hours, giving it extended search and targeting capabilities.

Tonight, Captain Shigetoshi Miyazaki sat at the controls behind the cockpit. Miyazaki, commanding the seaplane-equipped Yokohama Air Group, was stationed on Gavutu and Tanambogo, commanded by Commander Masaaki Suzuki, Japanese commander on Tulagi. Miyazaki and his airmen had scoured the ocean for remnants of the American fleet that escaped Pearl Harbor and could threaten Japanese bases at Guadalcanal and Tulagi.

If Miyazaki got a clear shot, he would sink at least one of the American ships, possibly more.

But tonight, the weather made search conditions difficult. He climbed down below the lower cloud cover for a look at the ocean. Every time he went down through the clouds and then climbed back up, the aircraft took a beating from the turbulence. When he got down low enough to see the ocean, barely five hundred feet above the surface, the low altitude meant limited visibility.

If the American fleet was under that cloud cover, they might get lucky again, like at Midway. The American navy might prove to be a problem for the Japanese defenses on the islands. But if Miyazaki and his men found the fleet, the Americans' luck would have run out.

Miyazaki checked the fuel gauge. Only thirty minutes left of flying time, just enough fuel to duck below the cloud cover for one final sweep before returning to base.

But no matter. He intended to have his planes up in the morning, searching, if the weather permitted. If the Americans were down there, either tonight or tomorrow, Miyazaki and his men would find them and sink them.

Chapter 5

The South Pacific
USS *Neville* (APA-9)
Course 040 Degrees
On Approach to the Solomon Islands (Nearing Guadalcanal)
August 7, 1942
0130 Hours Local Time

The roar of *Neville*'s engines droned on through the night. As the clock swept past midnight, General Rupertus tried to sleep, but that wasn't happening. Not tonight.

The heaviest load in battle always fell on the commander's shoulders. The commander had to consider everything—before, during, and after the battle. Lives depended on him, and his Marines' lives would depend on his decisions both tonight and in the morning.

The midnight hour had arrived for the ships steaming through the waters toward the Solomon Islands. It was now D-Day, Friday morning, August 7, 1942, the day of their attack on Tulagi.

Within the next eight hours, his Marines, the men with him aboard this ship, would see their first action. They would launch a bloody counteroffensive against the Japs in these islands after sunrise.

As he replayed the battle plans in his mind, he could not stop thinking about Sleepy and Patrick back home in DC. He often did mental calculations, wondering what they were doing in real time.

Under normal circumstances, a sixteen-hour time gap separated the Solomon Islands and Washington, DC. But in 1942, the United States had adopted Daylight Saving Time for the entire year to accommodate the war effort.

Just west of the International Date Line, the adjusted fifteen-hour time gap put Bill and his Marines one day ahead of Sleepy, little Patrick, and everybody else on the East Coast of the United States.

Sleepy was a great Marine Corps wife, especially considering the rampant death, carnage, and war they had endured together during their time in Shanghai. Although twenty-two years his junior, she displayed wisdom,

Admiral Harry Yarnell, USN, greeting Sleepy and Colonel Bill Rupertus at the French Club, Shanghai, China.

Rupertus, Sleepy, and Doris Masters (far right) at the French Club, Shanghai.

toughness, and maturity beyond her years, the product of growing up as a naval officer's daughter. The cream of the crop at all military, political, and social functions in Washington, she gave Bill a renewed purpose—a purpose he lost after losing his first family.

He decided to go up top, to the deck, for some fresh ocean air.

He checked his watch: 0130 hours local time, Friday, August 7, and just past 1030 hours, Thursday, August 6, in Washington, DC. Sleepy would be up, with Patrick running around the house like a whirlwind. By now, she would have finished her morning coffee, chatted with her sister Jo, and scoured the paper for all the social events, ready to take Washington by storm.

When he stepped out onto the starboard passageway, into the night air, the cool sea breeze refreshed his face. He wanted to light a cigarette so bad he felt his veins screaming for a smoke. But the task force ships remained in a blackout on approach. Even flickering cigarette ashes might alert a Japanese patrol boat somewhere out at sea.

Bill leaned on the guardrails, absorbing the moment's serenity, the peace before naval gunfire would explode over the first morning light.

The crescent moon had not yet risen. But way off the ship's starboard, lit by the stars peeking through cracks in the cloud cover, Guadalcanal's dark outline appeared in the distance, its black, mountainous silhouette blocking the stars on the low eastern horizon. Somewhere off in those dark islands, the Japanese waited, their machine guns in place, their mortars and rockets ready for launch, their planes poised to sink American ships.

Rupertus knew the Japanese all too well. But for a second, he dismissed those thoughts. This moment's serenity would be short-lived, for sure, perhaps for the rest of the war. And the quiet, peaceful, black ocean night reminded him of another peaceful place, far away—Arlington Cemetery.

During his year spent commanding the Marine Barracks at 8th and I in Washington, he often visited Arlington Cemetery to sit at the graves of his first wife, Marguerite, and his children, William Jr. and Ann Rodney, all robbed from him by scarlet fever in China. Like the air at Arlington, tonight a strange, false peace filled the ocean air, calm with a fictitious promise that he would see them again in this lifetime.

The peace over these darkened waters was the respite before the shedding of blood.

The past two years had been a blurry rush. On September 18, 1940, just twenty-three months earlier, he had boarded USS *McCarley* at Norfolk, bound for Guantanamo Bay, to take command of the Marine Barracks at the

William H. Rupertus Jr. and his sister, Ann Rodney Rupertus.

Major Rupertus, Peking, China, 1930. (USMC PHOTO)

Garde d'Haiti Marine and government officials. Rupertus is on the right.

Naval Air Station and the 4th Defense Battalion. But "GTMO" wasn't his first Caribbean assignment.

In 1919, he had arrived at Port-au-Prince, Haiti, with the USMC 1st Provisional Brigade. He and his Marines trained the national police force, the "Garde d'Haiti," which later became a significant political force.

Like the Haiti tour, when he took his first wife, Rita, on the Guantanamo assignment, his new wife, Sleepy, and infant son Pat could accompany him. He never knew whether irony, coincidence, or fate placed both his first wife and then his second wife with him first in China and then in the Caribbean.

Sleepy and Pat, who had just turned fifteen months old, arrived at Guantanamo, joining her friend Doris Masters and Doris's toddler "Champ." Doris and her husband, First Lieutenant James Masters, were also stationed at GTMO.

He loved holding Sleepy in his arms and bouncing Patrick on his knee. But the memory of losing Rita, Ann Rodney, and William Jr. on an overseas tour constantly haunted him. True, Guantanamo sat 518 miles off Miami, much closer to home than China. But Guantanamo Bay also sat amid a foreign country.

If fate had brought them together again, Bill didn't want to tempt it. Sleepy fell into a dangerous situation in Shanghai, and in Cuba he had watched Sleepy and Patrick like a hawk. Their time at GTMO marked the best months of their marriage. But less than a year later, orders came to leave Guantanamo Bay and proceed to San Diego by the end of November 1941.

The life of a Marine, owned by the Corps and country. And Rupertus loved it.

In San Diego, he became chief of staff to the commanding general, Major General William P. Upshur, a Marine legend, Medal of Honor winner, and longtime friend of General Vandegrift and Commandant Holcomb. Holcomb recommended Rupertus to Upshur and asked Upshur to prepare Rupertus to take command. He looked forward to working for General Upshur, who was seven years his senior.

But when the Japs bombed Pearl Harbor, they ordered General Upshur to San Francisco and gave Rupertus command of the Marines in San Diego, where thousands of American boys flooded into the Marine Corps, eager to avenge over two thousand Americans killed on December 7. Between December 8 and January 1, 1942, more than nine hundred recruits flooded into the Marine Corps Recruit Depot daily.

Seeing these young Marines pour into San Diego lit a fire in Rupertus to teach them how to defend themselves, considering the danger they faced, a danger far greater than they knew. Never had he seen people more barbarically determined to kill, maim, or destroy than the Japanese army had shown in Shanghai.

Dead Chinese bodies on Shanghai's streets—not just dead Chinese soldiers but also women and children—were burned into his memory. He never shook the powerful, putrid ammonia-like stench of death, which caused men to puke.

Bombing of Shanghai.

The Battle of Shanghai lasted from August 13 until November 26, 1937, becoming one of the bloodiest battles in world history.

The Chinese defended themselves mainly with small-caliber weapons. But strik-ing from the air, land, and sea, with heavy-armored vehicles,

Rupertus and Sleepy, Shanghai, 1937.

the Japanese, using superior force, killed some 187,000 Chinese in Shanghai alone and wounded another 85,000. This massacre happened over three months, one week, and six days.

Rupertus and his Marines witnessed the entire slaughter. Yet they were ordered to "hold your fire."

He still dreamed of Japanese tanks and aircraft blowing explosive holes through well-defended Chinese infantry lines and Jap ships shelling the Shanghai harbor, spraying geysers of red blood skyward.

Perhaps more than any other general officer in the US military, Rupertus knew what American forces faced if war came against the Japanese. America could defeat them, but at a high price.

The Marine Corps would need something to motivate them, a rallying cry, to get through possibly the most challenging time in American history. One day, as he thought of these young, new Marines, he picked up his smooth rifle, examined it, and remembered his years competing on the Marine Corps Rifle Team and later as an instructor. He began thinking about the right words that he, as their commanding general in San Diego, could say to motivate them.

From his experience in China with the Japanese, Rupertus knew the danger these Marines would face, and he knew that their rifles would protect them and ensure the success or failure of the mission.

He called Captain White, the base public relations officer, into his office. White sat down in front of Rupertus's desk, as Rupertus stood, walked around, and spoke about his concern for how casually his men approached their rifles. "The only weapon standing between them and death is the rifle . . . they must understand that their rifle is their life. It must become a creed with them."

Captain White suggested an editorial in the *Marine Corps Chevron* titled "My Rifle Is My Life." Rupertus, who had won the Distinguished Marks-manship Badge as a second lieutenant in 1915, liked the title but disagreed

☆ MARINE CORPS ☆
CHEVRON

PUBLISHED BY THE UNITED STATES MARINES IN THE SAN DIEGO AREA

| Vol. 1, No. 10 | Saturday Morning, March 14, 1942 | Page 1 |

THE OBSERVATION POST
By Li'l Spud

We Trun . . .
A bouquet of roses, this week, to those hard-working DI's of the recruit depot area. If'n youse guys don't think they put out for their monthly stipend, just follow them from 0430 in the morning till they're through at night—that'll be about taps—or after.

We Were . . .
Surprised to learn how few people in the service know what the ribbon worn to indicate possession of the Congressional Medal of Honor looks like. The gadget is a blue field interspersed with small white stars. We've noticed only one on the Base; it belongs to Captain Iams, of the Pay Office, who won it for conspicuous bravery in Haiti.

Harold (Who . . .
Hains to be called Harold) Quinn, of the Recruit Depot, is that fourth-cruise salt whom you see working with "Tex" Walters. Quinn spent so much time in China that he will invariably greet you with "Saidee fong chee?"

One Of . . .
The most energetic guys in the Marcon Corn is John Miller; you'll see him every night (if'n you go there every night) in a beer garden, clearing away empties. The following morning, assuming that you're up and about that early, he may be found on, of all things, a streamlined garbage truck. John's been trying to beat another fellow to his favorite "pickins" for weeks, but, as he puts it, "the early bird gets the worm and I ain't had a worm in years".

Let Us . . .
Repeat our request for more personal contact with all the men in the area. We know that you'd rather read about your buddies than some imporessed article but it is impossible for the staff members to get any of the dope we want if we're not tipped off from the outside. In other words, drop us a line or call on us in the office—we're glad to hear from you!

Just Received . . .
A very interesting letter from one of our old pals: First Sergeant Jimmie Bradley. Jimmie is currently recruiting in one of the northern states and if'n you guys want to write him let us know and you'll get his address. The state is so sparsely populated, says Bradley, that "The crows have to take on a heavy flying order for 'tween town flights to keep from starving to death!"

What With . . .
All the letters we're receiving from guys we wondered about, we're tickled pink—only thing that has us stymied is the answer to the missus. Would anyone like to do some cumshaw stenography?

Three Housing . . .
Bronx cheers to the obnoxious fellow Marine who replied to the Sergeant who told him to button up his blouse while he made himself noticed in one of the nicer nitespots, "I don't see why I should, you're not my Sergeant". We'd like to be his sergeant—for just a few minutes.

And "Nick" . . .
Nixon received a letter from a friend in the Navy. He brought the epistle to a close with "Knit one, Pearl Harbor!"

* Free.

Navy Lauds Marine Base Transport Personnel

Local Marine Corps Transport Men Cited

SURROUNDING MAJ. JAMES M. RANCK, Jr., Base Transport officer, are men of his command who were commended for salvaging a naval landing boat. Left to right are MarGun. C. A. Price, Cpl. R. Massey, MarGun. N. D. Kent, Lt. C. E. Dobson, Cpl. C. E. Ledford, Lt. R. G. Chambers, Cpl. R. C. Hall, MTSgt. C. Eschliman, Cpl. H. A. Greason and MTSgt. O. F. Niles. Eighteen Marines participated in the operation.

New Artillery Range Named For Marine Officer

Imperial Valley Practice Ground Honors Memory of Gen. Robert H. Dunlap

NILAND, CALIF.—Mar. 12—(Special to the Chevron)—This new artillery range has been officially named Camp Dunlap in honor of Brig. Gen. Robert Henry Dunlap, famed Marine Corps artillery officer.

PROMISING LEADER
Regarded by many as a probable future leader of the Marine Corps, Gen. Dunlap was killed by a landslide, May 19, 1931, while participating in rescue work at Cinq-Mars-La-Pile, France.

Gen. Dunlap began his active career in 1898 when he was appointed a second lieutenant in the U. S. Marine Corps at the age of 19. From that time until his death he served through the various ranks of the Marine Corps.

SAW DUTY
The officer saw active duty early in his career when he took active part in the Philippine Insurrection and the Boxer Rebellion. He participated in practically all of the Marine Corps expeditions to Spanish-American countries.

Although his main interests were in his regular duties as a Marine Corps infantry officer, he was considered an authority on artillery weapons. During the World War he commanded regiments of artillery.

He was born in the District of Columbia on December 22, 1879.

Order Voids All Expired Passes

All personal passes to enter the San Diego Marine Corps Base issued in 1941 became void Monday, 9 Mar. Those entitled to passes must renew same at the Base Intelligence office in the Administration building.

My Rifle

The Creed of a United States Marine

Suggested By

Brigadier General William H. Rupertus,
Commanding, The Marine Corps Base

1. This is MY rifle. There are many like it but this one is MINE.

2. MY rifle is MY best friend. It is MY life. I must master it as I must master MY life.

3. MY rifle, without me, is useless. Without MY rifle, I am useless. I must fire MY rifle true. I must shoot straighter than my enemy who is trying to kill me. I must shoot HIM before he shoots ME. I will . . .

4. MY rifle and myself know that what counts in this War is not the rounds we fire, the noise of our burst, nor the smoke we make. We know that it is the HITS that count. We will HIT . . .

5. MY rifle is human, even as I, because it is MY life. Thus, I will learn it as a brother. I will learn its weaknesses, its strength, its parts, its accessories, its sights and its barrel. I will ever guard it against the ravages of weather and damage as I will ever guard my legs, my arms, my eyes and my heart against damage. I will keep MY rifle clean and ready, even as I am clean and ready. We will become part of each other. We will . . .

6. Before God, I swear this creed. MY rifle and myself are the defenders of MY country. We are the masters of our enemy. We are the saviors of MY life.

7. So be it, until Victory is America's and there is no enemy, but peace!

Heroic Act Wins Praise

Navy Commends Marines For Fine Salvage Work

The Marines have landed! Not only did they land, but they did so at the request of the United States Navy, which realizes that when there's a difficult job to be done, the leathernecks can do it.

EIGHTEEN CITED
For their action in salvaging a valuable Navy landing boat, stranded on Coronado Island 12 Feb. 1942, six officers and 12 enlisted men of the San Diego Marine Corps Base received commendations this week from Capt. Frank A. Braisted, commander of Train Squadron Four of the United States Pacific Fleet.

CALL ON MARINES
Realizing that equipment was not capable of salvaging the boat, officials of the Navy called on the Marines who immediately responded in their true tradition.

Rushing to the scene of the wreck, Marines under the direction of Maj. James M. Ranck, Jr., Transportation Officer, set up their

(Continued on Page 5)

USMC Artists Eligible For LIFE Contest

Local Brush-Wielders Get Chance At Fame and Cash; Subjects Cover Corps Work

Marines who can wield a pencil or brush as deftly as they can a rifle are urged to enter LIFE Magazine's art competition for service men.

With prizes totaling $1,000, the contest closes May 4, and shortly after a select group of judges, are are outstanding American artists, will pick the winners.

OPEN TO ALL
Although open to all branches of the armed forces of the United States, Marines have been especially urged to submit their works. Subject matter must deal with some phase of training or combat in the Corps.

Selections will be made regardless of mediums which include oil, water color, gouache, pencil and other standards. Sculpture, cartoons or photographs will not be accepted.

SEND ENTRIES
Send all entries prepaid to: Pictorial Branch, Bureau of Public Relations, War Department, Washington, D. C., and label on the outside of the front "For LIFE Magazine Art Competition".

North Island Man Values Training

(NAVAL AIR STA., Mar. 12)—William (Bill) Foote, Marine at North Island, places a high value on his training.

When interviewed by a reporter from a San Diego newspaper, Bill said:

"I wouldn't take a million dollars for what I've got out of the service in the 19 months I have been a Marine. My brother is in the Navy, but I'll take the Marines any day."

The brothers' mother recently spent two weeks here on a visit from S. Paul, Minn.

with the idea of an editorial, which he thought might sound like a sermon. Instead, Rupertus advocated a rifleman's creed that should be "something so deep, a conviction so great, a faith so lasting, that no one should have to be preached to about it."

Rupertus penned a piece called "Creed of a US Marine" and gave it to Captain White, the magazine's new editor. White published it in the *Chevron*, and the article spread like wildfire. And thus the "Rifleman's Creed" was born.

Within a few short hours, his men, the first Marines going into combat, would be the first of thousands to recite it. By the grace of God, he hoped like hell it would save lives.

Bill closed his eyes and enjoyed the cool Pacific breeze caressing his face as the flotilla continued its course on its rendezvous with destiny. He looked out over the dark waters and checked his watch.

0133 hours.

Five hours to sunrise.

Five hours until he could light a cigarette.

Five hours until battle.

* * * * *

USS *McCawley* (APA-4)
Flagship, Task Force TARE
Squadron X-Ray
The South Pacific
Course 360 Degrees (Course Due North)
August 7, 1942
0224 Hours

The thin, waning crescent moon hanging over the watery horizon provided just enough light to reveal Savo Island's vague outline off in the distance, its volcanic peak rising some fifteen hundred feet above the water.

Savo Island, a twelve-square-mile volcanic pancake sitting in waters of the central Solomon Islands, would serve as the breakpoint for the two US Navy squadrons carrying the entire US 1st Marine Division.

US Navy Captain Charlie P. McFeaters, an Annapolis grad and Scottsdale, Pennsylvania, native, commanded the *McCawley*, which carried Rear Admiral Richmond K. "Kelly" Turner, who commanded the entire amphibious force, dubbed Task Force TARE. Turner was known for his grizzly head, beetling brows, and ferocious language.

As a navy captain and director of war plans in the Office of the Chief of Naval Operations, Turner had issued a written warning in November 1941 of an imminent Japanese attack against American forces. However, for reasons never explained, Turner never forwarded the intercepted Japanese radio messages of an impending Japanese attack against the Hawaiian Islands to Admiral Husband Kimmel, then US Pacific Fleet commander in chief.

The navy relieved Kimmel of command for reasons beyond his control and not his fault. They promoted Captain Turner to rear admiral, and he now commanded all US naval amphibious ships leading the assault on the Solomons.

Major General Alexander Vandegrift, commanding the 1st Marine Division, and 1,200 of his Marines joined Admiral Turner on the *McCawley*. For Vandegrift and his assistant division commander, Brigadier General Rupertus, aboard USS *Neville* steaming several miles to the north, and some 18,000 US Marines under their command, their job had not yet commenced. That would change in the next seven hours. Rupertus and his men would first attack Tulagi, and then Vandegrift and the rest of the division would attack Guadalcanal.

The strength of all the Marine units included 956 officers and 18,146 enlisted men.

As a young officer, Vandegrift had fought in three separate battles during the Banana Wars and at the Battle of Veracruz during the Mexican Revolution.

But now the pressure to succeed exceeded anything he had ever experienced. No one doubted that America would dominate its Latin American opponents. But Japan posed a different challenge. Except for the navy's great victory at Midway, the Japanese had so far dominated the war in the Pacific. That had to change, and it had to change now.

Vandegrift stepped onto the deck of the *McCawley*, brought his binoculars to his eyes, and gazed at the horizon. Six miles to the north, leading the way, the amphibious ships of Squadron Yoke, whose Marines were under the immediate command of Vandegrift's next-in-command, Brigadier General Bill Rupertus, would lead the ground attack at daybreak.

Rupertus began as Vandegrift's assistant division commander. In Vandegrift's estimation, he was the best damn commander in the whole Marine Corps to lead the initial American counterattack against the Japanese on the ground, which was why Vandegrift had hand-selected him for the job. Rupertus's resume made him look like a super Marine. First in his class at Command Staff College at Leavenworth, an expert rifleman and member of the Marine Corps Rifle Team, multilingual, and he knew the Japanese like the back of his hand from his two tours in China.

Rupertus needed to destroy the Japanese at Tulagi and Florida Island to clear the way for Vandegrift to move onshore at Guadalcanal. If any American general could kick the Japanese's collective asses for what they had done at Pearl Harbor, Bill Rupertus was that man.

Vandegrift's biggest worry at the moment? A Jap submarine slipping inside the navy's destroyer screen, firing torpedoes at the vulnerable transport ships carrying his Marines.

Infiltration by a single Jap sub could spell disaster.

Vandegrift commanded the Marines on board some fifteen US Navy transports, each crammed with young leathernecks, many still teenagers, all headed to Guadalcanal.

Rupertus commanded Marines on eight transports bound for Tulagi, designated Squadron Yoke, steaming out in front, six miles north of Vandegrift's ship.

Vandegrift's Marines would invade Guadalcanal once Rupertus hit Tulagi and got the Japanese there under control.

If the navy could keep the Japanese subs at bay for the next seven hours, those Japs on Tulagi and Guadalcanal would find out what it's like to look down the gun barrels of over eighteen thousand US Marines.

No commander could sleep in the hours before an attack, and so Vandegrift stepped out on the ship's deck for some fresh air.

"Beautiful night, isn't it, sir?"

Vandegrift turned and saw his chief of staff, Colonel Gerry Thomas.

"Feels better out here," Vandegrift said. "Breeze feels nice, if nothing else."

"How are you feeling, General?"

"Never better," Vandegrift said.

"Sir, why don't you try to get some sleep? I'll wake you with time to prepare."

Vandegrift gave Thomas a half grin. "Thanks, Gerry. But I won't sleep for the same reason you won't sleep. And I guarantee you General Rupertus isn't sleeping either. But thanks for the offer."

"Understood, sir," Thomas said.

"However, I do think I'll head to my quarters for a few minutes. Just a couple of personal things I need to take care of."

"Aye, sir. I'll hold the watch 'til you get back. If you need anything, just let me know."

"You're a good man, Gerry."

Vandegrift patted Thomas's shoulder and then headed down to his quarters. Even for the commanding general over the entire 1st Marine Division, the cramped crew quarters made movement difficult. Vandegrift pulled open the small metal drawer in the desk right beside his rack and pulled out a pen and pad.

> *My Dearest Mildred,*
> *Tomorrow at dawn, we land in our first major offensive in the war. Our plans have been made. May God grant that our judgment be sound. Whatever happens, you will know that I did my best. Let us hope that the best will be good enough.*
> *Love,*
> *Archer*

* * * * *

USS *Neville* (APA-9)
Squadron Yoke
The South Pacific
Course 360 Degrees (Course Due North)
August 7, 1942
0230 Hours

The weather had cleared, at least a little bit. The rain had stopped, and Bill Rupertus found himself out on the deck again, gazing at the stars through a few openings in the clouds. Tonight, Bill reflected on his Catholic faith, and the beautiful sky reminded him of the psalms he learned as a boy. "The heavens declare the glory of the Lord." Tonight, and tomorrow, and for the rest of the war, he would depend on his faith more than ever to protect his men in battle and to protect Sleepy and Pat back home.

Together, something about the stars and the sea, even mixed with the clouds, provided nature's peace more than any other combination.

Bill Rupertus loved the ocean—so much that after three years at the Washington, DC, National Guard, he started his military career in 1910 as a cadet in the US Revenue Cutter School, renamed the US Coast Guard Academy in 1913.

Rupertus had excelled at Revenue Cutter School, graduating second in his class with Frank Gorman, brother of his future first wife, Marguerite "Rita" Gorman. Rita Gorman lived in Washington, DC, where the two met as family friends, dated, and fell in love. Her father, Terrence, was deputy

US Revenue Cutter Class of 1913. Bill Rupertus kneeling, second row on far right.

customs commissioner for the US Treasury in Washington, DC. One thing led to another, and soon he proposed to Rita.

However, after graduation Bill faced a life-changing crossroads beyond his control. Despite having excelled among his classmates, the Revenue Cutter Service rejected him on medical grounds.

They called it "Bright's disease"—the name at the time for a severe kidney complication. Bright's disease would lead to heart failure, they claimed. They told him he had five years to live. He would still graduate. But the news stung, shattering his dream of becoming a Revenue Cutter Service officer.

But the disappointment did not deter his determination to marry his girlfriend and serve his country. With a degree from the prestigious Revenue Cutter School, he applied to the Marines, earned a commission as a second lieutenant, and went on to make history.

In the Marine Corps, he kept his love of the sea. But rather than commanding cutters, he now commanded men, which started back on the USS *Florida*.

Rupertus tried clearing his mind as he waited for the sunrise. Between the cracks in the clouds, above the cloud cover somewhere, a million bright stars stretched from horizon to horizon. And without the moonlight, the celestial panorama cast a false calm over the waters.

For the sailors aboard on watch, and the Marines unable to sleep, as the dawn drew closer, they saw that no place on Earth were the heavens so glorious than at sea.

For the Marines, although protected by the mighty firepower of three aircraft carriers, thirteen heavy cruisers, one battleship, and some twenty-two destroyers, every Marine on the troop transports would see bloodshed before the stars rose again.

Cadet Bill Rupertus, US Revenue Cutters School, 1913.

U.S.S. FLORIDA, 1918

Standing: Workman, Rupertus, Murdock . . . Perry . . . . Whitehead, Willett, Westfall, Blandy, Calvert, Simons, Selman, Brantley, Ring, Field, Jenkins, Cox, Brown, Graf,
Sitting: Bennett, Smeallie, Watson, Washington, Bulmer, Reed, Brainard.

Rupertus and a Marine detachment, USS *Florida*.

A weather clearing, even a partial clearing, made the armada more visible for Japanese search planes overhead. He decided to go below decks to check on his men. Then, maybe, he would stretch out on his rack and try to rest.

He took a final look at the sea and the skies. The slight clearing in the weather revealed the waning moon's thin crescent. Off in the distance, Savo Island's faint outline rose from the sea.

Four hours until sunrise, when the sound of explosions would ensure that nobody would sleep. The time had arrived.
*****

Bridge, USS *Neville* (APA-9)
Squadron Yoke
The South Pacific
Course 040 Degrees
August 7, 1942
0255 hours

After dozing for thirty minutes, Captain Bailey got up to return to the bridge for the next major course correction.

"Captain's on the bridge!" the officer of the watch called out.

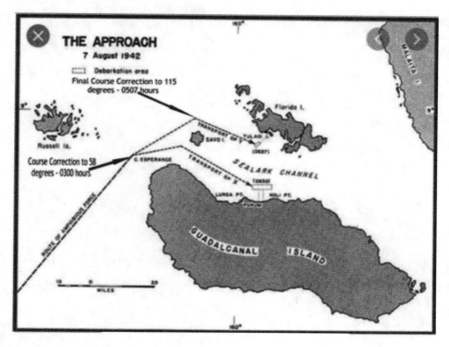

"As you were," Bailey responded. "Status?"

"Clear seas. No sign of the enemy."

Bailey glanced at the clock on the bulkhead: 0258 hours, local.

"Very well. Stand by for course correction to zero-five-eight degrees."

"Aye, Captain. Standing by for course correction to zero-five-eight degrees."

Bailey checked the clock again: 0300 hours.

"Helmsman. Make your course zero-five-eight degrees. Steady as she goes."

"Aye, sir. Making my course zero-five-eight degrees."

Neville began a slight turn in the water, to starboard, as Bailey checked his navigational charts.

One final correction, in two hours, one-one-five degrees for the final assault on Tulagi. Three minutes after that, warplanes on the USS *Wasp* would launch initial airstrikes before the Marines hit the beaches.

Chapter 6

IJN Radio Communication Center
Tulagi Island
August 7, 1942
0402 Hours

The darkness of the night hung over the Pacific. Then the sounds of Reveille blared from the bugler's horn. All over the island, Japanese sailors and soldiers scrambled from their racks, jumped into their uniforms, and began preparing for the day.

However, their first duty would be worship, for the emperor was worthy of their worship, their attention, and their lives.

But Petty Officer Third Class Yosmu Yamaoka did not need to be awakened by Reveille, nor would he be able to worship this morning with his comrades. Yamaoka had been on duty in the Imperial Japanese Navy radio communication center on Tulagi Island since after midnight. Yamaoka would have liked to worship or take a break. But it could not be. A thick tension had hung in the air all night. The concern started at around 2100 hours, when radio clerks in the communication center had received unusual signals from the enemy.

Yamaoka listened for every squeak and crackle that came over the airways. But since the last radio traffic at 2100, the Americans had gone silent, which proved more troubling than the sporadic radio traffic they had picked up earlier in the evening. An imposed radio silence might mean the Americans were up to something. Or it could be nothing at all.

Chapter 7

USS *Neville* (APA-9)
Commanding General's Quarters
August 7, 1942
0429 Hours

Knowing that sleep would be impossible, Bill Rupertus lay on his rack, hoping to get some rest. That ended when the bells started to ring on the ship's loudspeaker at 0429 hours.

"General quarters! General quarters! General quarters! All hands to battle stations! General quarters! General quarters! General quarters! This is not a drill."

On a US naval vessel, even a troop transport like the *Neville*, sounding "General Quarters" required every sailor to move to battle stations and prepare for combat. The General Quarters alarm probably sounded because the armada had now moved into Japanese-controlled waters and, hopefully, not because an enemy plane or sub was spotted.

Still, the call for General Quarters, over the constant ringing of alarm bells all over the ship, captured every man's attention from bow to stern.

Rupertus pushed himself up on the rack and swung his feet around. He needed to prepare for a final logistics meeting with his staff. With his men set to invade in less than four hours, the war had arrived.

*****

USMC General Staff Meeting
Rupertus Staff
USS *Neville* (APA-9)
August 7, 1942
0500 Hours

Bill Rupertus glanced at his watch and then studied his staff. There was still an hour and a half before sunrise. In his quarters, a faint incandescent bulb hanging overhead provided the only light.

"Anybody sleep last night?"

"Negative, sir."

"Not much, General."

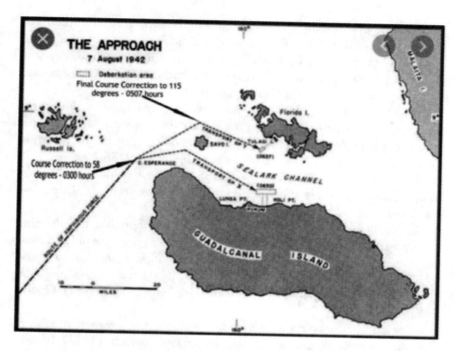

"I didn't think so," Rupertus said. "Okay, listen up. I just talked to Captain Bailey. We're on course and scheduled for our final course correction in about seven minutes from now. Now, take a look at this map."

Rupertus unrolled the navigational chart map to explain the flotilla's current positioning.

"Okay, gentleman, it is now 0500 hours. In seven minutes, we'll execute our final course correction leading us into combat. You can see on the map," he tapped the arrow on the map noting the final course correction, "here, we'll turn to one-one-five degrees, on the course south-southeast, for a final straight shot into Tulagi. We expect the Japanese to discover us before we land." He looked up at his staff. "We've been lucky so far with the cloud cover blanketing us from Japanese aircraft most of the night. But our luck won't continue indefinitely. Be prepared for all contingencies. Any questions?"

"Negative, General."

"No, sir."

"Very well. About an hour after we turn to one-one-five degrees, the navy will start battering the hell out of shore positions on Tulagi, Gavutu, and Florida Island with naval gunfire from our destroyers and cruisers and air assaults from our carriers. If the Japanese haven't discovered us by then, you can bet your last dollar they'll know we've arrived."

"Now hear this. Now hear this," came over the ship's loudspeaker system, known in the navy as the 1MC. "We are commencing our final course change into Tulagi. Be ready, and good luck, gentlemen."

Rupertus looked up. His staff stared at the gray bulkheads during the announcement as if they were waiting to feel the ship's turn in the water. A moment later, *Neville* began listing, and the officers felt her right turn in the water. Five other US Navy transports, including the USS *Heywood*, USS *Little*, USS *Colhoun*, USS *Gregory*, and USS *McKean*, would follow *Neville's* course change. All these ships carried the 3,900 Marines under Rupertus's command.

Up until this point, the entire mission had felt more like the planning stage. Steaming through the night toward the western coastline of Guadalcanal, it seemed as if the mission had not yet begun. Now, with the final course set for Tulagi and three hours until combat, reality started sinking in.

"All right, gentlemen. We're in the final leg before commencing 'Operation Ringbolt.'"

Operation Ringbolt was the code name for the invasion of Tulagi, Gavutu, Tanambogo, and Mokambo, all located just off Florida Island's southern shore.

"Let's recap the game plan. First, the navy bombs the hell out of our targets. We then move onto Florida Island. 1st Battalion, 2nd Marine Regiment goes in first, where we meet our Australian ally, Lieutenant Frank Stackpole. The Japanese aren't heavily fortified on Florida. At least we don't think they are. But they have a seaplane base we must secure and take out.

"Then, at my order, 1st Ranger Battalion, under Lieutenant Colonel Edson, and 2nd Battalion, 5th Marines, under Lieutenant Colonel Rosecrans hit the beach on the South Shore, move to the east, and attack down the length of the island. After that, the 1st Parachute Battalion, on my command, hits Gavutu and Tanambogo, and we go from there.

"Now, as you know, gentlemen, I've seen the Japs up close and personal in China. They're fierce bastards and have no regard for any norms of civility in combat; they ignore any ethics of war, act like savages, and will fight like the devil."

Rupertus tapped his finger on the desk. "I'll tell you something, men. The Japanese have yet to face the fury of the US Marine Corps. We're going to take it to the Japs and ram it down their throats. Within the next forty-eight hours, we're going to give America her first combat victory on the ground in this war."

He eyed each of his officers as they hung on his every word. "I have never been so proud of a group of officers and men as I am right now." He paused for a second. "Any questions?"

"No, sir, General!"

"No, sir!"

"Very well. Return to your duty stations, return to your men, check your rifles, check your equipment, and await my order."

Chapter 8

USS *Wasp* (CV-7)
The South Pacific
Twenty Miles South of Guadalcanal
August 7, 1942
0530 Hours

"Turn the *Wasp* into the wind. Prepare to launch aircraft."

"Commence turn into the wind. Aye, sir."

"Fighter Squadron 71. Prepare for launch on my command."

"Fighter Squadron preparing for launch on your command."

With those commands, first from the commanding officer of the aircraft carrier USS *Wasp*, Captain Forrest P. Sherman, and then from the Air Support Force commander, Rear Admiral Leigh Noyes, the US military initiated the final order sequence launching the pre-invasion naval bombardment phase in the invasion of the Solomon Islands.

Ten minutes later, sixteen planes—F4F Wildcats—from Fighter Squadron 71 began taking off in sequence from the *Wasp*'s flight deck.

Lieutenant Commander Courtney Shands, US Navy, commanded the squadron. A Ferguson, Missouri, native, Shands had left his Midwestern home, graduated from the Naval Academy in 1923, and was commissioned in 1927, the same year he married his precious Elizabeth in Birmingham, Alabama.

Shands played on the Naval Academy football team as the starting center and swam as captain on the Academy's water polo team. But this marked his first time in combat, in the Pacific, leading his squadron in the first air battle of the Solomons campaign. These navy warplanes would pave the way for General Rupertus and his Marines later in the morning.

This was everything he had trained for. As he pulled his Wildcat up into a climb, Shands glanced at the picture of Elizabeth.

Once his fighters were airborne, they would be joined by fifteen attack planes of the torpedo bomber squadron on board the *Wasp*, VS-71, commanded by his good friend Lieutenant Commander John Eldridge.

The warplanes circled above the carrier as they assembled in attack formation, Shands, the flight leader, checked his navigational chart.

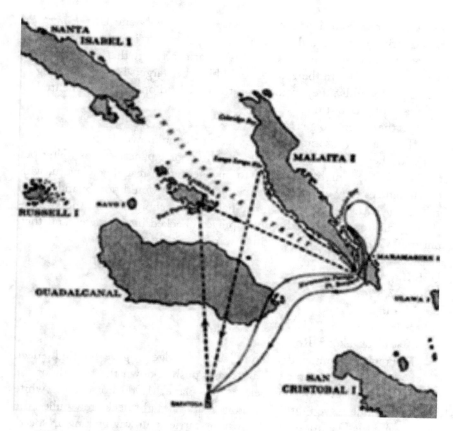

Within the next few minutes, more planes would be launched from the *Wasp*'s sister carriers, USS *Saratoga* and USS *Enterprise*, the three American aircraft carriers spearheading the Air Support Force for the invasion.

Wasp was the flagship for the Air Support Force. As such, she would launch the initial air assault against Tulagi, Gavutu, and the smaller surrounding islands.

Shands's mission, per his group commander, was "to attack and neutralize Japanese seaplanes moored around Gavutu before they take off and threaten the American fleet."

Lieutenant Commander Eldridge's dive-bomber squadron would hit the shore batteries on Gavutu. They would set a course almost due north, fly over the middle of Guadalcanal, and then hit their first targets on Tulagi, Gavutu, Tanambogo, Halavo, Port Purvis, Haleta, and Bungana.

Warplanes from their sister carriers, USS *Saratoga* and USS *Enterprise*, would strike Japanese military buildings at Port Purvis on Florida Island, paving the way for General Rupertus's Marines to hit the beaches in less than two hours. From there, they would hit other targets before returning to the ship. Hopefully, they would drop their payload on target and neutralize Japanese anti-aircraft fire.

But there were no guarantees.

They were flying into the battle, facing the unknown. In the worst-case scenario, they might face multiple squadrons of Japanese Zeros flying out of Rabaul. They might be forced to engage before reaching Gavutu, with no guarantees they would survive. Some probably would not. Shands again glanced at Elizabeth's picture, taped below the tachometer and the rate-of-climb indicator. He uttered a quick prayer, checked his altimeter, and then put the Wildcat into a bank as other warplanes flew off the *Wasp*.

*****

USS *Wasp* (CV-7)
August 7, 1942
0555 Hours

"Clear for takeoff, sir!"

"Clear for takeoff. Roger that."

Lieutenant Commander John "Jack" Eldridge Jr. gave his flight deck chief a thumbs-up, returned a salute, and pushed down the throttle of the SBD-3 "Dauntless" dive bomber. As the plane's 1,000-horsepower white Cyclone engine revved into a sonorous roar, the flight deck crew pulled the chocks, and the Dauntless rolled down the carrier's runway, picking up speed. A moment later, the dive bomber cleared the flight deck. Eldrige pulled up on the stick, putting the Dauntless into a climb.

Three hundred feet.

Five hundred feet.

One thousand feet.

He banked left and turned into a circling pattern, looking down over his shoulder as the other planes in his squadron began lifting off from the carrier.

There were fifteen scout bombers altogether, the US Navy dive bombers of Squadron VS-71. Along with the sixteen F4F Wildcats of VF-71, they were the first wave of American airpower in the invasion of the Solomons.

Japanese forces in this section of the Solomons were concentrated on the islands of Tulagi, Gavutu, and Tanambogo.

This morning, they would lead the first dive-bombing attack against hostile positions on Gavutu and Tanambogo. Once the planes headed north away from the *Wasp*, for the United States, the hot part of the war against the Japanese had begun.

Chapter 9

Sealark Channel
The South Pacific
USS *Neville* **(APA-9)**
Course 115 Degrees (Course Due North)
On Approach to Tulagi Island
August 7, 1942
0555 Hours

The sun had not yet crested the eastern horizon, and a gray mist hung over the water from last night's weather. Rupertus felt excitement as the night's darkness morphed into the morning's gray glow.

He stepped out onto the ship's starboard deck, reached into his right trouser pockets, pulled a Zippo lighter, lit a Camel cigarette, and took a draw. The smoke he inhaled was damn good. And just what he needed. A jolt of nicotine after a long, sleepless night.

0600 hours.

Rupertus, already in his battle helmet, knew the battle plan well. By now, dozens of warplanes from the three American aircraft carriers off the southern coast of Guadalcanal would have taken to the skies, hopefully before the Imperial Japanese Air Force responded. The landing craft were in place, ready to launch Marines onto Florida, Tulagi, and then Gavutu after the navy bombed the hell out of their targets.

He pulled from his pocket a single black-and-white snapshot revealing the most beautiful woman he'd ever laid eyes on. A silent prayer followed for Sleepy and Patrick. He stuck her picture back in his pocket and made the sign of the cross.

Off the ship's starboard, Savo Island passed from left to right. The Japs were there. Rupertus knew it. He looked through his binoculars out toward Savo. The Japs were probably looking back at him. But from this distance, the island resembled the shape of half a watermelon rising from the sea, full of lush green trees and vegetation.

He rechecked his watch: two minutes until 0600 hours.

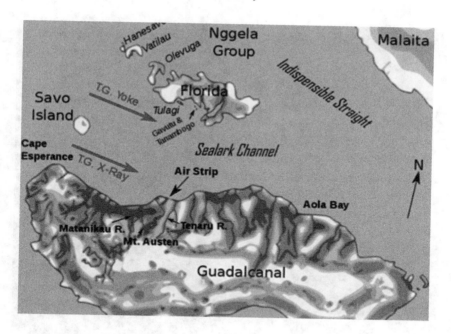

He brought his binoculars back to his eyes and gazed at the horizon, looking into the skies just above the water, to the left of Savo Island.

"See anything, General?" The question came from Colonel Robert Kilmartin, affectionately known as "Killy" by Rupertus and other officers closest to him in the Corps.

Rupertus kept the binoculars to his eyes. "Nothing yet, Killy. Just a bunch of gray water and green overbrush out there. But just because I haven't seen 'em doesn't mean I don't smell 'em."

"I take it you mean the Japs, sir?"

"They're out there. I know it. I can smell Japanese from six miles away, which I learned out of necessity from witnessing their brutality in Shanghai in 1937."

"Understood, sir."

"You wouldn't have believed, unless you saw with your own eyes, how they murdered thousands of innocent women and children."

"I can't imagine it, sir."

"Want a cigarette?"

"Thank you, sir." Kilmartin reached out and took a single cigarette.

General Rupertus and Colonel Kilmartin aboard the USS *Neville*, August 7, 1942. (US NAVY)

"Light?"

"Yes, sir."

Rupertus dropped his binoculars and offered Kilmartin a flame from the Zippo. "The Japs' only morality is savagery. I pray that most Americans never see what I've seen."

"We'll take care of business, sir."

Rupertus scanned to the left of his previous position, searching for US naval warplanes approaching the area from over Guadalcanal.

"I wish we could stop and wipe them off Savo before we wipe them off Tulagi."

"General, I guaran-damn-tee we'd wipe them off the face of the earth at Savo before taking care of business at Tulagi."

Rupertus allowed himself a smile. "Something tells me that you're right on mark, Killy." A moment later, eight black dots appeared in the air, off the southern horizon. "Well, I'll be damned."

"What have you got, General?"

"Navy aviation is right on time this morning, Killy. Look." He handed the binoculars to Kilmartin.

"You're right, sir. I'm counting one, two, three, four—eight dive bombers coming over the southern horizon, sir. American! Every damn one!"

"Your mathematical computations are on the mark this morning, Killy." Rupertus took another drag from the cigarette. "Now, let's pray that our airplanes hit 'em before their airplanes take off."

"Aye, sir."

"Tell the men the navy bombardment is under way. Perfect timing. We're less than fifteen minutes from the debarkation area. Prepare to board the landing craft on my order. Tell Colonel Edson and the other commanders that we're thirty minutes from my order to land the landing force."

"Aye, sir."

Chapter 10

Savo Island
Japanese Lookout Post
August 7, 1942
0600 Hours

Somewhere behind the gray clouds, the sun had already started rising on the eastern horizon, but being pre-dawn, the sea and the sky were primarily gray.

The Japanese lookout on Savo Island, under the command of Lieutenant Yoshimoto, had been on watch for the night. So far he had seen nothing except inclement weather, followed by a slight clearing.

When he first saw the flotilla of gray ships on the horizon, out in Sealark Channel, he thought the fleet was a Japanese military convoy bringing men and weapons to resupply Japanese positions on Tulagi. The fleet steamed through the water from his right to his left, probably from the Japanese naval base at Rabaul.

Finally. Lieutenant Yoshimoto, his direct commanding officer, would be pleased, and the observer looked forward to breaking the good news. The lieutenant, having been replaced by Lieutenant Commander Suzuki, would board one of these ships and return to the homeland tomorrow. Now that he thought about it, the appearance of the ships today made more sense.

The lieutenant would be happy, and all the men on Savo, Tulagi, Gavutu, and the other islands, which they occupied for the emperor, would be delighted. The Imperial Japanese Navy had been awaiting these supplies for weeks.

The lieutenant was a good man. In his early fifties, he was older than many of these men's fathers, which placed him in an honored position. The spotter would tell the lieutenant that the ships had come to take him home!

He looked through his binoculars again, scanning the convoy for the Rising Sun flag, which was flown from Japanese warships as the Imperial Japanese Navy ensign. The flag of the Rising Sun, fluttering from the great gray ships of the Imperial Japanese Navy, always brought goosebumps to his neck and arms.

Yes, this would be a good day. There'd be fresh food—fruits and vegetables from the homeland—perhaps saki for the men.

He kept scanning with his binoculars. So far, he saw only images of the gray morning water through his high-powered lenses. He changed the angle. The bow of the lead ship came back into view. He swept the binoculars to the ship's superstructure. A tall mast rose into the air about one-third of the way back from the bow, just in front of the bridge.

What? The lookout readjusted the focus on his binoculars. Something seemed odd. He waited for the wind to unfurl the flag in full view.

What in the hell was that?

Hot, electric fear jolted his body.

Stars and Stripes!

"American warships!"

Chapter 11

IJN Radio Communication Center
Tulagi Island
August 7, 1942
0602 Hours

Behind the mist filling the sky, the sun began rising over the Sealark Channel. Since midnight, Petty Officer Third Class Yosmu Yamaoka had been on duty in the Imperial Japanese Navy radio communication center on Tulagi Island.

Still nothing. Two hours had passed since Reveille on Tulagi. Through the windows, Yamaoka saw the darkness turning to light. His comrades who had earlier worshipped the emperor were now at their duty stations.

Yamaoka wanted to go worship. He wanted to take a break. He thought about the nervousness that had permeated the night, starting around 2100 hours when radio clerks in the communication center intercepted the unusual signals from the enemy, sending tensions soaring. The Americans were up to something, but no one yet knew what.

"Petty Officer Yamaoka!"

Yamaoka turned just as the observer burst through the door, shouting, "American warships! Off Savo Island!"

Sudden knots twisted his stomach. He instinctively ran to his radio. "All personnel on Tulagi, Gavutu, Tanambogo, Savo, and Florida! Enemy warships! This is not a drill! Enemy warships off Savo Island!"

Chapter 12

Japanese Seaplane Base (Adjacent to Tulagi)
Gavutu Island
August 7, 1942
0604 Hours

Rumors spread of American naval activity in the area. Most of the concern arose in the communication center and the watch stations. But so far, the fears stemmed only from spotty evidence and gossip. Outside the communication center, no one knew that the radio operators were nervous.

By contrast, a festive, celebratory atmosphere filled the rest of Tulagi, marked by the arrival of Lieutenant Commander Noboru Sato the previous day. Sato had arrived by air aboard a large Kawanishi H8K seaplane, which the Americans called the "Emily" flying boat. He brought provisions needed by the Japanese troops and sailors on Tulagi: beer and saki, much of it consumed at the Kasen Unit Club last night. But his most important cargo was the aircraft oil, brought to refuel the seaplanes of the Yokohama Air Group.

At the moment, fifteen Japanese seaplanes floated at anchorage off Tulagi harbor. Commanded by Captain Shigetoshi Miyazaki, the air group consisted of a combination of bombers and fighters at anchorage off Tulagi and Florida Islands. The planes provided the principal air defense for this sector of the Solomons, including Tulagi, the islands around it, and Guadalcanal.

While his fellow officers celebrated Lieutenant Commander Sato's arrival, Miyazaki had flown scout patrols last night looking for Americans, but found nothing except lousy weather and spacious seas. Miyazaki had no time for celebrating.

He had come up empty in his search for the American fleet. Still, Miyazaki knew in his gut that somehow, somewhere, the Americans were about to strike. He had to get his planes in the air.

He walked down to the wooden pier stretching into the harbor to inspect his seaplanes. Despite the spotty weather in the area the last two days, he had to get his planes flying this morning. Several were already running at anchorage.

Good.

The first plane should be airborne within the next few minutes.

"Air raid! Air raid! Air raid!" The warning blared over the loudspeaker system.

What the hell? Miyazaki looked up into the low-hanging clouds as sirens began blaring throughout the base. The sound of approaching aircraft engines began drowning out the air raid siren. Suddenly, six warplanes bore down on the seaplane base.

"American Wildcats! Get those planes in the air! Now!"

The sound of multiple machine gun bursts followed. Fifty-caliber bullets splashed the waters all around him.

Two of his planes exploded. A third burst into flames, and then a fourth. The entire harbor erupted into a fiery inferno. Flames leapt into the sky. Black smoke gushed and billowed high above the flames.

Sato reached for his rifle, chambered a round, and then began firing into the sky at the American planes as his planes burned in the harbor. But the black smoke rising into the air blocked his view of the Wildcats destroying his base. He could only fire toward the sound of roaring aircraft engines.

Chapter 13

Japanese Headquarters
Tulagi Island
August 7, 1942
0610 Hours

The celebration had gone late into the night, with much drinking and revelry. He had thanked and praised the emperor for the new provisions to his troops on Tulagi.

Lieutenant Commander Suzuki's job was to welcome the emperor's representative, Lieutenant Commander Sato, who had flown in with the provisions last night. Suzuki had gone to bed late and, knowing Captain Miyazaki's planes would be in the skies early, protecting the ceilings around Tulagi, decided to sleep a few extra minutes before starting the day.

He rolled over and glanced at the alarm clock: 0600 hours. Another 30 minutes. He could roll out of the rack at 0630 hours and still assume his command duties for the day.

A thunderous shaking knocked him from his rack and onto the floor.

"What the hell?" His first thought—"Earthquake!"

But the rattling and broken glass yielded to the roaring sound of approaching aircraft. Americans!

He grabbed his pistol and ran outside his hut. Billowing smoke rose from the direction of Gavutu against the relentless roar of aircraft engines. The American bombs kept falling. Suzuki left his hut and sprinted toward the bomb shelters Lieutenant Yoshimoto had constructed in the limestone caves.

His first objective—survive the attack.

Chapter 14

USS *Neville* (APA-9)
Squadron Yoke
Sealark Channel (between Guadalcanal and Tulagi)
Course 360 Degrees (Course Due North)
August 7, 1942
0630 Hours

Brigadier General Bill Rupertus stood on the bridge, watching the action through his binoculars, as US naval aviation delivered an aerial pounding of the target area.

A light fog settled across the water under low-hanging cumulus clouds. Through binoculars, Rupertus saw smoke rising above the target area. Good. The navy's Dauntless dive bombers and F4F Wildcats were inflicting damage on the enemy.

Across the way, he could see the cruiser USS *San Juan* and destroyers USS *Monssen* and USS *Buchanan* pounding Tulagi and Florida Islands with multiple rounds.

So far, so good.

Hitting the enemy from the sky and the sea was risky enough. Hand-to-hand combat would provide a different, more dangerous challenge.

"How's it looking out there, General?"

"Navy's doing their job, Killy," Rupertus said. "Some damn fine pilots out there. Brave as hell, too. It's great seeing those bastards on the receiving end of American firepower."

He pulled his binoculars down. "How are the men?"

"Chomping at the bit to fight."

"I'm chomping to get 'em in the fight. I want these boys on Tulagi before some Jap sub figures out we haven't gotten off the ship yet."

"General." Bill turned and saw one of his lieutenants holding a message. "From USS *McCauley*. Admiral Turner, sir."

"Very well." Rupertus opened the message.

"TOP SECRET: From Commander Task Force TARE, to Commander Squadron Yoke. Commence operations. Land the Landing Force. Richmond Turner, RADM, USN."

He turned to Kilmartin. "Killy. Send out the order. On my command. Land the landing force."

"Aye, sir. Copy. Understood. Land the landing force."

"Notify the *Zeilin*, the *Heywood*, and the *President Jackson*. I'll take care of *Neville*."

He turned to his right. "Captain Bailey."

"Yes, sir, General."

"We've been ordered to commence operations. I need the 1MC."

"Aye, sir. Stand by, sir." The ship's commanding officer turned to his right. "Petty Officer Jones. Ready the 1MC."

"Aye, Captain. Ready on the 1MC, at your pleasure, sir."

"Now hear this. Now hear this. This is the captain speaking. Stand by for the commanding general, Task Force Yoke." Bailey handed the microphone to Rupertus.

"This is the commanding general," Rupertus began. "To all US Marines and naval support personnel. Commence Operation Ringbolt. Land the landing force. I repeat. Land the landing force. Good luck, and Godspeed."

He handed the microphone back to Captain Bailey. "This is the captain speaking. All engines stop. General quarters! General quarters! All hands to battle stations. All hands to battle stations."

Rupertus checked his watch: 0637 hours.

He had given the order right on time, hopefully marking the initial phase of America's first victory on the ground in the Pacific. It came at a potentially high price—the lives of his Marines. But Vandegrift had selected Rupertus and his men because they were the best America had to offer.

"Captain Bailey."

"Yes, sir, General."

"I'm going to the main deck to see my men off. I'll be back in a bit."

"Aye, sir. And Godspeed to you and your men."

Chapter 15

USS *President Jackson* (APA-18)
Sealark Channel
Off the Coast of Florida Island
The Solomon Islands
West of Tulagi
August 7, 1942
0700 Hours

"Company B, Combat Team A! Move! Move! Move!" Captain EJ Crane, from Galveston, Texas, waved his arms and fingers toward the ship's side. "Over the side, men! Board that landing craft. We've gotta move."

The men moved in a quick stream, descending the net-rope bridges down to the landing craft bouncing on the water below.

Although the invasion of Tulagi was primarily a 1st Marine Division operation, the 1st Battalion of the 2nd Marine Division also supported the operation. Captain Crane had replayed General Rupertus's words in his mind a thousand times.

"Your men will be the first on the ground of all the men in the task force, Captain," the general had told him. "Company B, Combat Team A is the tip of the spear. Your mission is to launch an assault against Florida Island, immediately east of Haleta. Florida Island is four hundred yards north of Tulagi. We must secure it to secure the perimeter against Japanese attack as we move onto Tulagi. In other words, you and your men will have our flank. Otherwise, when we hit Tulagi the Japanese could be reinforced by troops from Florida Island, and we don't want them retreating from Tulagi across the channel to Florida, where they could regroup and counterattack."

"Are you with me so far?"

"With you all the way, General," Crane had responded.

Rupertus had stopped and looked into Crane's eyes with a long, almost hypnotic stare, as if the general could read his soul, to judge whether he was worthy of the task. The general's piercing blue eyes and powerful stare created an air of intimidation, comfort, and inspiration, all at the same time.

Rupertus, it seemed, possessed an innate ability to read a man's mind and to test his leadership by a simple glance.

A moment later, Rupertus had broken the stare. "We need you and your boys to hit the beach, and then seize that village at Haleta. We need you to have our backs when we land on Tulagi. Stay focused. Are we clear?"

"Yes, General," he had said.

"Son," Rupertus had placed his hand on Crane's shoulder. "You'll make the Marine Corps proud. And you'll make Texas proud, too. There's a reason we selected you to lead the first boots on the ground."

Rupertus exuded a calm, sharp confidence that would motivate his men to march into hell and back.

"Keep moving men!" Crane yelled. "Remember! Hands vertical, feet horizontal! Let's get the hell out of here before the Japs figure out we're here."

He watched his Marines in battle helmets with rifles strapped over their shoulders and bullets in their belts, put their boots over the ship's side and begin climbing down the net ladders into the boats below.

When the last Marine climbed over the side, Crane approached the ship's side, swung over the banister, and stepped onto the wide net bridge to climb down toward the water. A moment later, he stepped onto the landing craft, bobbing in the waves.

"Sir, all men are present and accounted for."

"Very well," Crane responded to his gunnery sergeant. "Okay, sailor, let's move out!"

"Roger that, Captain," the landing boat's coxswain pilot responded. "Push away from the ship!"

A couple of sailors pushed off against the hull of the *President Jackson*, and the boats lined up, rocking in the water, with their engines running.

Off in the distance toward Tulagi, black smoke rose in the air, mixing with the clouds. Booming sounds rolled across the water, like loud thunderclaps. The landing craft engines revved, and some of the distant explosions were drowned out by the engines' roar. Then the landing crafts began a straight-line movement north, toward Florida beach.

Crane checked his watch: 7:04 a.m, right on time. Now their fate rested in the hands of God. "Our Father, who art in heaven . . ." Crane began reciting the Lord's Prayer. Others joined in. Then almost all the Marines in the landing boats: "Thy Kingdom come, thy will be done, on Earth, as it is in heaven."

Chapter 16

USS *Neville* (APA-9)
Squadron Yoke
Sealark Channel (between Guadalcanal and Tulagi)
Course 360 Degrees (Course Due North)
August 7, 1942
0710 Hours

After ordering commencement of Operation Ringbolt, Rupertus quickly moved down from *Neville*'s bridge to her main deck, to see his Marines as they stepped off the ship and climbed down into the landing boats.

He was sending some of them to die. Death's ever-looming presence was never far removed in his mind. He thought of the tombstones at Arlington—Rita, Ann Rodney, and William Jr.

Freedom's price—if America could preserve freedom—would be high. He owed it to them to see them off personally. With his battle helmet secured, Rupertus stepped out onto the main deck, where his men were already heading over the ship's side.

"Attention on deck!" someone shouted as he approached the line of Marines stepping over the ship's side.

"Carry on." Rupertus checked his watch: 0717 hours.

Some one hundred men of the 1st Raider Battalion were climbing down the net ropes along the ship's side into the landing boats waiting below. Their target: Beach Blue on Tulagi. They would hit their target once Captain Crane and his men secured the beaches on Florida Island.

In war, timing was everything. At the moment, Crane and his men were hunkered down in their landing craft, crossing the water to Florida Island. These Raiders would follow ten minutes later, to Tulagi.

Out of eight hundred Marines in the 1st Raider Battalion, these one hundred were chosen to spearhead the assault at Tulagi. They were part of Combat Team Number 2, commanded by Lieutenant Colonel Merritt Edson, whom Rupertus had hand-picked for the assignment.

Edson had earned his nickname, "Red Mike," from his red beard while serving in Nicaragua. He was a no-nonsense Vermonter with combat experience, having fought in France and Germany in World War 1. Edson had earned his wings as a Marine aviator but excelled in ground combat, so Rupertus named him commander of the Raider unit assigned to first take the battle into the teeth of Japanese resistance.

Intelligence reports predicted fierce Japanese resistance. But Merritt Edson was the man Rupertus trusted most to prosecute this battle. Edson stood on the deck, in full battle gear, watching his men go over the side. Rupertus stepped over and placed his right hand on Edson's shoulder.

"This is the moment we've been training for, Mike.

"With men like these, we can't lose," Edson said. "We won't lose."

For a moment, both officers stood together, watching their Marines step over the ship's gunwale side, as distant naval gunfire thundered in the air. In pairs, the Raiders crossed the gunwale and then descended net-rope ladders leading to the landing craft in the water.

"Damn right, we won't lose," Rupertus said. "Not with officers and men like you."

"We won't let you down, General."

"I know you won't, Mike. I wish I could go with you in the first wave. But I will join you on the beach soon enough."

"We'll keep the lights on until you arrive, General." A confident grin crawled across Edson's face.

Rupertus nodded. "The lines are getting short, Colonel. You better get moving. We got some Japs to kill."

Edson turned and gave his commander a salute. "See you on the other side, sir."

Rupertus returned the salute. "Godspeed, Mike."

Edson dropped the salute, turned, and jogged to the ship's side. Rupertus watched Edson step over the side and begin climbing down. He walked to the side and looked down as the colonel stepped into one of the four troop transport boats, each carrying twenty-five Marines. They were all aboard the landing craft below, ready to depart the ship.

Over the engines' roar and the explosions on Tulagi, Rupertus heard voices below. And the words he heard, from the men headed into battle, sounded familiar:

This is my rifle. There are many like it, but this one is mine. My rifle is my best friend. It is my life. I must master it as I must master my life. My rifle, without me, is useless. Without my rifle, I am useless . . .

One by one, the boats pulled away from the ship. As they began pulling away, all the men joined in.

I must fire my rifle true. I must shoot straighter than my enemy, who is trying to kill me. I must shoot him before he shoots me. I will. My rifle and I know that what counts in this war is not the rounds we fire, the noise of our burst, nor the smoke we make. We know . . .

Their voices began to fade, drowning out by the whipping wind and the boat engines. They moved on toward their target areas, across the water, reciting the "Rifleman's Creed" that Rupertus had authored in San Diego six months ago:

Before God, I swear this creed. My rifle and I are the defenders of my country. We are the masters of our enemy. We are the saviors of my life. So be it, until victory is America's and there is no enemy, but peace!

Their voices faded as they moved away from the *Neville*, in a straight line heading across the water toward Tulagi.

He glanced at the horizon before heading up to the bridge.

Chapter 17

Lead Landing Craft
From USS *President Jackson*
August 7, 1942
0730 Hours

The US Navy LCM (2) landing craft transporting the Marines in battle were forty-five feet long and fourteen feet across at the brain. Each carried four navy crew members, including a coxswain, an engineer, and two seamen.

The lightly armed vessels had two Browning 50-caliber machine guns. Against Japanese troops who might attack from the beach with small-arms fire, the machine guns could be effective. But against a submarine or enemy naval gunfire, the machine guns were worthless.

From the lead landing craft, over the roar of the boat's engines, Captain Crane watched the promontory that marked Florida Island come closer into view.

The destroyers *Monssen* and *Buchanan* had lined up along the approach route between the *Neville* and the landing zone to guide the landing craft to their target. US Navy scout planes had also dropped smoke bombs into the water, essentially smoking directional buoys into the target area.

The low-hanging clouds produced little wind, and swells were calm. On the final voyage over, his men were introspective, for the most part, with some gripping their rifles and repeating General Rupertus's "Rifleman's Creed." Others prayed.

They had now closed within 2,700 yards of the beach. It was 0730 hours. On the mark, the USS *San Juan* began shelling the small island, just south of Haleta village.

The loud booms from *San Juan*'s guns thundered across the water as the landing team moved closer to the shore.

After the *San Juan* opened fire, the destroyer USS *Buchanan* joined in, firing multiple rounds onto the peninsula west of the targeted landing zone. *Buchanan*'s guns joined the USS *Monssen*, which was shelling a hill on the promontory overlooking Tulagi's westernmost tip.

Closer to the water, the explosions seemed louder, more thunderous, more shattering than they sounded from the deck of the *Neville*.

The smoke rising from the promontory over Tulagi, just off to the right, painted a panoramic view of the battle areas the Marines were entering. As the boats chopped through the water to their destination, now fifteen hundred yards away, Crane turned around and looked at his men. Their jaws were set; their eyes were steely. A couple made the sign of the cross.

A few sat a little high in the boat for comfort.

"Stay low, men! Use the steel side of the boat for protection. Don't give Jap snipers any easy targets!" He turned around and looked forward again.

"Five hundred yards, Captain!" the forward lookout announced.

"Roger that, Petty Officer."

Crane turned forward, stayed low, and tightened his chin strap. He lifted his eyes just above the edge of the landing craft. So far there were no signs of the enemy, at least not on the beach. That could be a good sign or a bad sign. The Japanese were notorious for fighting back by opening up with sniper fire from unknown locations.

"Three minutes, sir. Three minutes."

He turned around and yelled at his Marines, "Three minutes, men! Lock and load! Three minutes!"

The landing boats continued their path through the water. As they got closer to the beach, the boats started bobbing up and down in the breakers as the water got rougher.

"One minute, Captain!"

"One minute! One minute! Get your rifles ready, men! Fix bayonets!"

Crane felt his heart pound.

"Thirty seconds!"

"Thirty seconds, men! Here we go!"

"Landing craft, it's touching the bottom!"

Crane felt the boat's bottom scraping against the sand.

"Stand by to open the front door!"

"Get ready, men!" Crane shouted.

He looked forward, above the front of the boat. The vegetation on the island and the beach came into view, and then the front section scraped against coral, in shallow waves.

"Let's go!" Crane brought his rifle into firing position, lowered his head, and leaped over the side of the landing craft.

The sounds of the crashing waves drowned the landing craft's engines, and water soaked his boots and pant legs as he pushed through the breakers and sprinted up onto the sand.

"Heads down! Spread out! Stay low!"

Chapter 18

Lead Landing Craft
From USS *Neville*
August 7, 1942
0730 Hours

These men of the 1st Raider Battalion were anxious to get in the fight. The Raiders had formed as a special force's unit for raids against lightly defended Japanese-held islands. The initial interest in creating the Raider units stemmed from President Roosevelt's interest in the British Commando units, including the Royal Naval Commandos headquarters at Ardentinny, Scotland.

FDR's interest in Special Forces did not progress further until Admiral Chester Nimitz, commander in chief of the US Pacific Fleet, requested an elite unit of Marine commandos trained for critical-mission amphibious assault. With Nimitz's request, the Raiders were born. The USMC commandant chose the term "Raiders" to describe the new commandos.

The Corps commissioned the 1st Raider Battalion on February 16, 1942, followed by the 2nd Raider Battalion on February 19.

A message was intercepted the day before the Raider's first mission, on August 6: The woman's voice coming over the radio waves taunted them and called them out.

General Rupertus made sure the Raiders were aware of "Tokyo Rose."

Before they had departed the *Neville* to board the landing craft, Lieutenant Colonel Edson read them the intercepted radio message from the Japanese, broadcast from Tokyo: "Where are the US Marines hiding? The Marines are supposed to be the finest soldiers in the world, but no one has seen them yet."

Within minutes, the Japs were going to find out where the US Marines were "hiding." In the process of strategic battle planning, examining aerial photographs of Tulagi, General Rupertus had chosen Beach Blue as the invasion point because the Japanese might least suspect it.

Unlike other areas on Tulagi, which would have provided a smooth, sandy beachfront approach, Beach Blue, full of sharp coral reefs that would not let the boats reach the sand, forced the landing crafts to stop at the coral reefs, away from shore. The Raiders would have to jump overboard in water, possibly up to their necks, and then slosh in to the beach.

This approach was risky, in part because of unknown water depths and sharp coral reefs. In the words of Major Justice Chambers, who would lead in the first batch of Marines, "Everybody had to plunge into the water and wade to shore. This is no fun, as we found out during our training in Samoa. Because coral reefs are dotted with holes, at any moment you are likely to step into water that is over your head."

But General Rupertus calculated that the Japanese would concentrate their defenses on the serviceable beach areas on the southeast side of the island, expecting the Americans to land in an area with quicker, easier access.

Like America's greatest generals, Rupertus was an audacious combat leader, committed to offensive warfare and embracing the element of surprise.

If the general's plan worked, they would land on the western coast and then press southeast through the jungle to take the enemy by surprise.

Tulagi, four thousand yards long and one thousand yards wide, featured a ridge that rose 350 feet above sea level and ran the island's length, broken up by a ravine. Other than a few feet of sand that lapped from the water to the jungle, making a small beach around the island, not much was there, except an army of mosquitoes.

American intelligence varied about Japanese troop numbers. Some intelligence reports speculated that fifteen hundred Japanese were on Tulagi. Others estimated as many as eight thousand.

The United States needed Tulagi in large part because of its excellent harbor. The operation was planned in three phases—first, the landing at Haleta on Florida Island to protect the left flank of the main thrust.

After seizing the main objective, Tulagi, Rupertus's Marines would attack and capture the twin islands of Gavutu and Tanambogo.

But Tulagi presented a tremendous tactical challenge. First, the coral reefs that surrounded the island on three sides. The Japanese had fortified the island with the coral in mind, by placing their top defenses in the east and southeast, opposite the coral reef perimeter.

The Japanese were depending on the coral reef as a natural defense against an invasion. Rupertus was playing a high-risk game of poker by sending his men through the coral reef to surprise the Japanese.

Rupertus was concerned that he was not sure of the size of the Jap force they would face, though his men would never know it. The general displayed

an iron jaw and a steel face, cool as a cucumber, with a contagious fearlessness in his darting blue eyes. Soon these men would know whether their general's gamble, invading on Beach Blue, had paid off.

The 1st Raider Battalion, Combat Team 2, commanded by Lieutenant Colonel Edson, had been ordered to land on Beach Blue on the southwest coast of the island. The Marines would move in on the western side of the island, near the site of a small cemetery.

As Captain Crane and his men were hitting the beaches on Florida Island, transports attached to the USS *Neville* prepared for the assault against Beach Blue. The Raiders had climbed down into patrol boats provided by the USS *Zeilin*.

On approach to the landing zone, the Raiders would receive fire support from four US Navy destroyers: the USS *Little*, *Gregory*, *Calhoun*, and *McKean*.

As the Raiders departed the *Neville*, the destroyer escorts stood in a line in the water, guiding the Marines in toward their target area, the reefs off Beach Blue.

In the front of the lead boat, Major Justice Chambers regurgitated the Tulagi battle plans in his head. Chambers, a West Virginia boy from Huntington, had attended college for three years at Marshall before enlisting in the Naval Reserve. From there, he joined the Marine Corps Reserve as a private. Two years later, the year Franklin Roosevelt was elected, Chambers received his commission as a Marine officer. In the summer of 1940, while attending summer camp with the reserves, his battalion was called to active duty.

They assigned him to the Raiders, and now here he was, in the front of a combat boat, a West Virginia boy on the other side of the world, about to lead his men into direct combat with the fiercest enemy in the world. Chambers had been recommended by Lieutenant Colonel Edson and approved by General Rupertus himself. He would not let them down, and he would not let his country down.

The sounds of naval gunfire broke his concentration. Chambers checked his watch: 0740 hours.

He looked up as USS *San Juan* fired round after round of pre-suppression naval gunfire on Tulagi. The *San Juan*'s target was Hill 208, rising high above the island's southwest coast. They targeted the hill to suppress and eliminate Japanese sniper fire, which would rain down on the Marines once they landed.

"Twenty-seven-hundred yards, Major!"

"Copy that," Chambers repeated. "2,700 yards!"

The boats continued to move inward, under the thunderous booms of *San Juan*'s canons. A moment later, USS *Monssen* and USS *Buchanan* moved in close behind the landing crafts and opened fire on Tulagi.

In two landing boats, the first wave consisted of Company B, which Chambers commanded, and Company D, commanded by Chambers's friend Major Lloyd Nickerson. The landing craft churned closer to shore, as three US Navy destroyers blasted the landing area. A young Marine yelled out, "Here's where the Japs find out where the Marines have been hiding!"

As the three destroyers continued pounding the island, a squadron of dive bombers from USS *Wasp* struck the island's northeastern side with heavy bombs, drawing Japanese attention and sending a false signal that the invasion would come from the opposite side, just as General Rupertus planned.

A moment later, more scout planes dropped smoke bombs along the route through the water leading up to the debarkation point.

"One thousand yards, Major!"

"Copy that! One thousand yards!"

Powerful surges of adrenaline shot through Chambers's arms and stomach. He muttered a quick prayer under his breath, squeezed his rifle hard, and softly repeated the Creed. "This is my rifle. There are many like it, but this one is mine."

In the US military, the terms "D-Day" and "H-Hour" are used for the day and hour on which a combat attack or operation is to be initiated. Under

General Rupertus's designated battle plans, H-Hour was to be at 0800 hours in this operation.

Chambers glanced at his watch: 0755 hours. He looked back at his men and signaled, "Five minutes, men! Five minutes!"

Just then the destroyers ceased fire, as planned, to avoid raining friendly fire onto the Raiders once they hit the beach. Now, only the sound of the engines and the waves entered the landing craft. A moment later, disaster nearly struck. USS *San Juan* spotted an enemy submarine, just outside Gavutu Harbor. *San Juan* increased her speed and, four minutes later, began dropping depth charges. Booms echoed across the water as submerged bombs sprayed geysers in the air.

Chambers and his men were caught in the midst of a naval war even before they hit the ground or fired a bullet. If that submarine got loose and torpedoed any American ships supporting the invasion, a colossal disaster would follow. A moment later, a large oil slick appeared in the water as the *San Juan*'s depth charges found their target.

"Be ready, Major! Here we go!" the forward lookout shouted.

"Stand by, men! Chambers yelled to his Marines in the back of the landing craft. The engine slowed, and the boat scraped the bottom before coming to a stop. It was 0800 hours, right on the mark.

"Okay, men! This is it! In the water! Let's go!"

Chambers reached over the gunwale, pulled himself up, and dropped down into the water. For a second he thought he might be in over his head. But his feet found the bottom of the reef, and his head bobbed above the warm water, barely. He held his rifle high over his head and waded across the reef to the beach, which looked about fifty yards from the landing craft.

The thick coral prevented even a single landing craft from reaching the shoreline. The beach on this side of the island rose steeply from the water. No one was around. It appeared the Japanese were surprised, though not completely.

As the Marines approached the beach, sniper fire cracked the air. One Marine took a bullet. Then the sniper stopped firing. So far, General Rupertus's "Coral Landing" strategy had worked.

"Let's go, men! Into the tree line!" Major Chambers motioned with his arm, signaling his Marines to hustle.

The actual beach on Tulagi was a sand strip only a few yards wide. Above that, jungles and hills covered the island, with the jungle stretching down to

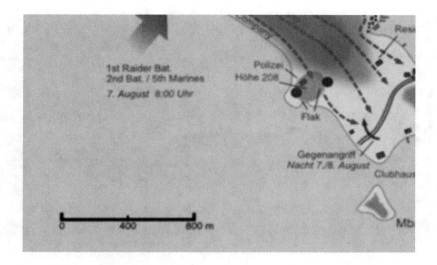

within a few yards of the beach. Major Chambers pulled his men inside the tree line and called them around him for instructions.

"Okay, men, here's an aerial photograph of Tulagi. We've just hit the beaches here and are moving inside this tree line. The jungle, as you can see, is thick. This vegetation is a ripe environment for snipers, as we have already seen. So be on your toes. Keep your eyes peeled and prepare to engage the enemy at any second. We believe they're concentrated on the southeast sector of the island, with heavy fortifications around Hill 280. We expect them to have automatic weapons and be largely dug inside caves under the hill.

"Once we cross this Phase Line A, the base of that hill, we expect it to get pretty hot in there. Be prepared to take fire at any time, as I suspect there are snipers in those trees, and the Japanese may decide to take the offensive and try to come down and attack us before we get there. Let's hope we still have the element of surprise. Either way, within the next couple of hours, the Japs will know we're here.

"Hill 280, the highest point on Tulagi, has already been targeted this morning by naval gunfire. But if the Japs are dug in caves under the ground, we can expect many have survived. We're going to have to root them out ourselves. Our plan now is to move up in the center of the island and then turn to the southeast to begin moving on the entrenched Japanese positions. We want to wipe them all out.

US Marine Corps Raiders coming ashore on Beach Blue, Tulagi, August 7, 1942.
(US NAVY PHOTO)

"It's liable to get bloody." He looked into all their eyes. Their steely determination gave him confidence. "Any questions?"

"No, sir, Major!"

"No, sir!"

"Remember Pearl Harbor! Let's go kill some Japs!"

"Very well, gentlemen," Chambers said. "Follow me."

Chapter 19

IJN Military Headquarters
3rd Kure Special Naval Landing Force (SNLF)
Southeast Sector of Tulagi
August 7, 1942
1100 Hours

Commander Masaaki Suzuki, commander of the SNLF unit on Tulagi, picked up the telephone to the Yokohama Air Group headquarters on Gavutu Island.

An answer came from the other end. "This is Captain Miyazaki."

"Shigetoshi. What is the condition of your planes? Can we get any of them in the air?"

"The situation is not good, sir," the commander of the Yokohama Air Group responded. "We have two in the air somewhere from before the attack began. But all my planes are burning in the harbor. The American dive bombers have hit us hard."

Suzuki let that news sink in. "Our situation is equally dangerous. Their naval gunfire has been overwhelming as their bombers continue to strike us. We've received word from one of our snipers that their Marines invaded from the western sector of the island."

"What are your orders, Commander?"

"These are my orders. Destroy all equipment and papers. I will notify Admiral Sadyoshi on Rabaul. Meanwhile, we will fight them all to the death. There should be no surrender. We shall give our lives to our emperor. That is all."

"Very well, sir." The line went dead.

"Petty Officer Yanmaoka. Take down this message for Admiral Sadyoshi. Transmit immediately upon completion."

"Yes, sir."

From Commanding Officer 3rd Kure Special Naval Landing Force (SNLF) to Commander, IJN 11th Fleet, Commander, IJN 25th Air Flotilla, Rabaul.

Be advised the enemy forces have launched overwhelming air, land, and sea attacks against the central Solomon Islands, focusing their attack upon Tulagi and Gavutu.

Have issued orders destroying equipment and papers.

Bombs dropping near IJN radio transmission facility. Heavy bombing. Expect to lose communication soon.

Enemy troop strength is overwhelming; we will defend to the last man.

Respectfully,

Masaaki Suzuki, Commander IJN

"Let me see the draft."

"Yes, sir." The clerk ripped the draft message from the typewriter and handed it to Suzuki.

Suzuki took the draft order and read it. "Very well. Send it. Now."

"Yes, sir."

Chapter 20

USS *Neville* (APA-9)
Off Tulagi Island
Operation Ringbolt Command Post
August 7, 1942
0915 Hours

Rupertus walked into the command center, lit a cigarette, and sat down.

"Okay, Killy. What's our status?"

"So far, so good, sir," Colonel Kilmartin said. "We had some problems with the coral reefs, as expected. We couldn't land any landing craft on the beach. But both Raider battalions are on the ground, with Colonel Rosecrans's group holding down the west side of the island and Edson's four companies moving to the southeast. Additionally, we just landed two tanks on the ground from USS *President Jackson*, just a few minutes ago, in fact, at 0900 hours."

"Great news. No casualties, and we're going to need those tanks for the move up the island."

"Seems the plan to surprise the Japs worked, at least so far."

"Casualties?"

"Minimal, sir, at least so far. One of our men got hit by a Jap sniper, but we didn't lose him."

"Good news," Rupertus said.

"Hopefully, the rest of the day goes as smoothly as the first part, General."

"I hope you're right, Killy. But I wouldn't put any money on it if we were playing craps."

"Poker either, sir."

"It's going to take them at least two hours to press through all that heavy jungle underbrush and get in position to attack. It's going to be a long couple of hours, Killy. And we still don't have any information on Japanese troop numbers?"

"No estimate yet, sir, except one sniper."

"Very well, then. Killy, prepare a report for my signature to General Vandegrift: 'Both Raider battalions ashore. Surprise achieved, preparing to advance. No casualties on landing.'"

"Aye, sir."

Chapter 21

USS *Heywood* (APA-6)
Sealark Channel
Off Gavutu Island
August 7, 1942
1000 Hours

Major Robert Williams, commanding the 1st Marine Parachute Battalion, the battalion known throughout the Marine Corps as "paramarines," had spent the last two hours preparing his Marines for their amphibious assault against Gavutu Island. His men were ready to go.

A landing craft shortage had delayed their departure. And being stuck on a hot ship for four hours on the morning of D-Day with their fellow Marines already in combat made them antsy and dripping with perspiration.

Plus, they were being held back for an emergency, delayed in their principal mission of attacking Gavutu to possibly support the Marine Raiders on Tulagi, if the Raiders called for backup. Although Williams had complete faith in the plan, waiting was still nerve-wracking.

But Gavutu had to be taken by a combination of naval airpower, followed by Marine Corps ground power.

Located four thousand yards off Tulagi and off the southern coast of Florida Island, Gavutu housed the dangerous seaplane base that provided Japanese aerial cover not only for Tulagi but also for Guadalcanal.

Some good news had come to his Marines this morning. US Navy dive bombers from USS *Wasp* had damaged or destroyed most of the floating Mitsubishi Japanese Zero aircraft, which were moored in Gavutu's harbor awaiting takeoff.

The navy dive bombers had not eliminated the Japanese forces on the ground. That dangerous task devolved on Major Williams and his men, scheduled to assault Gavutu at high noon, some four hours after US Marine Corps Raiders had launched their initial assault on Tulagi.

General Rupertus had carefully planned the overall assault against Tulagi and the surrounding islands to be executed in stages.

Navy dive bombers executed the first stage by hitting Japanese aviation assets in the area and other Japanese gun positions.

Rupertus then ordered a combat team from the 2nd Marines onto Florida Island to cut off potential escape routes from Tulagi and quell Japanese resistance from the flank. That landing occurred first, at a little after 0730, Major Williams was told. Florida Island appeared to be secure. At 0800, Rupertus ordered Marine Raiders onto Tulagi, the operation's principal target.

Part three of the operation, the ground attack on Gavutu, would commence at noon, four hours after H-Hour on Tulagi. Rupertus staggered the times and kept Williams's Marines in reserve if they needed to be called onto Tulagi in an emergency to relieve the Raiders. Williams's principal mission was to root the Japanese off the seaplane bases in Gavutu and either kill or capture the Jap soldiers. Although his group was a parachute battalion, on this attack they would move into the target by sea and not by air.

One reason for the planned sea-based attack involved topography. At their base, Gavutu and its twin islet, Tanambogo, located a thousand yards north of Gavutu, were connected by a land bridge. They were high-rising coral islands with small, shallow beaches surrounding each.

Parachute landings are best executed on smoother surfaces. The islands' small size and sharp, high-rising topography made a parachute landing impossible.

Gavutu, only 500 yards long and 250 yards wide, presented little maneuvering room. Tanambogo was even smaller. The two coral islets were connected via a stone causeway, 500 yards long, built through the shallow coral waters, and just 8 feet wide.

The twin islets sat 3,000 yards across shallow waters east of Tulagi Island. They were visible by the naked eye from Tulagi's eastern tip.

Each islet featured single, high-ground areas that the Japanese would defend. On Gavutu, the Marines' principal objective would be Hill 148, and on Tanambogo, the target would be Hill 121.

Williams and his paramarines would first hit Gavutu. Later in the afternoon, the 1st and 2nd Battalions of the 2nd Marines would strike Tanambogo. Though he had studied it a thousand times already, Williams took another glance at the overall operational map.

As was the case on Tulagi for the Raiders, the unknown calculus was the unknown Japanese troop numbers. They could be facing huge numbers. Charging up these hills to take these islands could be a bloody proposition.

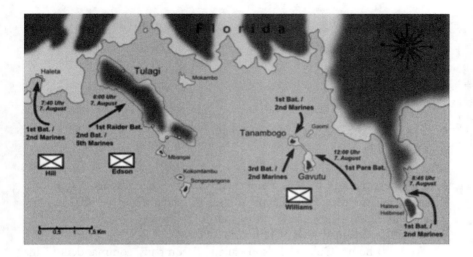

At 1000 hours, the cruiser USS *San Juan* had begun to shell Gavutu, Tanambogo, and their twin peaks. But the navy's shelling would alert the Japanese the Marines were coming.

Unlike the Raiders' surprise landing on Tulagi, a surprise landing on Gavutu would prove impossible. On Gavutu, everything was visible. His men could not slip in on the backside, unseen, as the Raiders had done at Beach Blue.

It was almost two hours before they were to hit the beaches at Tulagi, but it was now time to board the landing craft to begin the journey to the attack point.

Williams checked his watch. "Okay, men! Line 'em up! Time to get off this damn ship and board the landing craft. Let's get a move on."

Chapter 22

Tulagi Island
Near the Shoreline Northwest of Hill 208
August 7, 1942
1055 Hours

For the last two hours, Edson's Raiders had cut their way through hot, humid jungles in the middle of the island. All four Raider companies—Baker, Dog, Able, and Charlie—now stretched in a long line from Carpenters Wharf to the shoreline just northwest of Hill 208.

At 1100 hours, Colonel Edson called all company commanders to his command post, atop the ridge, for final briefings before the assault against the Japanese.

"Okay. One company will attack the south side of the ridge. The other company will attack the north side. We're supposed to get continued naval shelling by our ships. But remember, they most likely have machine guns on that ridge. Mortars, too. Attacking first, we surprise the bastards and eliminate those machine guns before they know what hit 'em. Be ready. When I give the green flare signal, we start the assault. It may take several hours to fight through to the base of that hill. But we start here."

Edson looked into his company commanders' eyes. Their faces reflected steely determination. "Any questions?"

"No questions, Colonel."

"Very well. Return to your respective companies. Be on the lookout for the green smoke flare."

"Aye, sir."

"Okay. Get back to your men and be ready for my signal."

Chapter 23

USS *Neville* (APA-9)
Off Tulagi Island
Operation Ringbolt Command Post
August 7, 1942
1115 Hours

On board USS *Neville*, Colonel Robert Kilmartin walked into the command center with a message in hand.

"Sir. New message from Lieutenant Colonel Edson."

"About damn time," Rupertus said. "What have we got?"

"Updated information, sir. May we go to the map?"

"Certainly."

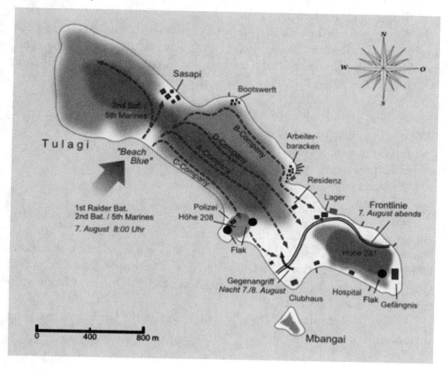

Kilmartin rolled out a black-and-white map with grease pencil markings showing troop positions on the battle space.

"First, as can be seen here, 1st Raiders, 2nd Battalion has climbed over the 350-foot peak running down the island and come down on the other side to Sasapi village, which we now occupy."

"Which officer commanded the capture of Sasapi?"

"Major Lloyd Nicholson, sir."

"Make a note to put a commendation in Nicholson's file."

"Aye, sir."

"Please continue."

"Lieutenant Colonel Edson, as you can see, has divided his four companies into four straight columns running into the occupied southeast part of the island. As you can see, Baker Company and Charlie Company will be moving parallel to one another down the coastline. Meanwhile, Dog Company and Able Company will straddle opposite sides of the ridgetop, with all four companies moving southeast, at the same pace, so the Japs can't get around our positions and hit us from the backside."

"Roger that," Rupertus said.

"What you see here is the projected columns for the attack. We last heard from Lieutenant Colonel Edson just a few minutes ago; his man and, notably, Charlie Company, had advanced just to the northwest of Hill 208, which USS *San Juan*'s been bombarding all morning.

"As you can see, our projected lines show Charlie Company going through and around Hill 208." Kilmartin paused and glanced at Rupertus. "We need to kill a lot of Japs to get around that hill."

Rupertus took a satisfying drag from a cigarette. "Hill 208. Where the rubber first meets the road."

"Yes, sir, General. And if I may?"

"Certainly."

"Now this particular aerial photograph doesn't show all four companies, only Able at the top and Charlie on the right side of the ridge. Hill 208 isn't marked by the grease pencil on this photograph, but if you look at Charlie Company advancing down by the water line, if you note the point where Charlie Company will do a snaking maneuver to the left, about halfway up their arrow, that's Hill 208."

"I see it," Rupertus said. "It's where they bank to the left before resuming their original course."

"Once they clear Hill 208, all four companies will be converging into the battle space on Hill 280. Some of our maps refer to Hill 281. But Hill 280 and 281 are the same thing."

"Yes," Rupertus said. "We'll have to overrun that hill, likely filled with automatic weapons in dugout caves, to take the island."

"Yes, sir."

"When does Colonel Edson expect to make his move?"

"By 1130 hours."

Rupertus checked the clock on the wall. "Almost that time." He shifted gears. "Okay, what about our situation with the Gavutu landing force?"

"We heard from Major Williams. The boats have been in the water for a little over an hour now. They are about twenty minutes from initiating their final run into the battle space. Right now, they are on track for a noon landing."

"Great." Rupertus again glanced up at the clock on the bulkhead. "I wish I could have figured out a way to land those guys undetected, like we did on Tulagi."

"I understand. But you have trained these men well, sir. They will not let you down."

"I believe that, Killy."

"Oh, and sir?"

"Yes."

"There's one other thing."

"Let's hear it."

"I'm sorry to inform you that we have lost a Marine."

Rupertus's stomach twisted. Although he had seen far more death than any man should ever have to face, the news of another death, and especially of a family member or a Marine, was hard.

"Sniper fire?"

"No, sir. Not sniper fire. Accidentally discharged his weapon while aboard ship waiting to transition to the landing force."

"Damn." Rupertus thought for a second. "Get me info on his next of kin."

"Aye, sir."

A call came in. Vandegrift had broken radio silence to reach Rupertus, who gave him a verbal report.

"Several enemy targets, including the Japanese seaplanes in the Tulagi harbor, have been bombed. The scheduled gunfire destroyed nine Zero seaplanes and nine Japanese bombers in the water."

Chapter 24

Charlie Company
The Battle for "Hill 208"
August 7, 1942
1130 Hours

"Sir. Green smoke flare is up! Out to our left."

Major Kenneth Bailey, company commander for Charlie Company, had taken his company along the southeast tract along the seawall, almost to the base of Hill 208.

So far, Bailey had no reason to believe the Japs had spotted them. The heavy, thick jungle vegetation had its advantages for a Marine company moving under cover for a surprise attack.

Bailey turned his binoculars toward the ridge above them. Just as his gunnery sergeant reported, green smoke rose in a plume from the center of the ridge, over toward Colonel Edson's headquarters. That signaled only one thing.

"Okay, men! We got our signal. Let's move out! Prepare to engage!"

A second later, rifle fire cracked the air. Bullets whizzed by the Marines' heads.

"Take cover!"

Although USS *San Juan* had pounded this hill with over 1,505 five-inch shells, the Japanese crawled out of caves, like swarming hornets, firing their Arisaka rifles.

"Get down!" Bailey yelled. "Fire's coming from the lookout post by the ocean. Give it back to him and hotter than they're giving it. Let's kill those Jap sons of a bitch."

Two bullets whizzed by Bailey as he pulled the lever to chamber a round in his M1903 Springfield rifle. He pulled the trigger. One Jap slumped and fell down the hill.

Bull's-eye!

"Get some mortar fire on the hill! Now!"

"Roger that, Major!"

Each mortar had a firing pin in the bottom of the tube. They had practiced this a thousand times, and now they would employ the mortars in combat. When the Marines dropped a 60-millimeter shell down the tube, the firing pin would strike the ignition cartridge in the shell's tail, which detonated the cartridge. Explosive gases blew out the base of the shell when the cartridge fired. The 60-millimeter shells could strike accurately between 200 and 325 yards away, well within the Japanese bunkers atop Hill 208.

General Rupertus had drilled them on close-in mortar support during training at New River. "These mortars will cover our men charging across open ground." Rupertus had constantly hammered this point, even as the 1st Division trained at New River. "The key is rapid mortar fire and accurate mortar fire."

Charlie Company needed to take that hill, and they would need to cross open ground to get to its base. They would need the mortars to cover them as they prepared to rush toward the hill and try to take it.

At Bailey's command, the Marines opened up a heavy barrage of 60-millimeter mortar fire on the hill at the Japs as Charlie Company continued to pour on heavy rifle fire. The loud *swoosh* from the M-2 mortars was followed a few seconds later by the sight of smoke pluming on the side of Hill 208, followed by the sound of explosions on the hill. The mortars were striking their targets.

Now came the real challenge. To take Hill 208 and advance toward the Japanese stronghold in the southeast, a platoon would have to charge straight across an old cricket field, which looked like the greens on a golf course. That would involve sprinting at least, Bailey estimated, a hundred yards.

"Listen up!" Bailey waved his platoon leaders in toward him. "Now, as you see, the only thing between us and that hill right now, which is full of Jap snipers with automatic weapons, is that cricket field out there. I wish there were some way to get to the hill without crossing the field. But there's not. And you know what that means . . ."

"We're ready to go, sir."

"Let's take 'em. That's why we're here."

"Okay," Bailey said. "On my command, we're charging across that field. We've got plenty of mortar fire covering us. Hopefully that pins down the Japs while we cross.

"When we cross that field, we move up the hill, killing any Japs that get in our way, and we must eradicate those dugouts where the Japs are hiding.

Use grenades, use automatic fire, use your bayonets if you have to. But I want every Jap killed within the next hour. Are you with me?"

"Yes, sir!"

"On your order!"

"Very well. Return to your ready positions and await my signal. I'll move out first."

As his platoon leaders returned to relay his instructions, Bailey uttered a quick prayer under his breath. He knew that men would die crossing that field. He might die himself. He gave his platoon leaders two minutes to get into position.

"Follow me!"

Bailey gripped his rifle and, headfirst, charged out onto the cricket field, firing rounds at the Japanese and yelling expletives as he sprinted.

Thank God his mortars were firing to give them cover, but the mortars weren't stopping the enemy's hailstorm of bullets. His men were getting hit to his left and right, but they had to keep running forward, to reach the vegetation at the base of Hill 208.

"Keep moving, men!"

Bailey continued firing. Japanese bullets struck the ground around his feet and whizzed by his ear.

I'll never make it.

A moment later, through whizzing bullets, he reached the other side and dove for cover into the jungle vegetation on the side of the hill. Bailey turned, looking back out onto the field, and frantically motioned his men to quickly join him. Many raced ahead and dove for cover. Others lay dead on the cricket field, their heads exploded into pieces from Japanese bullets. But there was no time to recover the bodies.

"Okay, men," Bailey said. "Spread out and move up this hill." He pointed up. "We've got to take the Japs out of those bunkers."

The next hour would prove to be a hot, bloody shootout as the Marines exchanged fire with elite Japanese Rikusentai forces, determined to hold the hill. Japanese snipers were hiding everywhere, it seemed. They were so small they could conceal themselves up in the branches of coconut trees.

Nothing produced more anxiety for a Marine than taking sniper fire without knowing the origin of fire.

Charlie Company now faced two deadly sources of fire from the Japanese: sniper fire and machine gun fire. In a slow grind, they began crawling through the thick underbrush and up toward the top.

Although putting up a fierce firefight, some Japs began retreating to the southeast, abandoning their position on the hill. But the machine gun dugouts were a problem.

"Let's drop grenades in these machine gun bunkers, boys! I'll take this one," Bailey said. "Get the grenade ready!"

He ran up behind the dugout and kicked hard on the door. The door burst open.

Gunfire.

"Aaahh!"

A single shot from a Japanese rifle struck him, and he fell over bleeding.

Chapter 25

Dog Company
Tulagi Island
"Phase Line A"
August 7, 1942
1135 Hours

"What do you think, Bill?" Major Justice Chambers, company commander of Dog Company, stood alongside his executive officer, Captain William E. Sperling, of Bound Brook, New Jersey.

"Looks like a ravine to me, sir. It's got to be our stop point," Sperling said.

"I think you're right, Bill."

Up until about 1130 hours, Dog Company had moved to the southeast along the ridge's highest point on Tulagi but had met with only limited resistance from occasional sniper fire. The plan was to advance along the top center spine of Tulagi, toward the southeast, to a predetermined point known as "Phase Line A."

Phase Line A marked the end of the ridgeline, at about the midway point of the island, and just before they were to move into the heavily Jap-infested southeast sector.

Before their landing, Lieutenant Henry Josselyn, Royal Australian Naval Reserve (RANR), had briefed the Marine Raiders on the island's terrain. Lieutenant Josselyn once lived in the area, knew the island's terrain, and provided some maps and photographs.

Looking down at the ravine, Chambers felt confident that they were in the correct spot, where they were to halt.

When they reached the line, they were to fire green starburst flares into the sky to notify the US Navy to begin bombarding the eastern sector of the island. The bombardment should soften Japanese defenses as the Marines moved down into the ravine prior to the final major assault on the main Japanese stronghold, Hill 281.

Major Justice Chambers brought his men to a stopping point at the edge of the ravine. "Looks like the phase line to me." Chambers said. "Why don't you pull out the aerial photo to make sure we're properly oriented?"

"Yes, sir."

"Looks right to me, sir; that's got to be Hill 281 on the other side of the ravine," Sperling said.

"Agreed," Chambers said. "All right. The battle plan calls for us to fire flares to alert the fleet to bomb the hell out of those Japs on the other side. Pass the word down to the platoon leaders. We'll hold up here as ordered, launch the flares, and wait."

"Roger that, sir."

Chambers waited for a few minutes as his second-in-command carried out his instructions. Sperling returned shortly.

"Platoon leaders have been informed, sir. Would you like me to carry out the order to launch flares now?"

"Yes, launch flares!"

"Aye, sir."

A moment later, multiple *poof* sounds flooded the area. White smoke clouds billowed across the ground as numerous flares were launched, climbing high into the gray sky above the island. The flares exploded into green starbursts, stretching out into large green streaks. The streaks remained visible for about thirty seconds until the breeze whisked them in different directions.

Chambers turned to Captain Sperling. "Great job, Bill."

"Thank you, sir. Let's hope the navy responds with a shitload of firepower."

"I hope you're right, Bill. Because either way, we're going to cross that damn ravine. And I've got a feeling Colonel Edson won't delay more than an hour or so. Let's have the men ready to move out on short notice either way."

"Aye, sir."

Chapter 26

Lieutenant Commander Suzuki returned to his headquarters from the dug-outs, hoping that the bombing from the American navy had ended. He needed to assess and reassess the situation.

The American Marines had been on the island now, he estimated, for at least three hours. Suzuki had read about this General Rupertus, author of the American Marine Corps' "Rifleman's Creed."

By their tactical maneuvers this morning, Rupertus had shown flashes of daring, audaciousness, and technical brilliance. His Marines had invaded from the backside, completely surprising Suzuki and his men. The Marines' front lines had closed to within a few hundred yards of the Japanese position. But his men had fought bravely and slowed their advance.

Suzuki loved his men. They would die for him, and he would die for them. And they would all die for Hirohito, their divine emperor.

They had survived the first bombing wave by the American warplanes this morning and the shelling from American warships offshore. Because he obsessively feared the Americans, Lieutenant Yoshimoto had built excess bomb shelters on the grounds. As it turned out, Yoshimoto's obsession with building caves and bunkers had allowed them to survive this morning's onslaught.

At age fifty-three, Yoshimoto was scheduled to leave Tulagi today and return to Japan, retire from the service, and live in peace with his family. Now Yoshimoto faced the foes he feared most, the American navy and the Marine Corps. Yoshimoto, along with most of the men on the island, would probably never see their families again.

The question now was, could he hold out long enough until help arrived from Rabaul? If it ever arrived.

Suzuki knew that help might not arrive in time to save his men. They had lost their air cover from Gavutu and would need immediate air support to hit the Marines from the backside to slow their advance and perhaps defeat them.

At this point, only one tactic might fortify the Japanese position on Tulagi.

He would concentrate his firepower atop Hill 281 and move his remaining forces along the ravine at the south end of the island, to mount his last stand against the Marines when they crossed it.

If the Americans took Tulagi, it would be over the bodies of every Japanese soldier and at a high price in American blood.

Chapter 27

Tulagi Island
Field Headquarters, 1st Raider Battalion
August 7, 1942
1145 Hours

"What the hell is going on with Charlie Company?" Lieutenant Colonel Edson fumed that the four companies under his command were not moving as fast as he planned. Charlie Company, seemingly stalled under heavy fire on Hill 208, lagged behind the others in their advance against the Japanese lines.

"They've gotten bogged down, sir," his platoon sergeant responded. "Hell of a lot of shooting going on over there."

"Gunny, send somebody down to find out what the hell's going on with Charlie Company. Report back to me immediately."

"Aye, sir. I'll check it myself."

"Very well." Edson pulled a Zippo lighter from his pocket and lit another cigarette. "Corporal, see if you can reach General Rupertus on the radio."

"Right away, sir."

Edson took a drag from the cigarette and then brought up his binoculars to look at his main target, Hill 281. If his Marines could take Hill 281, they could control the entire island—the rest of them out on mop-up operations.

"Sir," the corporal said. "I have General Rupertus on the radio."

"Thank you, Corporal." He took the radio. "Good morning, General."

"What have you got for me, Edson?" Rupertus said.

"Sir, your plan for the surprise landing on Beach Blue worked beautifully. We caught them by surprise. But the Japs know we're here now. They are catching hell from us and vice versa."

"What's your current position?" Rupertus asked.

"General, we're almost at the base of Hill 281. I've got those Jap suckers in my binoculars. We started shelling them with mortar fire, and we're hitting them with rifle fire. But there's a bunch of them up there, and they're dug in. Right now, we've got Charlie Company bogged down on my right flank, and I sent the gunny to see what's going on.

"We need them covering our right flank."

"They are engaged on Hill 208. Right?" Rupertus asked.

"Yes, sir. We've gotta nail that down before we can go after Hill 281. Otherwise, the Japs will circle our point, go right down the hill, and hit from behind."

"Understood," Rupertus said. "Let us know if you need more firepower from the navy. We've got the *San Juan*, the *Monssen*, and the *Buchanan* on standby."

Just then, the gunnery sergeant came running back up the ridge from Charlie Company.

"General, my apologies, sir, but I gotta jump off. Urgent situation here."

"Very well," Rupertus said. "Let us know if you need more naval shelling."

"Yes, sir."

"Rupertus out."

Edson looked up. "Gunny, what have you got?"

"It's rough down there, sir." The gunny was panting from the sprint. "They're making slow progress. Thick firefight. We've got several Charlie Company KIAs out on the cricket field, and Major Bailey has been shot and is wounded."

Tulagi's cricket ground burns during the August 7, 1942, invasion of the Japanese-held island. (US NAVAL HISTORY AND HERITAGE COMMAND PHOTO)

"How bad?"

"Pretty bad bullet leg wound, sir. He's bleeding pretty bad. Shot while routing a Japanese machine gun dugout. Captain Thomas is taking over command for the time being, but it's slow going right now, Colonel."

"Damn!" Edson slammed his burning cigarette to the ground and stomped it. He thought for a second and then turned to his executive officer, Major Sam Griffith.

"Sam, Captain Thomas is a good man and a fine officer. But he may need a little help. Go down there and take command of Charlie Company. Check on Major Bailey. We may need to evacuate him. But go down there, take that hill, and clean out those Japs."

Griffith saluted his commanding officer. "Roger that, sir. We'll wipe 'em off the hill, and I'll make sure Bailey's okay."

"I'm depending on you, Sam."

"Aye, sir. I won't let you down."

Chapter 28

Ambush!
Baker Company
Tulagi Island
August 7, 1942
1145 Hours

Baker Company, commanded by Major Lloyd Lionel Nickerson, had climbed through thick underbrush over the 350-foot ridge, pushing all the way across to the island's side, and captured the village of Apassi. Then, like the other three companies, it turned to the southeast. Baker Company's immediate goal—to join the four other companies in the assault against Hill 208.

For Major Nickerson, born in Canada before his family moved to Texas and then Massachusetts, the privilege of fighting for his adopted country, the United States, was a special honor.

Like the other company commanders in the 1st Raider Battalion, Nickerson had supreme confidence in both the operational commander, Brigadier General Rupertus, and the 1st Raider Battalion commander, Lieutenant Colonel Edson.

Besides his company having to wade through more than a hundred yards of water, walking across coral on the bottom to reach the beach, Baker Company had faced no opposition. Capturing Sasapi had not been a capture at all. The small fishing village on Tulagi's northwestern shore had no Japanese defenders, and the natives welcomed the Marines with open arms.

Like his friend Major Kenneth Bailey, whose Charlie Company would push up the southern seaside flank of the island, Nickerson and Baker Company would mirror Charlie Company and cover the northern seaside flank.

Only about 1,200 natives lived on Tulagi, and now General Rupertus was sending US Marines to their island to battle an unknown number of Japanese.

In some ways, the initial assault and capture of Sasapi was too easy. Despite not yet losing any of his men, Nickerson felt queasy in his stomach. The stifling hot weather did not help, and the warm ocean breeze to his left did not cool.

Every step to the southeast felt like the calm before the storm. His Marines had never been in combat. Most had never been shot at or fired a shot in anger.

A loud popping cracked the air.

"Take cover!" someone yelled.

"Sniper fire! Sniper fire!"

Nickerson hit the deck, along with his men, as a hail of rifle shots filled the air.

"Man down! Man down!"

"I got him!" Nickerson looked up. One of his platoon leaders, Lieutenant Eugene Key, from Conroe, Texas, got up and charged toward the injured Marine lying on the ground, bleeding, on the other side of a rock wall.

Key jumped across the wall, and as he did, another shot rang out.

The bullet struck Key in the chest. Blood saturated his uniform. Yet somehow he pulled himself up, pulled a grenade from his belt, and tossed it toward the Japanese snipers. The grenade detonated. Then Key slumped over and fell to the ground, dead.

Key was a brave young officer, only twenty-five years old.

"Let's get some fire on those snipers!"

The Marines unloaded a dozen rounds toward the vegetation where they believed the snipers were hiding. Then silence, only distant gunfire from across the island, and the sound of waves lapping against the seashore below.

Charlie Company still had a bleeding Marine beyond that wall.

"Let me go, sir!" yelled Private Thomas F. Nickel, of Lansing, Michigan.

"Okay. But keep your head down, Nickel," Nickerson said.

Private Nickel jumped up, sprinted forward, and, following Lieutenant Key's path, leaped over the stone wall. Another shot ran out. Nickel's head exploded into a bloody goo. He fell to the ground, dead, not far from Lieutenant Key's body.

Nickerson winced at the young private's body lying beside Lieutenant Key. He wanted to vomit. He just lost two Marines in a matter of minutes, and his men could not see the enemy. Meanwhile, the first Marine lay out in the open, possibly bleeding to death.

The Marines had a motto they lived by: "no man left behind."

"I'm going myself," Nickerson said.

"No, sir!" said one of the company commanders.

"Sir, you can't do that," said the gunnery sergeant.

"I can't let my men get shot and killed, Gunny."

"Sir, that's what the Japs want you to do." The gunnery sergeant looked into his eyes. "They want to smoke out and kill our officers. You're in command here, sir. If they take you out, many more of us will die. Sir, you're more valuable to this company alive than dead."

The gunny was right. Nickerson knew it.

"Let me go." This was JG Samuel Miles, a navy lieutenant and the battalion's junior surgeon.

"Doc, if we let you go and something happens, we're down to only one surgeon. We may need you both."

"Understood, sir, but that Marine may be dying out there. I'm trained and qualified to help him, medically."

As much as Nickerson hated to send him, Lieutenant Miles had a point. "Okay, men, here's what we're going to do. On my command, I want you to commence fire, and keep pouring on the fire at that tree line and don't stop until my command. Let's give the lieutenant a chance to get across the wall."

"Aye, sir."

"Yes, sir."

He looked again at Miles. "You sure you want to do this, Lieutenant?"

"We're at war, sir. It's my job."

"Okay, stand by until I give the commence firing order."

"Yes, sir."

"Marines, on my command, commence fire!"

A wave of bullets poured into the tree line. The Marines kept firing.

"Okay, Miles, go!"

Miles took off running, following the same route as the lieutenant and private. As he leaped across the wall, two shots rang out from the trees, striking him in the head and the throat. Miles fell to the ground, lifeless.

"Damn it! Cease fire."

Now what to do? An unidentified sniper, or snipers, was pinning down Baker Company, and nobody knew where the shots were coming.

"Hey, I see the son of a bitch!" Nickerson heard gunshots from his rear. He turned as his Marines fired into the tree line just to the right of the suspected target area. One Jap dropped from the tree line, falling dead in a bleeding lump on the ground. Another one fell nearby.

"Got 'em," a Marine said.

"Damn bastards."

Nickerson exhaled. Hopefully, those shots took care of the problem. "Sergeant!"

"Yes, Major."

"Form a detail. Dispatch two Marines to transport the injured man back to Beach Blue. Have the others get the dog tags off Lieutenant Key, Lieutenant Miles, and Private Nickel. Get their weapons, their ammunition, their grenades. Bring the dog tags to me but leave no weapons behind. Move their bodies off to the side. We don't have time to bury them now. We'll do that later.

"Okay, men, prepare to move out."

Chapter 29

USS *Neville* (APA-9)
Off Tulagi Island
Operation Ringbolt Command Post
August 7, 1942
1200 Hours

"Any more news from Edson, Killy?"

"No, sir. Not yet."

"How about Major Williams and the force approaching Tulagi?"

"Nothing since our last report, but they should be storming the beaches right about now."

"Which means they may already be in a firefight or will be within a few short minutes."

"Yes, sir," Kilmartin said.

Rupertus sipped black coffee. The *Neville* mess crew had offered lunch from the galley. But the general wasn't hungry. His men were battling in the initial wave on Tulagi and now about to land on Gavutu, battling for their lives. Some had already died. Food was the last damn thing on Rupertus's mind.

Only black coffee. And cigarettes.

Rupertus set the coffee on the table, got up, and walked over to the map of the island on the ship's bulkhead, like a geography professor about to deliver a lecture.

"I tell you, Killy," he said, staring at the map, "based on Edson's last transmission, I don't have a great feeling about what's going on." A drag from the cigarette. "Especially with Charlie Company bogged down at Hill 208." He pointed to the map, to Charlie Company's last reported location, and then said (tapping twice at the ultimate target), "I've got a feeling Suzuki will concentrate his firepower atop Hill 281."

"Well, sir, we've known from the beginning it's going to be a hot situation."

"You're right, Killy," Rupertus said. "But it's not what we know that counts in war. It's what we don't know. What we don't know is anything about Japanese troop numbers on the southeast side.

"It's kind of like invading Florida. You cross the Florida-Georgia line and march down to Palm Beach, and you haven't seen anybody at all, except a few alligators, snakes, and palm trees. And then you got to go into Miami, and you know there are a lot of people you haven't seen along the way, but you don't know how many you're going to find. Could be a hundred thousand of them. Could be a million. Could be two million." He tapped the Tulagi map again. "Smaller example, same principle. And much more deadly."

"But sir, to your credit, we didn't know what to expect when you ordered our landings across the coral reefs at Beach Blue. And that paid off. Minimal casualties so far. A stroke of genius, if I might add."

Rupertus smashed his cigarette into the ashtray. "You know the difference between winning and losing a war, Killy?"

"I hope I never learn the difference, sir."

"It can be the difference between insanity and pure luck. Or, in this case, maybe the grace of God. If my so-called brilliant plan had backfired, I'd be the biggest goat in the Marine Corps, and General Vandegrift would have my ass. You know what they say: 'Victory has a thousand fathers, but defeat is an orphan unto itself.'"

"Yes, sir."

Rupertus looked at Kilmartin. "Anyway, we can't dwell on that right now. I'm not worried about what happened two hours ago. I'm worried about what's happening right now."

"Understood."

"Anyway, my gut tells me that Colonel Edson will call for that naval gunfire, and probably sooner rather than later."

Kilmartin nodded. "I think your gut might be correct, General."

"Okay. Here's what I want you to do. Copy this down."

"Aye, sir."

"Notify Admiral Turner on the *McCawley*. Also, notify the commanding officers of USS *San Juan*, USS *Monson*, and USS *Buchanan*. Based on our assessment of the situation on the ground, we expect a request for naval gunfire support to be imminent. Expect targets of opportunity to be Hill 208 and Hill 281. Please prepare to avoid delay. Please remain on standby for further notifications. Respectfully, W. Rupertus, BGEN USMC, Task Force Yoke."

Kilmartin finished taking the message. "Copy that, General. I will get this off immediately."

"Thanks, Killy. And let me know the second we hear from Colonel Edson."

"Aye, General."

When Vandegrift learned from Rupertus that they were still trying to land on Tanambogo and needed help, he sent his D-1, Jim Murray, to ask Admiral Turner to release the reserve to Rupertus, telling Turner, "I know Bill well enough that he would 'not tilt at the windmills.'"

Chapter 30

At 1026 hours, a little over an hour and a half earlier, twelve US Navy landing craft carrying the the 1st Marine Parachute Battalion departed from the USS *Heywood*, including the battalion's ground commander, Major Robert Williams, whom General Rupertus had selected to head the mission on the ground.

A thirteenth landing craft departed from the USS *Neville*, and it would rendezvous with the others at 1141 hours for the final voyage to the enemy-held island for the assault on Gavutu.

There were 397 of them altogether, elite warriors of the 1st Marine Parachute Battalion. To a man, they were fiercely loyal to the Marine Corps, to their country, and to their commander, General Rupertus.

When they arrived in the waters off the island, they would attack in three waves, at staggered times, each wave with four transport boats carrying 130 Marines each, and the third wave also having a torpedo boat.

Under the attack plan, the first wave, assigned as "Company A," would land at 1200 hours at the Japanese seaplane ramp. This would give the Marines a concrete ramp with stable footing to move onto the island to take an offensive posture. After Company A moved into position, Company B would land at the seaplane ramp and move into position to reinforce Company A.

Company C would remain in the water a bit longer to provide fire support to the initial assault companies and then land on Gavutu at the end of the five-hundred-yard causeway that connected Gavutu to Tanambogo. From here they would intercept any Japanese attempt to reinforce Gavutu from Tanambogo.

So far the Marines' journey across the water in the transport boats had been rough. As the late morning breeze through the sound increased, the seas had gotten choppy, and half the Marines got seasick on the transit over. The Higgins boats rolled heavily in the water, with salt water spilling over the side, drenching the men and their weapons.

Major Williams felt himself getting queasy several times during the trip. Somehow he managed to keep his breakfast in his stomach. But many of his Marines opened their mouths and vomited without restraint.

Each landing craft was spaced at five-minute intervals, each rolling in the waves, each taking on water—and vomit from the Marines' uneasy stomachs.

Aside from the fact they had not been shot at or thrown overboard, the seven-mile transit across the water from the gathering point to the local waters around Gavutu could not have been more miserable.

But as the first wave, containing Company A in the lead landing craft, entered the shallower waters just northeast of the island, the waters calmed. As they passed Tanambogo, on their way to the seaplane ramp at Gavutu to the south, rifle sounds popped in the air as they drew sniper fire from Hill 121 on Tanambogo.

"Stay low, men." Major Williams motioned his men down. "Don't make it too easy on the bastards."

The sniper's shots splashed in the water around them. Luckily, the bullets missed. A few minutes later, the firing stopped. As they moved in, closer to the concrete seaplane ramp, they saw the direct results of US naval firepower.

The bombed-out and shot-out hulks of Japanese fighter and bomber aircraft smoked in the harbor. Oil slicks pooled on the water. On the shoreline, smoke rose from the relics of small buildings.

Except for a few coconut trees that the US bombers missed, the navy had blasted the living hell out of the whole area, which now looked like a bombed-out crater on Mars. "There's no way anybody could have survived this," Williams mumbled to himself.

Gray smoke. Gray water. Orange flames licking into the sky—a desolate landscape.

"Don't be fooled by what you see, men. We've already drawn sniper fire from Tanambogo. We don't know what's on top of that hill."

He pointed toward Hill 148. "Keep your eyes peeled and your rifles ready. Remember the 'Rifleman's Creed.' It's not the rounds we fire. It's the targets we strike. Not a matter of if we engage these bastards. It's a matter of when."

Steering between the burning, smoking seaplanes half sunk in the water, the Higgins boats moved in closer, toward the ramp. Commanded by Navy Lieutenant R. E. Bennick, the first wave of landing craft slowed to cruising speed, navigating between the wreckage of damaged aircraft in Gavutu Harbor.

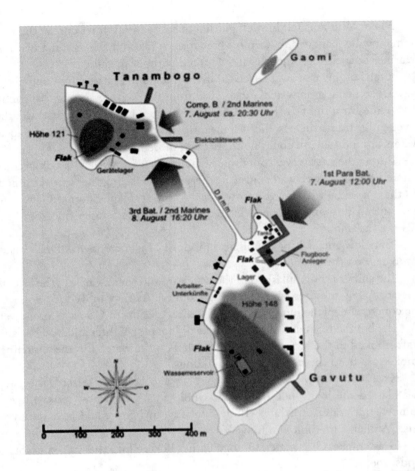

The smoking wreckage looked like a moment suspended in time. A Jap plane's wings stuck up out of the water, with the rest of the plane submerged. On others the back end of the fuselage rose from the water with the aircraft nose and propellers submerged.

On the wings and the back of the fuselages was a large red circle, the symbol of Japanese air power: the Rising Sun. The same damn symbol flew on the Jap Zeros that had attacked Pearl Harbor.

The US Navy had delivered a hard blow this morning. The vast destruction brought personal satisfaction that the navy had done its job, to hit, sink, and destroy Japanese aircraft—to essentially eliminate the threat from these Japanese warplanes, which could sink any ship in the American fleet.

Major Williams thought back to Pearl Harbor, to the image of the sinking burning ships—USS *Arizona*, USS *Oklahoma*, and other vessels and planes destroyed by the damn Japs. He remembered his friends who died there, only eight months ago.

The destroyed Jap planes ignited a moment of American pride. Damn right! The navy had bloodied the Japs' noses. But Williams needed to keep his head in the game. His Marines were about to engage in a mortal combat, planes or no planes.

"Major," Lieutenant Bennick said, "this bombing has strewn so much debris in the harbor that we can't land on the seaplane ramps as planned. A huge concrete block has fallen in the water, blocking access to the ramps."

Bennick was right. The harbor hosting the seaplane base had turned into a watery graveyard. Parts of destroyed Japanese planes rose from the water like metal tombstones.

"What's your plan, Lieutenant?" Williams asked.

"Over there." Bennick pointed to an area along the shore just north of the bombed-out seaplane ramps. "That small beach beside the concrete pier. I don't see any obstacles in the water blocking our approach."

Williams gave a thumbs-up. "Looks good to me, Lieutenant."

The landing craft cruised by the wreckage of the concrete landing ramp. A moment later, the engine slowed, and the lead craft came to a halt, about twenty-five yards from the beach.

"This is about as close in as we can get, Major," Lieutenant Bennick said. "It's not ideal, but the water should be shallow enough to wade onto the beach."

"Not a problem, Lieutenant. We work with what we have."

As the boat came to a halt in the water, Williams turned to his Marines. "This is as far as we can go, men. We're going over the side of the boats and head quickly into the beach. Everybody ready?"

"Yes, sir!"

"Very well. Lock and load, I'll go first."

Williams strapped his rifle around his back, put his foot over the side of the Higgins boat, lifted onto the side, and dropped into waist-deep, warm water. Behind him, he heard dozens of splashes as his men pulled themselves over the side and fell into the water themselves. Williams stepped toward the beach, scanning the hills for snipers.

Chapter 31

Japanese Machine Gun Encampment
Hill 148
Gavutu Island
August 7, 1942
1205 Hours

Captain Shigetoshi Miyazaki, commanding the Yokohama Air Group on Gavutu and Tanambogo, had made his way up to Hill 148 to take command of the Japanese defenses on Gavutu.

He had already radioed Admiral Sadyoshi on Rabaul to report the dire situation his airmen now faced. They were without their principal weapons, the powerful aircraft that had been sunk by the American surprise attack that morning.

Miyazaki radioed Lieutenant Commander Suzuki over on Tulagi, and they agreed that, without fast reinforcements from Rabaul, they had no chance. But either way, they would fight until the death.

Miyazaki was joined by his comrade, Lieutenant Mitsuwa, the Japanese infantry officer on Gavutu Island, who commanded the 13- and 25-millimeter machine gun units on the island.

Between their locations on Gavutu and Tanambogo, 886 Japanese were prepared to fight until the end. Through his binoculars, Miyazaki looked down at the American Marines disembarking from their landing boats and wading through the water to shore.

"Hold your fire until my command," he ordered his gunnery officers. "Make sure they are all out of the landing craft and have no escape route."

"Yes, sir, Lieutenant."

Miyazaki continued to watch.

"Patience, men."

Down below, the Marines sloshed their way from the water and onto the beach. Miyazaki wanted enough space between the landing craft and the Marines that the boats could not be used as rescue vehicles. But he did not want to wait so long that the Marines moved out of his line of fire.

"Stand by men. Just a few more seconds." The Marines were now beginning to assemble on the beach.

"Stand by!"

As more Marines gathered on the beach below, they became more vulnerable to ambush.

"Be ready." Miyazaki held up one finger. "On my command."

A second later, "Hassha o Hajime!" (the Japanese phrase for "Commence firing!").

Chapter 32

Dog Company
Tulagi Island
Atop the Ridge
Approaching the Southeast Sector
August 7, 1942
1205 Hours

From high atop the 350-foot-long ridge on Tulagi, Dog Company remained halted at the steep ravine that they would need to cross to advance into the southeast sector and, eventually, Hill 281.

Dog Company had met light resistance thus far. They had stopped here only because of the steep ravine.

Charlie and Baker Companies were moving parallel to the southeast, near the opposite seawalls of the island. By contrast, Able Company and, more so, Dog Company had held the high ground near or atop the ridge.

In warfare the advantage always starts with the high ground. And for most of the morning, Dog Company had controlled and enjoyed the high ground. That was about to change.

"Still no bombardment from the navy on the hill over there," Chambers said.

"Maybe they didn't see the flares, sir."

Chambers thought for a second. "That makes no sense. The flares were clear, visible, and burst a thousand feet up in the air. We got at least three ships out there, two destroyers, and a cruiser. If they didn't see the flares, maybe the watchstanders missed the signal on all three ships?"

He inhaled more nicotine into his lungs. "No." He thought a second. "That's impossible."

"Well, it's been thirty minutes, sir, and they sure haven't started shelling at all."

"Nope." Chambers stamped his cigarette out on the ground. "And I am not waiting around here all day, Captain. Our ships were supposed to fire on that hill after we launched our flares. But for whatever reason, they haven't executed their orders."

"No, sir, they did not. At least they haven't yet." Sperling responded.

"Well, Captain, navy or no navy, we have our orders." He stopped to light another cigarette. "Our orders are to take that hill over there and to kill any Japs that get in our way."

"Yes, sir."

Chambers looked down into the ravine, and then across it to the target hill on the other side. "Have you ever seen a ravine like that before?"

"Well, let me put it this way, sir," Captain Sperling said, "I don't think there's a ravine that big anywhere in the state of New Jersey."

"Well, Captain, I'm from West Virginia," Chambers said, "and that ravine doesn't look any different from a typical drunk coal miner's backyard in West Virginia. Piece of cake, walk in the park."

"With respect to the major, sir, my guess is if the major takes a stroll down a ravine in a coal miner's backyard, he doesn't have to worry about Japs in the Appalachians, with high-power rifles." Sperling grinned.

"Captain, have you ever seen a drunk moonshiner with a shotgun?"

"No, sir. Moonshining's illegal in Jersey."

"Well, I have." He took a drag from his cigarette. "And frankly, given a choice, I'll take a Jap machine gun over a drunk West Virginia moonshiner with a shotgun thinking you're about to steal his liquor still."

Sperling chuckled. "I admire the major's courage and humor."

"It will take courage to win this battle and win this war, whether the courage is real, or a front for us officers to display for our men."

"Agreed, Major."

"Besides, moonshining might be against the law in New Jersey, but it is the official hobby, religion, and mandatory pastime of West Virginia."

Sperling broke into a big grin. "In that case, sir, I hope the major will extend me an invitation to visit West Virginia when the war's over. Sounds like more fun than Jersey."

"Consider it done, Captain. Now gather the platoon leaders together. Tell them that we will move through this ravine, up the hill on the other side, and re-take the high ground. There's a gun emplacement over there, near the beach. The colonel wants us to secure it. Tell them that I expect to take heavy fire. So let's hit the Japs harder than they're dishing it out.

"We'll move out on my command and establish perimeter positions on the other side." Chambers tossed his cigarette onto the ground. "Tell the men to spread out and not move together in bunches. I don't want to become easy targets for the Japs. Any questions, Captain?"

"No, sir!"

"Very well, Captain. Be swift, as we have no time to waste. We don't want to give the Japanese any time to fortify their defensive positions on the other side. Let me know when the platoon leaders have been briefed."

"Yes, sir."

Chambers brought his binoculars up and scanned across the ridge. "No sign of the enemy over there," he said.

Of course, Japs could hide behind coconuts and then pop out, fire, and hide again. Despite his efforts to calm Captain Sperling's nerves, Chambers knew damn well that it would be a dogfight to get through that ravine.

Chambers thought for a second about ordering mortar fire on the other side of the ravine, to shake things up. But with no identifiable targets yet, that might waste too much ammunition, which would be needed later.

No, they would try to fight their way through as best as possible and do their utmost to identify snipers and take them out.

"Sir." Chambers looked around and saw Captain Sperling. "Platoon leaders have been briefed, and I'm ready to move on your command."

"Very well. On my command, move out!" Chambers motioned his arms and stepped down into the ravine.

"Move out! Follow me!"

He moved deeper into the ravine, heading down toward the bottom. Other than the blowing wind, the only sound was the men marching, of boots against dirt, rocks, and weeds. When he reached the final slope into the bottom of the ravine, rifle shots rang out, and bullets fell like hard rain in a thunderstorm.

"They're up on the ridges! Return fire!"

The Japanese had waited until Dog Company reached the bottom of the ravine before starting their ambush. Chambers ran to a coconut tree to take cover. Just then, a bullet struck the tree so hard that he first thought it was a mortar round.

Damn.

"Keep moving, men! Pour it on!"

Sprinting through a fire of bullets, Chambers crossed the base of the hill and began climbing up the other side. As he climbed, he looked to his right. Major Bailey's company was taking heavy fire from Hill 208.

"Get some damn mortar fire on Hill 208! Take out those Japs!"

A blinding flash blew him onto his back. Flying shrapnel struck his chest and legs.

He was hit. He knew he was going to die.

*****

USS *Neville* (APA-9)
Off Tulagi Island
Operation Ringbolt Command Post
August 7, 1942
1210 Hours

"Sir, it's Lieutenant Colonel Edson on the radio. Your instincts were correct again, General."

"I'll take it," Rupertus said. "Colonel Edson. What's your situation?"

"It's getting hot over here, General. I've got both Baker Company and Dog Company pinned down in some pretty fierce dogfights. The slugging is going rather slow right now. We need more fire support, General, concentrated on Hill 281. We're taking casualties. Repeat, we are taking casualties."

"Copy that, Colonel," Rupertus responded. "We've got the navy on standby. We're calling fire support. Give us a few minutes."

"Roger that. Thank you, sir."

*****

Dog Company
Tulagi Island
Atop the Ridge
Approaching the Southeast Sector
August 7, 1942
1215 Hours

"Major! Are you okay?"

Major Chambers looked up. Several dark human silhouettes wearing helmets appeared against the sky. He blinked his eyes and heard muffled voices. But his ears were ringing so bad that he couldn't make out who was saying what.

"Sir, a pretty bad mortar shell exploded beside you. You've taken a lot of shrapnel. Let us give you a hand."

"Say again?"

"Sir, we need to evacuate you. We need to get you to the ship."

"Bullshit!" Chambers snapped. "I'm here to lead my men and kill Japanese. I'm not leaving!"

"Major. Sir." The blurring in his eyes had subsided to the point that he recognized his next in command, Captain Sperling, standing over him. "Sir, you're in pretty bad shape. Your left wrist is smashed up, and I think your right wrist is broken. Your upper left leg looks like somebody carved it out with a steak knife. Sir, we need to get you to a medic and back to the ship."

"That's a negative, Sperling! Help me get my ass back on my feet. We got an island to take, and a war to win." Chambers, squinting his eyes to try and orient his vision, could see Sperling shaking his head.

"All right boys, let's see if we can get the major on his feet."

One of his Marines crouched down and started lifting him by his shoulders.

"Aaaah! That hurts like hell!"

"Sorry, sir."

"I don't care, get me on my feet!"

"Aye, sir."

"Sir, with your hands in that condition, I don't think you can handle a rifle."

"I can handle it. Let's go Sperling. We didn't come over here to discuss my medical condition."

"Aye, sir."

"Sir," this was the company corpsman. "At least let me get a bandage on your leg to try to stop that bleeding."

Chambers sighed, frustrated. "Okay, but make it fast."

The corpsman kneeled down and doused Chamber's leg wound with alcohol, which burned like hell. He wrapped a bandage around the wound, which sent another jolt of searing pain through his leg and up into his stomach.

"That should do as a makeshift, sir, but we'll need to look at it later."

"Okay, thanks, let's get moving."

Sperling and the corpsman got Chambers back up on his feet.

"Let's go!"

As his men exchanged fire with Japanese snipers, and fighting through intense pain, Chambers hobbled up the hill, his men surrounding him and following him. The damn Japs would pay for taking a pound of flesh from his leg and ambushing his men.

Chapter 33

Gavutu Island
August 7, 1942
1220 Hours

"Get down! I said get the hell down!" Major Williams yelled at his men as they ran into Japanese machine gun fire and mortars, fired from the two high points on Gavutu and Tanambogo.

Company A had landed unopposed in the initial wave, the Japanese allowing them to move in about seventy-five yards toward Hill 148.

But Companies B and C faced a wave of Japanese bullets as they rushed through the water to get to the shore. Several officers had died, and at least 10 percent of the Marines in the Gavutu invasion force had already been killed.

Major Williams, an Ohio State graduate from Arbor Vitae, took cover under a rock as his men scrambled to avoid fire from the Japanese machine guns. With a cigarette hanging from his mouth, Williams turned to his battalion executive officer, Major Charles Miller.

"Chuck, I know the fire's heavy, but we've gotta take that hill. Is everybody ready?"

"Yes, sir, it's rough going."

"Needless to say, Chuck, but if anything happens to me, you're in charge. And no matter what," he looked up at Hill 148, "we must kill those Japs and get them off those hills."

"Sir, I'll follow you to the top, and we'll kill those Jap bastards and take control of these islands."

"You're a good man, Major Miller."

"Back at you, sir."

"Okay, men!" Williams turned and yelled back at his men. "We're going to take that damn hill! We're moving out now. I'll go first. Follow me!"

Williams got up, and crouching, gripped his rifle and began running, head down, toward the base of Hill 148. Bullets whizzed around his head so close that he felt the rushing air against his ear.

"Aaaaaaaah!"

The bullet struck him hard in the chest. The pain seared like fire surging through his chest and into his body. A powerful dizziness overcame him. The last thing he remembered was falling against the rock. Then nothing but darkness.

*****

USS *Neville* (APA-9)
Off Tulagi Island
Operation Ringbolt Command Post
August 7, 1942
1230 Hours

"General, we just got an urgent message from Gavutu."

"Let's hear it, Killy."

"General, we're taking heavy fire casualties. Several officers KIA. Our ground commander, Major Williams, just got shot, sir. He's out of the fight."

"Damn it! Any word on his condition?"

"Major Charles Miller, Williams's XO, has taken command on the ground. Miller says the fire's so heavy that they can't reach Major Williams to recover him. But they think he's alive. Meanwhile, they're moving into the fire toward the base of Hill 148."

"Any requests for airstrikes or reinforcements?"

"Not yet, sir. Major Miller will remain in contact and request, as necessary."

Rupertus stood up, walked over, and stared at the map of Gavutu hanging on the bulkhead. He crossed his arms and thought for a second.

Rupertus's stomach twisted in a tight knot for Major Williams. Vandegrift had given Rupertus the cream of the 1st Marine Division and the most elite forces available to the Marine Corps for Operation Ringbolt.

Rupertus's forces, the Raiders, and paramarines, who were now carrying out combat operations in Tulagi and Gavutu, were considered more elite than the forces now moving on Guadalcanal. They were chosen because the immediate Japanese threat came from Tulagi and Gavutu, as the airfield on Guadalcanal was not yet complete.

Guadalcanal would heat up later. But for the time being, Tulagi and Gavutu marked the immediate flashpoints. That's why Rupertus and his hand-picked men were selected to become the tip of the American arrow. If they did not first wipe out the Japanese on Tulagi and Gavutu, the operation against Guadalcanal would probably fail.

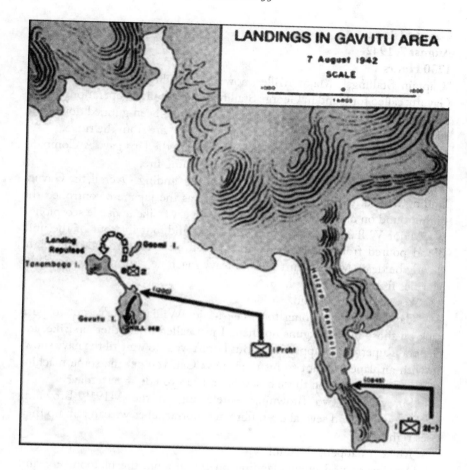

Rupertus had hand-selected Major Williams as one of the elite force commanders for the mission. Williams, in Rupertus's mind, had all the grit to lead the Gavutu strike.

Now Rupertus worried about having to write a letter home to Williams's family. He uttered a silent prayer for his major and turned back to the chief of staff.

"Very well, Killy. Alert me if anything else comes from Gavutu."

"Aye, sir."

*****

Gavutu Island
August 7, 1942
1230 Hours
"Captain Stallings!" Major Miller, now commanding the paramarines on Gavutu, called for Captain George Stallings, the battalion's operations officer.

A Company went in with 102 men. Many had been gunned down, and all were pinned down from Japanese machine gun fire from the ridge.

B Company had fared worse because at least the Japs gave A Company a few minutes to get on the ground before opening fire.

The Japs hit C Company the hardest during landing. Overall, the Gavutu landing had turned bloody for the Marines, as the Japanese controlled the high ground on both hills and were hidden in caves like invisible scorpions.

Major Williams lay sprawled on the ground, out in front of the unit. Blood poured from his stomach and pooled onto the ground. He might already be dead. Miller didn't know. Heavy machine gun fire prevented the Marines from approaching him.

"Yes, sir!" Stallings said.

"Captain, if we're going to rescue Major Williams, we've got to push back on those machine guns up there. I just called in another airstrike, and General Rupertus has approved it. But I don't want to wait 'til the navy shows up with airplanes. I want to hit them now. Can you get me some machine guns and mortar fire on those bastards, and can you do it yesterday?"

"Sir, we got two Brownings"—referring to the M1919 Browning machine gun—"and several 60-millimeter mortar tubes we can ram up their asses right now."

"Make it happen, Captain!"

Dancing around bullets landing on the ground, the platoon sergeants passed on Miller's firing instructions. The Marines deployed the Brownings. A moment later, the sound of American machine gun fire exploded, spewing 30-millimeter bullets at five hundred rounds per minute, pouring lead into the caves in the hill where the Japs were firing. Miller looked through his binoculars. Some of the Japanese were falling over, hit, and dying from the American fire.

"Hell, yeah!" Miller pumped his fist.

A minute later, four blue US Navy Avengers flying in formation roared in toward the island.

"Keep pouring on the fire, boys!"

The Avengers flew over the top of Tanambogo and started dropping bombs over the Japs. Miller watched the bombs falling through the sky toward their Japanese targets below.

A second later, explosions shook the earth. The Japanese fire subsided. "Okay, men. Grab Major Williams! Let's go!"

"I'll get him, sir." This was Lieutenant Norman R. Nickerson of Niagara Falls, New York. Nickerson, a great athlete and outstanding college basketball player at the University of Buffalo, rushed out to Williams and shielded him from the Japanese bullets. Navy Pharmacist Mate Second Class Les Farrell, ducking down, also sprinted out to the bleeding battalion commander.

"Hang in there with me, sir," Farrell said. "I'm going to put some sulfanilamide powder on that wound, get you bandaged up, and get you the hell out of here."

Farrell went to work. A few seconds later, he and Lieutenant Nickerson got the major onto a stretcher. Keeping their heads low, they headed back toward Major Miller and the other officers.

"Take the major to the command post, down by the dock area. Get him on the first boat out of here."

"Aye, aye, sir."

"All right, men. Move out. We've gotta push those Japs off the hill."

Chapter 34

USS *Neville* (APA-9)
Off Tulagi Island
Operation Ringbolt Command Post
August 7, 1942
1256 Hours

"Admiral, Lieutenant Colonel Edson is on the radio from Tulagi."

"Thank you, Killy." Rupertus took the telephone from Kilmartin. "Colonel Edson. What's our update?"

"Sir, we're advancing to the southeast. But the Jap sniper and mortar fire is pretty heavy. We need more naval bombardment. Recommend heavy naval shelling. Target of opportunity is Hill 281."

"Copy that, colonel," Rupertus said. "We're calling in your fire support. Stay strong and stand by."

"Copy that. Thank you, sir," Edson said.

"Killy," Rupertus turned to his chief of staff.

"Open a channel to the USS *San Juan*."

USS *San Juan* was a navy cruiser, larger and more powerful than the two destroyers off Tulagi, the *Buchanan* and the *Monssen*.

"General. USS *San Juan* on the line. Captain Maher for you, sir."

"Thank you, Killy," Rupertus took the phone. "Captain Maher. General Rupertus. Captain, I know it's been a busy morning, but my Marines on Tulagi need more firepower."

"Copy that, General," Maher's voice squawked over the radio frequency. "Will need fire coordinates."

"Same as earlier, Captain. Principal target is Hill 281. The sooner, the better."

"Got it, sir. Will commence shelling in less than one minute."

"Copy that. Thank you, Captain." Rupertus turned to his executive officer. "Killy. Get a message to Edson. Help is on the way."

"Right away, sir."

*****

Tulagi Island
Field Headquarters
August 7, 1942
1257 Hours

Colonel Edson was watching the top of Hill 281 when he heard the familiar voice of his executive officer, Major Sam Griffith, returning from Charlie Company. "You see anything up there, sir?"

"I see the Japs reinforcing their position up there, Sam. They're rolling more gun emplacements into position and there's a lot more troop activity." He brought his binoculars down and looked over at his CO. "It's gonna be some hard slugging when we hit that hill."

"They're tenacious little bastards, for sure, sir, "Griffith said.

"How are things at Charlie Company?"

"They're in a slugfest, Colonel, trying to route the Japs out of those bunkers on Hill 208. Captain Thomas is in charge and is doing a hell of a job. But I'm happy to go back down there if you would like me to, Colonel."

Edson thought for a second. "If Captain Thomas has it under control, let's leave him in command. I need you here as my exec. I may send you back down in a while to check on their progress. Besides, Captain Thomas can raise us on the radio if he needs us."

"Roger that, sir."

A shrill whistling sliced through the air, followed by a loud, thunderous explosion from Hill 281. More shrill whistling. Then another explosion.

Edson brought his binoculars back up to his eyes for a closer view. Two plumes of white smoke billowed from the hill, one from the top and one from the right side, about two-thirds of the way to the top.

More shrilling sounds whizzed through the air. More explosions. A third shell struck the top of the hill and shook the ground from hundreds of yards away. Japanese soldiers scrambled like tiny fire ants, taking cover as exploding shells from USS *San Juan* flew in from the south.

"General Rupertus, you brilliant, beautiful son of a . . ." Edson caught himself. "Sam, I talked to the general less than two minutes ago, and already he's got the navy pounding the hell out of that hill. Damn, the man is efficient."

"That he is, Colonel," Griffith said. "We're lucky General Rupertus is running this operation, sir. Brilliantly executed plan, so far. Hopefully this new round of shelling buys us more time to advance."

"Sam, you read my mind." Edson dropped his binoculars. "Alert the company commanders. Let's move in closer to the base of that hill while we have cover from the navy's shelling. I know Charlie Company is still bogged down at Hill 208, but let's at least get Able and Dog Companies moving forward, and let's get Baker Company moving too."

"Roger that, sir. Would you like me to alert them now?"

"Yes. Immediately."

"Aye, sir." Griffith saluted Edson and then left to alert the company commanders.

*****

USS *Neville* (APA-9)
Off Tulagi Island
Operation Ringbolt Command Post
August 7, 1942
1319 Hours
General Rupertus was reviewing his notes when the ship's 1MC began blaring.

"General quarters! General quarters! All hands to battle stations! Enemy aircraft sighted and approaching from the southwest. All hands to battle stations, prepare anti-aircraft guns. General quarters! General quarters! General quarters! This is not a drill."

"I'm surprised it took them this long." Rupertus strapped on his battle helmet. "Get my rifle, Killy?"

"Yes, sir. Where are you going, General?"

"I'm going down to the deck to watch. Let's hope the navy gets those Hellcats out there on those Zeroes before they sink the fleet. But if they get too close, this ship will need every rifle we can muster firing on the bastard. I can bring one of them down, even if they put a torpedo in the ship's side."

"But, sir," Kilmartin protested, "do you think it might be better to keep you below decks, out of the line of fire?"

"If the ship gets sunk, what difference will it make?"

"I believe you, General." Kilmartin grabbed Rupertus's Springfield rifle from against the bulkhead and handed it to his boss.

"Thanks," Rupertus said. "You coming with me, Killy?"

"Would not miss it, sir."

During any General Quarters situation on board a US Navy warship, all personnel rush to preassigned spaces where they are to remain at battle. Of course, if one were a brigadier general in command of a Marine unit, with no specific military duties in the event of a naval attack other than to make sure his men had life preservers on, Rupertus could go anywhere on the ship he pleased.

Rupertus moved out of the command post, headed up to the starboard main deck, and looked out in the vicinity of Guadalcanal, from where the Japanese pilots in the aircraft would be approaching. All around him, members of the ship's crew were wound up as tight as a ticking alarm clock.

The ship's armament of twenty-two machine guns, including four 50-caliber, two 40-millimeter, and 16-millimeter machine guns, could take down one or two aircraft that flew in close enough for a shot. But the lightly armed *Neville*, standing alone, would not stand a chance against an armada of heavily armed warplanes.

Rupertus knew his 1903 Springfield rifle would not improve the ship's anti-aircraft armament. But then again, one lucky shot might.

Rupertus and Kilmartin, in full battle gear, jogged out onto the starboard deck. There, just above the horizon, off in the direction of Guadalcanal, enemy planes, maybe thirty of them altogether, appeared as blackbirds of prey in the sky. The twin-engine bombers approached in a line abreast.

Neville's 50-caliber anti-aircraft guns opened fire.

"Damn, General," Kilmartin said. "Looks like they're sending the whole Imperial Japanese Air Force out to sink us."

As the enemy planes bore down on the ship, *Neville*'s 40-millimeter and 16-millimeter weapons opened up. The explosive rattling of thousands of bullets spewing lead over the Sealark Channel rattled the ship. So far, there was no evidence that *Neville*'s anti-aircraft fire was having any effect on the enemy planes.

Several squadrons of Japanese Zeros appeared out of the clouds, providing cover for the Japanese bombers.

"I'm seeing dive bombers and Jap Zero fighter escorts," Kilmartin said, in a loud voice, talking over the sound of multiple machine gun fire.

"Agreed, Killy."

"Sir, if the Zeros reach our position, and right now I don't see anything to stop them, they're liable to strafe the deck. You might be safer below decks if those Zeros start strafing."

"I'm okay, Killy. Thank goodness most of our Marines are no longer on board this ship. If the ship goes down, at least with a few Marines on hand with their rifles, they stand a fighting chance."

They could hear the roaring sound of aircraft engines coming over the ship's port side. Rupertus craned his head back and looked straight overhead as eight US Navy F4F Wildcats broke through the gray clouds and roared overhead, several hundred feet in the air, crossing the path of the *Neville*. With their distinctive bluish-gray-painted color, with a single white star in a blue circle painted on the bottom of their wings and fuselages, the Wildcats streaked out to meet the inbound Japanese planes.

"Hell, yeah!" someone yelled. As the Wildcats moved over the ship's starboard side, *Neville's* anti-aircraft machine guns ceased fire to avoid accidentally shooting down the US Navy planes.

The Wildcats converged on the Jap planes, and shots began to fly. Several enemy bombers burst into flames and dropped into the sea.

A moment later, a second squadron of Wildcats appeared in the sky, ducking down through the clouds and racing out to join the dogfight. Several of the Japanese bombers managed to fly closer to the *Neville*, with the navy F4Fs following them all the way in.

Rupertus watched through his binoculars as an incredible dogfight unfolded over the water. This developing air battle was between the Imperial Japanese Navy's finest aircraft, the Mitsubishi A6M Zero, versus the US Navy's F4F Wildcats.

The Zeros and the Nakajima B5N "Kate" bombers had inflicted much damage on the American fleet at Pearl Harbor and inspired Rupertus to pen the now-famous Marine Corps "Rifleman's Creed." This time, though, the Japanese planes were more than meeting their match.

The Wildcats tried pouncing on the Jap bombers as the Zeros maneuvered to defend their bombers. Rupertus watched as several planes burst into flames and dove into the water. However, because of the distance and the fire and billowing black smoke blockng his vision, he could not tell whether the burning planes were American or Japanese.

The Japanese bombers were dropping bombs and torpedoes in the water. But so far, *Neville* had not been touched. After several burning planes fell into the sea, many Japanese planes appeared to break off and begin to leave the area.

"The Japs are starting to break off, sir."

"Good!" Rupertus said. "But you can bet they'll be back."

One of the F4F Wildcat fighter planes, smoke trailing from its engine, came roaring in over the starboard side of the ship.

"He's been hit, sir," Kilmartin said.

The Wildcat flew out several hundred yards off the ship's starboard side before crash-landing into the sea. Rupertus and Kilmartin watched as the single-engine plane bobbed on the top of the sea.

"Now hear this! This is the captain!" The voice of navy captain Carlos Bailey boomed over the ship. "Stand by for rescue operations. Initiate man overboard protocol. We're going to maneuver to pull that pilot out of the water."

The ship began to turn, steering toward the location of the downed plane, which was still afloat. Sailors rushed to the ship's starboard side, with ropes, life rafts, and lifeboats on standby.

A few minutes later, rescue crews brought the downed pilot into a lifeboat and began heading back toward the ship.

"Well, we dodged a bullet, Killy."

"That we did, sir."

"Let's get back to the command post."

*****

USS *Neville* (APA-9)
Off Tulagi Island
Operation Ringbolt Command Post
August 7, 1942
1400 Hours

Rupertus paced back and forth across the deck in the shipboard command center, glancing at the maps of Tulagi and then Gavutu and Tanambogo.

It was the loneliest of feelings, sending men into battle, knowing some would die, and yet not being on the front lines with them. Rupertus was a general. But first and foremost, he was a Marine. He was a warrior.

Rupertus needed to remain in the command center on board the ship to orchestrate the overall operations everywhere his Marines were deployed—on Florida Island, on Tulagi, on Gavutu, and soon, on Tanambogo. He had eaten nothing all day and had sucked down one cigarette after another.

Colonel Kilmartin rushed back into the command center. "General, we just got an updated message from Tulagi. From Major Miller."

"Let's hear it, Killy."

"Sir, our boys are taking heavy fire. We have multiple casualties. The good news—we've clawed our way up Hill 148 and hope to take it within a matter of hours. Maybe within the next few minutes."

"That's a big deal." Rupertus allowed himself a brief smile.

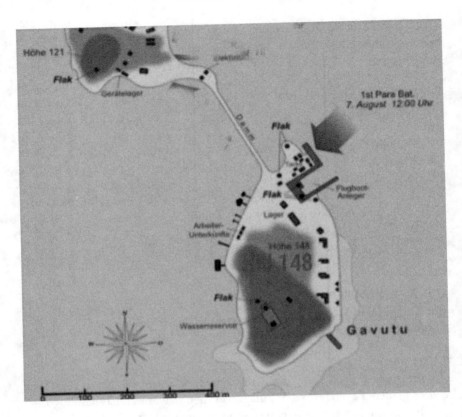

Kilmartin continued, "The Japanese have consolidated their position on Tanambogo. A number have crossed the causeway connecting the two islands. Our acting ground commander, Major Miller, requests additional airstrikes against Tanambogo, specifically against Hill 121."

Rupertus looked up at the map showing Tulagi-Tanambogo, and identified Hill 121.

"Very well," Rupertus said. "Notify Admiral Turner and the commanding officer on USS *Wasp*. Request airstrikes on Tanambogo, effective immediately. The specific target is Hill 121. Please provide firing coordinates."

"Aye, sir. On it immediately."

"And Killy?"

"Yes, sir?" The chief of staff turned around.

"Any word on Major Williams?"

"They were able to retrieve him under fire and carry him to the back of the lines. He's with medics, and they expect to evacuate him out tonight. He is alive, though he's lost a lot of blood."

*****

USS *Neville* (APA-9)
Off Tulagi Island
Operation Ringbolt Command Post
August 7, 1942
1430 Hours

"General, the latest round of airstrikes against Tanambogo have been completed. At this point, Major Miller requests additional reinforcements."

Rupertus thought for a second. "How much additional manpower is he requesting?"

"Doesn't say, sir. But he wants reinforcements for their ground assault against Tanambogo, and specifically against Hill 121."

"Any ideas on Japanese troop strength remaining?"

"We don't know for sure, sir, but Major Miller estimates several hundred."

"Let me think." Rupertus studied the map. "Okay. Let's order in one company from 1st Battalion, 2nd Marines off Florida Island to reinforce our guys on Gavutu."

A raised eyebrow from Kilmartin. "Sir, permission to speak?"

"Of course, Colonel."

"Well, sir, do we believe that one company will be sufficient for reinforcements?"

"Has Major Williams requested more than one company?"

"No, sir, he's only requested reinforcements."

"Hmm. Well, we're already short on manpower. Most of our Marines are with General Vandegrift landing on Guadalcanal. We already have a light force on Florida. And although they haven't met with resistance, we need them there to deter the Japanese from escaping from Tulagi and Gavutu. I'm concerned that if I pull more than one company away right now, I'll leave our defenses there too thin."

Kilmartin nodded his head. "Yes, sir."

"Let's go ahead with one company. If Major Miller requests more reinforcements, we can evaluate at that time."

"Aye, sir."

Chapter 35

Gavutu Island
August 7, 1942
1500 Hours

The five landing crafts from the USS *President Jackson* moved toward the northeastern shoreline of Tanambogo. The boats carried men from Company B, a combat team of the 2nd Marines, who earlier in the day, under the command of Captain Crane, had landed on Florida Island and occupied Haleta.

On Florida Island, they had met no resistance. That was about to change. General Rupertus had assigned them a new, deadly mission—to cross the water and establish a beachhead on Tanambogo.

They hoped to make a landing on Tanambogo and pressure the Japanese from the backside, to help open the causeway that Major Miller and his Marines had not been able to reach.

As the landing crafts started to approach the shoreline, the sound of shrill whistling shells flying over their heads was followed by massive explosions along the island's eastern shoreline. The shelling was delivered courtesy of the destroyers USS *Monssen* and USS *Buchanan*. The naval gunfire, meant to soften the resistance near the beachhead ahead of Company B's landing, shook Tanambogo.

A shell from one of the warships struck an enemy fuel dump, lighting the sky and exposing the Marines in the water. As a result, Company B was cut to pieces.

D Company, from the 4th Platoon, moved in close enough to set up to machine guns on the pier. But the enemy fire was overwhelming, and they had to withdraw.

Captain Crane and thirty of his men somehow made it through and landed on Tanambogo. But the heavy enemy fire also forced them to withdraw and head back out to sea. Twelve of Crane's men were evacuated under fire. The boats turned and headed back north toward Florida Island to wait out the naval bombardment.

Chapter 36

"What do you think, Colonel?" Major Sam Griffith, executive officer of the 1st Raider Battalion, posed the question to his boss, Lieutenant Colonel Merritt Edson.

It had been a long, hard day for all four companies of the 1st Raider Battalion. Japanese snipers hidden in coconut trees, and the fact the Japanese had dug themselves in deep, hiding in tunnel caves dug out of limestone cliffs on the side of hills, had slowed the Raiders' progress. Further, the Japs had set up machine gun pits outside the dugouts protected by sandbags, delaying the Marines even more.

The navy had pounded Hill 281, which, like the other hills in the combat zone, was named Hill 281, as General Rupertus had requested, because it rose 281 feet above the sea. During the naval bombardments, the Jap machine gun fire had partially subsided as the Japs took cover. During these times, the Marines could advance against a reduced level of resistance.

It was a bloody day, with dozens of Marines killed. Colonel Edson had not yet gotten an up-to-date body count. But this he knew: Between the direct fire on the ground, combined with the navy's bombardment from the sea, as the day ended, more Japanese had been killed than Marines.

And at the end of the day, that's what counted—more dead Japanese than dead Americans.

Edson and his men could not have gotten better support from both the navy and their ground commander, Brigadier General Rupertus.

The Japanese were feisty bastards and worthy opponents. Their fighting spirit was admirable, even if they displayed the morality of a nation of dogs. They had fixed their defenses atop Hill 281 and burrowed themselves in a ravine at the island's southeast end.

Edson had brought his Marines into a position a few hundred yards from the Japanese defenses. The Japanese were in a better place than the

Marines had anticipated. They held the high ground, dug into hidden machine gun perches and pillboxes built out of concrete. Foxholes and caves were everywhere.

The Japs were not going to surrender and would fight to the death of the last man. Still, the Marines had won, and the Japanese had lost the first day.

"I'm sorry, what did you say, Sam?"

"I was asking about your thoughts, your plan. And if you have any additional orders at the moment, Colonel."

Edson checked his watch. "Well, we're about to lose our daylight, and we can't take the hill in the dark, not given the chronological situation. I think at this point we dig it in for the night. Then, in the morning, those Japs will wish they had never heard of the US Marine Corps."

"Aye, sir."

"Sam, pass the word to the company commanders. We're holding up here. Set defensive perimeters and set watches. Plan on moving out for an all-out assault on that hill at daybreak."

Chapter 37

Gavutu Island
Hill 148
Old Glory Raised!
August 7, 1942
1800 Hours

Grasping his M1903 Springfield rifle in his hands, with a round chambered and ready to fire in case a Jap sniper popped up from inside a cave, Major Chuck Miller walked along the zigzag path to the top of Hill 148.

His men had controlled Hill 148 for the last couple of hours. All the Japanese survivors of the Marines' onslaught retreated over to Tanambogo, across the narrow, five-hundred-yard causeway where they continued to snipe at his Marines with rifle fire and mortar fire. Gavutu, however, was now under the control of the US Marine Corps.

Miller had served in the Marine Corps for more than ten years, but he had never seen anything like this. Between the navy's initial bombardment of Gavutu, followed by the intense, bloody firefight between his men and the

Gavutu and Tanambogo Islands. (US NAVY PHOTO)

Japanese occupying the A-line, Gavutu smoked like a burning oven with a gallon of grease spilled in the bottom.

After the day's battle, smoke filled the air everywhere, it seemed.

Everywhere he turned, bodies of dead Japanese soldiers were strewn over the ground. Some were lying dead with their eyes and mouths frozen wide open. Some had died with contorted looks of excruciating pain on their faces. Some lay there, stumps of what they once were, without arms, legs, or hands. Many dripped blood from American bullets.

The Japs deserved what they got, as far as Miller was concerned. They had started this war, and they would get what was coming to them.

It wasn't the Japs Miller worried about; it was his Marines—they had taken heavy casualties. And while he did not yet have a report on the number of Americans killed, he estimated the death toll to be one out of every ten Marines. And that wasn't counting those severely wounded, like Major Williams, the battalion commander being attended to by navy corpsmen down by the bombed-out seaplane ramp. Major Williams had been badly injured and might not survive.

He stepped onto the summit of the hill, where he found more of the same. Dozens of dead Japanese lying around, and his Marines standing atop Hill 148 with their guns, some smoking cigarettes, looking tired as hell, and some looking dazed.

Miller walked over to one of the Japanese machine gun embankments and glanced at the bodies. One of the bodies appeared to be the Jap commander.

He stopped to light a cigarette. The first full day of battle had ended. Tanambogo, with its Hill 121, would hopefully be finished off tomorrow. Tomorrow would bring another bloody day. His Marines would need reinforcements, and he planned to ask General Rupertus for more manpower.

But for now, Miller had one thing he needed to do. It was just before 1800 hours, and the sun would set in thirty minutes or so. Still, it was not too late. "Sergeant. Round up a color guard."

"Yes, sir! With pleasure, sir!" The sergeant turned to a couple of his men. "Corporal. Private. Come with me."

The Japanese flag had flown at the summit of Hill 148 since the beginning of the occupation. Marines had already pulled the flag down, and now a new flag was about to be raised.

"Security details, take your positions on the perimeter of the summit," Miller ordered.

"Attention on deck!"

The Marines inside the security detail came to attention.

"Present arms!"

The Marines snapped their rifles into the honor guard position, presenting the underside of the firearm toward the flag.

"Hoist the Colors."

"Hoist the Colors! Aye, sir."

Miller snapped a sharp salute as the makeshift honor flag raised Old Glory on Gavutu.

The battle for Tanambogo was far from over, but what a damn fine sight to see!

Chapter 38

With his Marines from the 1st Parachute Battalion now in control of Gavutu and the major battle for Tulagi to commence after sunrise, General Rupertus made a command decision.

Rupertus wanted to be on the battlefield with his men and not on board the ship. He had remained on board because, as commander, he was overseeing two simultaneous amphibious invasions, one on Tulagi and the other on Gavutu, by two separate Marine combat teams.

The general needed to remain in his central location on the *Neville* to devote his full attention to both teams during the initial stages of the invasion. At various times, both Colonel Edson on Tulagi and Major Miller on Gavutu had made requests for targeted airstrikes, and now Major Miller had requested additional ground forces for Tanambogo.

Rupertus had approved all those requests. He had received communications from his commanders on the ground that the Raiders had suffered up to 22 percent casualties. That sickened his stomach, and he dreaded reporting those numbers to General Vandegrift.

Rupertus walked over to one of the navigational charts to study the position of the warships and landing ships positioned off Tulagi.

He then took another look, focusing only on the position of the *Neville* and its three sister transport ships off Tulagi.

The *Neville*, the flagship for Operation Ringbolt, was on station as the southeastern corner of four ships, alongside the *Heywood*, the *President Jackson*, and the *Zeilin*, anchored about four and a half miles from Beach Blue.

The boats traveling onto Beach Blue from the four transport ships were cutting a course approximately south of northeast.

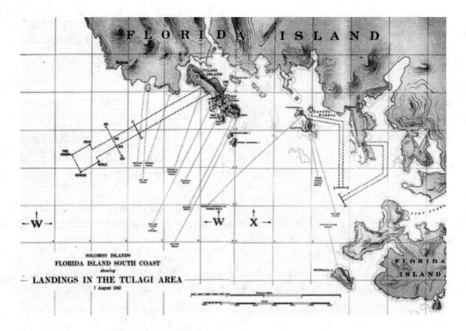

It had been a hard day for Marines and those on board the ships, with the air attacks and enduring heavy fire from Japanese forces on both Tulagi and Gavutu.

"Colonel," Rupertus said to his chief of staff, Colonel Robert Kilmartin, "I'm ready to move our command post to Beach Blue on Tulagi."

"Yes, sir. As you know, sir, Tulagi is not yet fully secure."

"Which is precisely the point. Our Marines need their commander on the field. Now I understand we had to remain behind during the initial stages since we were commanding movements on two fronts—in both Tulagi and Gavutu. But now we're beyond the initial stages and have established beachheads in both battles."

"Understood, sir."

"Notify Captain Bailey. We're moving our command post. Prepare a landing craft and notify the beachmaster at Beach Blue. I'll meet you down on the deck by the boats."

"Aye, sir."

Rupertus strapped on his battle helmet, grabbed his rifle, and headed down to the starboard deck. When he arrived, a small navy crew met him by the rope ladder, which went over the ship's side down to the landing craft.

The sailors came to attention and snapped a short salute. "Good evening, General," a chief petty officer said. "We heard you're looking for a boat ride to Tulagi."

"Sooner the better, Chief."

"Your landing craft is already down there, engine running, a crew aboard and waiting, sir."

"Thanks. I'm waiting on my chief of staff."

"Aye, sir."

Colonel Kilmartin arrived in full battle gear with his rifle, accompanied by the general's aide and one other officer with their rifles and in battle gear.

"Ready, Colonel?"

"Yes, sir." Kilmartin said. "Just spoke to the beachmaster on Beach Blue. They're ready for us but cautioned about snipers moving in the area. Said we might face Jap sniper fire on approach."

"Who's the beachmaster?"

"Navy lieutenant. Lieutenant Jorgensen. Officer on the *Neville*. Beach Blue is the only beach open, sir. The lieutenant has been able to do that under heavy sniper fire. We control that part of the island, and we've rooted out all the Japs from the coconut trees. And it's harder at night."

"Have you relayed my orders for the rest of the staff to follow?"

"Yes, sir, General. They will stay on board the ship until a little before midnight, and then will join us with the rest of the communications equipment and everything else we need to establish our new command post.

"They will first dispatch your situation report to General Vandegrift and then request a release of an additional combat team from the division. Also, per your orders, sir, they'll send out the message ordering the withdrawal of Combat Team A from East Florida Island to report to Beach Blue in the morning."

"Okay," Rupertus nodded. "Let's give it a shot and see how it goes."

"After you, sir." Kilmartin motioned to the ladder.

Rupertus climbed down into the boat, accepted a salute from the navy crew, and took a seat in the middle of the boat. The Higgins boat had a US Navy crew of four, including a coxswain, an engineer, a bowman, and a sternman.

A moment later, once Colonel Kilmartin and two of the other general's aides had climbed aboard, they cast off from the side of the *Neville* and moved through the dark waters to the north, headed to the northwest sector of Tulagi.

The wind had died down earlier in the day. The smooth surface of the sea provided a calm ride across the waters to the south.

"We're getting close, General," the US Navy coxswain said. "Maybe ten minutes out." A moment later, the coxswain pointed over the dark waters, where several lights became visible.

"There. That's Beach Blue, General. Remember, sir, there's heavy coral in the area. You'll have to wade into the beach like the guys did this morning. Coral is sharp and can be as bad as poison when it gets ground into a cut."

"Copy that, Chief."

Rupertus flipped his cigarette overboard, as the glow might provide a visible target point for Japanese snipers.

They moved in closer, and the dark silhouette of Tulagi, with its 350-foot spine running down the middle, emerged from the dark of the night.

As they came in, perhaps one hundred yards from the now dark shoreline, the coxswain slowed the engines on the Higgins boat.

"This is about as far as we can get you, General, because of the coral. She's already scraping under the front hull of the boat."

"So, this is where we get off?"

"Yes, sir. But please be careful, it's dark out there, sir."

"Let me go overboard first," Kilmartin said, "to make sure we have solid footing on the bottom."

"Not necessary, Killy. I'm not as old as you think I look."

Rupertus started to step over the side of the boat. The sound of a rifle shot cracked the air. Then another. And another.

"What the hell?" exclaimed Kilmartin.

The shots whizzed by their heads in the air, hitting the water all around and splashing in the boat. "General, get down!" Kilmartin yelled. Then to the coxswain, "Get us the hell out of here!"

Chapter 39

Command Post
1st Raider Battalion, Combat Team 2
Tulagi Island
August 7, 1942
2200 Hours

Shortly before dusk, the Marines came upon a deep ravine running east and west, cutting across the island.

They decided to anchor their company lines along the perimeter of the ravine and then dig in deep for the night. Intelligence officers began scanning written materials taken from the dead Japanese, soon discovering that their encampment along the perimeter of the ravine was on the edge of the core of enemy resistance.

Except for occasional sniper fire, the 1st Raider Battalion and each of its four companies had been spared from heavy combat since about sunset.

By 2200 hours, the battalion had pushed down almost to the base of Hill 281, and Lieutenant Colonel Edson had commandeered a house known as "the Residency" as his temporary command post.

The Residency, a large white wooden building built by the British, once served as the home of the highest British official, the High Commissioner, governing the Solomon Islands. Set between the two ridges, the Residency was complete with all the amenities—tennis courts, golf links, and the cricket field where Charlie Company had earlier engaged in intense combat.

Inside the Residency, Colonel Edson and his men found valuable intelligence, including maps detailing the Japanese position on the island and other written materials that revealed the island's Japanese war plans.

Colonel Edson stood at a desk inside the residence and pulled out some papers that appeared to be handwritten in Japanese. "Lieutenant Erskine," he called out to his Japanese language specialist, Lieutenant John "Tiger" Erskine.

"Yes, sir, Colonel."

"This map has some writing on it. Translate this for me, will you?"

"Aye. Let me take a look."

Edson watched as Erskine studied the document.

"Sir, these are military planning documents, left behind and signed by Lieutenant Commander Suzuki, the Japanese commander on the island. If this information is accurate, it's a gold mine."

"Well, I'll be damned." Edson struck a match and lit a cigarette. "Tell me what we've got, Lieutenant."

"Very well, sir. It appears Commander Suzuki has set up his current headquarters here," Erskine pointed to a specific position on the map, "in this ravine. As you can see, it's west of the hill, almost in line with where our southernmost company, Charlie Company, is lined up."

"He's holed up out in front of Charlie Company, but in the ravine on the other side of Hill 208?"

"That's correct, sir. Also, sir, they have two machine gun batteries set up for an ambush. Machine gun batteries are located right here, at the foot of the hill, behind the hospital." Erskine pointed out that position on the map.

"They also have two more-powerful 8-millimeter anti-aircraft batteries positioned right here"—he again pointed to the map—"right on top of the southeast promontory. Commander Suzuki refers to this position as 'Bird Hill.'"

"Son of a bitch." Edson took a drag from a cigarette. "Bird Hill, eh?"

"Yes, sir," Erskine said.

"Now I know how General McClellan felt when he found General Lee's battle plans at Antietam." He glanced over at his executive officer, Major Sam Griffith. "But I'll tell you what, Sam. You can better believe my Marines will be a hell of a lot more aggressive than McClellan ever was."

"Should we try and hit them tonight, Colonel?"

"Too dark for a large, organized assault. But we sure as hell will hit them in the morning. Pass the word along to the company commanders, Sam. We hold up here until sunrise, and then we hit and hit hard. And we'll hit those machine gun embankments and any anti-aircraft embankments with aircraft first thing. Once we take those out, we should be able to find a way to the top of that hill and take it."

"Understood, sir."

"And Sam, tell them to be on the lookout. The Japanese could try something during the night."

"Aye, sir."

Edson, in his gut, had a feel for the Japanese. He had served with his commanding general, Brigadier General Rupertus, in Shanghai in 1937 and saw the way they had slaughtered the Chinese army and Chinese citizens in Shanghai.

Their time together in Shanghai was one of the reasons General Rupertus had selected him for this mission. And, in Edson's opinion, Rupertus knew and understood the Japs better than any flag officer in the entire US military.

Rupertus was chosen to lead the first Marine ground assault against the Japanese partly because of what he witnessed in Shanghai in 1937—absolute barbarianism and mass murder by the Japs.

Edson had studied the Japanese tactics, warning his men about the Jap propensity for surprise and attacking in the middle of the night. First, they would send scouts, moving in the darkness, to survey the perimeter. The Japs scouted for weaknesses, like open areas between units on the defensive perimeter. Once they scouted the position, the Japs attacked from a single direction to avoid confusion within their ranks.

He and General Rupertus had seen this in Shanghai, as the Japs used these nighttime tactics not only against the Chinese military but also against civilians. And so he warned his men. Every Marine had grenades nearby, and defensive machine gun posts would remain manned throughout the night.

*****

1st Raider Battalion, Combat Team 2
The Gap between Able and Charlie Companies
Tulagi Island
August 7, 1942
2300 Hours

At 2300 hours, in the gap between Able and Charlie Companies, the Japanese struck.

They had found a gap between the two companies and came rushing into the opening, firing guns and running into the outer lines of the defensive perimeters of each company.

Once inside the gap, the Japanese began to crawl on the ground toward Able Company, launching a slew of grenades and rifle fire. On the other side, Charlie Company began striking back. Suddenly, the Marines had the Japs pinned in a crossfire between the two companies.

Lieutenant Colonel Edson, trying to grab a little shut-eye in the rack, popped up and grabbed his sidearm. He rushed toward the sound of the shooting, heading along the path from his temporary headquarters toward the direction of Able and Charlie Companies. A few minutes later, he met his chief of staff, Major Griffith, who was walking up the pathway from the direction of shooting.

"What have we got, Sam?"

"Sir, these Japs may not be as clever as we had given them credit for."

"What do you mean?"

"They tried to infiltrate Able Company but moved into the gap between Able Company and Charlie Company. They got caught in a vise, and we crushed them. I guess they had no idea Charlie Company was right behind them. Twenty-six Japs killed and counting."

Not long after Able and Charlie Companies had foiled the midnight attack, the Japanese struck again. This time, they infiltrated the lines and tried to retake the residence where Lieutenant Colonel Edson had set up temporary quarters.

During the night, the Rikusentai launched two more significant attacks and five separate smaller attacks near the command post area. They came out of their caves, screaming, whistling, making loud cricket noises, all in an attempt at psychological intimidation.

The Japs' antics did not surprise Colonel Edson. He had seen their mind-game shenanigans before in Shanghai. This time, the Japanese were tangling with an enemy much more formidable than the Chinese army, which they had crushed in 1937.

Captain John Sweeney, of Columbus, Ohio, was in command in defense of the command post. By 2330 hours, a light rain had turned into a heavy downfall. The weather did not deter the Japanese attacks in the least. During their final major assault against the command post, they slipped into a tiny house nearby on the property, in an attempt, perhaps, to secure shelter as they prepared to try another assault on the principal residence.

The night and heavy rainfall made it difficult to see. But through his binoculars, Sweeney spotted a group of about a dozen Japs entering the small white house.

"You see those Japs squeezing into that little white house over there?" he asked his gunnery sergeant.

"I see somebody, Captain. And it ain't our guys."

"They think they are sneaky little bastards. Think they're going there and hide, and then, at the last second, pour out and mow down a bunch of Marines."

"You want me to take a firing squad over there and root them out, Captain?"

"Hell no, Gunny. That'd waste valuable energy. Tell your men to train their machine guns on that building."

"You want to waste the building with them inside, sir?"

"When the snakes are in the pit, Gunny, what are you going to do? You burn the hell out of the snake pit!"

"Aye, sir." The gunny turned to two of his men. "Corporal. Private. Train your machine guns on that little building over there. On my command, commence fire. Don't stop 'til I tell you to stop."

Sweeney waited for a couple of minutes until the last one appeared to have gone in.

"Okay, Gunny. Tell the men to blast the hell out of that place."

"Corporal! Private! Commence fire!"

The Marines' dueling machine guns burst with a powerful rat-a-tat-a-tat-a-tat-a-tat into the night, firing through the rain and riddling the little white house with holes like a slab of Swiss cheese.

When the firing started, some of the Japanese tried to run out. But the Marines gunned them down. Payback.

Screams and moans sounded from inside the shack, like something from a Halloween horror movie. A moment later, as the machine guns kept pounding, everything went silent.

"Cease fire, Gunny."

"Cease fire!"

The firing stopped. For a moment, the only sound was the rain.

"Good shooting, Gunny. You've trained your men well."

"Thanks, we took out quite a few of them, Captain. What do you want to do with the bodies?"

"Tell you what. Get some of the guys and have them drag those Jap bodies back into the house. Then, after that, we're gonna burn this damn place to the ground."

"You're going to torch the place, sir?"

"That's right, Gunny. I hate to leave a bunch of messy Jap bodies out here, almost in the colonel's front yard. Also, I want to send a message, a bright, loud, and clear message, to any Japs out there that might be watching in a coconut tree, about what might happen if they screw around with the US Marine Corps."

"Aye, sir."

"Okay, let's get those bodies in the house, and get this place torched. And get me a body count before you torch the place, will you, Gunny?"

"Aye, aye."

Sweeny watched as his Marines dragged the Jap bodies back into the wooden house and then poured gasoline around the perimeter. As the Marines went about their work, the gunnery sergeant came back over.

"We've got your body count, sir—thirteen altogether."

"I guess that's our lucky number tonight, Gunny."

"Yes, sir. Charlie Company got thirteen earlier. I guess we're running a tie."

"I guess we are, Gunny." Sweeney stopped to light a cigarette. "Okay, Gunny. Tell the boys to light them up."

"Aye, sir." He turned to the Marines standing around the white house. "Light 'em up, men."

One of the Marines held a burning torch down to one of the corners of the house. Despite the rain, flames engulfed the place in a quick swoosh. A moment later, more flames leaped into the sky, lighting the entire area.

"Let's hope the Japs get the message, Gunny."

"I guess we will find out in the morning, sir."

"Yes, we will."

Chapter 40

Operation Ringbolt Command Higgins Boat
Off Beach Blue on the Tulagi Coast
August 8, 1942
0615 Hours

The night was long, and General Rupertus had not counted on spending most of it in a boat in the water, trying to penetrate the beach to establish a command post in the battlefront.

Yet Rupertus considered it essential to establish a command post on the ground, near the battlefront, as a morale boost for his men, if nothing else. When his Marines waded ashore yesterday morning, they had caught the Japanese off guard and by surprise. Only occasional, sporadic sniper fire had greeted the first wave coming in.

But now, the sniper fire had gotten worse. Though the Marines controlled the entire western section of the island, including Beach Blue, Japanese snipers had infiltrated into the trees and weeds and were hard to pin down.

The snipers' potshots came at a rapid pace throughout the night.

Rupertus wanted to push onto the beach, even in the face of the sniper fire. The others aboard the Higgins boat, particularly Colonel Kilmartin, argued that the general's safety and importance to the war effort did not justify the risk.

And Killy was right, which was one of the things that made him a great chief of staff. Killy shot it straight and was not an ass kisser always eying his next promotion. Rupertus could carry on his duties on the *Neville* for a bit longer.

At midnight, the rest of his staff, the rear echelon of the general's command post, had boarded another Higgins boat and made their way to the waters off Beach Blue. They brought additional communications equipment so that Rupertus could contact General Vandegrift and other associated commands.

After the first onslaught of bullets, the navy coxswain had pulled the general's boat out, away from shore, far enough beyond the effective range of the Japanese rifles.

When the second boat arrived on the scene, carrying the rest of the general's staff, the Japs unleashed another round of sniper fire, forcing the second boat to take evasive maneuvers to get out of sniper range.

But since the second boat brought onboard communications equipment, Rupertus could communicate as necessary with Vandegrift throughout the night. As a result, the entire command post remained afloat all night, off Beach Blue and outside the range of Japanese rifle fire.

By 0600 hours on the morning of August 8, the second day of the joint operations against Tulagi and Gavutu, Rupertus made a decision concerning the Beach Blue command post.

"Let's think about this, Killy. We moved our men in without too much sniper fire all day yesterday, and then the snipers go ballistic overnight. Is that how you read it?"

"Yes, sir, and that is consistent with what we're hearing from our beachmaster, Lieutenant Jorgensen."

"Well, here's the way I'm reading it. It's a hell of a lot easier for the Japs to move around in slime and coconut trees at night because they know it's a lot harder for us to see them."

"A reasonable theory, sir."

"Okay, why don't we try this: Let's move back into the drop-off point. If we don't draw fire, let's see if we can get you onto the beach along with several men to start establishing the command post. Why don't you take Captain Powell and Captain Seeley?"

"Aye, sir."

"If this works, I'll go back to the *Neville* to check overnight messages, and then I'll organize two more combat teams here at Beach Blue, and one more to send over to Gavutu. I plan to return with one of the two combat teams to shore up support for our command post on the beach."

"Ready to give it a shot when you are, General."

"Very well. Chief," Rupertus said to the navy coxswain. "Let's navigate back to the drop-off point and see if we draw fire from those bastards this morning."

"Aye, sir. But to be safe, respectfully recommend that everyone stay low."

"Thank you, Chief."

The coxswain revved the engine, and the Higgins boat cut through the water toward the beach. Rupertus enjoyed the morning breeze whipping around his face.

As they moved in closer, Rupertus reflected that Beach Blue looked different in the daylight hours than it had late at night, when he had seen only lights coming from the beach. Now he saw several tents erected inside the tree line, and a number of his Marines stood guard, patrolling out front.

"Isn't this about where we started drawing fire last night, Chief?"

"Just about, sir. I made several runs in here yesterday, and we're almost at the coral reef area, which is our drop-off point. But we're in their range if they start shooting."

"Steady as she goes, Chief."

"Aye, sir."

The coxswain slowed the boat. Rupertus again felt the scraping against the front hull as they came to a halt. Still no shots. "Okay, sir," the coxswain said. "We're at the drop point, and if anyone wants to go ashore, now's the time."

"I need to first get back to the ship, to check on messages from General Vandegrift, check on Major Williams, and review classified message traffic. Also, we need to get more firepower out here." He looked at Kilmartin. "What do you think, Killy?"

"Agreed, sir."

Rupertus turned to his third in command, Major William Enright, an operations officer for the staff. "Major Enright? I want you to head over to the beach, take a few men, and start setting up our command post. Colonel Kilmartin and I have to head back to the ship, but we should be back a little later in the morning."

"Yes, sir, General," Enright said. "It will be my honor, sir." Enright, a 1932 graduate of the US Naval Academy, served as commanding officer of the 1st Battalion, 5th Marines.

"Very well." Rupertus turned to the cockswain. "Chief, I know we're in range of their snipers, but I want you to keep us here until Major Enright and his men make it to the beach, so they have a way off if the snipers open fire."

"Aye, sir."

Enright and his team went over the boat's side, dropped into the water, and began to wade toward the shore. The calm water, with no currents or breakers, helped them move quickly to the beach.

A moment later, Enright reached the beach, turned, and gave the general a thumbs-up.

"Outstanding!" Rupertus said. "Very well, Chief. Let's turn this baby around and head back to *Neville*. We'll be back in an hour or so."

"Aye, sir."

The coxswain turned the boat, and they cut a course to the south toward the *Neville*. Rupertus first wanted to get a full briefing of overnight combat activities and check on any messages from General Vandegrift.

*****

Higgins Boat Carrying Commander, Operation Ringbolt
Approaching USS *President Hayes* (APA-24)
August 8, 1942
0645 Hours

During the evening, Rupertus was in touch with *Neville* and the beachmaster at Beach Blue with the US Navy model TBY-8 transceiver, referred to as the "TBY."

The TBY was a portable, high-frequency transmitter-receiver that allowed two-way communication by either voice (telephone) or MCW (telegraphy). For security, the TBY operated on 131 different channels in four bands with a frequency range of 28 to 80 MHz. It was battery-powered, and an antenna could be set up for operation in a minimum of time. It weighed thirty-eight pounds and could be carried as a knapsack load and operated by one man while mounted on his back.

For the last few hours, USS *Neville* had remained anchored in the transport area, a little over four miles off Tulagi Island, remaining in Condition of Readiness 1-A, the highest level of readiness just short of going to General Quarters and immediate battle stations. The too-close-for-comfort Japanese air raid on the afternoon of August 7 kept the entire crew on edge all night long.

During the night, as Rupertus waited in the water just off Beach Blue for an opening to establish a command post on Tulagi, he was monitoring the military situation of both Tulagi and Gavutu on the TBY radio system he had with him in the Higgins boat.

The situation on Gavutu-Tanambogo remained one of Rupertus's biggest concerns. Major Miller's request for additional reinforcements could not yet be fulfilled due to the logistical issues with the company of 2nd Marines on Florida Island. The company had started its amphibious landing on Tanambogo just as naval gunfire commenced, but it never established a beachhead. And while Major Miller's men had captured Gavutu, victory came with a price.

Company A had unloaded on the beach before being ambushed by Japanese machine gun fire. Companies B and C, which landed four minutes and seven minutes, respectively, after Company A, had taken severe casualties, especially the officer corps.

Major Williams, the battalion commander, was evacuated late last night and brought to the *Neville* for medical attention. Rupertus wanted to check on Williams on board the *Neville* before returning to Beach Blue. But some of the other officers in the Gavutu invasion force had not been as lucky as Williams.

Captain Richard J. Huerth, of Jacksonville, North Carolina, company commander for Company C, took a bullet through the head just as he rose from his boat to lead his Marines onto the island. Huerth's bleeding body fell back into the Higgins boat, into the laps of his men.

Captain Emerson E. Mason of Augusta, Maine, the battalion intelligence officer, was shot and killed as he reached the beach. Though he had seen so much death in his lifetime, Rupertus felt sick to his stomach every time one of his Marines fell.

Like Williams, Huerth and Mason had been either selected or approved by Rupertus for their missions. That added to the sting, but Rupertus had to push on.

As things now stood, Major Miller's Marines controlled Gavutu. Still, Japs remained entrenched on Tanambogo, one thousand yards away and separated by the narrow rock causeway.

Rupertus knew, and so did Miller, that the Marines on Gavutu could not charge across that five-hundred-yard causeway without being mowed down by the Japanese on Tanambogo. Miller needed more men, and Rupertus would find additional help for Tanambogo even if he had to go to General Vandegrift.

Plus, the battle on Tulagi still raged on. Lieutenant Colonel Edson had made progress in taking control of most of the island. The bloodiest battle for Hill 281 would probably commence this morning.

Rupertus had monitored the situation involving numerous banzai attacks over the evening against Edson's men, camped on the front lines a few miles from the new command post at Beach Blue. Edson and Lieutenant Colonel Rosecrans, the 2nd Raider Battalion commander at Tulagi, would need reinforcements, and sooner rather than later. Tulagi might fall today.

Rupertus needed to get more boots on the ground, on both Tulagi and Gavutu. Based on overnight events, Rupertus asked for three additional combat teams for the two islands, requesting two additional combat teams for Tulagi and a third for Tanambogo.

Vandegrift was reluctant to release additional teams, but based on the events transpiring overnight, including the dire situation on Tanambogo and the banzai attacks against Colonel Edson's Raiders on Tulagi, Vandegrift changed his mind.

Rupertus wanted to head out to the ships to brief his combat team's commanding officers about the situation on the ground.

The Higgins boat pulled up alongside the USS *President Hayes*, one of the transport ships carrying Marines just off Red Beach at Guadalcanal. The *Hayes* had steamed over to the Tulagi staging area at the request of Rupertus, authorized by General Vandegrift. It was now 0645 hours, and as they arrived alongside the rope ladder leading up to the deck of the ship, Rupertus turned to his chief of staff.

"Killy, radio Major Pressley and let him know that we're ready."

"Aye, sir."

Kilmartin picked up the TBY. "This is Colonel Kilmartin. Please inform Major Pressley that the general is ready for him."

"Aye, sir," a voice squawked over the radio.

"I see him, sir." The coxswain pointed up, and Rupertus craned his head back.

In full battle gear, the US Marine had begun to descend the ladder on the outside walls of the ship. A moment later, Major O. K. Pressley, from Lowrys, South Carolina, stepped into the bottom of the boat, saluting the coxswain, and said, in a thickly drawn southern accent, "Permission to come aboard, sir."

"Permission granted."

The Marine officer then turned and saluted General Rupertus. "Good morning, sir."

"Major Pressley. Welcome aboard."

"Thank you, sir." Major Pressley was the commanding officer of Combat Team B, and Rupertus wanted to have a few words with him before ordering him onto Beach Blue.

"I understand you were an All-American center on the Clemson football team, Pressley?"

"I've been accused of that, sir. From back in 1928. Long time ago, sir."

"Well, your personnel jacket is impressive, and you're gonna need some of that athletic ability for the mission we have for you."

"I'm ready, sir."

"Major, I'll cut to the point," Rupertus spoke as the Higgins boat pulled away from the side of the *President Hayes*. "Our boys on Tulagi had a long day yesterday."

"So, I've heard, sir."

"And on Gavutu, we brought 351 Marines and officers to the fight yesterday to face whatever opposition we found on both Gavutu and Tanambogo. We have a few Reising submachine guns, some Browning submachine guns, rifles, and not much more. Not until we can get tanks on the ground.

"Anyway, we have a shot at taking Tulagi today if we can root the Japs off Hill 281. But if we're going to do that, we need more firepower."

"Understood, sir."

"Cigarette?"

"Thank you, sir."

Rupertus extracted a pack of Camels from his front pocket and handed them over to Major Pressley. Pressley took a cigarette, struck a flame with a Zippo lighter, lit and pulled a drag from the cigarette, handed the pack back to Rupertus, and then leaned against the gunnel of the boat.

"Last night, around 2200 hours, I radioed General Vandegrift and requested additional firepower from our Marines still on board ship just off Guadalcanal."

"That would be my men and me, sir."

"Yep. Lieutenant Colonel Hunt's battalion also. His men are now getting under way. He doesn't know it yet, but I'm thinking about diverting his men from Beach Blue to Gavutu."

"Sir, we heard all the action was at Tulagi and Gavutu, while our Marines got zero resistance yesterday coming ashore at Guadalcanal. It's hard waiting on a ship and not getting into the action. Sir, my team is ready for action, and we're ready to go straight to Hill 281 if you give the order."

"It might come to that," Rupertus said. "But I wanted to take a few minutes here in the boat to lay out our plans for your team."

"Yes, sir."

Rupertus took a swig of water from a canteen. "I am sending two additional combat teams to Tulagi this morning. This will include Combat Team A, which should be landing at 0945 hours, and then your team, Combat Team B, landing a little over an hour later, at 1115 hours. You with me so far?"

"Yes, sir."

"Now, Combat Team A, Lieutenant Colonel Hunt's team, will break left and reinforce the northwest sector of the island, assuming I don't change my mind and send them Gavutu instead. That's the section we already control."

Rupertus took another swig of water. "But when your team lands, you will break to the right and head to the southeast sector of the island, where you will provide direct fire support for the Raider teams already there, commanded by Lieutenant Colonel Edson. Still with me?"

"Yes, sir."

"Two additional combat teams will move in to secure the landing area at Beach Blue to make it easier to bring supplies in until we clear these Japs out, which I hope happens today. Those combat teams can also reinforce our efforts here.

"Okay. Before you sweep down to the southeast sector, we have an important job for you—that is, to help secure Beach Blue."

"Yes, sir."

"And here's what I mean. Part of the problem is we had a bunch of Jap snipers up there last night firing away, hiding up in the coconut trees, behind vines, in caves, or anywhere else they could squeeze.

"We didn't have many snipers firing yesterday during the initial invasion. But last night, they slipped in during the dark when we couldn't see them. The sniper fire was so intense last night that we couldn't come in with the boats long enough to make a landing.

"This morning wasn't as bad as last night. We got Major Enright, my operations officer, and a few of my other staff members on the beach to set up our forward command post.

"Keeping that command post in that beach area will be crucial until we wipe the Japanese off the island. When you arrive on the beach, I first want you to report to Major Enright to clear the snipers out before releasing you to Lieutenant Colonel Edson.

"I have already given orders to Combat Team A to start the process when they land at 0900. They're going to sweep up to the left and kill Japs anywhere from the landing point to the island's northwest tip. But you, Major, are batting cleanup. Anything they miss, I want you and your men to kill every damned Jap you find, anywhere within one mile of that beach, before we release you to do anything else. Are you with me?"

"Yes, sir," Major Pressley replied. "My men will wipe every Jap sniper out of that area. If any snipers are in there, or any Japanese soldiers are within a mile of that beach, we will make them regret testing the resolve of the US Marine Corps."

Rupertus smiled. "I like your attitude, Major."

"Thank you, sir."

Rupertus looked up and saw they were approaching the port side of the *Neville*.

"I have to jump off here at the *Neville* to take care of some duties before I return to Beach Blue. I'm leaving you in the capable hands of my chief of staff, Colonel Kilmartin. You all will proceed to Beach Blue from here, where you will wait for your men to arrive. I'll see you both within the next couple of hours."

"Any questions so far?"

"No, sir."

"I realize we had a hell of a night last night. Maybe your men haven't got much sleep at all because of those bastards with their banzai attacks. But we stuck it to them and killed close to a hundred of them altogether."

The Higgins boat pulled up alongside the ladder leading up to the deck of the *Neville*. Four ropes dropped over the ship's side, and the navy crew on board the Higgins boat grabbed the ropes to secure the boat. Rupertus stood to depart on the boat as Kilmartin, Pressley, and the other boat crew members stood to offer salutes.

Rupertus returned the salute. "As you were, gentlemen."

He grabbed hold of the ladder and began to climb up the ship's side. A moment later, he stepped onto the deck and exchanged salutes.

"Welcome aboard, sir," the navy lieutenant serving as the officer of the deck at the top of the ladder saluted as Rupertus stepped onto the main deck.

Rupertus snapped a return salute. "Lieutenant, take me to sickbay, please. I need to check on Major Williams."

"Aye, sir."

Chapter 41

Command Post
1st Raider Battalion
Tulagi Island
August 8, 1942
0730 Hours
"Okay, men. Gather around."

Lieutenant Colonel Merritt "Red Mike" Edson had gathered his company commanders around him to discuss the day's plan. He looked them all in the eye. Their faces showed intensity and an eagerness to get in the battle.

"First, I heard from General Rupertus on the TBY. He received authorization from Vandegrift for more reinforcements today. The general has established his forward command post at Beach Blue and will personally be on the ground sometime later this morning.

"As most of you know, General Rupertus and I served together in Shanghai and watched them up close when they brutalized the Chinese. They're small, they don't sleep, and they have a limitless supply of personal energy. They hide everywhere and pop out from under the smallest leaf on the ground. So we must watch our blind side every second." A drag from a cigarette. "Here's the good news. When we captured this 'Residency,' as they call it, we found their plans and learned where they pre-positioned their machine gun batteries and anti-aircraft weapons.

"That's why they were so pissed off. We've got their battle plans. This may be why they attacked multiple times to get back to the Residency before Captain Sweeny decided to light them all up like a bunch of fried chicken in the frying pan."

Chuckles arose from the company commanders.

"Now we've blown up a map here to explain the intel we got last night, through our interpreter, Lieutenant Erskine, and I'm going to ask Griffith to step out and explain the relevant positions that you need to be aware of as we move forward this morning." Edson glanced over at his executive officer. "Sam?"

"Thank you, sir."

Major Sam Griffith stepped into the middle of the group as Lieutenant Erskine positioned a large map on the bulletin board, displaying the southeastern section of Tulagi.

"Okay, note the locations of these batteries. The Japs have two machine gun batteries located right here, at the foot of the hill. Behind the hospital. Can everybody see that?"

"Roger that."

"Copy that."

Heads nodded.

Griffith continued. "As you can see, they have two badass 8-millimeter anti-aircraft batteries right here, on top of the southeast promontory. The Japs call this position 'Bird Hill.' Y'all see both of those gun emplacements?"

More nodding of heads.

"If those gun embankments are still there, we want to hit them first, to take 'em out, and make it as hard on the Japs as possible."

"Copy that."

Griffith turned back to Lieutenant Colonel Edson. "Colonel?"

Edson stepped back in front of his company commanders.

"Now I know you gentlemen have been in firefights all night long with these bastards. This morning, we're all ready to finish the job. We must wait for another hour or two, both for reinforcements, which General Rupertus is sending our way, and also at the general's request, the navy is sending a couple of squadrons of dive bombers to bomb the hell out of that hill. Then we move in and kick their asses back to Tokyo."

Cheering. "Oorah!"

"The Japs better enjoy the early part of the morning while they can because they're about to get a full dose of US naval firepower, followed by the clenched steel fist of the US Marine Corps!"

"Oorah!"

"When I give the command to attack, we're first going to have companies Echo and Foxtrot of the 5th Marines join our own Dog Company. Then we will attack the downslope of Hill 281, and then swing right toward the enemy pocket of the ravine."

Edson pointed to the map. He looked over at Captain William Sperling, who had replaced Major Chambers as company commander when Chambers was evacuated after getting shot on the cricket field. "That's you, Captain Sperling. I know that y'all don't have hills like that in Jersey, son, but are you up to leading our Marines up that hill?"

"With respect, damn right, sir! And if I might add, it will be a pleasure to kick their asses for what they did to Major Chambers."

"Atta boy, Captain," Edson said. "Okay, men. Let's get 'em. Move out!"

*****

Tulagi Island
The Assault on Hill 281
August 8, 1942
0800 Hours

At Edson's command, the Raiders began their assault on Hill 281 in the southeastern quadrant of the island.

Edson sent Companies E and F of the 2nd Battalion, 5th Marines, to position themselves on the northeast slope of Hill 281. The other companies remained on the perimeter of the ravine.

The assault would begin with the weapons company. Captain George W. Herring, of Rockmart, Georgia, a 1940 Naval Academy graduate, served as the battalion's weapons officer. Herring's company oversaw the concentrated firepower from the 60-millimeter mortars attached to each of the assault companies.

The final movement on Hill 281 would start with Herring's command.

"Captain, commence fire," Lieutenant Colonel Edson's voice boomed over the TBY radio.

"Aye, sir, commence fire!"

Herring turned to his men. "Commence fire! Commence fire!"

First swooshes and then explosions filled the air as the Marines began pouring round after round of 60-millimeter mortar fire onto Jap positions. They pounded the Jap headquarters position. They struck the machine gun batteries discovered the night before with the capture of the residence. They poured mortar fire onto everything in sight.

Following the initial attack with the 60-millimeter mortars, the 2nd Battalion, 5th Marines, opened up with heavier 81-millimeter mortars. The heavy mortar barrage continued throughout the morning.

A little after 1100 hours, manna from heaven appeared!

Eleven SDB A-24 Dauntless dive bombers from USS *Wasp* swooped in low over the horizon. These were the same warplanes that, just sixty days earlier, were responsible for sinking the bulk of the Japanese fleet, including Japanese aircraft carriers, during the US Navy's stunning victory in the Battle of Midway.

Each SDB can carry bombs weighing more than two thousand pounds. These were the bombs that sank the Japanese aircraft carriers *Akagi*, *Kaga*, *Sōryū*, and *Hiryū*. And now, the Japanese elite forces, the Rikusentai, were catching some of the same furious hell their fleet had caught at Midway between June 4 and 7.

The navy dive bombers dropped payloads of bombs after bombs on the Japanese positions.

Colonel Edson watched through his binoculars as great plumes of smoke rose throughout the Japanese positions. He allowed himself a satisfying grin.

"Hell yeah!" An explosion. Another explosion. More smoke rising from atop Hill 281. "Take that, you sons of bitches."

The Marines watched with nervous anticipation from every company in the southeast sector of the island as the navy planes rained down hell on the Japs. The ground shook with fury, almost as if bombs were exploding below their feet. Anything not bolted down rattled.

After the fierce shelling and bombing finished, Colonel Edson gave the order.

"All companies! Advance! Okay, move, men! Move!"

Responding to Edson's command, the company commanders and Company G, 5th Marines, began pushing through the ravine. This movement started their full charge into the southeast sector of the island, shooting at Japanese troops now rattled by the continued mortar and aerial bombardment.

Chapter 42

Beach Blue
Tulagi Island
August 8, 1942
1100 Hours

Before departing the *Neville*, Rupertus called in additional airstrikes from the navy, at the request of Colonel Edson, and checked on a few of his men who were hospitalized. His final sickbay stop—Major Williams.

"How's he doing, Doc?"

"Sir, he was shot through the stomach by a Japanese machine gun, but the bullet did not lodge in and went through him." Lieutenant E. B. McLarney was the navy physician and medical officer assigned to Rupertus's staff. "Our corpsmen have stabilized the bleeding. They got sulfanilamide powder in the wound, and that helped. No signs of infection. We've just begun transfusions."

"Will he make it?"

"If I were a betting man, I'd bet on it."

"Thanks, Doc."

"My pleasure, General. See you on Tulagi soon?"

"I'm headed there now, Lieutenant. Once we get the place a little more secure, I'll send for you. Unfortunately, we have plenty of business for you."

"Aye, sir."

With his business on the *Neville* completed, General Rupertus commandeered another Higgins boat, instructing the coxswain to take him back to Beach Blue.

By 1100 hours, Combat Team B had already arrived on Beach Blue to help secure it, sweeping to the north to clear the area of Japanese snipers.

Rupertus arrived at the same time as members of Combat Team C, under the command of Major Pressley, whom the general had briefed early that morning.

"This is as far in as we can get, because of the coral, General."

"We should have the other side of the island cleared soon to give you some better landing areas, Chief."

"Aye, sir. Good luck, General."

Rupertus stepped over the boat's side into waist-deep water and waded in toward the beach. At the same time, members of Major Pressley's combat team also waded ashore.

If a sniper were out there at that moment, Rupertus presented a clean target. But he wasn't worried about that. Right now, he needed to find Colonel Kilmartin and get everything up to speed.

A couple of minutes later, he stepped onto the beach. Kilmartin and Major Enright greeted him.

"Welcome to Tulagi, General," Kilmartin said.

"It's about damn time, Killy; have we got the command tent set up yet?"

"Yes, sir. Right this way, sir." Kilmartin led Rupertus and Major Enright across a narrow beach, which Rupertus noted could not have been any more than ten feet wide, and the jungle came right up to the edge of the little beach.

The green-colored command post tent, guarded by a platoon of Marines on all sides, was erected just inside the tree line. They stepped inside. A single incandescent bulb lit the interior of a tent that was already hot and muggy, the price of fighting a war in the tropical South Pacific in the damn middle of nowhere. The front flaps were wide open to let some fresh air in.

"Sir," Kilmartin said, "I assumed you would want an immediate briefing upon arrival, so we set out the updated map of the current battle space." He pointed to a map on the table.

Rupertus walked over to have a look. "It would appear we've got everything updated through about 1000 hours today."

"Yes, sir," Kilmartin said. "Should I continue with the updated briefing?"

"By all means."

"I'll start with Gavutu, okay, sir?"

"Fine."

"Sir, as you recall, last night at 2200 hours, General Vandegrift approved your request for an additional combat team to this sector. At 0330 hours this morning, USS *President Hayes* and USS *President Adams*, with 2nd and 3rd Battalions of the 2nd Marines, departed their station off Beach Red at Guadalcanal and steamed to our position off Beach Blue.

"This morning, you ordered the 3rd Battalion, 2nd Marines, under Lieutenant Colonel R. G. Hunt, to divert from Beach Blue and head to Tulagi.

"Now, as you can see here from the map, sir, those landings began at 1000 hours this morning, on the west side of Gavutu.

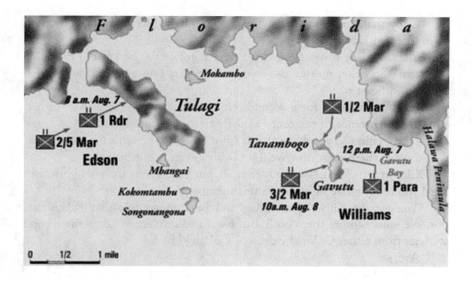

"Colonel Hunt's men are still landing, but the colonel is on the island and he relieved Major Miller of command."

"Great. Major Miller did one hell of a job taking Hill 148 when Major Williams went down. Speaking of which, Killy, I visited Major Williams in the sickbay on the *Neville*, and the doc thinks Williams will pull through."

"That's great news, General."

"Yes, it is. Please continue your brief, Killy."

"Yes, sir. Lieutenant Colonel Hunt's men have drawn fire on approach. But because we control Gavutu today, unlike yesterday, we've been able to eliminate the threat of ambush at short range from Hill 148."

"Go on."

"Yes, sir. We still haven't established a beachhead on Tanambogo. And ordering our men across that narrow causeway right now would create an easy turkey shoot by the Japs."

"Let's try again a bit later today, when Colonel Hunt's men are all on the ground at Gavutu. Who has the colonel designated to command that landing?"

"Sir, the colonel is thinking about ordering Captain Tinsley, company commander for Company I. The landing will be supported by gunfire from USS *Buchanan*, and we're going to try to get tanks on the island today."

"Copy that. Let's make it happen. Switching gears to Tulagi, anything from Colonel Edson?"

"Sir, according to your order, the navy bombed the hell out of Hill 281, and we have a heavy mortar assault now underway. I'm moving now to finish off the southeast sector."

Rupertus thought for a second. He crossed his arms and then turned toward the entrance of the tent to inhale fresh air from outside. "You know how I am itching to get down to the front lines and be with the men, but if we go down there right now, we'll probably get in Edson's way."

Kilmartin nodded. "Not only that, sir, but Lieutenant Colonel Hunt will need you today as we fight to secure Tanambogo."

"You're right, Killy. Again. Tulagi and Tanambogo dominate Tulagi harbor. We must capture them both. But I want you to let me know the second we hear from either Colonel Edson or Colonel Hunt."

"Aye, sir."

Chapter 43

"Okay, men. Let's review the plan." Captain W. B. Tinsley, company commander for Company I, in the lead Higgins boat on approach to Tanambogo Island, turned around and addressed his Marines.

"Colonel Hunt has ordered us to establish the beachhead on this island, and we're going to do just that. Remember, we must establish a presence on the backside of the hill to engage the Japs so Marines can cross that causeway from Gavutu on the other side.

"Now, when we hit the beach, we separate. I'll take one group, and we'll move on the right side and fight our way to the eastern side of the slope. The other group, you guys move in the opposite direction and on the southern side of the hill.

"We've got one tank over there, and the navy has been shelling the heck out of that hill. But we're expecting heavy fire. Stay low, move fast, Marines, and kill Japs! Are we clear?"

"Clear, sir!"

Suddenly, multiple gunshots started to ring out. Bullets splashed in the water all around them.

"Japs! Stay down, men!"

"Aaaaaaaaaaaaaaaahh!"

"God!" Tinsley turned around and looked back. A couple of his men had taken bullets. Blood gushed like geysers through the uniforms.

"Captain, this is far as we can go," the coxswain said.

"Okay, men! This is it! Out of the boat!" He turned to the coxswain. "Chief. Take these wounded Marines back to Gavutu."

"Aye, sir."

Tinsley jumped out of the landing craft. Waving his arms, he led his men onto the beach. "Okay, break now!"

Staying low and keeping his rifle out front, Tinsley broke to the right, taking his men with him.

"Aaah!"

"Oh God!"

"I'm hit! I'm hit!"

Bullets hit several of his men.

"Captain, we're taking fire from Gaomi!"

Gaomi, a tiny island east of Tanambogo, was separated from Tanambogo by shallow water, a couple of hundred yards from Tanambogo's beach.

Tinsley looked through his binoculars. Jap soldiers lined the beach, firing with long rifles and machine guns. "Take cover and return fire, men! Gunny! Get me on the TBY to Gavutu."

"Roger that, Captain."

Tinsley opened fire from a prone position along the beach, shooting across the bay at the Japs on Gaomi. A couple of the Japs' heads exploded, and they fell over, dead.

A second later, the gunnery sergeant returned with the PBY. "Colonel Hunt on the line, sir."

"Colonel. Captain Tinsley."

"What's your situation, Captain?"

"Sir, the east flank of the company is taking heavy fire from Gaomi Island. Also, heavy fire from the top of Hill 121. We're pinned down from two directions. Multiple casualties. Request immediate naval fire support against Gaomi."

"Roger that, Captain. I'm contacting General Rupertus. Stay strong, Tinsley. Help is on the way."

"Yes, sir."

*****

Beach Blue
Tulagi Island
Operation Ringbolt Command Post
August 8, 1942
1630 Hours

"Sir, urgent message from Colonel Hunt on Gavutu."

"What is it, Killy?"

"Two platoons from I Company are pinned down by unexpected fire from Gaomi Island. Request comes from Captain Tinsley, I Company commander."

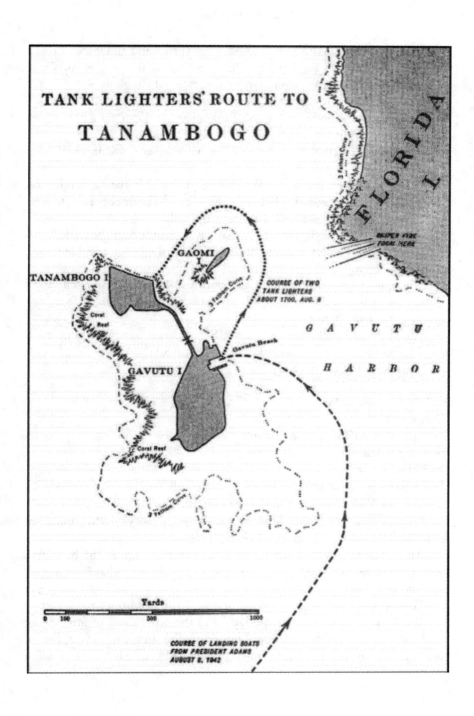

TANK LIGHTERS' ROUTE TO
TANAMBOGO

FLORIDA I.

GAOMI I.

TANAMBOGO I.

Coral Reef

GAVUTU I.

Coral Reef

Gavutu Beach

COURSE OF TWO
TANK LIGHTERS
ABOUT 1700, AUG. 8

SNIPER FIRE
FROM HERE

GAVUTU

HARBOR

Yards

0   100   500   1000

COURSE OF LANDING BOATS
FROM PRESIDENT ADAMS
AUGUST 8, 1942

"Send a FLASH MESSAGE to Admiral Turner and all US Navy combatants in the area. 'Requesting immediate suppressive fire on Gaomi Island. Signed, William Rupertus, Commander, Operational Ringbolt.'"

"Roger that, sir. Going out immediately."

"Let me see the updated map on Tanambogo, so I can get a better idea of what's going on at Gaomi."

"Aye, sir. Map's right here. As you can see, they are catching hell from the flank."

Rupertus studied the map. "Yep. We've got to eliminate every Jap on Gaomi to secure that causeway between Gavutu and Tanambogo, and to protect our guys trying to take the east side of the hill."

Kilmartin responded. "Hopefully that naval gunfire does the trick."

"Let's hope." Rupertus threw his cigarette on the ground and stomped it out.

Rupertus stepped just outside the tent and checked his watch: 1635 hours. Less than two hours to sundown. Less than two hours to continue with any effective offensive.

"Sir, just heard back from the navy. USS *Gridley* is moving into position and will commence fire on Gaomi as requested, ASAP."

"Excellent. Thank you, Killy."

*****

Mobile Command Post
Company I
On Approach to Tanambogo Island
August 8, 1942
1645 Hours

"Lieutenant, get some more mortar fire on the hill."

"Aye, sir. We're moving as fast as we can, sir."

Foof! Foof! The whooshing sounds were Tinsley's men launching 60-millimeter mortars up at Hill 121.

An explosion. The first mortar landed somewhere up on the hill. Then more explosions from additional mortars, followed by the hard rattling of machine gun fire.

"Take cover!"

The Marines fired back at the Japs, and the acrid smell of gunpowder filled the air, mixed with the tropical humidity. The smoke was thick, almost choking. Half of Company I remained pinned down, caught in the crossfire on two sides, taking bullets from the Japs on top of Hill 121 and also from Gaomi. If they could just eliminate the threat from Gaomi.

"Where the hell is the navy?" Tinsley wondered aloud.

"Oh shit! I'm hit! I'm hit!" Tinsley turned around. One of his men was shot.

"Medic!" Tinsley yelled. "We need a medic. Now!"

A shrill, piercing sound cut through the air. The massive explosion on Gaomi shook across the narrow, shallow waterway to the beach at Tanambogo.

"Hell yeah!"

More shrill whistles pierced the air. More explosions. The navy had arrived, and the ground shook and shook some more. Once the naval bombardment began, the firing from Gaomi Island stopped cold turkey.

"Damn better late than never!"

"Sir, Lieutenant Colonel Hunt on the line for you." The gunnery sergeant handed Tinsley the TBY.

"Captain Tinsley here."

"How are you making out, Tinsley?"

"A bit better at the moment, sir," Tinsley said, "now that the navy blasted the hell out of those Japs on Gaomi."

"Well, you can thank the USS *Gridley* and General Rupertus for the assist."

"I'll buy the general and the skipper a drink if I ever get the hell out of this place alive, sir."

"You will, Tinsley. And probably with a promotion. Now listen up. With the Japs on Gaomi eliminated, we're sending in the 1st Platoon of K Company to secure the causeway. The target time is 1700 hours. The causeway is exposed, and that's a dangerous assignment.

"So get your men moving again, to charge that hill, distract the Japs, and give K Company room to operate."

"Aye, sir. Out now."

Tinsley turned to his men. "Okay, guys, the threat from that island has been eliminated. Let's hit that hill. Move out!"

Chapter 44

Beach Blue
Tulagi Island
Operation Ringbolt Command Post
August 8, 1942
1700 Hours

Rupertus stood up, stretched his legs, and paced back and forth in the command post with his arms crossed. His men had made progress on all fronts, but at a heavy price.

Meanwhile, across the sound in Guadalcanal, General Vandegrift had not yet run into opposition. That would come later. But for now, the light resistance on Guadalcanal allowed Vandegrift to free up additional forces for the ongoing assaults against Tulagi and Gavutu.

Rupertus pulled out his wallet and extracted her picture. She always made him smile, and now was no exception. Fortunately, Sleepy didn't know what was going on here. It was good she wasn't with him. She'd insist on strapping on a helmet, grabbing a rifle, and charging the Japs herself.

That brought another smile.

After losing his first family to scarlet fever in China, he had thought he would never find love again.

Then along came Sleepy.

His reminiscing was interrupted by his chief of staff. "General, Lieutenant Colonel Edson is on the line for you, sir. He says it's important."

"Very well," Rupertus said. He stepped over to the communications table and picked up the telephone on the TBY.

"Rupertus here. What have you got, Colonel?"

"Great news, sir. I am pleased to report that Tulagi has fallen."

"Say again, Mike?"

"Tulagi has fallen, General. Our Marines control all of Hill 148 and the entire southeast sector of the island. Most of the Japs are dead, and while we're weeding out a few Jap stragglers, we're now in total control. Congratulations, sir."

Rupertus let that sink in. "Copy that, Colonel. Great work. I'll inform General Vandegrift. I'll be down to see as soon as I can break away. Keep me posted."

"Roger that, General."

Rupertus hung up the phone. "Killy."

"Yes, sir."

"Prep a message to General Vandegrift."

"Ready, sir."

From ADC 1st Marine Division
To Division Commander
Subj: Status of Combat Operations, Tulagi-Gavutu/Tanambogo
Date: 8 August 1942
1. Lieutenant Colonel Edson reports that Tulagi has fallen.
2. Tulagi southeast sector fully controlled by USMC Raiders.
3. Most enemy combatants believed KIA. Will continue to search for and eliminate holdouts.
4. Preparing to move Tulagi command post to the southeast sector.
5. Combat operations continue on Tanambogo. Expect continued fighting tonight and into tomorrow.
v/r
W. H. Rupertus
Brigadier General, USMC

"Message sent." Kilmartin turned around and faced Rupertus. "Congratulations, General. You just won America's first battle against the Japanese on the ground. That is a historic feat."

"Thanks, Killy. But there is no 'I' in team, and I haven't won anything. Yes, this is a historic victory, but all of our men won it, and that includes you too. We still have work to do on Gavutu, and if we don't win this war, this victory will become an irrelevant footnote. But thank you for the comments. Anyway, no time to celebrate. Got to get back to work."

"Aye, sir."

Chapter 45

Bridge, USS *Neville* (APA-9)
August 9, 1942
0130 Hours

"Captain to the bridge! Captain to the bridge!"

The announcement blared over the ship's 1MC, prompting Captain Carlos Bailey, commanding officer of the USS *Neville*, to roll out of his rack. Bailey, resting in his full khaki uniform, jumped to his feet and grabbed the telephone connecting with the bridge. "This is the captain. I'm on my way."

A few minutes later, the commanding officer stepped onto the bridge of his ship.

"Captain's on the bridge!"

"Carry on. Lieutenant, what've we got?"

"Two things, sir. The whole Jap fleet showed up. It appears we have a major naval battle that started past Savo Island. Out there, sir," the lieutenant pointed. "To the west."

Bailey lifted his binoculars to his eyes. Just as he brought the horizon into focus, two huge red flares streaked through the sky to the west, near the Florida and Guadalcanal Islands entrance about five miles away. The flares appeared to have been dropped by Jap aircraft and lit the horizon. Immediately, naval gunfire commenced near the flares and farther out to sea.

"Damn."

The flares illuminated the shapes of warships, and soon searchlights and gunfire could be seen coming from the ships around Savo Island. The American warships in that area were stationed to guard against Japanese naval forces entering the Sealark Channel and interfering with US military operations against Tulagi and Guadalcanal.

"Not a good situation," Bailey said.

He continued to watch through the windshield of the ship's bridge as the action unfolded. He saw large splashes in the water behind the ship nearest to *Neville*'s position.

"Have we heard from Admiral Turner?"

"Yes, sir, Skipper. Both Admiral Turner and Vice Admiral Fletcher are monitoring the situation. We've also heard from General Vandegrift, sir."

"General Vandegrift?"

"Yes, sir. General Vandegrift has left Guadalcanal and is on a Higgins boat headed our way to come aboard this ship."

"Aboard the *Neville*? Vandegrift wants to come on board tonight?"

"Yes, sir. And apparently, they have had some navigational problems trying to find us. They made it out to the USS *Southard* and are now back at sea trying to find us."

"Any indication as to why the general is coming out?"

"Sir, I believe he wants to check on the progress of unloading materials and ammunition and supplies to Tulagi and Gavutu."

"Understood. Still, I get nervous that the entire task force ground commander is out in a Higgins boat in the middle of the night with a naval battle unfolding and having navigational problems. "

"Aye, sir."

"Notify the officer of the deck to let me know the moment the general steps on board."

"Aye, sir."

Captain Bailey continued to monitor the situation to the west. If the American warships out there did not hold, the Japanese could penetrate the Sealark Channel and sink every transport ship anchored off Tulagi and Guadalcanal. In times like this, he wished he commanded a battleship.

"Captain! Look!"

Bailey checked the clock mounted on the rear bulkhead of the bridge: 0155 hours. Two large fires burned on the surface of the water, out in the distance.

"Are those planes burning on the surface of the water?" asked the lieutenant.

He looked again. "No. Shit! Those are ships on fire!"

Gun flashes in the direction of Savo Island appeared to be from Japanese warships. More flares lit the night sky over Savo, and they could now see warships across the sea.

"Damn! What just happened?"

About 0200 hours, a violent explosion and flames appeared under the flares. A ship had blown up. Two more green flares lit the skies over the *Neville*.

"Are they marking those flares for us, skipper? Are we the next target?"

"I sure as hell hope not, Lieutenant," Bailey said. "But they're dropping those flares to illuminate targets. We have a lot of cargo to unload onto Tulagi before we can go anywhere. It's not looking good." Another ship burst into flames off in the distance. "Damn. I hope that's not one of ours."

"Do you think it might be, sir?"

"I'm worried it might be." Bailey thought for a second. "Lieutenant, bring up the navigational chart showing our cruiser and destroyer screens out there."

"Aye, sir."

Bailey glanced at the assigned position of the cruiser and destroyer escorts protecting the transport ships off both Tulagi and Guadalcanal.

To guard against the Japanese navy coming in and interfering with the landings of military operations against both Tulagi and Guadalcanal, the US Navy had assigned fifteen destroyers and cruisers in three separate clusters to guard the Sealark Channel and the defense's transport ships.

These included the Northern Force, which protected Tulagi, the *Neville*, the *President Jackson*, the *Heywood*, and the other support transports in the area. The Eastern Force guarded both transport groups against any approach from the east. The Southern Force guarded the transport ships waiting off

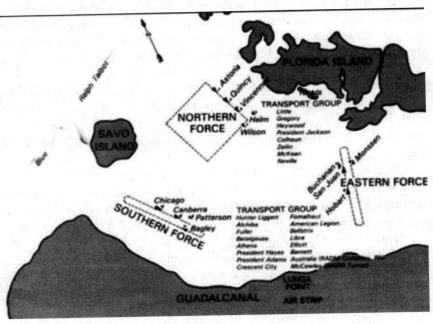

Guadalcanal. The USS *Blue* and the USS *Ralph Talbot* were stationed to the north of Savo Island, in the direction of Rabaul, from which a Japanese naval attack might most likely originate.

A few minutes later, the gunfire appeared to draw farther away. Perhaps the attacking ships were retreating.

"Skipper, the boat carrying General Vandegrift has just pulled alongside."

"Great," Bailey said. "Let's get him aboard and get him up here ASAP!"

Vandegrift arrived on the bridge with his staff. "General's on the bridge!"

"Welcome aboard, General," Bailey said. "We were concerned about you, out there in the dark, sir."

"Well, it was a hell of a journey, Captain. Other than crossing twenty miles of ocean water in the dark and not being able to see a damn thing except for ships blowing up on the horizon, it was a great voyage." Vandegrift said.

"*Southard* radioed and said you were on the way," Bailey said. "Anyway, how may we be of service to you, General?"

"I wanted to see how the offload is going, and I need to see General Rupertus. We were trying to reach him from the Higgins boat, but no luck. Would you try to contact Beach Blue and get the message to Rupertus? I would like to see the general and Colonel Kilmartin here, on the *Neville*, immediately."

"Aye." He turned to one of the junior officers on the bridge. "Lieutenant?"

"Take this message to the radio room. 'Message to Beach Blue. General Vandegrift is on board *Neville* and requests to see General Rupertus and Colonel Kilmartin immediately. Boat being sent for transport. Out.'"

"Aye, sir."

*****

Bridge, USS *Quincy* (CA-39)
The Sealark Channel
Between Florida Savo Islands
August 9, 1942
0200 Hours

"They're hitting us with searchlights, sir! There must be ten ships in a single column!"

"Commence fire! Now!" Captain Samuel N. Moore, commanding officer of the New Orleans–class cruiser, USS *Quincy*, issued the orders to fire.

At 0613 hours on August 7, the *Quincy* was the first American warship to open fire against Tulagi as a prelude to the Marines' invasion.

In the predawn darkness of the early morning hours of August 9, the *Quincy* was under heavy fire, caught in a crossfire between three Japanese navy warships, which had appeared out of nowhere, and without notification.

Quincy was patrolling along with the USS *Astoria*, USS *Vincennes*, USS *Helm*, and USS *Wilson* just to the west of Florida Island to protect the transport ships and US Marines in the United States' operations against Tulagi.

"Why the hell aren't we firing on these bastards?" Captain Moore screamed.

"Don't know, sir. We relayed that order to the gun crew."

"It's taking too long to fire! Repeat the order! Commence fire!"

"Commence fire! Aye, sir!"

At that command, several rounds thundered from all nine of *Quincy*'s 8-inch guns. "Bull's-eye, sir! We scored a hit!"

"About damn time!"

Multiple enemy shells hit their target, and the front part of the ship burst into flames.

"Left full rudder!"

"Left full rudder! Aye, sir."

"Set course for Savo Island! Mark your course two-seven-zero degrees. All ahead full!"

"Set course for Savo. Marking my course two-seven-zero degrees. All ahead full!"

Captain Moore was attempting a desperate run over to Savo Island to save his ship and get out of the enemy crossfire that had surfaced in the dark of the night.

Another explosion rocked the front of the ship.

"Sir, we've been hit by torpedoes!"

Another explosion broke the glass windshields, with sharp shards of glass exploding into the bridge. Fire quickly consumed the bridge. Captain More staggered and tried to orient himself. Through his blurred vision he saw hazy images of dead bodies all over the bridge: dead sailors, glass, and blood. The fading images would be his last memories as he lapsed out of consciousness.

*****

Beach Blue
Tulagi Island
Beachmaster's Tent
August 9, 1942
0230 Hours

Lieutenant Herman Jorgensen, US Naval Reserve, had worked almost non-stop, often under fire, since the first echelon of Marines arrived early on the morning of August 7. Tulagi had fallen, and after a message had come in from the *Neville* at about 0045 hours that new ammunition, food, and water were to be unloaded at Beach Blue, Jorgensen decided to lie down in his tent to catch an hour of sleep while his men prepared to receive additional supplies.

He had just started to doze, maybe for a minute or two, when one of his men rushed into his tent.

"Lieutenant! Lieutenant! You gotta see this!"

"What the hell?" Jorgensen rolled out of the rack and followed the petty officer down to the beach.

"Out there, Lieutenant!" The petty officer pointed to the right. Several miles over the waters to the west, there were explosions in the sky and ships off in the distance firing rounds.

The battle had opened with a brilliant light. A giant flare streaked across the night sky and illuminated the American warships. Firing back, the flashes of guns from the American ships lit the night sky.

"The damn Jap navy is headed this way!" Jorgensen said. "Probably from their base in Raboul."

"Should we alert the general, sir?" the petty officer asked.

"Whatever is going on out there, it's a hell of a lot of ships," Jorgensen said. "I'm sorry. What did you say, Petty Officer?"

"I asked if we should alert the general, sir."

"I'll leave it up to the Marine Corps to wake General Rupertus. But I will alert Colonel Kilmartin."

*****

Bridge, USS *Vincennes* (CA-44)
The Sealark Channel
Between Florida and Savo Islands
August 9, 1942
0238 Hours

For the last thirty minutes, Captain Frederick Lois Reifkohl, commanding officer of USS *Vincennes*, was battling for the life of his ship. Riefkohl was the first Puerto Rican to ever graduate from the US Naval Academy and was one of the navy's most decorated sea captains, including winning the Navy Cross in 1917 for his work in battling an enemy submarine.

But now, none of that mattered. The *Vincennes* and her sister warships, the heavy cruisers *Quincy* and *Astoria*, had become trapped between two moving columns of Japanese warships that had appeared out of the night and somehow surrounded the American cruisers in a surprise move maneuver.

The Japanese had not been picked up on radar and had materialized, it seemed, out of nowhere. Already, *Vincennes* had received multiple hits and the sea was a flaming inferno. Captain Riefkohl did everything within his power to control his ship and fire back.

"Right full rudder!"

"Right full rudder! Aye, sir."

"On my command, stand by to commence fire!"

"On your command, sir."

"Stand by, stand by." Reifkohl waited for the Japanese warship to roll into his gun sights. "Now! Commence fire!"

"Commence fire! Aye, sir."

The *Vincennes* shook as her 8-inch guns thundered into the night, blasting multiple rounds at her Japanese attackers. But with the numerous hits his ship had taken so far, Reifkohl worried that the counterattack might be too little, too late. The aircraft hangar on his ship was struck, and flames lapped high into the night. The ship's firefighters struggled against the massive flames.

The night sky lit up, first by bright flares exploding in the sky, dropped by Japanese planes to illuminate the position of American warships. Fires on board the *Quincy*, the *Astoria*, and his ship also lit the skies over the entire battle space.

"Captain! The *Quincy*! She's going down, sir!"

"What?" Captain Reifkohl swung his binoculars over to the right side of the bow. His sister ship, USS *Quincy*, was bow-down under the water, her stern raised high. A couple of seconds later, she slipped below the surface.

He checked the clock on the bulkhead. "Mark it for the log. USS *Quincy* went down at 0238 hours."

Somehow, Reifkohl sensed that his ship would meet the same fate. But he had to keep fighting.

*****

Beach Blue
Tulagi Island
Operation Ringbolt Command Post
August 9, 1942
0327 Hours

"General! We just got a message from General Vandegrift. He's on board the *Neville* and wants to meet us. He's sending a boat right now."

"On the *Neville*? Rupertus asked.

"Yes, sir. They're sending a boat to pick us up, per General Vandegrift's order."

"Forget that, Killy. We'll commandeer one of our boats and head out to the *Neville*. Let's go."

"Aye, sir."

Like everyone else on Beach Blue, Rupertus had been watching the naval battle unfold on the horizon for the last two hours. The streaking lights and flashes across the dark water had made it impossible to ignore. But at this point, no one had any information on how the battle was unfolding.

However, all night long, boats had been going back and forth between Beach Blue and the *Neville*, unloading additional supplies that the Marines would need to occupy the island on a long-term basis.

Rupertus and his chief of staff, Colonel Kilmartin, commandeered one of those boats and ordered the coxswain to take them out to the *Neville* immediately.

*****

USS *Neville* (APA-9)
August 9, 1942
0500 Hours

The Higgins boat bearing the assistant division commander of the 1st Marine Division, Brigadier General William Rupertus, and his chief of staff, Colonel Robert Kilmartin, pulled alongside the USS *Neville* just before 0500 hours.

Rupertus respected Vandegrift more than anyone in the US Marine Corps and had great affection for the man. The two men went back a long way. They both had served in Haiti and China in the same time frame and had crossed paths on many occasions.

Just a little more than six months ago, Vandegrift had tapped Rupertus to be his assistant division commander. Together they assembled, trained, and prepared the Marines of the 1st Marine Division for war. Then, in planning the execution phase of the Solomon Islands campaign, Vandegrift again, in planning the initial invasion into Tulagi and Gavutu, where the Marines would meet their stiffest resistance, gave Rupertus the best crack forces in the Marine Corps to carry out the assignment.

Rupertus would march to hell and back for General Vandegrift. And if Vandegrift wanted to meet in the middle of the night or early in the morning on a transport ship in the middle of a naval battle, Rupertus would be there, come hell or high water.

"Can I help you with the rope bridge, General?" the coxswain aboard the Higgins boat asked as the boat pulled alongside the *Neville*.

"No. But thank you, Chief."

Rupertus climbed up the rope ladder, scaling the ship's side, and stepped on board the deck. Kilmartin followed behind. One of Vandegrift's aides met them on deck.

The aide popped a sharp salute. "Sir, General Vandegrift is on the bridge with Captain Bailey. He sent me to escort you there."

"Very well, Lieutenant."

A moment later, Rupertus, accompanied by Kilmartin, stepped onto the bridge and exchanged salutes with Vandegrift.

"Bill, Killy, come in," Vandegrift said. "First off, congratulations on your victory at Tulagi. You just made history, my friend. The first American ground victory against the Japanese in the war."

"Thank you, sir," Rupertus said. "The victory was a team effort, sir, and we could not have done it without your support. But I feel you did not call me here to discuss the future rendition of American history books."

"You know me well, Bill. We have a problem, and I'll cut to the chase."

"I'm guessing the problem has to do with all those fireworks in the waters around Savo Island between midnight and 0300 hours."

"Correct," Vandegrift said. "Lieutenant, roll out the nautical chart showing ship positioning for General Rupertus."

"Aye, sir."

"Okay, as you know and as you can see here, we had three heavy cruisers, USS *Astoria*, *Quincy*, and *Vincennes*, making up the bulk of the Northern Force to guard this ship and your Marines landing on Tulagi."

"Yes, sir."

"Well, as of this morning, all three of those ships lie on the bottom of the ocean. We've lost over a thousand men."

"Damn."

"And in the Southern Force, guarding Guadalcanal, the *Chicago* has been hit and taken out of commission, and the Australian cruiser, the *Canberra*, has been hit so hard she may not make it. So, the bottom line is, right now we're vulnerable to being sunk by the Japanese without any frontline defense from any cruisers."

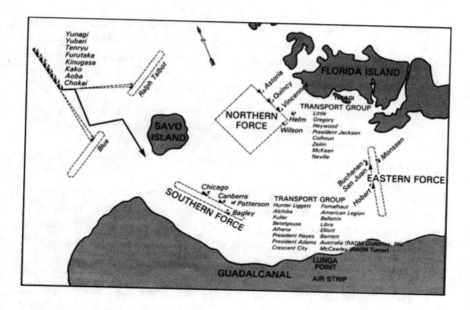

Rupertus thought for a second. "We still have our air cover from the three carriers south of Guadalcanal."

"Only for a few more hours. The navy is getting ready to pull out."

"Say again, Archer?"

"Bill, our ships just got hit by the Imperial Japanese Navy's 8th Fleet, out of Rabaul. Because our navy destroyed most of their carriers at Midway, they had to come in during the night to avoid being spotted by our carrier planes. They probably turned and left and did not destroy these transport ships, including the *Neville*, because if they waited too long, our carrier-based planes would have a chance to sink every one of them once the sun started to rise. So they came in the dark of the night and surprised us. We're lucky they didn't try to sink us all.

"But here's the problem. The three carriers we have stationed off the south coast of Guadalcanal, the *Wasp*, the *Enterprise*, and the *Saratoga*, are preparing to leave the area," Vandegrift said.

"When?"

"In an hour."

"An hour?"

"That's right. And they're taking the transport ships, too, including the *Neville*. Which means we're going to have to throw this unloading process into overdrive and get everything we need onto the beaches, both Tulagi and Guadalcanal."

"On whose order, sir?"

"Direct from Admiral Ghormley," Vandegrift said. "The navy only has a handful of carriers left, and most of them have been in support of our operation. They don't want to risk the carriers any longer."

Rupertus thought a second. "So the whole amphibious force is now vulnerable to air attack."

"Correct," Vandegrift said. "When we planned this operation, we expected the transport ships to remain in the area for four days. Now they're pulling out, which puts us in a bind. So we've gotta work double-time to get the Henderson Field airstrip ready on Guadalcanal. We have no time to waste."

"Sir, what's the operational status of Henderson Field?"

"We captured the airfield without any real opposition. Right now, it's almost ready for use by both fighters and dive bombers. And that's Admiral McCain's goal, to get us several fighter squadrons and bombers on the ground so that we don't risk our carriers in the area.

"But we have no barbed wire, and the airfield right now is defenseless. The Japs all withdrew to the bush, but we expect them back. So we can probably use the field now, but since it's defenseless, it's vulnerable to attack. We must get to work, and fast."

Vandegrift continued, "There is a probability the ships are leaving at once, which means we must unload any essential supplies immediately. The *Neville* is scheduled to pull out at around 0700 hours."

Rupertus looked at Captain Bailey.

"I'm afraid that's right, General. Unfortunately, we have our orders. It's not what I want to do. But right now, if those Jap ships decide to show up again, we've got no defenses. Not with our cruisers sunk."

"Understood, Captain. But our Marines in battle on Tanambogo all need cast rations," Rupertus said, referring to the godawful "C-Rats" (the prepackaged food prepared for the troops, consisting chiefly of smelly, canned corned beef or stale bacon). Rupertus continued, "And we need all ammo unloaded and landed immediately, before the ships leave."

"We'll do the best we can, General," Captain Bailey said, "in the limited amount of time that Admiral Ghormley is giving us to withdraw."

General Vandegrift looked up again. "Which is why we've got to light a fire under these unloading operations, now."

"Yes, sir."

"What's our updated situation on Tanambogo, Bill?"

"Sir, the naval bombardment we requested late yesterday afternoon and supplied by the USS *Gridley* has turned the tide. The *Gridley* blew the Japs off Gaomi, which allowed Captain Tinsley's company to move up Hill 121 from both sides. 1st Platoon, Company K, moved across and secured that dangerous causeway, establishing a beachhead on the Tanambogo side, where they remained throughout the night while our warships were under fire off Savo Island.

"By 2100 hours last night, our guys had secured two-thirds of Tanambogo. I'm moving Major Miller to Beach Blue this morning, and the rest of our parachute battalion—leaving Lieutenant Colonel Hunt in charge. I expect 3rd Battalion, 2nd Marines, to finish off the job sometime today, sir."

"Thanks, Bill. I feel better about that. But in light of the attacks, and with the Japs surely planning to mount a major counteroffensive on Guadalcanal, we'll need to have some elements of your 3rd Defense Battalion and support. Your Marines have taken Tulagi and hopefully finished off Gavutu and Tanambogo today. But the battle for Guadalcanal has not yet begun."

"Understood. My Marines will be ready as necessary to transfer across the channel to Guadalcanal to prosecute the war effort there."

"We may need some of them, but hopefully not all of them. We must hold Gavutu now that we've taken it. But we'll need some of your Marines pretty soon, Bill."

"Aye, sir." Vandegrift stood and offered his hand, and Rupertus took it. Their handshake was strong, and it lingered for a moment. They were both generals, but beyond that, they were brothers in arms. They were Marines.

"Good luck, Bill. Let's stay in close contact."

"Will do, sir."

With that, their meeting ended. Rupertus stepped off the bridge with Kilmartin. "Killy, let's check on some of the wounded guys in sickbay. We'll have to make it quick."

"Yes, sir."

They headed below deck for a quick check on the wounded Marines. Some would have to move to the hospital. With no time to spare, Rupertus returned to Beach Blue on Tulagi.

*****

Beach Blue
Tulagi
August 9, 1942
0700 Hours

As soon as he stepped off the boat, he directed all beaches and the government wharf to be used for landing supplies. The good news, now that his men controlled the entire island, was that they were no longer restricted to Beach Blue. The natural harbor in the beaches on the southeast sector was also available for unloading.

Rupertus ordered his logistics officer, Captain Gober, to organize a working party. At 1030 hours, he held a conference with his battalion commanders: Colonel Edson, Lieutenant Colonels Rosecrans and Hunt, and Majors Pressley, Hill, and Miller.

He lit a cigarette, took a long draw from it, and thanked every one of his men.

"Gentlemen, I am damn proud of every one of you. What you and your men have accomplished in the last forty-eight hours is beyond description. Together, you have achieved the first American ground victory in the Pacific. I'm proud of you, General Vandegrift is proud of you, and the president is proud of you. What you will have accomplished for the morale of our fighting forces and the morale of the American people.

"But there is no rest or sleep for the weary. We're in a tight time frame, gentlemen. The fleet is pulling out, leaving us vulnerable for days, and the Japanese are on the march. We expect continued air raids from Rabaul, and we'll be lucky if the Japanese fleet doesn't return tonight."

Rupertus continued, "We need to continue mopping up on Tulagi, Gavutu, and Tanambogo. And one other thing: We don't need another situation where the Japs get hold of one of these small islands again, like they did yesterday at Gaomi when they pinned down our paratrooper company on Tanambogo. I need the 2nd Battalion, 2nd Marines, to attack both Songonangong and Mokambo and organize a defense of Tulagi."

Songonangong and Mokambo were small islands around Tulagi and Gavutu. Rupertus wanted to make sure the Japs didn't drop personnel off there in the middle of the night to take potshots against Marine positions at Tulagi and Gavutu-Tanambogo.

He then assigned each battalion commander a specific sector to oversee. Colonel Edson would oversee the eastern sector of the island. Major Hill would be responsible for the southwest sector. Major Pressley would take the northwest sector, and Lieutenant Colonel Hunt would remain in command on Gavutu-Tanambogo and Mokambo.

Major Miller, who had so ably taken command for Major Williams on Tulagi, which led to the island's capture the day before, was moved back to Tulagi and would be in charge of Force Reserves, headquartered in the vicinity of Sesapi.

Colonel Pepper of the 3rd Defense Battalion would take charge of anti-aircraft defenses for the islands. General Vandegrift earlier in the morning had mentioned that the 3rd Defense Battalion would soon be transferred to Guadalcanal.

Before they all dispersed, General Rupertus posed for a quick photo with his immediate staff.

Front row, left to right: Lieutenant Colonel O. K. Pressley, Colonel Merritt A. Edson, Lieutenant Colonel H. E. Rosecrans, and Lieutenant Colonel R. E. Hill. Middle row, left to right: Navy Lieutenant E. B. McLarney, Brigadier General W. H. Rupertus, Colonel R. C. Kilmartin, and Major William Enright. Back row, left to right: Captain Ralph Powell, Captain Daryle Seeley, and Captain Thomas Philpott.

At 1100 hours, following Rupertus's orders, Combat Team V landed on Mbangai, Songonangong, and Mokambo. By 1500 hours, Marines had secured all three of the small islands and wiped off any Japanese resistance.

Meantime, *Neville* and the other transport ships remained behind and continued to unload ammunition and supplies for the Marines, even though the three aircraft carriers had pulled out of range. The carriers' absence put those transport ships at mortal risk from a Japanese air raid from Rabaul or any other position in the area.

By the middle of the afternoon, there was good news from Tulagi and Tanambogo: Colonel Hunt and the 3rd Battalion, 2nd Marines, had secured both islands. Now the challenge became getting enough supplies off the ships to sustain the occupation until more American airpower and supplies arrived in the area.

Though the *Neville* continued unloading throughout the morning and into the early afternoon, communications on the PBY remained spotty. The PBY problems had started the previous night when General Vandegrift was unable to reach Rupertus until 0327 hours in the morning, which delayed their meeting on the *Neville* until 0500 hours.

So the supplies kept coming from *Neville* throughout the morning, without meaningful communication from the ship. Rupertus kept his command post on Beach Blue, in part to facilitate better radio communications across the water. A breakthrough in communications came around 1500 hours on August 9.

"General," Kilmartin said. "We've got PBY communication with *Neville* again. Captain Bailey wants to know if we would like vehicles unloaded on the island."

Rupertus thought for a second.

Commanding officers of troops were responsible for the complete unloading of their ships, and basic priorities for landing supplies and material were established in this order: (1) ammunition, (2), water, (3) combat transportation, (4) rations, (5) medical supplies, (6) gasoline, (7) transportation other than combat, and (8) miscellaneous.

Rupertus had Marines still on board the ships, and he needed to get them off, too, ASAP. It would be great to have a few jeeps to drive around the island's perimeter, but Rupertus did not want to delay the *Neville* any longer than necessary.

"Killy, tell Captain Bailey thanks, but that's a negative on the vehicles. We'll confiscate whatever the Japanese left behind and use those if we can.

But tell him we need food, ammo, water, and weapons, and we also need those two batteries—Battery 'E' off the *Neville* and Battery 'I' off of the *Hayes*."

As the sun descended over the Pacific, sometime after 1800 hours, the *Neville*, the *Hayes*, the *McCawley*, the *President Jackson*, and all the other transports pulled out. Everything they could unload, and everyone who could be unloaded, had been unloaded.

Rupertus stepped out of his command post, struck a cigarette, and looked over the waters, out toward Guadalcanal, where, somewhere across the way, his friend and commanding officer Archer Vandegrift, awaited the onslaught of Japanese.

His men had won the first ground victory in the war against the Japanese, recapturing the British colonial capital of the Solomon Islands and capturing a valuable deep-water port for the navy to use later on. And if America won this war, their feat would go down in history.

But their victory came with a high cost. The preliminary death count showed that he lost over 120 of his Marines. Another 200 injured. They had killed 863 Japanese and captured another 20, many of whom were sent away on the *Neville*. But the losses the navy suffered at the Battle of Savo Island were staggering. Over a thousand American sailors had died, with four heavy cruisers sunk. That marked nearly half the number of sailors lost at Pearl Harbor in one blow.

His job, now, was to secure these islands and stave off Japanese attacks until the Marine Corps called him elsewhere. That "elsewhere," most likely, would be twenty miles away, to the south, across the waters of the Sealark Channel.

The Battle of Tulagi was won.

The Battle of Guadalcanal was about to begin.

Chapter 46

"Hicks House"
New ADC Command Post
Tulagi Island
August 11, 1942
Morning

With the navy pulling out and supplies low, Rupertus began moving his headquarters on Tulagi from the Beach Blue command post into the "Hicks House," in an area next to the hospital. Rupertus decided to merge Colonel Edson's headquarters with his own to simplify the communications and administrative personnel operations to improve efficiency. He ordered the parachute battalion in reserve and to occupy the ridge adjacent to the Hicks House. Rupertus then had a conference with all battalion commanders and made slight adjustments to their sector duties, including making Major Edson assistant chief of staff working under Colonel Kilmartin.

But the real point of urgency (for the Marines) at both Tulagi and Guadalcanal was Henderson Field. The airstrip was named in honor of US Marine Corps Major Lofton Henderson, killed during the Battle of Midway, the first Marine aviator to perish.

By August 11, Rear Admiral John S. McCain, commander of the US Navy South Pacific Air Forces, sent his pilot/aide in a PYB plane to Guadalcanal to see whether Henderson Field was ready for flight operations—a welcome sign for Rupertus, General Vandegrift, and the Marines. The absence of the three American aircraft carriers was a continuing worry, making both Tulagi and Guadalcanal vulnerable to air raids.

McCain knew that things needed to move faster. Within days, McCain sent a convoy and a US Navy Seabee unit to speed up the construction of the airstrip.

The next few days, Guadalcanal remained relatively calm. But naval intelligence showed that the island would soon explode. Admiral Turner had alerted Vandegrift that the Japs were planning a significant counterattack within days. Hopefully McCain's fighters would arrive in time. With Tulagi mostly secure, Vandegrift asked Rupertus to transfer his 1st Raider Battalion,

1st Parachute Battalion, and 2nd Battalion of the 5th Marines to Guadal-canal to lead the 1st Marine Division's defense around the inside perimeter of Henderson Field and whatever else might be needed to respond to the Japanese attack. He ordered the Marines slated for Guadalcanal to prepare for departure.

Even as Rupertus continued operations on Tulagi and thought of his next mission, Sleepy remained in his heart. He wondered what she knew and hoped that she didn't worry too much. Of course, Sleepy was tough as nails and safe back home in the nation's capital. She had endured Shanghai in 1937, and she would survive this, too.

He missed her more than he realized, especially in the lull moments when the Japanese were not attacking. Holding a burning cigarette, he pulled out her picture and gazed at it for a moment. He hoped the war would be over sooner rather than later. The harder he fought, and the harder his men fought, the sooner they'd go home

*****

"Hicks House"
New ADC Command Post
Tulagi Island
August 12, 1942
Day 4 of the US Occupation

The morning of August 12 brought good news from the US Navy. The Japanese cruiser *Kako*, believed to be one of the Japanese ships from Rabaul that had attacked and sunk three US Navy cruisers on the night of August 9, was attacked and sunk by the American submarine USS *S-44*. The *Kako*'s sinking happened the day after Savo Island, on August 10, and news trickled into Tulagi of the *S-44*'s victory.

The news did not atone for the loss of the three American cruisers—the *Astoria*, the *Quincy*, and the *Vincennes*—and the Australian cruiser HMAS *Canberra*. In fact, the loss of the three American warships and their crews cast a solemn shadow over the great victory the Marines had won on Tulagi and Gavutu.

The Japanese had lost most of their carriers at Midway, and now a navy submarine had sunk one of their cruisers, which constituted the bulk of Japan's remaining naval firepower. The *Kako* sinking marked one less damn Japanese cruiser that Rupertus had to worry about firing on his men on Tulagi.

The news of *S-44*'s victory provided a nice morale boost to start the day.

Rupertus received a message that three boats were on their way over from Guadalcanal.

As he stepped out on the hill from his command post, he spotted the boats, and a Jap sub on the surface racing toward them.

He picked up the phone. "E battery. Open fire on that sub chasing those boats."

"Aye, sir."

Four short blasts filled the air, and four splashes hit in the water all around the sub. It broke off and stopped its pursuit of the boats.

After the Japanese sub left the area, the three boats motored into the calm waters of Tulagi harbor, walled by green vegetation. At 1200 hours, the boats arrived on the beach. On board were Captain Murray, Marine Gunner Banta, and two nerve-wracked AP reporters, including *Guadalcanal Diary* author Richard Tregaskis.

Murray, Banta, and Tregaskis made their way to the command post. The close call with the submarine had scared the hell out of the reporters.

When they found Rupertus, he greeted them warmly and summarized the fighting in Tulagi, Gavutu, and Tanambogo.

"The toughest job has been to clean out scores of dugout caves filled with Japs. Each cave," he said, "was a fortress in itself filled with Japs who were determined to resist until they were all killed. The only effective way to finish off these caves was to take a charge of dynamite and thrust it down the narrow cave entrance. After we blasted the cave, we could go in with a submachine gun and finish off the Japs inside."

The Japanese dugout "dungeons" on Tulagi and Gavutu were numerous. Exterminating them was a tedious job, particularly on Tulagi, where only yesterday the last of them had been finished off.

"You've never seen such caves and dungeons," said Rupertus. "There would be thirty or forty Japs in them, and they refused to come out, except in one or two isolated cases."

Rupertus went on, "The bravery of our men. There should be forty or fifty congressional medals awarded to these people. I don't know how to express it. I think the United States should be just as proud as these people who gave their lives." Then he paused. "Who gave their lives to the most wonderful work in our history. When it comes to bravery, there isn't anybody in the world that can beat us. I don't think the United States has an episode in its history that can touch what's been done here."

The group also interviewed Colonels Edson and Rosecrans, Captain Stallings, Pilot Officer Spencer of the RAAF, Chaplain Fitzgerald, and others. Just as they were about to leave, the Japanese sub surfaced again, ten thousand yards off the coast. It was far too dangerous for the crew from Guadalcanal, so Rupertus told them to stay the night.

On this same day, division command sent a message that meals on Guadalcanal would be rationed to two a day and those on Tulagi would continue at one a day. For the time being, the Marines would have to fight lean, hungry, and smart.

They would be facing the Imperial Japanese 17th Army, commanded by Lieutenant General Harukichi Hyakutake, just a year older than Rupertus, who had been ordered to retake Guadalcanal. Hyakutake would oversee the Japanese 17th Army's 28th Regiment, under the command of Colonel Kiyono Ichiki, which was stationed closest to Guadalcanal at the time.

Rupertus knew the enemy well. When the attack came in full force, it would be brutal.

Chapter 47

Henderson Field
Guadalcanal
August 19–20, 1942

General Rupertus had already sent some of his best commanders, including Lieutenant Colonel Edson and his Raiders, to Guadalcanal. Their mission, first and foremost: secure the airfield on Guadalcanal.

That airfield, which Japanese laborers and Korean conscripts had initially constructed, was located on Lunga Point, a promontory on the northern coast of Guadalcanal.

Nearly eleven thousand Marines had landed, without serious opposition, on Lunga Point on August 7, as General Rupertus led the first American amphibious assault of World War II against Tulagi that very day.

That the Marines had not yet faced a full Japanese onslaught on the ground on Guadalcanal remained a bit of a mystery. General Vandegrift speculated that the overwhelming force of eleven thousand Marines descending on the island, concentrated in a single area, had spooked the Japanese to head inland, where they would wait until reinforcements could arrive.

In Rupertus's opinion, Vandegrift was correct. But the general also knew it was only a matter of time. The airfield presented too grand a prize for them to abandon it without a bloody fight.

While Tulagi proved valuable for its deep-water port facility, Guadalcanal would be fought over because the strategic airfield, its prized possession, was a game-changer in the war.

The Marines, including many of the men who had fought to capture Tulagi, moved quickly, securing the perimeter with initial defensive lines by August 12, the day the first American aircraft landed on the field, a PBY patrol bomber. Still, the area was not ready for large-scale air operations until August 18.

By August 19, the Japanese began pouring supplies and men into Guadalcanal, on the opposite side of the twenty-mile-wide island from where the Marines had landed, to prepare for the battle to recapture Henderson

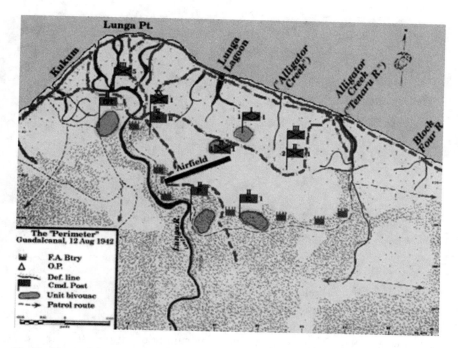

Field. These fast convoys, bringing troops, supplies, and weapons, shipped from Rabaul to Guadalcanal, became known as the "Tokyo Express."

Since the Marines had captured the airfield and established an aviation presence on Henderson Field, the Japanese could not use slower transport ships to bring forces into Guadalcanal.

Therefore, to deliver troops and supplies, they used faster-moving cruisers and destroyers steaming down a body of water known as "The Slot," the colloquial name given to the New Georgia Sound, the waterway that runs northwest–southeast through the middle of the Solomon archipelago.

On August 19, an advance detachment of about nine hundred Japanese soldiers from Ichiki's 28th Regiment landed on Guadalcanal before the rest of the regiment.

Most of these men of the 28th Regiment were veterans like Rupertus and Vandegrift and were fighting in China and Shanghai at the same time Rupertus was in Shanghai in 1937–1938. Rupertus knew that some of the same men from the regiment had bombed, raped, and pillaged Chinese citizens and their homes.

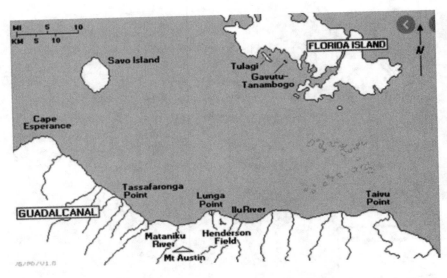

This first group, including Colonel Ichiki, arrived onshore at Taivu Point, some twenty miles to the east of Henderson Field.

The Japanese were accompanied by Destroyer Squadron 2 of the Imperial Japanese Navy. With only a seven-day supply of rations, supplies, and ammunition, Ichiki left one hundred of his men to set up camp and protect the supplies near the beach while he headed with the rest of the men to set up camp in the jungle, nine miles away.

Seeing no Americans, he radioed his headquarters that he had succeeded in the invasion. He was ordered not to take the airfield without the rest of his regiment he had left behind.

Meanwhile, on August 19, that same day that the Japanese began landing on Taivu Point, Rupertus and his men faced a military challenge again on Tulagi, from the Imperial Japanese Navy.

Japanese destroyers opened fire on Tulagi and the government wharf, killing a Marine and injuring three USS *Wasp* Air Group officers. The Japanese bombardment of Tulagi harbor by destroyers continued into August 20.

To counter the Japanese, the Americans continued pouring forces into the area. The following day, August 20, thirty-one Marine Corps F4F Wildcats and STB Dauntless dive bombers landed on Henderson Field. This was the beginning of what became known as the "Cactus Air Force." With the Japanese dropping troops into the other side of the island, the arrival of the warplanes could not have been timelier.

Rupertus knew in his gut that he would join that fight, sooner or later. As of August 20, his mission was to remain in charge of the islands his men had conquered. The air raid sirens, harassing Japanese subs, Jap bombers, and aircraft constantly taking shots at the Marines ensured that Tulagi and Gavutu would not enjoy a moment of peace.

Chapter 48

Tulagi Island
Headquarters
September 9, 1942

One month and two days since US forces first invaded Beach Blue on Tulagi, the Japanese had continued to harass the American troops on the island, primarily through naval gunfire and air power. The Marines had secured the islands but were subjected to mortar and other incoming enemy fire at any time.

After the attack on Pearl Harbor, the United States needed a small naval craft to patrol up and down the coast of the United States and along the Panama Canal. The navy brought a small flotilla of converted tuna boats designated as "YPs," the acronym for Yard Patrol boats. Most were built with a wood frame and had little to no ability to defend themselves, and yet they could transport 150 men.

To ferry sailors and Marines back and forth between Guadalcanal and Tulagi, the navy brought a small flotilla of these boats into the Solomon Islands combat theater. Ever since the Marines had secured Tulagi and Tanambogo, they were in use daily, crossing the channel between the two islands.

Rupertus had a soft spot for the YP operators, who placed themselves in constant danger every time they crossed the channel. On September 9, 1942, in the early morning hours, the Japanese attacked one of the American YP boats as it crossed the channel, just before it reached the shore on Tulagi. On the one-month anniversary of his victory at Gavutu, General Rupertus wrote in his diary, describing the event in his own words:

> *At about 2 AM we turned in and were awakened by someone screaming from a nightmare. Then heard voices of men shouting on the wharf, a shot and then a bluejacket killed, and at the same time lights lit up the harbor.*
>
> *I beat it out of the house to see what was going on, and as I was running to the road, guns opened fire from Japs in the harbor and I threw myself down flat into a ditch . . . lots of water—pack and belt all wet—then as fire slackened, I made a run for the battle CP, where our 5" using star shells were being used as a spotlight to illuminate the sky and find the Japs (firing at them).*

Society of Red Tape Cutters Award by Dr. Seuss.

The general jumps from a YP onto the dock at Tulagi, believed to be in September 1942. (USMC PHOTO)

The Japs had fired on the YPs, damaged the hospital—and eight men were slightly wounded and removed to safety. At about 2 AM, reports that cries for help were coming from the YP—sent Higgins boat to meet it, and they brought survivors back to me . . . they deserve a lot of credit for their job (YPs transported Marines every day over dangerous 20 miles on sea back and forth from Guadalcanal to Tulagi). Went out to the ship to get an estimate of casualties . . .

Four days later, on September 13, Rupertus wrote in his diary a sad note about the dedication of American cemeteries on foreign soil, thousands of miles from home, to hold American bodies:

All clear here and Cactus. Dedicated a cemetery here—a US cemetery. Next Sunday, dedicate another one, also dedicated one at the golf course. Got to mass and communion, also will dedicate a cemetery at Gavutu—again at Police HQ next week. Air raid signals at Cactus 2:20–3:20 PM and 6PM–6:10. Japs dropped bombs on the north coast of Florida!
*****

Burial at cemetery on Gavutu. (USMC PHOTO)

Tulagi
Command Post
War Cemeteries
September 20, 1942

Sunday, September 20, 1942, marked the forty-fifth day since Rupertus's Marines initiated the invasion of Tulagi and the forty-fourth day since the first American victory on the ground in the Pacific. Over on Guadalcanal, the ground battle heated up as the Japanese struck at the Tenaru River, attempting to crack Vandegrift's perimeter at Alligator Creek and pour more troops onto the island.

From September 12 to September 14, Lieutenant Colonel Merritt Edson had served under Rupertus at Tulagi but was then shipped across the sound to Guadalcanal with Marine Raiders and USMC paramarines to engage in a bloody struggle on a ridge overlooking Lunga Point. The Marines defeated the Japanese 35th Infantry Brigade and the 28th Infantry Brigade, fighting on the ridge, which became known as Edson's Ridge. Edson's victory marked another great ground victory for the Marines, following Tulagi and Gavutu.

While the navy took advantage of Tulagi's deep-water harbor, the YPs continued to transport men, supplies, and equipment back and forth across the channel as the needs of the Marine Corps on Guadalcanal and Tulagi dictated.

Over the past few weeks, most of the Japanese attacks came from ships, submarines, or planes stationed at Rabaul, in New Britain, the source of the attack on the night of August 9, when the Japanese navy steamed in the middle of the night to surprise the American cruisers guarding the entrance of Savo Island.

As part of the daily security routine on the islands, Rupertus sent Marines on patrols throughout Tulagi and Gavutu, as well as some of the smaller islets like Gaomi, to ensure that no Japanese forces from the Tokyo Express infiltrated overnight via submarine or other means. Many Japanese troops swam from Tulagi to Florida Island during the Marines' initial invasion and returned at night to slaughter Marines. Japanese snipers who had escaped to Florida also presented a continuing threat.

In addition to Gaomi, the Marines ran daily combat missions to Mbangai, Kokomtambu, Mokambo, and Songonangong, all within a couple of thousand yards of Tulagi.

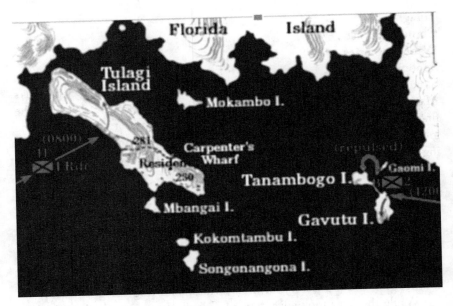

September 20 started as a normal day on the tropical Pacific island in the middle of a war zone. Following the typical routine, a YP left Tulagi harbor headed for "Cactus," which was the code name used for Guadalcanal, specifically Henderson Field.

At 1020 hours, an air raid siren bellowed across the island, but no Japanese planes were spotted. Once the "all clear" sounded at around 1100 hours, General Rupertus dedicated a cemetery on the grounds of the police barracks, where several Marines were already buried. He hoped that all their bodies would eventually return to America.

For now, burying them on an isolated foreign island was the best they could do. At least they would be buried with their American brothers in arms.

In the early afternoon, the YP carrying Major Enright arrived from Guadalcanal. The major carried a letter each for Colonel Kilmartin and Rupertus.

"Sir, could I see you for a second?"

Rupertus looked up and saw his trusted chief of staff, Colonel Robert Kilmartin.

"Absolutely. Come in."

"Sir, General Vandegrift asked me to show this letter to you." Kilmartin handed an envelope to Rupertus.

Rupertus unfolded the letter.

My Dear Killy,

This is a tough letter for me to write and I believe you will accept it in the way it is meant. We now have fourteen colonels in the Division, Gerry Thomas just having received a field promotion to that grade. We have orders from the Marine Corps commandant to send all excess officers, over and above our authorized allowance, back to the states at the earliest practicable date so that we may use them to organize and command new units now forming. This has worried me greatly as I hate to lose any of the Colonels in the Division.

After careful consideration, I thought that the fairest way to do it was to send them out according to the date on which they joined the Division. This, I believe, is the fairest to everyone and certainly is beyond criticism as to favor one person over another. You can realize that this is so when I tell you that Roy Hunt, one of my closest friends I have in the service, comes within that category.

You have done excellent work, and it will give me great pleasure to put it both on your Fitness report and in a letter of recommendation.

Please tell Rupertus that, for the time being, he will have to use his "3" officer as his chief of staff. I hope you can get over here before you leave. In fact, you will have to as you will leave from here.

My kindest regards to all on Tulagi.

Sincerely,

A. A. Vandegrift,

Commanding General, 1st MarDiv.

Rupertus folded the letter and handed it back to Kilmartin. "Major Enright bought me a letter from Vandegrift, too. You've been my right arm, Killy, and you have been a major factor in our victory on Tulagi. I hate to lose you, but I'm glad for you. You're going home to be with your family."

"The Marine Corps is also my family, sir, and if I had my druthers, I'd stick by your side until the end."

"Yes, I know you would, Killy. And if I had my way, I keep you right here, and we'd finish the whole thing off together."

"Major Enright is lucky to serve as your new chief of staff, sir, and I know he will do an excellent job."

"Yes, Enright will perform well. But you'll be missed, Killy."

"Thank you, sir."

"Please ask Major Enright to step in."

"Aye, sir."

After a meeting with Enright, Rupertus penned a response to his old friend and boss, Major General Vandegrift.

Dear Archer,

Received your letter via Enright (incidentally, you wrote on the envelope "Kindness to "Lieutenant Colonel" Enright). Enright says that's a field promotion and in your handwriting! I'm sure sorry that Killy is leaving us—he has been a tremendous help to me, and I shall miss him. He says now I'll have no one to pick on! I usually saved a tin can alarm to get him to line up in the a.m. and other wisey tricks on him. Killy is getting his things together tomorrow, is setting his affairs, including eight cuts he owes me or I/O him, and will leave for cactus on the YP boat on Tuesday morning. Enright is worth his weight in gold and can do both jobs well. He is a go-getter and never stops where he meets obstacles until the job is done.

Next time you suspect ships in this channel—open with star shells about 1000 yards this side of the target also the next time that Jap plane flies over here at night, we will open fire on him (if we can see his exhaust). He flies right over the center of the island! Natives came in, and they reported they found 16 dead Japs as a result of the last encounter—some of them must have been killed by the bullets getting them in the woods.

We counted seven only in the open. Patrols out to the East point of Florida will return tomorrow. I'll get that damn little boat if I can only get a tip from the native police I have out. Surely, we had our 180 men back that friendly cat Fuller ran off with. By Wednesday or Thursday, if all is clear, here I'll send word for the Duck to come over (or before) if you tell me. From Enright's description, I don't know which CP of yours is the best, and both have their disadvantages. All well here. My best to Capers, Roy, George, and Jim.

Sincerely, Bill.

Rupertus closed his day with an entry in his diary:

YP boat 0630 to Cactus—Dedicated Cemetery at Police Barracks at 1100—Air raid alarm at 1030 AM. No Jap planes seen or bombing. Enright returned with letters to Killy and me from AAV. Killy is to go back. Also Roy, George, Bill.
*****

Tulagi
USMC Command Post
September 21, 1942

In the days since his forces had occupied Tulagi, Rupertus first secured the islands and then began building diplomatic relations with the natives. In particular, he worked on his relationship with the native chiefs to recruit native guides, to get their support and intelligence against the Japanese on Tulagi, Guadalcanal, and throughout the Solomons.

The natives preferred the Americans to the untrustworthy Japanese and welcomed the American forces on the first day of the invasion when Major Nicholson brought his Marines into Sasapi. Rupertus never took occupying their land for granted. He worked to gain their trust, to assure them that his Marines would protect them against the Japanese.

The Marines also needed the natives' eyes and ears on the islands. Rupertus penned a letter to the native teacher he knew, David Maesiedi, to promote a partnership.

On September 20, Maesiedi responded with a letter to Rupertus in English, requesting weapons from the Marines to defend themselves against the Japanese:

> *To the Right Honorable*
> *The General*
> *at Tulagi Belagais Village*
> *September 27, 1942*
> *Dear Sir,*
>
> *Excuse me as I beg to inform you of a few words. As to remind you that my ways back from all your soldiers, when I was with them to look for the Japanese at Gale on Friday last.*
>
> *I gather together with all the chiefs all on this side of the Floridas which I was. And I told them a few orders which I received from the Captain of the Soldiers [sic] to remind them about it. Then after that Sir, I began to ask all the Chiefs and village people if they kindly helped me some days next week looking for these Japanese at Gale; to find out how many were killed and how many will remain in the bush. And also, Sir, I would like to make sure where they have made their new home at present. Then Sir, all the chief and the village people agreed with me together, and they said we will be seeking these Japanese on Tuesday next week.*
>
> *Sir, I am now beginning to choose out which of the good boys that will be going with me. Start from Belaga's Village right up to Soa and Uti Mamon. Although I would remind you Sir, if suppose any person of whom I have chosen to go with me, and he doesn't want to go with me, I will write down his name and bring it to you, Sir. Sir, another thing all of the Chiefs on this side of the Floridas told me to write, and mention to you, so that you will say something to all your Air Force, about us, that we will go looking for the Japanese at Gale on Tuesday next week. Sir, otherwise, they will think that we are Japanese if they see any of us there at Gale. Sir, please can you send me one or two guns with a few cartridges with it, if you think that is all right to take guns with us? But if not, doesn't matter Sir. I have the honor to be kin [sic]."*
>
> *Your humble and obedient servant, J. David Maesiedi*

Rupertus and Marine officers greet native chiefs in a formal ceremony on Tulagi. (USMC PHOTO)

Rupertus and a coastwatcher talk with native chief on Tulagi. (USMC PHOTO)

Rupertus shakes hands with young boy on Tulagi. (USMC PHOTO)

*****

Tulagi
Farewell to a Friend
September 22, 1942

Tuesday, September 22, 1942, the forty-fifth day of the Marine Corps' occupation of Tulagi, was the day General Rupertus had dreaded. Saying goodbye to a friend, and especially a friend and comrade in battle, was always sad. Such was the life in the US military, and especially the US Marine Corps.

The departure happened early in the morning when Colonel Kilmartin boarded a YP at 0600 hours for the voyage across the channel to Guadalcanal to begin the first leg of his journey home. It was a bittersweet moment for Rupertus—happy Kilmartin could go home and yet saddened at losing the man at his right arm during the Marines' first victory.

To protect his friend as he began his journey, Rupertus had called in a US Navy SBD Dauntless dive bomber to circle overhead and guard against any enemy threat to the boat carrying Killy. It was the least Rupertus could

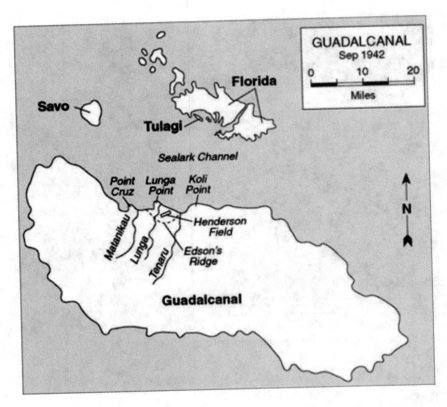

do for his trusty aide. What a damn shame it would be for Kilmartin to come this far and then get sunk on the first leg of his voyage home.

With that, Rupertus lost his trusted chief of staff. He liked and trusted Enright. But the order relieving Killy had come down from above, from the commandant's office. And that was life in the military. Here today, gone tomorrow. Much like life itself, fleeting as a vapor, precious, and to be cherished. But Rupertus and his men would push on. Victory demanded it. As for Kilmartin, Rupertus knew their paths would cross again.

Chapter 49

USMC Command Post
Guadalcanal Island
Nimitz and the Navy Cross
October 1, 1942

In the weeks since his Marines had scored the first decisive combat victory against the Japanese on the ground in World War II, General Rupertus had, for the most part, remained on Tulagi, continuing to command the occupying force there.

Tulagi, however, had become a valuable operational base for the Allies, particularly its deep-water harbor. Numerous warships and other vessels stopped in from time to time, which drew the Japanese navy's fire.

On October 1, Rupertus crossed over to Guadalcanal, where he met with Admiral Chester Nimitz. The commander in chief of the Pacific Fleet had come to check on the Marines and award the Navy Cross to General Vandegrift and General Rupertus.

Rumors flew that Nimitz and MacArthur, the two five-star officers overseeing the prosecution of the Pacific War, were jockeying for control of forces as the Marines began their island-hopping campaign. With the Marine Corps being part of the Department of the Navy, Rupertus's natural affinity was to Nimitz, although he had great admiration for MacArthur.

For the time being, the navy ran the offensive operations in the Solomon Islands, and Vandegrift and Rupertus came under the operational command of Admiral Nimitz. They were looking forward to spending a few moments with the great admiral.

Rupertus and his crew arrived early in the morning and were escorted to the hut where Admiral Nimitz was waiting along with General Vandegrift. After a few moments of chit-chat, the award ceremony began.

Rupertus stepped forward first and saluted Admiral Nimitz. "It's great to see you again, sir."

"The honor is mine, Bill. At ease."

"Yes, sir."

"On behalf of the president of the United States, it is my honor to award you the Navy Cross for extraordinary heroism in command of our forces in the capture of Tulagi, Gavutu, and Tanambogo, America's first victory on the ground in the Pacific. Congratulations, General." Nimitz, in a long-sleeved khaki uniform, pinned the Navy Cross on Rupertus's chest.

"Thank you, sir."

Nimitz awarded the Navy Cross to Vandegrift. Then the admiral proceeded to pin another fourteen Navy Crosses and eleven Distinguished Flying Crosses on the chests of US Marines and naval aviators for their valiant heroism in the Solomon Islands campaign.

As Nimitz pinned medals to the men's uniforms, he told them they were heroes and an inspiration to all the American armed forces. To each man, he said, "Good work; more power to you."

Afterward, Vandegrift, Nimitz, and Rupertus discussed the general war planning strategy. While the Japanese had made several attacks against the Marines' position at Cactus, Henderson Field remained under the control of the Marine Corps, the primary strategic asset to the Allies in the Pacific Theater.

All three men agreed. The Japanese would soon launch a major offensive to recapture it.

One topic that came up involved the possibility of the army relieving the Marines on Guadalcanal. General MacArthur, it seemed, was anxious to get more directly in the fight. Rupertus got the feeling that Nimitz was not MacArthur's greatest fan. And, of course, the notion of having a five-star flag officer sharing command in the same theater could be confusing.

But that was FDR's call, and Rupertus kept his thoughts to himself, especially in front of Nimitz. There were no immediate plans for either the army to relieve the Marines on Guadalcanal or General MacArthur to take command of any Marine Corps units.

After the meeting with Nimitz, Rupertus took a YP back across the channel to Tulagi. A few days later, a black-and-white photo arrived from Guadalcanal, showing Nimitz pinning the Navy Cross on his chest. Rupertus looked at the picture, smiled, and then put it in an envelope to mail to Sleepy. She would appreciate this sort of thing more than he did.

Diary, Thursday, October 1
Up at 5:30 AM. Breakfast at 0600. Lined up with Edson, Pollock and about 20 others. AAV received the Navy Cross and so did I. AAV says I'll still get the

Admiral Nimitz pinning the Navy Cross on Rupertus, October 1, 1942, Guadalcanal.
(USMC PHOTO)

DSM. Got in a bit of discussion about relieving us by the Army. I spent all day with Colonel P looking over defense battalion activities. Back to CP by 1:45 PM and sat around and talked with AAV, Peck and Thomas. Nimitz party off in B17 at 2 PM. Carlson for conference on task. After supper sat around and gassed some more. Moved guest tent with aide to AAV, Lieutenant Larrant and Peck. At about 9 PM Jap plane dropped two bombs on the airfield. Searchlights to look for wounded planes. Our planes bombed four Jap destroyers in late p.m. We turned in at 9 PM after the air raid. At 4 AM, awakened by the cry of "air raid"—was still in undies. Three Jap planes dropped bombs on an area near Raiders. Several drums of gas set a fire near new fighters. No sleep.

Received orders from Cactus to attack Garabussa where Japs were congregating. On October 6 sent Enright to Cactus to find out about the operation. October 8 had a conference with Col. Arthur, Lt. Colonels Hill and VanNess and Major Enright about the attack. Hill left the next day with 2 YPs and 8 Higgins in what turned out to be a dangerous operation.

Diary, October 10
At 10:45 got a message from Hill that his YP boats had landed at Aola. Also that one boat capsized and 50% of the men lost. YP seven miles north of Taivo Point to come into Aola and land troops. Hill plans time operations as planned. Have notified division—continuing to unload Fuller, establish defense in Hills sector with Marines Fuller bought. 1330 air raid alarm. No Jap planes; both YP's returned at 1900 with 14 men from the capsized boat. 4 cruiser planes landed at Gavutu at 1 from Task Force. Enright left for Cactus in a Duck.

Chapter 50

In the Waters off Savo Island
Battle of Cape Esperance
October 11, 1942
Early in the Day

In the wake of the naval disaster suffered by the US Navy at the Battle of Savo Island, Norman Scott, the chief of naval operations, was determined to avoid a repeat of the navy being surprised by the single-line attack of cruisers from the Japanese navy base in Rabaul.

The Japanese continued running naval convoys of troops from Rabaul to Guadalcanal to launch attacks against Henderson Field. The US Navy expected the Japanese to try another surprise assault on the American fleet protecting Guadalcanal and Tulagi's waters.

Assigned to the Office of the Chief of Naval Operations in early 1942, Scott had a reputation as one of the most pugilistic and kick-ass commanders in the US Navy.

Scott was on board the USS *San Juan* during the Battle of Savo Island. *San Juan* was miles away from the Japanese surprise attack against the American cruisers, but close enough to watch, and Scott witnessed a large part of the battle. He took it personally. Scott knew the commanders and many officers of the warships that had gone down.

Scott, the man to shore up the naval operations of the US surface fleet around the Solomon Islands, was promoted to rear admiral and placed in command of Task Force 56. Hell would freeze over before Admiral Scott would allow such a disaster to happen again in his navy. Scott was known not only as a warfighter but also as an innovator in naval warfare tactics.

He advocated a tactic to defeat the Japanese known as "crossing the T," which he had studied while attending the Naval War College Senior Officers' Course at Newport, Rhode Island, in the 1930s.

The Japanese surprise attack and the Battle of Savo Island was effective because (1) enemy ships slipped up on the American flotilla guarding the entrance to the channel, and (2) the Imperial Japanese Navy moved in a single column, slicing through the middle of American warships, which were spread out, giving the Jap navy a tactical advantage.

Scott had a hunch the Japanese were coming back to try to pull off what they had done on the night of August 9 and sink a slew of American cruisers. They would try the same battle tactics, but this time, they would be met by the American fleet employing a new tactic.

"Crossing the T" is a naval warfare tactic whereby a line of warships crosses in front of a line of advancing enemy ships, almost in a perpendicular line, allowing the ships in the crossing line to bring all their guns to bear while receiving fire from only the forward guns of the enemy.

When Scott took command of Task Force 56, he met with his ship commanders and explained the tactic he wanted to employ when the Japanese returned.

"Okay, gentlemen, your attention on the board. Watch this. The Japanese will try to play out exactly what they did before. But this time we will be ready. Turn your attention to the chart, please. For those of you who have not been to war college yet, what you see here is a classic 'crossing the "T" formation.'

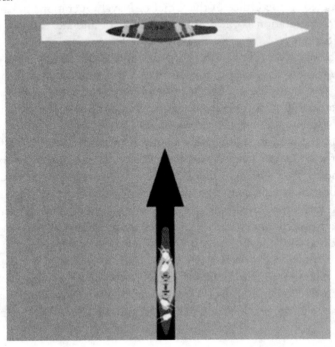

"I expect the Japanese to return, in a single column as they did during the Battle of Savo Island. They will try to split us down the middle T to divide and conquer. But this time," he tapped twice on the Fulton board with a pointer, "this time we'll be ready.

"Note in this diagram the Japanese armada is represented by the black arrow at the bottom of the diagram, moving from bottom to top. The cruiser is represented by the ship at top, perpendicular to the approaching Japanese ship, on the arrow moving from left to right. Now note the gun emplacements. In this single illustration alone, the Japanese cruiser has two of its four guns available to it. The American cruiser has all four gun emplacements available by firing from the broadside. So, in the single illustration alone, the American cruiser has double the firepower of the Japanese cruiser." He put down the pointer.

"Questions?"

"No, sir, Admiral."

"No, sir."

"Very well. Commander, would you please tack up the new diagram?"

"Aye, sir." The admiral's aide complied.

"Note what we're seeing on the board, gentlemen."

"Very well." Scott picked up the pointer and began tapping again. "Now, in this example, we've expanded out from the first diagram. The four ships traveling south to north represent the current Japanese battle tactics they used at Savo Island, where they try to get inside the American fleet and attack from both sides using a divide and conquer tactic.

"As they will face the American armada, up at the top of the 'T,' the only effective weapons in this configuration are the lead weapons on the forward deck of the lead ship. All the other Japanese warships, because they are in a single-file line behind the lead ship, are not able to effectively fire on the American fleet. If they fire forward, they're firing into the rear of their sister ships. All the American ships have an opportunity to open up from their broadsides and then angle on all the Japanese ships. The Japanese will have to break formation. This will be particularly effective if we can catch the Japanese by surprise. We will have all the guns on a broadside, trained against their column.

"Any questions?"

"No, sir."

"Okay, gentlemen, get back to your ships and be ready. The Japanese will try to strike from Rabaul again at any time."

*****

Bridge, IJN *Aoba*
Approaching Savo Island
October 11, 1942
2300 Hours

The Japanese navy had trained extensively in night fighting tactics before the beginning of the war. The US Navy had not, giving the Japanese a tremendous advantage that paid off handsomely at the Battle of Savo Island. Rear Admiral Aritomo Gotō felt confident that he would face no opposition from the US Navy.

US Navy warships had yet to attempt to halt any Tokyo Express missions to Guadalcanal. Therefore, Admiral Gotō was not expecting any opposition from US naval surface forces at night. Especially after the Battle of Savo Island, when the IJN's tactics sank three American cruisers and one Australian cruiser.

His mission tonight was to slip in under cover of darkness with three heavy cruisers under his command, bombard the American airfield (destroying the aircraft sitting on the runway), and then slip from the area before at the break of day, to avoid detection by the American navy.

Gotō's cruisers would follow a course parallel to the second convoy of Japanese warships to Guadalcanal. The second convoy, a supply convoy—referred to as the "reinforcement group" by the Japanese—was under Rear Admiral Takatsuga Jojima.

Jojima's convoy was on a separate mission from Gotō's, with Jojima's mission to reinforce Japanese troops on the ground, whereas Gotō was to attack and destroy the airfield. The reinforcement group was singing along an hour in front of Gotō's cruisers and reached the waters off Guadalcanal at approximately 2200 hours.

Jojima radioed Gotō, "No American ships sighted."

"Good."

From the flag bridge of flagship *Aoba*, traveling in the very front of the Japanese column, the admiral looked out from the bow through his binoculars. The moon had already disappeared for the night, and visibility was poor. Plus, rainstorms had further hampered visibility. But Gotō remained confident. The Americans would not be foolish enough to resist him, not at night. He would be in a position to fire upon and hopefully destroy the airfield within the next hour.

Gotō's flotilla had brought enough firepower to take care of any American ships, should they show up. With his big guns, he would finally destroy the airfield that the Americans had taken, which was rightfully the property of the Japanese empire.

Two other powerful cruisers, the *Furutaka* and *Kinugasa*, followed his flagship in a column, while the destroyers *Fubuki* and *Hatsuyuki* flanked the *Aoba* to the starboard and port.

"Do you see anything, Admiral?" his aide asked.

"There is nothing to see. All is well. We will carry out our mission to destroy this airfield as our troops destroy the Marines from the backside."

"Your leadership will make the emperor proud, sir."

Gotō smiled and nodded his head. "Our brave sailors and soldiers will honor our holy emperor. I am but one among many. Just the oldest one." He allowed himself a chuckle at his comment.

"I don't know about old, sir—perhaps the most experienced. We need experience at this hour. Your men would follow you into battle in any place and any time, sir."

"You are too kind, Commander."

"Is there any way I can be of service to you at the moment, Admiral?"

"Not at the moment, Commander. I don't believe the American navy is foolish enough to try anything in the dark. Not after we beat them so badly. We will be in battle soon enough when we attack that airfield. But for now, all is well."

*****

Bridge, USS *San Francisco* (CA-38)
In the Waters East of Savo Island
October 11, 1942
2335 Hours

Earlier in the day, at around 1445 hours, US reconnaissance aircraft had spotted a convoy of Japanese warships in the "Slot," racing toward Guadalcanal, approximately 210 miles from the western end of Guadalcanal.

There was no indication that the Japanese ships had spotted the American aircraft. The initial report showed at least two cruisers and six destroyers headed toward Guadalcanal.

This intelligence report convinced Rear Admiral Scott that tonight would be the night. And based on the direction and speed of the Japanese flotilla, he expected them to arrive in these waters any time between 2300 and 0100 hours.

With a flotilla consisting of two heavy cruisers, two light cruisers, and five destroyers, the admiral's forces steamed out to the west, hoping to lay a trap for the unsuspecting Japanese. The American cruisers included the *San Francisco*, *Boise*, *Salt Lake City*, and *Helena*, with the *Boise* and the *Helena* carrying an advanced radar system that had not been available to the American warships during the Battle of Savo Island.

Admiral Scott chose the *San Francisco* as his flagship, and at 2200 hours, his ships steamed past Cape Hunter at the northwest end of Guadalcanal, proceeding on a course to the west, determined to intercept the Japanese.

The Marines' success on Tulagi and Guadalcanal would largely depend on the US Navy's ability to intercept and destroy the Japanese naval power flooding in from Rabaul. The Imperial Japanese Navy posed the largest threat to Henderson Field. The Japanese navy had successfully transported more and more Japanese troops to Guadalcanal, which posed a threat to the Marines on the ground.

Since the Battle of Savo Island, a couple of the Japanese cruisers had been sunk by American submarines. But the American surface fleet needed to hammer the Japanese the next time they entered the waters around Guadalcanal.

At 2233 hours, Scott ordered his ships into battle formation. The ships under Scott's command included the USS *Farenholt*, *Duncan*, and *Laffey*, followed by *San Francisco*, *Boise*, *Salt Lake City*, *Helena*, *Buchanan*, and *McCalla*. They moved in tight formation, at a distance between five hundred and seven hundred yards apart.

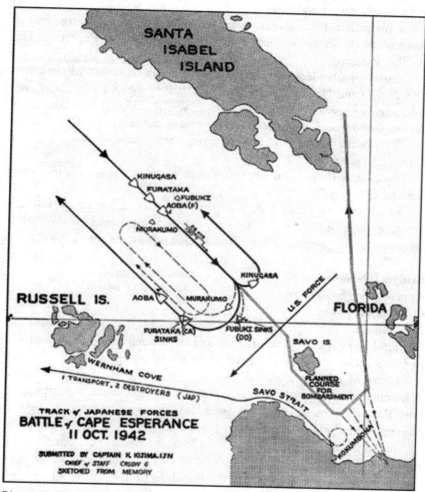

Diagram showing planned escape route of Japanese armada after the attack on Henderson Field. Diagram shows movement of US naval forces under Admiral Scott to cut off the Japanese advance of warships, cross the "T," and open fire on Japanese naval forces.

Twenty-seven minutes later, at 2300 hours, search planes from USS *San Francisco* spotted the initial Japanese landing force under Admiral Jojima. The pilots reported this back to Admiral Scott, but no cruisers were sighted.

Scott's cruisers could easily take out the Japanese destroyers, but he wanted to sink and disable Japanese cruisers. He needed to take out the cruisers to disable their naval threat.

In his gut, Scott knew that the Japanese warships would emerge through the clouds and rain squalls that dominated the night's weather pattern inside the Slot. Patience.

Thirty minutes later, at 2333 hours—a breakthrough. "Admiral. Both USS *Helena* and USS *Salt Lake City* have radar contact. Contacts believed to be enemy heavy cruisers emerging from squalls, heading in this direction. Bearing one-three-five degrees. They're coming out of the northwest, sir."

"Very well. Sound General Quarters. Set course to two-three-zero degrees. All ahead full."

"Aye, sir. Set course to two-three-zero degrees. All ahead full. Sound General Quarters."

Scott's task force executed a hard turn to the left. By setting a course for two-three-zero degrees, or southwest, Admiral Scott turned his ships into a line awaiting the Japanese column, to be prepared to cross the "T" as planned.

*****

Bridge, IJN *Aoba*
Approaching Savo Island
October 11, 1942
2343 Hours

"Admiral, our forward lookouts have sighted unidentified ships ahead. Our lookouts believe the ships to be American warships, sir."

Gotō thought for a second. "American warships? That must be wrong. Admiral Jojima has radioed us that there are no American warships in the area. Plus, the Americans have proven themselves incompetent to fight on the open seas at night."

He thought a bit more. Indeed, the lookouts were on edge and must be mistaken.

"The lookouts must have seen the rear ships from Admiral Jojima's convoy and mistaken them for American warships. To be safe, slow our speed to 26 knots, flash identification signals, and let us see how they respond."

"Flash identification signals?" said the commanding officer of the *Aoba*. "But Admiral, if our lookouts are right, and if the warships are American, would not flashing identification signals across the water help them target our position?"

Gotō smiled. "Captain, Admiral Jojima's lead surface vessels have already crossed these waters and tell us that no American warships are in the area, and I believe that for many reasons, and that our lookouts are seeing the trailing ships of Jojima's convoy.

"If we do not flash identification signals, we risk a collision at sea, which could affect our entire mission. The Americans are too far away to see our flashes. We will need the firepower of this cruiser and all the cruisers in our flotilla to destroy that airfield, which is our paramount goal.

"Now, Captain, please have your signal crew carry out my instructions to flash identification signals."

"Yes, sir, Admiral."

Admiral Gotō looked out to the water in front of the cruiser's bridge, to see what the two lookout scouts were reporting. Nothing came into view. Perhaps the scouts had imagined things. That sometimes happened to young sailors at sea, especially on battle missions. The mind could easily play tricks on a man out on the ocean, especially at night, and especially with younger sailors.

A moment later, the *Aoba*'s signal crew began flashing quick, bright lights across the water. The response would come any second.

A second later, a loud explosion rocked the front of the ship, spraying seawater high above the smokestack, knocking Admiral Gotō to the deck, and setting off fires in the front section of the vessel.

"Admiral! We're under attack!"

*****

Bridge, USS *San Francisco* (CA-38)
In the Waters East of Savo Island
October 11, 1942
2356 Hours

Admiral Scott watched through binoculars out the front of the *San Francisco*, and allowed himself a grin. A bright combination of smoke and fire rose over the waters surrounding the Japanese ships.

"Admiral, I think we surprised him. Your strategy of 'crossing the T' is working." Scott looked over his right shoulder and saw the commanding officer of the *San Francisco*, Captain Cassin Young, USN, who was having difficulty suppressing a smile.

"So far, so good. We've gotta keep it up. Do we have an initial battle damage assessment?"

"Best we can tell, and this is preliminary, sir, but *Helena, Salt Lake City, San Francisco, Farenholt*, and *Laffey* have scored multiple hits on their lead cruiser. We believe that is the IJN *Aoba*."

"The *Aoba*, eh? From the Battle of Savo Island?"

"Yes, Admiral," Captain Young said, "and she's turning around and trying to run."

"Good," Scott said. "Let's keep up the fire on them. Then we'll chase them back to Tokyo."

"Aye, sir."

Chapter 51

USMC Headquarters
Tulagi Island
October 12, 1942
0515 Hours

Rupertus's day started early at Tulagi on October 12, 1942. The US Navy destroyers USS *Southard* and *Hovey* had pulled into Tulagi harbor at 0517 hours, as rumors swirled that the US Navy had caught the Japanese flat-footed, scoring a huge naval victory last night on the other side of Savo Island.

Rupertus was on standby to send out YP boats to the waters off Savo Island to look for survivors. After inspecting PBYs Catalina aircraft with Rear Admiral Fitch's chief of staff, bad news arrived. Two of Rupertus's young officers and three enlisted Marines had been killed, shot in firefights with the Japanese while on patrols around the islands. An army aviator also died.

The Marines' conquest of Tulagi had not stopped the war and did not stop the killing. As several YPs arrived with the bodies of American service members, Rupertus made a note of the sad occasion in his diary:

> *October 12, 1942*
> *Four boats with troops returned from the Gurabuso operation. Losses, Captain Stafford, killed one private, killed Lieutenant Johnson, and three enlisted. One Lieutenant, two brothers killed. Another SOE is at Gavutu at 3 PM. SOE aviator reported being lost in the water. Boats sent out, brought back bodies of Captain Stafford, Lt. Stern (Army aviator), and one enlisted. Services for them were held at 4:30 PM at Police Barracks cemetery. YP 3 arrived with 3 boats and survivors from Aola (Lt. Col. Hill).*

Death was never easy, and Rupertus saw it every day. Captain Stafford and Lieutenant Johnson were fine young men and officers. Rupertus never knew Lieutenant Stern, the army aviator, as well as he knew the Marines. But that did not diminish the pain of burying and officiating over the interment ceremonies for all three.

"Thirty days in and feeling it" (Rupertus quote). (USMC PHOTO)

The most painful part came in penning letters to their families. From a personal standpoint, these letters cut at his heart harder than anything he faced in battle. With combat, he could be in control, at least to a degree. But

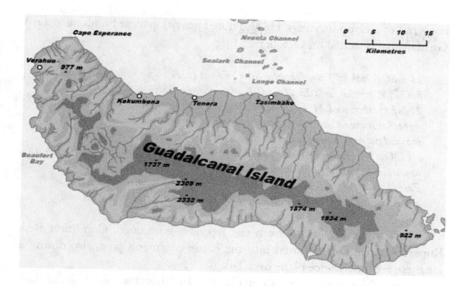

there was no control in a personal condolence letter. There was nothing he could write to bring back the lost son or the lost husband.

More news trickled in about the navy's decisive victory fought in the waters off Cape Esperance, the northwestern tip of Guadalcanal Island.

These naval battles were inextricably crucial to his own Marines' success in both Tulagi and Guadalcanal. Otherwise, the Japanese could continue to pour in troops and materials, supplies, and weapons by sea. Rupertus understood more than most that the control of sea lanes was vitally crucial to the war effort. If the preliminary reports were accurate, several Japanese destroyers and cruisers had been sunk in the battle. Rear Admiral Norman Scott commanded the American task force, and Rupertus made a mental note to buy the man a drink if they both survived the war.

After the Savo Island disaster, the "Battle of Cape Esperance" provided a mid-October morale boost for his men.

Later that afternoon, the phone rang. The navy was requesting YP boats from Tulagi to search the battle area. Their mission: to pick up Japanese sailors floating in the water. Rescue operations from the naval battle would last for the next two days.

Rupertus had noted in his diary the Marines returning from the Garabussa operation and the rescue operations on October 12 and 13 when he received information that six Japanese destroyers were sunk and sent YP boats out to pick up survivors. He also noted heavy Japanese bombing against Guadalcanal (Cactus) on October 13.

13 5 SOE took off from Gavutu. Sent YPs out to search for survivors off Savo. 8:45 AM service for a Lieutenant Ruff (injured aviator alone). At 12:05PM 21 Jap bombers and 24 Zeros over Cactus. At 2:15 twenty one Jap bombers and eight Zeros over Cactus—both times heavy fire- both from Cactus and convoy. Japs did not bomb convoy at either time convoy Zeiler and McCawley, 3-4 stackers DDs. No bombers down by AAV fire. Bombers never dropped here. Green condition. 2:35 PM red condition again at 2:50 PM green. 3:10 Jap bombers or Zeros this last time. 6:57 PM condition red. 7:55 PM condition green. No sign of enemy planes. YP returned at 8:48 PM. Three enemy DDs headed this way.

The barrage on Cactus from the Jap navy continued. Condition Red. Rupertus and his staff moved into the battle command post, also noting a Japanese reconnaissance plane over Tulagi.

As conditions cleared briefly on October 14, Rupertus's new chief of staff, Major D. W. Fuller, arrived from Cactus on the YP *Endeavour* to assume his new role.

Chapter 52

Imperial Japanese Army Command Post
17th Army Field Headquarters
Guadalcanal
October 20, 1942

Japanese General Harukichi Hyakutake had arrived on Guadalcanal from Rabaul on October 9. His mission: to take command of the Imperial Japanese 17th Army (consisting of some ten thousand Japanese troops on the island), to oversee forces and supplies flowing in from Rabaul, and to retake the Japanese airfield that the Americans had seized.

Hyakutake came from a proud military family. His older brothers Saburo and Gengo served as admirals in the Imperial Japanese Navy. As a student at the Imperial Japanese Army Academy, he was classmates with Generalissimo Chiang Kai-shek, the military leader of nationalist China, with which the Japanese government was now at war.

From classmates to sworn enemies—that became the fate of General Hyakutake and Chiang Kai-shek. Friends one day and mortal enemies the next, prepared to take each other's life.

Such was the nature of war. Hyakutake knew war. He knew how to kill the Americans occupying Guadalcanal and planned to do precisely that.

When he arrived on October 9, he had hoped to quickly move his armies into the captured areas. But his plans were delayed by an unfortunate and disastrous naval defeat suffered by the Imperial Japanese Navy on October 11 and 12 in the waters around Savo Island and off Cape Esperance.

The Imperial Japanese Navy lost one cruiser altogether, had another badly damaged, and lost a destroyer. Perhaps most significant, its commander, Rear Admiral Gotō, was killed in action.

Admiral Gotō had been friends with Hyakutake's brothers and had attended the Imperial Japanese Naval Academy only a few years after Hyakutake's brother, Vice Admiral Gengo Hyakutake.

In some ways, Hyakutake was envious of Gotō's sacrifice for their emperor. If he had to go, there could be no greater way than to die in a glorious battle for the emperor and the empire.

But at the end of the day, the emperor needed victory in battle.

Gotō's defeat and the defeat of the 6th Cruiser Division had already set back Hyakutake and his men in their quest to attack the airfield on Guadalcanal. Had Gotō succeeded in destroying the American airfield, or at least severely damaging it, Hyakutake could have moved to eliminate the Marine Corps remnant on the island days ago.

But now the task would take longer and be more difficult. As a student of war, the general knew his opponents well.

On Guadalcanal, he would face either Major General Alexander Vandegrift or Brigadier General William Rupertus. Like Hyakutake, both Rupertus and Vandegrift had served in China during the time of the Japanese army's offensive. They were likely to know Japanese battle tactics, and he had studied their tactics as well.

Hyakutake was not sure which one he would prefer to face in battle or prefer to avoid. Vandegrift was the senior of the two and rumored to become the next commandant of their Marine Corps. Both were battle-tested, and Rupertus had proved to be a vicious opponent in leading his Marines to victory at Tulagi and Gavutu.

None of that mattered. His duty and mission were to kill them all, which is exactly what he planned to do.

The general called his men together to explain the battle plan against the Americans.

"Gentlemen. This map shows the area that the Americans are occupying around Lunga Point, including the airfield. The Lunga River runs through the center of the map. The Matanikau River is off the map to the left. We have determined that a frontal attack along the coast would not be in our best interest, militarily. Therefore, we will attack from the rear, from the south side of their positions, where they will not expect it. The main thrust of our attack against the airfield will come directly from the south of their defensive perimeter.

"Our 2nd Division, under the command of General Maruyama," he nodded at Lieutenant General Masao Maruyama, 2nd Division commander, "will approach through the jungle along the east bank of the Lunga River. For purposes of this attack, we will divide the 2nd Division into three units.

"Our left-wing unit, advancing along the bank of the river, will be under the command of Major General Yumio Nasu. The right-wing unit, commanded by Major General Kiyotake Kawaguchi, will consist of the 230th

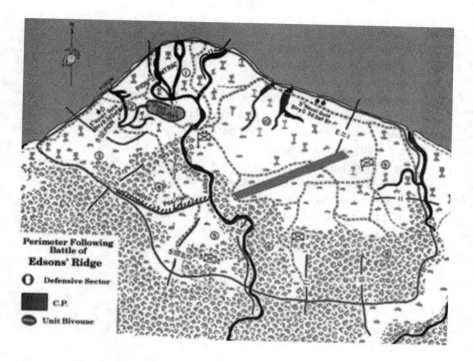

Perimeter Following
Battle of
Edsons' Ridge

O Defensive Sector

  C.P.

  Unit Bivouac

Infantry Regiment. The right wing will move north, parallel to the left wing, but farther out of the east.

"Lieutenant General Maruyama will command the Division Reserve, led by the 16th Infantry Regiment. Do we have any questions at this point?"

"No, my general."

"Very well. The Americans know that we have been concentrating our forces west of the Matanikau River. To provide distractions to allow our attack from the south to proceed, we will first initiate a heavy artillery barrage from the west, with our infantry moving in under the command of Major General Tadashi Sumiyoshi.

"Once the Americans commit to defending from the west, we will then pounce from the south, hit them by surprise, overrun them, seize the airfield, and kill them all. Our operations begin on October 22."

Hyakutake looked at all of his commanders. "You are the best battle commanders that the empire of Japan has to offer. And if you cannot win this battle, defeat the Marines, and defeat Vandegrift and Rupertus, then the task cannot be done. But this will be done. Victory is ours."

"Questions?"

"Sir," said Major General Sumiyoshi. "I believe that your plan to begin the attack from the west to distract the Americans is brilliant. This is our path to victory."

"Let's hope so, General. Surprise, when achieved, is often a key to victory in war. We surprised the Americans at Pearl Harbor and at the Battle of Savo Island. They surprised our navy at the Battle of Cape Esperance, which is why we have not attacked until now.

"The Americans have proven to be a worthy opponent, more powerful, deadly, and efficient than the Chinese, the British, the Australians, or any other opponent we have faced. We will see if the surprise is effective and efficient." He paused. "Now then, if there are no further questions, go back to your men and prepare them for battle.

"Victory is our only option."

Chapter 53

USMC Command Post
Guadalcanal
October 21–22, 1942

On Wednesday, October 21, word came to Rupertus that Lieutenant General Thomas Holcomb, the commandant of the US Marine Corps, had arrived on Guadalcanal as part of his Pacific tour. Holcomb was the highest-ranking officer to visit since Admiral Nimitz had come in early October.

But General Holcomb's visit would be short and with an agenda. In a brief meeting with General Vandegrift, Holcomb explained that he wanted Vandegrift to accompany him to see Admiral Halsey in Nouméa, in New Caledonia.

Their mission to Nouméa was critically important. The Japanese continued to pour troops and weapons onto Guadalcanal from Rabaul. The Marines needed replenishment, new supplies, and more firepower to finish off the Japanese. Together, Holcomb and Vandegrift would go to Nouméa and lobby Admiral Halsey about getting more supplies back in the picture for his Marines.

Rupertus received an order to report to Cactus (Guadalcanal) for five days. General Vandegrift wanted Rupertus to command all the Marines and support ground troops on Guadalcanal in his absence, while General Geiger would oversee the Cactus Air Force. Rupertus made an entry in his diary, noting a Japanese air raid against Tulagi on October 22, followed by his voyage with his staff across the channel to report to General Vandegrift and the commandant.

Diary, October 22
6:30 Jamestown PT [tender] arrived at 0700. DDs [Destroyers] over Cactus way shooting at Jap positions all a.m. Received orders to report to Cactus for five days duty x?? 12:52–1345, air raid. Ships in the channel opened fire on the plane. Out of here for Cactus at 6:33. Lieutenant Commander Painter, USN and I on PT left Ringbolt for Cactus. 8:15 p.m. reported to CP [Command Post]. Cmdt. USMC and staff there. I am to command in Arthur's absence.

Colonel John "Doggie" Arthur had command of Tulagi in Rupertus's absence.

After a conference with Vandegrift and the commandant, he learned that Vandegrift and Holcomb planned to leave on October 23 for the weekend conference with Admiral Halsey in Nouméa.

Later in the evening, Rupertus summoned Lieutenant Colonel Merrill B. Twining, the division operations officer, to give him a status report. As operations officer, part of his duties involved, when necessary, conveying orders from the division commander to the Marines in the field, particularly the battalion commanders.

Twining had previously served as a brigade advance team officer and had scouted both Tulagi and Guadalcanal back in July, flying reconnaissance missions and taking photographs as the Japanese Zeros were chasing his airplane. He knew the area better than any Marine, and Rupertus valued his judgment.

Late night on October 22, Rupertus paid a visit to Twining in the operation's dugout on Cactus. He brought along Corporal Walker "Shorty" Mantay, the assistant to the division chief, Technical Sergeant Raymond "Butch" Morgan.

Rupertus stuck his head in the dugout. "Mind if I come in?"

Twining immediately rose.

"Keep your seat, Merrill."

"Thank you, sir, and please, do come in."

"I thought you could use a little fresh coffee, so I had Butch whip up a batch, and Mantay here offered to deliver."

"You read my mind, General. And thank you, Corporal Mantay."

"My pleasure, sir,"

"Please have a seat, General."

"Thank you." Mantay began pouring coffee for both Rupertus and Twining.

"You know," Rupertus said, "one of the fringe benefits of taking command, even for a few days, is inheriting the general's cooking staff, and Butch Morgan is said to be the best cook in the world, and Mantay here is a close second."

Twining smiled. "Based on the few experiences when General Vandegrift has had me over for a meal, I have to agree. Nobody beats Shorty Mantay."

"Thank you, sir," Mantay said, smiling, as he finished pouring the coffee. "But all the credit goes to Technical Sergeant Morgan. He is the genius of the team."

"We appreciate you both, Mantay," Rupertus said.

"Thanks, sir. Will that be all?"

"That should hold us, Mantay. If Colonel Twining decides he wants another pot, or if he wants scrambled eggs, I'll let you know."

"Thank you, General." Mantay left the dugout.

"That's the easy part." Rupertus took a swig of coffee. "That's damn good coffee."

"Yes, sir," Twining said.

"Anyway, inheriting the world's greatest culinary team for three or four days is the easy part. The hard part is figuring out what the hell to do if the Japanese launched a major offensive."

"Yes, sir."

Rupertus and Twining talked about the battle and the loss of lives—officers and close friends. It was especially gut-wrenching to learn about the loss of Lieutenant Colonel Frank Goettge, the brave division intelligence chief and Twining's boss and close personal friend.

"This is the first time I've had a chance to talk to you in depth about Goettge. I know it's hard. Can you tell me what happened?"

Twining sipped his coffee, grimacing. "It's hard to talk about, General."

"Hey, if it's too tough, we can move on to something else."

"It's okay. He was your friend too. Telling the sad story might help you better prepare in case something happens while General Vandegrift is gone.

"Here's the official story, sir. Goettge was killed leading a twenty-five-man reconnaissance patrol on the night of August 12, west of the Matanikau River estuary, just three days after your men secured Gavutu.

"They planned to follow the Matanikau upstream and bivouac for a night, then head east, back to the Lunga perimeter. But the Japs heard the landing craft as it approached from Cactus and ambushed the entire patrol with machine gun fire. They could not see where the Japanese fire was coming from because of the dark, moonless night.

"Only three of the twenty-five Marines survived. They survived by swimming out to the ocean and then swimming five miles parallel to the beach before reaching American lines near Lunga Point."

Rupertus let that sink in for a minute. "What a damn shame. Frank Goettge was a good man and one of the best Marines I ever knew."

"Yes, sir, and a damn fine intelligence officer. Ironically, though, an intelligence failure got them killed."

"How so?"

"Well, Colonel Bill Whaling, the 5th Marine Regiment's XO, warned Colonel Goettge about Japs embedded in the area between Point Cruz and the mouth of the Matanikau River. Colonel Whaling urged Frank to land west of Point Cruz. But for whatever reason, the boat landed just west of the Matanikau River's mouth. The boat hit a sandbar, and the coxswain gunned the motor and headed back out to sea to keep the boat from getting stuck on the sandbar. The Marines disembarked on the beach around 2200 hours. Then the Japanese opened fire. The situation was hopeless."

"Any idea why they landed where they landed?"

"We've asked the coxswain. My guess is they were disoriented and probably thought they were west of Point Cruz."

Rupertus finished his cup of coffee. "The area west of the Matanikau River—are the Japs still concentrated out there?"

"Yes, sir. After we defeated them at Edson's Ridge, Major General Kawaguchi and his troops regrouped west of the Matanikau River. Of course, now General Harukichi Hyakutake is in overall command of Japanese forces on the island. He was in Rabaul during the Battle of Edson's Ridge, and they have brought him here to try and take back the island."

"Ah yes," Rupertus mused. "I know of General Hyakutake. Our time overlapped in China when I was serving there. A ruthless bastard, to say the least, for what he and the Japanese did to those innocent Chinese civilians."

"Yes, sir. They're all that way."

"Do you think they would attack from the west?"

"I'll put it this way. We know they're not as strong in the east. And when they tried to attack from the south at Edson's Ridge, things didn't go well for them."

"Could I take a look at your operational chart?"

"Yes, sir. And if the general would please allow me to explain?"

"Of course."

"We're right here in the center of the map, marked '1st Marine Division Headquarters,' affectionately known as Cactus. You can see the Lunga River, running from south to north, and just to the west of Henderson Field and west of our current position, right down the middle of the territory we control."

"Got it."

"Our main defensive perimeters to the south and to the east of where we are right now are about one mile from our current position, about one mile from our headquarters directly south to our southern defensive perimeter,

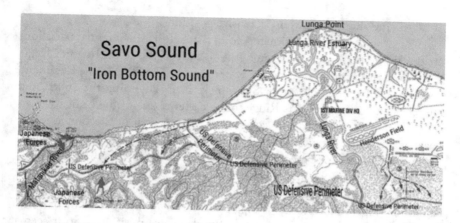

after Edson's Ridge. And if we look way out to the west, up to the mouth of the Matanikau River, we see heavy Japanese forces concentrated on the other side of that river. That river is a little less than four miles from here. The Japs out there are a little more than four miles to our west.

"Here's another map showing how we're currently situated on the perimeter, after the Battle of Edson's Ridge."

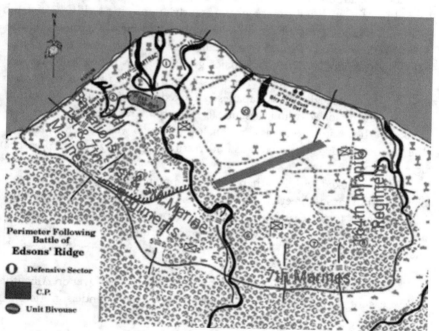

"Tell me about our current defensive positions."

"Sir, four American regiments comprising thirteen infantry battalions are defending the Lunga perimeter. As you can see, the 164th Infantry Regiment from the army is covering the eastern sector. The 7th Marine Regiment, commanded by Colonel Armor Sims, picks it up, adjoining the 164th, and stretches west across Edson's Ridge to the eastern bank of the Lunga River.

"Then, west of the Lunga, covering the sector west of the Lunga to the coast, we have the 1st and 5th Marine Regiments. Then, at the mouth of the Matanikau, where we expect the Japs might launch their next major attack, we have two battalions under Lieutenant Colonel William J. McKelvy: the 3rd Battalion, 1st Marines; and 3rd Battalion, 7th Marines. McKelvy's battalions are separated from the Lunga perimeter by a gap covered by patrols."

Rupertus took a second to study the defensive positions. "So it seems we've got everything covered, but the lines are thin."

"Yes, sir. Of course, if the Japs come pouring en masse across any given point, we're going to be thin on the lines and will need reinforcements to stop them from breaking through and grabbing the airfield.

"We've been running patrols throughout the area outside our defensive perimeter, including along the river, and we've had firefights ever since we landed in August. The Japanese are constantly attempting to hit the airfield by bombers coming out of Rabaul—or with destroyers and cruisers off the coast. We know they're going to make another run to try and take that airfield. They already launched two major ground battles trying to retake the field. The first attempt came on August 21, the Battle of the Tenaru. In that case, as you may recall, sir, the Japanese attacked with 917 commandos from the east and made a frontal assault at Alligator Creek. Colonel Kiyonao Ichiki led the assault. This was early on, less than two weeks after we landed. The Japanese's biggest mistake was underestimating the size of our presence here.

"They attacked with less than a thousand men, although damn fine soldiers, and ran into the teeth of eleven thousand Marines. We knew they had landing forces to the east at that time, so we prepped our defenses to meet any invasion. Alligator Creek was the eastern perimeter of our security, and they made the mistake of attacking it with an undersized force. Not smart."

"Agreed," Rupertus said.

"Here's where they hit us the first time on the map, sir. Over on Alligator Creek, east of the 1st Division headquarters and east of Henderson Field.

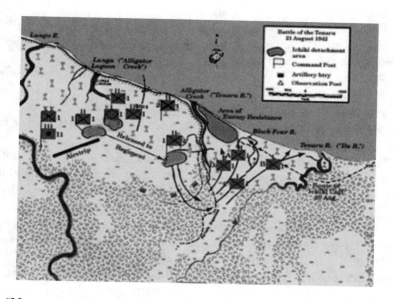

"Now as you can see, we pinned them down and surrounded them. But they thought they could make a rush at Henderson Field across Alligator Creek from the east. Here's a photo of dead Japanese on the beach at Alligator Creek the morning after the attack."

(USMC PHOTO)

Rupertus looked at the photo. "Not always as bright as they are vicious."

"Right, sir." Twining said. "Then the second major offensive attempting to retake the airfield came at the Battle of Edson's Ridge."

Rupertus chuckled. "You know, Colonel Edson was the very first officer General Vandegrift wanted me to send his way after we secured Tulagi. Guys like you and Edson make us generals look like geniuses."

"Thank you, sir. The colonel has done a hell of a job with the Raiders."

"That he has. Please continue your brief."

"Aye, sir. On September 12, the Japs came back again, with another attempt to take Henderson Field. But this time, they went with a larger force, with over six thousand men, over six times the size of the force they tried at Alligator Creek.

"They underestimated our strength, which at the time was about twelve thousand. Now the first attack, the Battle of the Tenaru, came from the east. This time the attack came from the south of the airfield. The Japanese Infantry Brigade commanded by Major General Kiyotake Kawaguchi carried out this attack. They hit us primarily from the south, and because they concentrated their forces, they initially broke some of our lines. And, if you hang on just a second, sir . . ."

"Sure."

"I have a map here showing where they hit us during the second offensive, now known as the Battle of Edson's Ridge."

"Thanks."

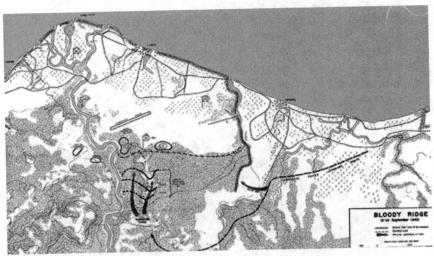

"As you can see, sir, they moved them from the east. One unit hit us from the east to create a diversionary tactic. Then the main thrust came from the south, after they made their way through the jungles to assemble at the launch point.

"They hit hard, fast, by night, and unexpectedly. Colonel Edson's men initially retreated to Hill 123, now called Edson's Ridge, and defended opposition from there, eventually wiping the Japanese out. It was pretty bloody.

"Here's a map showing how they penetrated the initial lines, and how Edson's men retreated to the ridge and fought the battle from there."

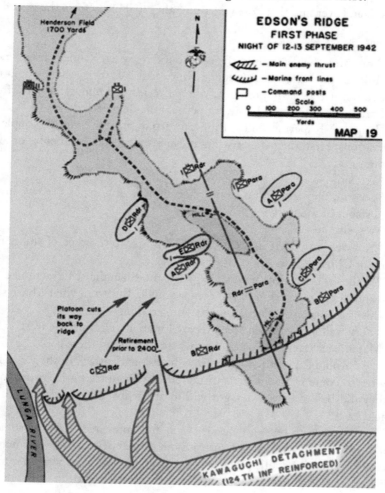

231

"So Company C, the 1st Raiders, retreated to defend the hill?"

"Yes, sir."

"That's too close to Henderson Field for comfort."

"Yes, sir."

Rupertus thought for a second. "Back on point. So, they hit us from the east. They hit us from the south. And the question is where will they hit us next time?"

"Yes, sir, I think that's the question."

"And we know this time they're mounting their forces to the west of the Matanikau River, and therefore we assume they will hit us from the west next time."

"That's the assumption, sir."

"You think they will hit in the next four days when Vandegrift is gone?"

"I doubt they know that General Vandegrift is leaving, but it would not surprise me if they strike tonight. What I've learned about the Japs, from Pearl Harbor right up until now, is to expect the unexpected."

"I agree," Rupertus said. "They can strike at any time. A couple of observations. First, they attack at night every time, often just before or after midnight."

"Yes, sir."

"Second, they are prone to use diversionary attacks, as we saw in the initial stages of the Battle of Edson's Ridge."

"Yes, sir."

"You were in China in 1925, Merrill. Similar to the type of stunts they pulled in China. Agree?"

"Well, sir, I was not there in 1937 for the Shanghai Massacre like you were and did not see them in full combat mode. But from what I have seen, yes, this is consistent with their mode of operation."

"Very well. I recommend we prepare for an attack from the west, out by the Matanikau River, but recognize that troop buildup there could be diversionary. I wouldn't be surprised to see a diversionary attack in the west. They may try to come in under the soft underbelly by attacking from the south, as they did before when they got within about two thousand yards of the airfield.

"So we need to be ready on all fronts, fully prepared from the south as well, because it also would not surprise me to see them attack with massive force again from the south. It's a lot closer from the southern perimeter to the airfield than it is from the western perimeter to the airfield."

"Yes, sir, it is."

"Who's in the defensive positions to the south?"

"The 1st Battalion, 7th Marines, under the command of Colonel Puller. And joining the 7th Marines, we have an army unit, actually a National Guard unit. The 164th National Guard Infantry Regiment, from North Dakota, under the command of Colonel Robert Hall, landed in October and occupied the eastern flank from Alligator Creek. They will swing all the way around, joining up with Puller's 7th Marines on the southern perimeter."

"National Guard? North Dakota, eh?"

"Yes, sir."

"One thing's for sure—if those boys were looking for a change in the weather from North Dakota, they sure got it here."

"Yes, sir."

"Please pass the word. I'll share my thoughts with General Vandegrift before he takes off tomorrow."

"Aye, sir."

"You've had a long day, Merrill. Thanks for the hospitality."

"Thank you, General. And welcome to Guadalcanal."

"Good to be here." Rupertus felt himself smile. "Try to get some sleep, Merrill. I'll see you tomorrow."

"Sir?"

"What is it, Merrill?"

"One other thing?"

"Sure." Rupertus squinted his eyes, inhaled the last drop from his cigarette, dropped it on the ground at the dugout, and smashed it out.

"If they attack while General Vandegrift is gone, we have full confidence in you, especially based on what you and your men did on the ground. What you and your men did in Tulagi was hellacious."

Rupertus nodded. "Thank you. My men get all the credit for what we did at Tulagi and Gavutu. We transferred a number of them over here, like Lieutenant Colonel Edson, who has performed brilliantly in battle here. But whether it's General Vandegrift or me, we're going to take the offensive and wipe these Japs off the entire island, instead of constantly worrying about defending against attacks on the airfield from the perimeter.

"Hopefully, Vandegrift and Commandant Holcolmb can persuade Admiral Halsey to get us the resources we need to finish the job. For the sake of men like Colonel Goettge and others, we need to wipe the Japanese off Guadalcanal, as we wiped them off Tulagi and Gavutu."

"Yes, sir, General. That we do."

Rupertus stood up. "Thanks for spending some time with me tonight, Colonel."

"My pleasure, sir."

With that, Rupertus left the dugout and headed back to Vandergrift's command post to spend the night with his staff and Colonel Enright at the 5th Marines command post.

*****

USMC Command Post—Cactus
Guadalcanal Island
October 23, 1942
The Japanese Counterattack

At dawn on October 23, with Major D. W. Fuller as chief of staff by his side, Rupertus took a jeep out to the Cactus airstrip on Guadalcanal, rendering salutes to the commander of the 1st Marine Division and the commandant of the Marine Corps. Each general boarded a separate DC3 Douglas twin-engine aircraft, which then, one behind the other, taxied down to the end of the airstrip. Already overhead, a squadron of F4F Wildcats was circling, prepared to give the generals' planes fighter coverage as they left the Solomon Islands airspace.

General Holcomb's plane was the first to take off. As it began to climb into the air over the Sealark Channel, General Vandegrift's plane rumbled down the runway and took off right behind it.

The planes turned, cutting a course south back over Guadalcanal, and disappeared out of sight. Rupertus watched until the aircraft were out of view; then he turned to his new chief of staff. "Well, Fuller, I guess it's you and me for the next few days, along with twenty-three thousand Marines itching for a fight. Hopefully General Vandegrift comes back with more supplies, bullets, tanks, and everything else he asks of the admiral."

"Yes, sir. Fortunately, the Japanese haven't started their major counteroffensive yet."

"We've been lucky. But they are liable to start when the general is gone, before he returns with supplies."

With Vandegrift absent, Rupertus, as assistant division commander, assumed temporary command of the entire division until Vandegrift returned. After visiting the front lines and catching up with Pete DeValle, Rupertus got cleaned up in the river and headed to the divisional headquarters to review intelligence reports on the current Japanese positions on Guadalcanal.

Not long after he arrived at headquarters, the air raid siren sounded. "What have we got, Fuller?"

"General, radar has picked up over forty Japanese aircraft inbound from Rabaul, believed to be a combination of Betty bombers in Japanese Zero fighter planes. They're headed our way. Cactus is scrambling twenty-four Wildcats."

"Very well. Let's hope our fighter pilots can do the job. But if any of those Jap bombers make it through our lines, send the order to have our men ready to hunker down until this firefight is over."

From the air and the sea, the attacks on Henderson Field had been constant, even in the weeks after Rupertus's Marines captured both Gavutu and Tulagi.

For this part of the world, Henderson Field was the most contested prize of the war. Whoever controlled it controlled a significant military advantage over the enemy.

On the evening of October 13, two days after the Japanese navy suffered a significant defeat at the Battle of Cape Esperance, two of their battleships advanced undetected, bombarded Henderson Field, and fired 973 14-inch shells into the Lunga perimeter. That attack from the Japanese navy severely damaged both the airfield runways, destroyed over half the Cactus Air Force, and killed forty-one Marines.

Despite the attack, one of Henderson Field's runways was operational again within two hours.

The latest attack by air, now underway, was expected.

By 1400 hours, starbursts were exploding over Henderson Field, drawing a barrage of Marine Corps anti-aircraft fire. Meanwhile, the Marine Corps pilots had taken off to challenge the Japanese Bettys and Zeros and had scored multiple hits, downed numerous Japanese planes, and, most important, got the Japanese air force off Rupertus's ass. At least for the day.

****

Japanese 4th Infantry Regiment Field Headquarters
West of the Matanikau River
Guadalcanal
October 23, 1942 (Day 1 of Battle for Henderson Field)
Dusk

Colonel Nomasu Nakaguma was gathering his forces of the Japanese 4th Infantry Regiment near Point Cruz, on the coast just west of the Matanikau River. His orders were to launch an attack commencing at dusk on October 23, and to his knowledge, there were no changes to those orders.

The Matanikau River attack was designed to distract the American Marines long enough for Japanese troops to attack from the south, penetrate the American southern defenses, and retake control of the airfield.

Hopefully his men would tie down the Americans long enough to give his comrades time to attack south of the Lunga perimeter with overwhelming force.

Nakaguma checked his watch: 1836 hours. Dusk would fall in one minute. Unless he heard from the Japanese high command to abort, he would launch his forces within sixty seconds.

"Major, notify all my tank commanders and company commanders. We will launch our attack in one minute, on my command."

"Yes, Colonel." The major complied.

Nakaguma watched as the second hand swept down. Thirty seconds. Fifteen seconds. Ten seconds. Five, four, three, two, one. "Major, transmit the order. Initiate attack."

"Yes, sir." The major picked up the radio's telephone. "All tank commanders, all company commanders, initiate attack! Attack!"

Immediately, nine Japanese tanks of the 1st Independent Tank Company headed out, rolling east across sandbars near the mouth of the Matanikau River. The tanks were followed by two battalions of the 4th Infantry Regiment, among the finest soldiers in the Japanese army.

Nakaguma watched with pride as his men in the tanks crossed the running water in the sand on their way into battle. The fateful Battle for Henderson Field had begun, and history would record that his brave troops laid the first blow and the first defeat of the Americans in the first engagement of the battle.

*****

Headquarters
First Marine Division
Guadalcanal
October 23, 1942 (Day 1 of Battle for Henderson Field)
1900 Hours

"General, Lieutenant Colonel Twining is on the phone. It's urgent, sir."

"Thanks." Rupertus took the radio receiver from Major Fuller, his chief of staff. "Merrill, what have we got?"

"It's started, General. We've got multiple tanks in at least two battalions crossing the Matanikau River right now. Headed this way."

"I'm not surprised. What's the situation with our initial defenses?"

"We're striking them hard with 37-millimeter anti-tank guns and artillery. It's pretty bloody at the moment, and we don't know how much firepower they're going to bring across the river, which goes back to our earlier conversation about their tactics. It could be a diversion or the real thing."

Rupertus thought about that. "Assuming this is the real deal and not a diversionary tactic, do we have enough firepower there to defend against a full-throttle invasion coming down the pike across the Matanikau River estuary?"

"Right now the 11th Marines are out there with the 1st Battery, 1st Special Weapons Battalion, defending with anti-tank guns. We also have the 3rd Battalion, 7th Marines, out there. But we will need reinforcements if that's where the main attack strikes."

"Who's closest on the perimeter that we could move in for fire support?" Rupertus asked.

"Sir, we could move the 2nd Battalion, 7th Marines, under Lieutenant Colonel Hanneken from the southwest sector. We stretch out 1st Battalion, 7th Marines, along the 2,500-yard line if we do that. Puller's guys would have to spread out and cover for Hanneken's men if we move Hanneken to Matanikau. That makes it thin for Puller's guys covering that stretch. But if the Japs look like they're striking from the west, it seems like the practical response."

"Okay," Rupertus said. "Let's monitor the situation. Meantime, alert Colonel Hanneken to be ready to shift over to the Matanikau River."

"Yes, sir."

By 0130 on October 24, Rupertus received reports that fighting had subsided around the Matanikau River estuary. His Marines in the front lines held their ground and repulsed the initial attacks. It appeared that his decision to avoid moving Colonel Hanneken's 2nd Battalion was the correct one.

"What do you think, Fuller?" Rupertus asked his chief of staff.

"Well, sir, we beat back their initial attack at the mouth of the Matanikau River, with no follow-up diversionary attacks to the south, at least not yet. The big question remains: Was the six-hour battle from dusk until about fifteen minutes ago an outlier, or was it a prelude to a major offensive?"

"I think you're asking all the right questions. Tonight they hit us only from the west, not from the south or anywhere else. So if this is a major offensive, the question becomes, where will they hit us next?"

"They're out there, somewhere; they've been building up their forces every day, almost nonstop, with these destroyer convoys from Rabaul."

"Tokyo Express," Fuller said.

"Yep," Rupertus said. "And the damn Tokyo Express has brought in enough Jap soldiers to bring them to division strength by now."

"Agree, sir."

"They're going to strike. And when they do, it will be with their entire 2nd Division, or the Sendai Division, as they call it."

"I have to agree, sir. It is not a matter of if but when."

"That's right, and when they do, we have to destroy them on the ground, on this island, to break the backs of their ground forces. We can leave it to the US Navy and General Geiger to finish them off on the sea and in the air. But our job is to destroy them on the ground."

In mentioning General Geiger, Rupertus meant Major General Roy Geiger, commander of the 1st Marine Air Wing, or the "Cactus Air Force," on Guadalcanal.

"Okay," Rupertus continued. "Let's hold our positions for the rest of the night and keep Lieutenant Colonel Hanneken and his men in place alongside Lieutenant Colonel Puller. We'll send out patrols in the morning to look for the Japanese positions. I'm sure General Geiger's pilots will be on the

Brigadier Generals Pete DeValle and Bill Rupertus on Guadalcanal. (USMC PHOTO)

lookout for the Japs and may pass on information about their positions, too. If we need to rearrange our forces tomorrow, if it appears they're planning a strike again from the Matanikau River, we can do that."

"Copy that, sir."

Rupertus retired to his quarters and made a note in his diary:

Diary, October 23, 1942

Now over at Cactus. 8:00AM T.H. with party and AAV left in D.C.'s for a White Poppy and Buttons. In a.m. visited Pete DeValle for a couple hours. Our planes strafed Jap positions—one plane down in the water, Michael Maguire Mahoney's body not recovered. Star shells at about 1440 with continuous artillery fire. Japs made three attempts to cross the Matakin river mouth by going further upstream around our flank and then again at sand spit at the mouth of the river. Luckily held them with half-tracks destroyed.

*****

Field Headquarters
3rd Battalion, 7th Marines
Hill 67
Guadalcanal
October 24, 1942 (Day 2 of Battle for Henderson Field)
Mid-afternoon

After the Japanese foray across the Matanikau River and the six-and-a-half-hour firefight that had followed, the morning of October 24 was quiet around most of the Lunga Peninsula.

But every Marine and soldier on the American side of the defensive perimeters expected another Japanese strike.

The 3rd Battalion, 7th Marines, had initially been formed at Guantanamo Bay, Cuba, on New Year's Day 1941. Only one month later, in February 1941, then–Colonel William Rupertus arrived at Guantanamo Bay to command the Marine Barracks at the US Naval Station.

That same month the 3/7 was reassigned to the 1st Marine Division. And now the 3/7 found itself half a world away, under Rupertus's command, in the middle of the hottest ground battle in the Pacific.

Out on the far western edge of the American defenses, right at the eastern bank of the Matanikau, 3rd Battalion, 7th Marines, served as the Marine Corps' defensive spear.

The men of the 3/7 had spent a good portion of the morning gathering the bodies of their buddies, the Marines who died in last night's firefight. The hardest part of their job was gathering their brothers for proper burial. They buried twenty-five Marines that day. However, at least six hundred Japanese had been killed, judging from the body count strewn along the beaches and the riverbed alone.

Part of the reason the firefight had been so one-sided in favor of the Marines was because of their 37-millimeter anti-tank weapons, which had repelled the nine Japanese tanks trying to cross the river to invade the 3/7's command territory.

One of the Japanese tanks had crossed the sandbars and crashed through the barbed wire on the perimeter of the American defenses.

When the tank penetrated the barbed wire, PFC Joseph Champagne, of Company M, 1st Battalion, 1st Marines, heroically charged the tank and slipped a live grenade in its tracks. The explosion disabled the tank's traction against the sand, at which point Lieutenant Thomas Matter opened fire at point-blank range, sending the tank into the surf of the ocean.

But even on the morning of October 24, except for intermittent fire from Japanese artillery, the forward command post of the 3rd Battalion 7th Marines, along Hill 67, was relatively quiet.

But the quiet would not last long. That afternoon, from Hill 67 the 3/7 spotted on the other side of the river what appeared to be a significant Japanese unit moving to the east, toward what was known as the Mount Austin Foothills.

"Sir, look at this!"

The lookout handed his binoculars to Lieutenant Colonel William K. Williams, commander of the 3rd Battalion, 7th Marines.

"Captain," Williams said.

"Yes, sir."

"Get General Rupertus on the line."

*****

Headquarters
1st Marine Division
Lunga Point
Guadalcanal
October 24, 1942
Mid-afternoon

"Sir, it's Lieutenant Colonel Williams, 3rd Battalion, 7th Marines."

"I'll take it," Rupertus said. He took the TBY-8 handset from his chief of staff. "General Rupertus."

"General, Lieutenant Colonel Williams, 3rd Battalion, 7th Marines."

"What's going on out there?"

"Sir, we spotted a large column of Japanese troops moving into position from the west, shoring up their forces on the west side of the Matanikau. It appears they are massing for a larger move out here, sir."

"Estimate on numbers?"

"Hundreds, sir. Hard to say. Could be battalion size."

"Do you have a specific location?"

"Sir, right now they are amassing forces across the river, in the Austin Foothills area."

"Very well. Thank you, Colonel. Stand by for further instructions." He turned and looked at his chief of staff. "Colonel Williams says we've spotted a Jap column moving into position out west, just beyond the Matanikau River."

Fuller grimaced. "Sounds like the same predicament we had last night, whether to move the 2/7 west to support against a possible invasion coming across the mouth of the Matanikau. Except this time we have intelligence of a potential buildup in the area."

Rupertus turned to one of the two sergeants in the headquarters with them. "Sergeant, would you please find Lieutenant Colonel Twining and ask him to report here immediately?"

"Aye, sir."

Rupertus trusted Fuller's judgment as much as Vandegrift did. But with General Vandegrift off the island, no one had superior knowledge of logistics or intelligence in the entire division than operations officer Lieutenant Colonel Twining.

A couple of minutes later, the sergeant returned with Lieutenant Colonel Twining, who stepped in the tent, saluted, and received a quick update from Rupertus.

"So, we have this one column of Japanese troops, possibly battalion size, moving into the west. What do you think, Merrill?"

"I think we must take the troop movement seriously, sir, unless and until additional intelligence suggests the Japs may be striking somewhere else along the perimeter."

"Our patrols have been out and about scouting but have seen nothing of the Japanese all day," Rupertus said.

"Not only that, sir," Twining added, "but General Geiger's planes have not seen much of them either."

"That's part of the problem when there's miles of jungle brush to hide in. You can't even see them from the air," Rupertus said.

"True, sir. But with all the aerial surveillance today, and our patrols, we've only spotted them moving in one area, out west."

Rupertus turned to Twining. "Merrill, if I order Hanneken's battalion to move to the west to support our forces at Matanikau, how bad will that spread out Lieutenant Colonel Puller's battalion?"

"Sir, the 1st Battalion, 7th Marines, which is Puller's battalion, has just a little over seven hundred Marines. If we move Hanneken over to cover the river delta, those Savannah Marines will stretch out over a distance of about 2,500 yards."

"Lemme think," Rupertus said. "That's seven hundred men stretched out covering a line of about a mile and a half from one end to the other."

"To be precise, 1.4 miles, General, but your math is practically right."

"Damn," Rupertus said. "That stretches out Puller's battalion a little more than I would like."

"Yes, sir," Twining said. "But if the Japs hit from the west, across the river delta, we're going to need the reinforcements, or they could come slicing right in from our western flank, straight into the airfield."

"And right now the only intelligence we have is that they appear to be massing to the west."

Rupertus thought for a second. "Okay. Contact Lieutenant Colonel Hanneken to move his battalion west to the Matanikau River delta to support the 3/7 under Colonel Williams. Alert Lieutenant Colonel Puller to stretch his battalion to the west to cover the territory now guarded by Lieutenant Colonel Hanneken's battalion."

*****

Imperial Japanese Army 2nd Division Field Headquarters
Guadalcanal
October 24, 1942
1600 Hours

Lieutenant General Masao Maruyama, 2nd Division commander, was ordered by the commanding general, General Harukichi Hyakutake, to approach the jungle along the east bank of the Lunga River and launch a major, full-throttle surprise attack against the Americans from the south.

At the commanding general's instruction, his division split into three units and moved into position for the surprise attack. Fortunately, it appeared that the Americans had not discovered the 2nd Division as they moved under cover of the thick jungle. All day long, they had heard American warplanes, under the command of General Roy Geiger, buzzing overhead.

But Geiger's planes were not taking a shot. After all, it was hard to shoot what you could not see. Of course, the thick underbrush cut both ways.

On the one hand, the dense, green canopy protected them from being bombed and strafed by the American warplanes. On the other hand, the thick vegetation slowed their march as they attempted to move into position for a surprise attack. The hard slogging through the jungle, in the tropical heat, had brought heavy fatigue to the troops, slowing their approach to the attack point.

The environment and the weather had already caused General Hyakutake to delay the initial attack until today, October 24. However, word had not reached Colonel Nakaguma's 4th Infantry Regiment. The diversionary attack from the Matanikau River had occurred on October 23, when it was supposed to have launched moments before the actual attack. Put another way, the first diversionary attack came twenty-four hours too soon.

The communication snafu by Colonel Nakaguma had infuriated General Hyakutake. But at the moment, his concern was getting his men in place for a large, frontal surprise attack, and the heavy rain now falling, like the thick jungle brush, would slow them even more.

Hyakutake wanted his forces in place to initiate the attack by 1900 hours. Maruyama doubted that his men could strike that soon because of the conditions. Once the heavy rain subsided, Maruyama could launch his full-frontal attack. As long as the attack came well before the sun rose, they should be able to achieve the element of surprise, destroy the Americans, and recapture the airfield.

The heavy rain pounded them. Again, a mixed bag. The rain would provide cover as they moved into position to attack. However, the wet conditions would make the attack more difficult to execute.

Nevertheless, they would attack and kill every American in their path to recapture the airfield for the emperor.

*****

Field Headquarters, Guadalcanal
1st Battalion, 7th Marines
October 24, 1942
2100 Hours

From inside his tent within his field command headquarters, Lieutenant Colonel Chesty Puller, US Marine Corps, sucked in a cigarette and studied the horseshoe shape of the Marine Corps' defenses around Lunga Point.

When 2nd Battalion, 7th Marines, commanded by Lieutenant Colonel Herman Hanneken, was deployed farther west, to the delta of the Matanikau River, Puller and his seven hundred men dispersed out to the right, to cover a front of 2,500 yards, almost a mile and a half, to defend against Japanese attack.

So his men were stretched thin as a result of covering Hanneken's position. The strategy was a gamble, based on the last known Japanese troop movement, which appeared to be moving toward the Matanikau peninsula.

Now Puller found his 1st Battalion of the 7th Marine Regiment stretched out along the line just to the east of the Lunga River, which flowed to the north, toward the airfield, and cut straight through the heart of the Lunga Peninsula before flowing into the Iron Bottom Sound.

But if the Japanese concentrated their forces in the single attacking column and hit along the lines his men were defending, that could become problematic.

Puller had met with his company commanders earlier and briefed them on the plan. "Men, our lines are going to be thin. If the Japanese break through and take that airfield, our orders are to move into the jungles and begin guerilla attacks to take it back."

He looked them in the eyes. "That's not going to happen. Hold the line."

"Aye, sir!"

The late afternoon rain had subsided, yielding to the canopy of the dark jungle and the sounds of a thousand strange insects chirping in the night. The Japanese were about to strike, Puller felt it in his veins. He couldn't see them, but Chesty Puller could smell a Jap approaching from a mile away.

The phone rang. "Lieutenant Colonel Puller."

On the other end, Platoon Sergeant Ralph M. Briggs, commander of the 1/7's outpost, spoke. "Sir, Platoon Sergeant Briggs here. We spotted the Japs."

"What have you got, Sergeant?"

"From what we can see, it looks like the whole damn Jap army, sir. Headed straight for our lines, coming up from the south, moving along the eastern banks of the Lunga River."

"Shit!" Puller thought for a second. "All right. Hold your fire until they have cleared the area. Then try to move your men across the Bowling Alley and out of the line of fire."

By "Bowling Alley," Puller referred to a huge, open field, several hundred yards wide and over two thousand yards long. The "Bowling Alley" stretched all along the lines held by Puller's 1st Battalion, 7th Marines. On the north perimeter of the Bowling Alley, the Marines had established their defensive position with 37-millimeter guns, machine guns, heavy coiled barbed wire, artillery, howitzers, and light infantry.

Across the way, along the southern perimeter of the long Bowling Alley, the thick jungle began. In the field that separated the northern and southern perimeters, weeds and high grass waved in the wind. The grass was not tall enough to conceal a man walking across, but the Japanese could crawl through the weeds undetected if it were dark enough.

If a Japanese assault came from the south, the Japanese would have to cross the Bowling Alley, at least in this area. An assault from the south, across the Bowling Alley, would put the Japanese in close proximity to the airfield that they so desperately sought. Puller knew this, and so did General Rupertus.

"Pass the word to all units to hold fire until the last possible second. Keep me posted. I've got to hang up and call division headquarters and General Rupertus."

"Aye, sir."

*****

Headquarters
1st Marine Division
Guadalcanal
October 24, 1942
2105 Hours

It was a calculated gamble. But the entire senior leadership of the division, including Lieutenant Colonel Twining and others, had agreed. All signs were pointing to a significant Japanese offensive to the west, by the Matanikau section. But the reinforced Matanikau section meant that 1st Battalion, 7th Marines, under Puller's command, would defend the entire southern perimeter on its own—too thinly spread for comfort if the major thrust came from the south.

"General, Lieutenant Colonel Puller is on the line. He says it's urgent."

"Thank you, Fuller." Rupertus took the phone from Major Fuller. "Puller, Rupertus here. What have you got?"

"Sir, intel reports large columns of Japanese troops moving up from the south, coming up parallel to the Lunga River along the east bank."

"Damn it!" Rupertus pounded his fist on the table. "Any idea on numbers, Puller?"

"There's a bunch of them, sir. Our scouts think division-size numbers, several thousand. One thing's for sure, sir. If they hit us with that full column, we're outnumbered. Big time."

"Sounds like Maruyama's sending the entire Sendai Division. Whatever we saw out west may have been a diversion."

"Could be, sir."

"Okay, Colonel," Rupertus paused for a second. "I'll order the reserve units from the 164th Infantry Regiment, the National Guard unit from North Dakota, to move into position to give you support. I know you'd rather have Marines, but their men are fresh, they've got these new M1 Garand rifles, and Colonel Moore"—he was referring to Colonel Bryant Moore, commander of the 164th Infantry—"is a tough, no-nonsense guy. He's a West Point grad commanding that National Guard unit."

The 164th Infantry Regiment, part of the North Dakota Army National Guard, had arrived on the island on October 13, with fresh troops and new M1 Garand rifles assigned to the army, which allowed for more rapid fire than the M1903 Springfield weapons that the Marines were using at the time.

"General," Puller said, "right now, I'll take help from anywhere I can get it."

"Copy that. It may take them several hours to get into place. You may have to hold the Japs off for a while."

"We'll beat them all single-handed, sir, even if we're outnumbered, whether the 164th arrives on time or not."

"I know you will, Puller. Hold the line."

"Yes, sir."

*****

Guadalcanal
Japanese Imperial Army
1st Battalion, 230th Infantry Regiment
Right Wing of the Sendai Division
October 24, 1942
2200 Hours

Less than twenty-four hours before, the Japanese 230th Infantry Regiment on Guadalcanal had been under the command of Major General Kiyotake Kawaguchi, in control of the six thousand Japanese soldiers defeated at the Battle of Edson's Ridge from September 12 to September 14.

Because of Kawaguchi's defeat at Edson Ridge, Lieutenant General Harukichi Hyakutake was dispatched to Guadalcanal, directly from Rabaul, to assume overall command of the Japanese forces on Guadalcanal. Hyakutake's arrival was hardly a vote of confidence in Kawaguchi's performance.

Kawaguchi was placed in command of the 230th Infantry Regiment for this great assault against Lunga Point, following General Hyakutake's battle plans.

But Kawaguchi believed the American defenses would be weaker farther east and ordered the 230th farther to the east of the position authorized by General Hyakutake.

That decision angered General Hyakutake, who wanted to keep his troops concentrated in a strong column to break through the American lines, with the Sendai Division punching through at a single point to spread out American defenses, much like a battering ram.

General Hyakutake relieved Kawaguchi for failing to carry out his battle plans and replaced him with Colonel Toshinari Shoji. Now Shoji would lead his men in the battle and fire the first shots against the Americans to recapture Guadalcanal for the emperor.

It was 2200 hours. The rain had stopped. Lead elements of the 1st Battalion, 230th Infantry Regiment, on the far-right flank of the regiment, had come to the edge of the tree line at the heavy jungle leading to the American position.

Across the way, perhaps three hundred yards across the open field, US Marines, defending their perimeter, were strung out in a line behind a double barbed-wire fence. By all accounts, the Marines were unaware the enemy had moved closer to their position.

Shoji brought his binoculars to his eyes, squinting in the dark to look at the Marines on the other side of the field.

This was the moment. Their destiny had arrived.

Colonel Shoji put down his binoculars and picked up his radio. "Commence fire! Attack! Attack!"

*****

Headquarters
1st Marine Division
Guadalcanal
October 24, 1942
2205 Hours

"General. Colonel Puller called. It's started, sir."

"Let's hear it, Fuller."

"The Japanese are attacking, sir, along the eastern side of Puller's flank. Almost at the juncture where the 164th Infantry Regiment is already in position."

"Damage or casualty reports?"

"Not yet, sir. The Japs are coming across the field toward our barbed-wire positions, and Puller's boys are hitting them with machine gun fire. The problem might be numbers, sir. So damn many Japs pouring into Puller's thinning lines."

Rupertus looked up at the positioning of his Marines along the area of the reported Japanese attack.

It had begun. Rupertus knew it. The Japanese were about to launch the largest land offensive yet, at Lunga Point with General Vandegrift in Nouméa. The challenge would fall on Rupertus to beat back the attack, possibly the final Japanese challenge on the ground. He had to get Puller reinforced and as quickly as possible, or the Japs might break through and take Henderson Field before breakfast.

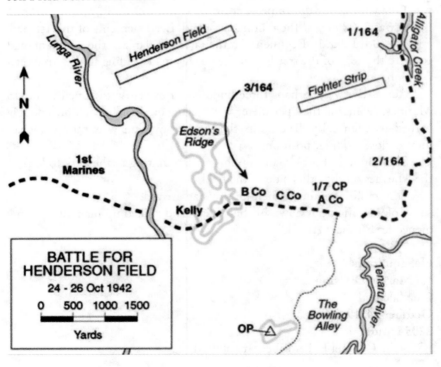

"Any additional requests from Lieutenant Colonel Puller?"

"Nothing as of yet, sir."

"Okay." Later, Rupertus made a quick entry in his diary.

Diary, October 24

(artillery got three more further to west on the road). Moved Hanneken's Bn. on the left of William. Put Col. Simms in command of the Matanikau sector. Pistol Pete still all night. Japs made assault on Pullers Bn. & Army Bn. Heavy fighting. Moved reserve bn into the line vacated by Hanneken.

Chapter 54

Lead Elements
29th Japanese Infantry
Approaching the Marine Defensive Perimeter Guarded by Able Company
Guadalcanal
October 25, 1942
0030 Hours

Several hundred yards to the west of the fighting underway between lead elements of the Japanese 1st Battalion, 230th Infantry Regiment, and the US Marines, lead elements of the Japanese 29th Infantry Regiment quietly moved to the edge of the jungle, looking out across the field that separated the thick jungle from the Marine Corps' defensive position.

The key now would be hitting the Marines in the dark and striking with the element of surprise. Of course, they could not achieve total surprise, but they could gain a tactical advantage if the 29th Infantry attacked before the Marines could recover and then blew through what appeared to be a thin defensive line.

The opening salvo by the 29th Infantry would come from 11th Company, 3rd Battalion, under the command of Captain Jiru Katsumata. The captain's men were under the overall command of the great General Yumio Nasu, who commanded the left wing of the Sendai Division for this operation, and under the immediate command of Colonel Massajior Firimaya, the direct commander of the 29th Infantry.

On behalf and under the command of both officers, Captain Katsumata of the 29th Infantry led the mighty Sendai Division into battle.

Katsumata was prepared to die for his emperor. His goal tonight was to charge the lines of the American Marines, kill them, and become the first Japanese officer to recapture the airfield the Americans had stolen. He would lead the charge of glory for Japan.

It had been an arduous, treacherous march for the Japanese army through the jungles south of the airfield. Their journey had begun on October 16, and the first day of the trek was unobstructed. The next day, they faced a dense forest with a trail so narrow they had to march single file, sometimes with heavy weapons slung over their backs, fighting through giant mosquitoes, strange insects, and island animals. They faced slick hills, slippery from the rain and covered in thick undergrowth, and hills so steep that blocks and tackles had to be used to haul their 70-millimeter cannons up the inclines. Japanese military engineers cut through trees and undergrowth, forging a path to the north, as the men moved through the jungle, lugging heavy machine guns, mortars, and boxes of ammunition.

Rotting trees lay fallen in their path. The strange insects in the jungle buzzed their heads and bit them during the march. Salty sweat dripped from their bodies, drenching their uniforms and inviting a feast of mosquitoes to bite them on their necks, arms, faces, and any other exposed area.

They had trekked by foot twenty-six miles through the thickest jungles on Earth to arrive at this position. His men were exhausted from the march. But they had made it to the attack position, and his men were honored to be at the tip of the spear to launch the major offensive.

For this to occur, in the final phase before the attack, Katsumata would need to move quietly in the dark through the thick underbrush of the open field and cut through the coiled barbed wire, and then kill the Marines on guard behind the barbed wire.

Against the sounds of a thousand chirping insects, the first platoon crawled on the ground through the thick underbrush, their bellies in the dirt, with rifles and wire cutters strapped to their backs. The weeds were dripping wet from the earlier downpour, and mud from the ground soaked into their uniforms. Even a snapped twig could alert the Americans to open fire before their job was complete.

So far, nothing suggested that they had been detected.

After a few minutes, they reached the outer perimeter of the barbed-wire barricade. They brought their wire clippers forward, put the wire in the devices, and clamped down. The barbed wire began to snap open, all along the lines.

The sounds of the jungle provided cover to help them silently cut through the barrier, carefully snipping one wire after the other.

Suddenly, a spotlight!

"Japs!"

*****

Able Company
1st Battalion, 7th Marines
Guadalcanal
October 25, 1942
0035 Hours

"Japs! Japs! Open fire!" said Captain Regan Fuller, the company commander for Able Company of the 1st Battalion of the 7th Marines serving under Lieutenant Colonel Chesty Puller. Like General Rupertus, Fuller knew more about the Japs than most junior officers in the Marine Corps.

The son of diplomats, he had grown up in China, where he saw the Japanese up close before returning to the States and graduating from the University of Virginia. Captain Fuller knew the Japs' offensive capabilities. The Japs must be killed, or his men would face not only death but also indiscriminate torture.

They had spotted the bastards crawling in the fields by Able Company's forward lookouts near the barbed-wire perimeter. Now they ran across the fields, charging in a raging banzai attack at the Marines of Able Company and their army counterparts of the 164th Infantry Regiment.

There were hundreds of them, perhaps thousands. Fuller's Marines and the soldiers of the 164th were vastly outnumbered.

Fuller's company hunkered down in their dugouts and opened up with machine gun fire and 37-millimeter guns with canister rounds. The canisters were essentially huge shotgun shells, almost the size of tiny ball bearings. The effect of a 37-millimeter blast proved devastating to the Japanese who came running in waves across the open field to overtake the Marines' position.

The 164th Infantry had been issued new, semi-automatic M1 Garand rifles, which turned out to be the superior weapon compared to the 1903 Springfield rifle used by the Marines. The critical difference favoring the Garand was the semi-automatic feature, allowing the soldiers to fire many more rounds in rapid succession by repeatedly pulling the trigger, rather than by individually working the bolt-action after every shot.

From his position in the dugout, Captain Fuller fired shot after shot into the stomachs of the Japs charging at them. He heard the sound of gunfire, exploding mortars, and explosions, and the cries of Japanese soldiers screaming as he shot them down. Streams of blood splattered everywhere. Marines were shot in the bellies, and others shot in the head, killed instantly.

But the Japs kept coming and were now almost on top of the Marines, even as his machine guns and 37-millimeter cannons tore through their stomachs and cut them down, shredding their bodies into bloody stumps.

The Marines had superior firepower but were inferior in numbers in the face of the massive Japanese waves coming across the field. The Marines needed backup, or they ran the risk of being overrun. It was a matter of numbers.

They needed help, and they needed it now.

*****

Japanese 9th Company, 3rd Battalion
Several Hundred Yards to the West of the Initial Attack
Guadalcanal
October 25, 1942
0110 Hours

Major General Yumio Nasu, commander of the Japanese 2nd Division, including its largest infantry battalion, arrived in the attack position a few minutes after 0100 hours. Along with Lieutenant General Masao Maruyama, commander of the feared Sendai Division, General Nasu commanded the bulk of the ground forces leading the attack against the Americans under the command of General Hyakutake, overall commander of the division and taking control of the right wing for purposes of this attack. Nasu's men, including the powerful 29th Infantry Regiment, took command of the left wing, moving north along the Lunga River.

While the battle had already begun slightly east of their current position, with a charge of lead elements of the regiment led by young Captain Jiro Katsumata now underway, Nasu arrived with the largest single infantry battalion about to be unleashed by the Japanese.

Nasu's powerful 29th Infantry Regiment, the largest regiment of the famed Sendai Division, would charge across the field as a great battering ram just east of the Lunga River.

While other elements of the Sendai Division would attack up and down these lines all night long, right here, right now, the great thrust would occur. Here they would break the American defenses and fight on to glorious victory.

Nasu stepped to the edge of the lower jungle line and brought his binoculars to his eyes. Through strained visibility in the darkness, he could make out the barbed-wire fences, and beyond those fences, the helmets of US Marines low in the dugouts, as the enemy waited for the massive Japanese onslaught that was about to hit them.

Since arriving on the island on August 7, the American Marines had proved themselves to be bold and courageous opponents. They had fought back Japanese forces first at the battle of Alligator Creek. In September, at the Battle of Lunga Ridge, not far from this position, the Marines had pushed back the powerful Japanese 35th Infantry Brigade, commanded by Major General Kawaguchi.

Vandegrift and Rupertus had trained their Marines well. The Imperial Japanese Army made a deadly mistake at both of those battles: the IJN had attacked with too few men.

This time, the Japanese navy brought twenty thousand troops to Guadalcanal, often landing east of the Americans' small Lunga Peninsula. After a massive buildup for the past three weeks, most of these troops under his command were ready to attack, in a concentrated manner, in an instant.

With their superior force and the Marines' lines spread out all around the peninsula, the outcome would be inevitable. His men had scouted the perimeter for days. His Japanese forces had launched diversionary attacks from the western part of the perimeter. They had lost a diversionary attack from across the Matanikau River to draw the Americans' attention and defense to a different area along the defensive front. The Marines were spread too thin, and resisting his force would be impossible. He would kill the Marines and kill their leaders, General Vandegrift and General Rupertus, and soon reestablish Japanese supremacy.

Nasu checked his watch and then conferred with his battalion commanders. The Sendai Division was ready to advance on his orders. He turned to his chief of staff. "Initiate attack."

*****

US Marine Corps Outer Defensive Perimeter
Company D
1st Battalion, 7th Marines
October 25, 1942
0111 Hours

From the inside of a dugout bunker, just a few yards north of the coiled barbed wire that stretched out in a formidable line in front of them for hundreds of yards to the east and the west, Staff Sergeant John Basilone chomped on an unlit cigarette and stared to the south, toward the direction of the thick jungle line. The sixth of ten children born to Italian American parents, the son of a tailor, Basilone was born in Buffalo before his family moved to Raritan, New Jersey, in 1918.

A devout Catholic, Basilone went to parochial school through age fifteen before dropping out to work as a golf caddy at a local country club. Wandering around Jersey trying to figure out what to do, he joined the Marine Corps in 1934 and got shipped to the Philippines, where he became a championship boxer.

He came home and left the Marines, but after serving a brief stint as a truck driver and in the army, the corps call was strong, and in 1940 he went to Baltimore and enlisted again. Frankly, he loved the Philippines so much that he hoped to go back. When the Japs attacked the Philippines, this struck home with Basilone. When the army surrendered in disgrace to the damn Japs, and MacArthur fled to Australia, Basilone took it personally.

Basilone was not just a championship boxer. He was a fighter at heart. With no use for the Japs, he would kill as many as he could without losing a moment's sleep. Hell, they had killed enough of his buddies on Guadalcanal already.

Tonight, Platoon Sergeant John Basilone served as a section leader with a weapons company in charge of four machine guns—heavy, water-cooled Browning machine guns. The tropical rain earlier in the night had drenched their position, bringing the mosquitoes out in droves. After the downpour, the night filled with the sounds of insects, crickets, and strange howling animals coming from the jungle.

By 2200 hours on October 23, with Basilone on watch, the telephone rang in the dugout. The battalion command post called to report large columns of Japanese soldiers heading somewhere in their direction. The command post was already surrounded by Japs. Could this be the famed Japanese Sendai Division about to strike?

Now, the only question was *where*. Where would the Japs strike in full force?

If the Jap army struck along these lines, the 1st Battalion had about three hundred men in the area—a thin line of resistance standing between any major Japanese assault and Henderson Field. Almost as soon as he hung up the telephone with the command post, hand grenades started flying out of the night. Mortar shells began to explode.

"Get those machine guns up on the left flank!"

Within seconds, Basilone's men were pouring four hundred and six hundred rounds per minute of machine gun fire toward the direction from which the mortar shells came.

They were out there, somewhere, and Basilone knew it. The fighting had already started toward the left side of the 1/7's perimeter, near the junction where the army's 164th National Guard unit picked up the defense.

Would they strike to the west, like they had yesterday? Or strike more to the east, where the fighting has begun earlier that night?

Were they engaging in diversionary tactics with mortars and hand grenades, or might they strike in full force right here? Right in the center of the southern line near the Lunga River, at a point that would put them closest to the airfield if they could break through.

If the Japs struck here, Basilone knew their defenses would be dangerously thin because Lieutenant Colonel Hanneken's 2nd Battalion, 7th Marines, had moved out to support against a possible invasion on the west side of the perimeter.

Basilone's group had dug in just to the east of Hill 80, at the southern end of Bloody Ridge, which Marines renamed "Edson's Ridge." On Guadalcanal, Hill 80 was surrounded by jungle on three sides and rose nearest to the perimeter line facing the jungle.

Basilone was stretched thin as a result and now commanded two separate machine gun units separated from each other along the lines. Hopefully, the machine gun fire from the Brownings would keep the Japs at bay and behind the lines.

As long as the Japs did not break through, if they attacked here, his men might be able to hold the lines, At least until reinforcements arrived. It depended on how many Japs decided to attack. One thing was for sure: Basilone would hold the line or die in the process.

*****

9th Company, 3rd Battalion
Sendai Division
Imperial Japanese Army
Guadalcanal
October 25, 1942
1114 Hours

"Captain." This was the executive officer of the 9th Company, 3rd Battalion, positioned inside the jungle directly across from the hill known by the Americans as Hill 80.

"What is it, Lieutenant?"

"General Nasu just issued the order, sir. Attack immediately."

"Very well. Notify all platoon leaders. There! Across from us. We must take out that machine gun battery to break through. Attack! Attack! Fire at will! Tell me the Marine position directly in front of us. We shall blow a hole through their defenses and head straight toward the airfield!

"Artillery, open fire! Charge!"

****

US Marine Corps Outer Defensive Perimeter
Company D
1st Battalion, 7th Marines
October 25, 1942
0115 Hours
"What the hell?"

"Japs! Japs!"

Blinding, flashing lights hit them in the eyes; the sound of a thousand fired bullets, with underlying thunderous explosions, filled the air. Some of the Marines fell in pain, bleeding. Others took shots to the head.

"Shit! They're everywhere!"

The Japs were swarming across the field like an army of locusts. It looked like there were thousands of them. The enemy quickly surrounded the American machine gun outpost.

Basilone's battery opened up in every direction, with all the Browning machine guns and everything else they had available—their machine guns, rifles, pistols. Waves of Japanese charged them in massive banzai attacks.

Men screamed. More loud sounds of gunfire, explosions, and inbound mortars filled the air.

Blood and body parts sprayed in the dark. The Japanese numbers appeared overwhelming.

"Keep the fire on 'em, boys!" Basilone yelled while firing round after round from his infield into the stomachs of Japanese who had cut through the perimeter wire and were within feet of breaching the dugout.

"Damn it! Sarge! My Browning's jammed!"

Basilone looked down to the left end of the dugout. The Marine operating the water-cooled Browning machine gun could not get it working, and the Japs were moving closer to the dugout.

"Hang on!" Basilone pulled his pistol out and fired to his right, toward the Japanese, as he ran to the other end of the dugout. Japanese bullets whizzed by his head. "Move aside!" he shouted at the gunner as he grabbed control of the machine gun. "Get your rifle and start firing!"

As bullets flew by his head, he fiddled with the trigger mechanism. The gun had jammed, and the Brownings were the only equalizer against the massive Japanese army pouring down on them. Adrenaline took over. He worked the firing mechanism, not even knowing exactly what he was doing.

A second later the 30-caliber machine gun began to fire again. "Keep feeding me ammo." Basilone took control of the weapon and began to fire and fire, and fire some more. It was as if adrenaline had caused a superpower to take control of him. Japanese bodies began piling up out in front. The bodies piled so high that Basilone had to reposition the machine gun to fire over the dead Japs.

A runner arrived in the dugout from the other machine gun section. "Our Browning's busted, Sarge!" Basilone knew that if he did not take action, his Marines in the other dugout would be overrun and killed, and the Japanese would have a straight shot at Henderson Field. "Corporal! Take over this gun!"

"We're running low on ammo, Sergeant."

Basilone picked up a spare machine gun and headed to the other end of the dugout. "Cover me!"

"Where are you going, Sarge?"

"To take this machine gun to the other squad. And find us some more ammo. Otherwise we're all dead men."

Basilone stepped out of the relative safety of the dugout, where at least most of his body was below the line of fire, and onto the field of battle, amid thousands of Japanese bullets whizzing around his head. Two other Marines followed. They headed down the narrow jungle pathway, toward their sister machine gun squad, carrying weapons and dodging bullets. A moment later, they were surrounded by a Japanese squadron and outnumbered eight to three. Using pistols, bayonets, rifles, and hand-to-hand fighting, somehow the three Marines managed to kill every member of the Japanese squadron.

They continued running through the jungle, dodging bullets until they reached the other dugout, where Basilone delivered the machine gun, gathered more ammunition, and began running back through the fire again to the first dugout to reinforce his men with the additional ammunition.

If they could hold the line until reinforcements arrived . . .

Chapter 55

1st Marine Division Headquarters
Lunga Point
Guadalcanal
Dugout Sunday, October 25, 1942
0530 Hours

Surrounded by his staff members and two key members of General Vandegrift's staff, Brigadier General Bill Rupertus took a swig of water from the canteen. His forehead broke out in a sweat, and he again wiped it with the sleeve of his shirt.

"You may want to take an atabrine, sir."

"Not now, Lieutenant," Rupertus responded to his staff physician, Navy Lieutenant E. B. McLarney.

Cactus had been under heavy assault for the last seven hours. Rupertus again studied the latest positions on the battle map on the wall. From all indications, the powerful Japanese Sendai Division, under the overall command of General Hyakutake, had made a strong thrust into the Marines' southern lines, being defended primarily by Lieutenant Colonel Chesty Puller's 1st Battalion, 7th Marines.

This was the Japs' most potent offensive yet. The initial attacks out west, which began on October 23, were a diversionary tactic in classic Japanese fashion.

Rupertus had reacted to the onslaught by ordering the 3rd Battalion, 164th Infantry, under the command of Colonel Robert Hall, to reinforce Puller's lines. Reinforcement began at about 0345 hours to stabilize the situation.

The situation was far from over. Now the Japanese were hammering Henderson Field and the perimeter. General Vandegrift was due back early in the morning from New Caledonia. Hopefully, the military situation on the ground would allow Vandegrift to land.

"Sir, Lieutenant Colonel Puller is on the phone."

"Thank you, Gerry." Rupertus took the phone from Lieutenant Colonel Gerry Thomas. "Puller, Rupertus here. How are we looking?"

"Damn, General. This has been their biggest thrust to date. Seems like we've been outnumbered ten to one. But so far, sir, somehow we're holding the lines. When the 164th showed up at 0345 hours, that helped, sir. The semi-automatic firing feature on the M1 rifle is a difference-maker. They can get their shots off a lot faster than our Enfields. A damn shame the army gets all the best toys first."

"That's General MacArthur for you," Rupertus said. "Tell you what. I'll put in a special requisition for some of those M1s for the 1/7. Maybe I can get General Vandegrift to endorse it."

"Appreciate it, sir."

"What else can I do to help you, Puller?"

"Well, there is one thing, sir."

"Name it, Puller."

"Come sunrise, we will need a mountain of shovels out here on the front lines, sir."

"Shovels?"

"Yes, sir. Not just to bury our guys, but we've got thousands of Jap bodies mounded in piles. I've never seen anything like it. One of our guys, Sergeant John Basilone, must have killed several hundred of them on his own. Once there's a break in the fighting, we'll need to get these bastards buried before the maggots and flies overrun us."

"Good point, Puller. I'll check with the army. I'm sure they have hundreds of shovels stashed at the bottom of wooden crates somewhere. They seem to have everything else stashed away. I will get them to deliver more shovels out to your men just as soon as things stabilize a little more, which I hope is sooner rather than later."

"Thank you, sir."

*****

1st Marine Division Headquarters
Lunga Point
Guadalcanal
October 26, 1942
0630 Hours

"Sir. Tower reporting. Vandegrift's plane is on its final approach."

Rupertus turned to Lieutenant Colonel Gerry Thomas, Vandegrift's chief of staff. "Gerry, would you like to greet your boss and give him a ride back here to headquarters? I'd love to go myself, but I better stay here to manage things until we turn control back over to the boss."

"Be glad to, sir."

Fifteen minutes later, someone announced, "Attention on deck!"

"At ease," Vandegrift said as he stepped back into the command tent for the first time in two days.

Rupertus managed a smile at the sight of his friend. "Hell, Archer, I have to say, sir, with respect, you're a sight for sore eyes."

"Bill, I wish I could say the same for you. You look like hell. Are you okay?"

"Just a little fever, sir. No big deal. Doc McLarney's been popping me all kinds of pills."

"I told you that you should have been nipping more out of the whiskey stash. It kills malaria every time."

"Should have listened to you, sir."

Vandegrift shook his head. "Can't go on vacation for even a couple of days without you guys throwing a party. What's our status?"

"Huge push by the Japs," Rupertus said. "They tried crashing straight through our southern perimeter, with massive force, just to the east of the Lunga, after we had reinforced to the west. It's been a hell of a night. But our boys are holding and we're beating them back. Puller called about an hour ago with a positive report. He says we've got thousands of dead Japs to bury. Asked me to find him a bunch of shovels to bury the bodies. I told him I would check with the army."

Vandegrift chuckled. "Sounds like Puller."

"Anyway," Rupertus continued, "I reinforced the southern lines with the 3rd Battalion from the 164th Army Infantry. They've got the new M1 rifles, which have been a lifesaver with their semi-automatic feature. Puller wants a bunch for the 1/7.

"Fighting continues, General, but it appears we've withstood their biggest blow and beat the hell out of them overnight."

"Great job, Bill. Let's talk for a bit to catch up. Are you ready to relinquish command back?"

"If you ask, sir."

"Very well. I've got the con." Vandegrift glanced at Lieutenant McLarney, Rupertus's staff medical officer. "Doc McLarney?"

"Sir, Rupertus has my okay. He can rest later. And must rest to beat any oncoming fever."

"Great."

"Take the general back to my quarters and give him whatever he needs to get him back up to speed. I'll be there shortly to review our trip and get a report on what the hell happened. We've got to keep General Rupertus in the fight."

"Aye, sir."

*****

US Marine Corps Outer Defensive Perimeter
Company D
1st Battalion, 7th Marines
October 26, 1942
0710 Hours

Lieutenant Colonel Chesty Puller, winner of two Navy Crosses for combat as a junior officer in the Banana Wars in Nicaragua, was never one to shy away from a battlefront.

Last night's massive fighting had not fully subsided, with rifle shots and mortar fire still cracking the air. It was not the smartest decision for a battalion commander to insert himself in the very front lines of battle—even a smoldering, subsiding battle—as a Japanese sniper might spot him from a coconut tree.

But Puller didn't give a damn. He wanted to see what happened last night. He strapped on his battle helmet, worked the action on his sidearm, and, with his intelligence officer Captain Francis Farrell and his staff gunnery sergeant, took the jeep down as far as he could to the front before moving out on foot to the base of Hill 80.

His destination was the machine encampment under the command of Staff Sergeant John Basilone. The closer they got to the encampment, the more Japanese bodies they had to step over and around.

"My God, this is a massacre," Puller said.

Silence. Then Captain Farrell managed to speak up. "We lost a lot of men last night, sir. But I'm sure as hell glad we're not the Japanese this morning."

A moment later, the machine gun encampment came into view.

The early morning light revealed more dead Marines than live Marines inside the dugout. And at the far end, Puller recognized Staff Sergeant John Basilone, his hands clutching a water-cooled Browning 30-caliber machine gun, scanning the jungle across the field, on alert for the enemy.

"Basilone."

No response. It was as if the staff sergeant were locked in a trance, and nothing would pull him from it.

"You want me to get him for you, sir?" Captain Farrell said.

"No." Puller motioned with his hand. "Leave him be."

The colonel stepped down into the dugout, where a young Marine, a private first class, sat in a daze on the near end, opposite of where Basilone still operated the machine gun.

"What's your name, son?"

"Phillips, sir. PFC Nash W. Phillips."

"Where are you from, Phillips?"

"Sir, I'm from Fayetteville, North Carolina."

"Your hand is shot up pretty bad, Phillips."

"Yes, sir."

"Are you in a lot of pain?"

"To be honest, I know it's bleeding badly, but I can't feel nothing, sir."

"Shock does that to you, Private."

"Yes, sir."

"Anybody else left alive?"

"No, sir. Just me and Staff Sergeant Basilone."

"Can you tell me what happened?"

"Staff Sergeant Basilone. I ain't never seen nothing like it. He's had his hands on that machine gun for almost three days. He's not slept a wink, sir. When he wasn't firing a machine gun, he ran back and forth between here and the other dugout to supply them with weapons and bring ammunition back, right out in front of the Japanese. He must have killed a thousand Japs by himself, sir."

"Cigarette, Phillips?"

"No, thank you, sir."

"See if you can get on your feet, son. I'm taking you back with me. We're going to get that hand checked out."

"Yes, sir."

*****

1st Marine Division Headquarters
Lunga Point
Guadalcanal
October 26, 1942
0745 Hours

Bill Rupertus woke up sweating profusely and breaking into shivers. Vandegrift was probably right: he should have been hitting the bottle a little bit harder. Neither Archer nor his staff had come down with any of this crap, and access to an occasional nip from the general's stash seemed to be their common denominator.

He tried to get up a few times to check on the status from the front. Each time, Doc McLarney had given him a shot of Vandegrift's whiskey, ordered him back to bed, and reminded him that General Vandegrift had returned and everything remained under control. Rupertus laid his head back on the pillow, closed his eyes, and tried to rest. He thought he felt himself dozing, perhaps the aftereffects of Vandegrift's whiskey, when he heard the doctor's voice.

"Sorry to bother you, General, but you have a visitor."

Rupertus opened his eyes, pushed himself up on the cot, and saw the commanding general of the 1st Marine Division standing there beside him.

"Sir."

"How are you feeling, Bill?"

"Slightly better than I felt an hour ago, sir."

Vandegrift smiled. "I didn't want to interrupt your recovery, but I have good news."

"Good news? I'm listening, General."

"Puller called. The Sendai Division is in retreat. Our men will pursue and attack them, but you have beaten them back, Bill. Congratulations."

Rupertus smiled. "That's great news, sir. But it wasn't me beating them back. It was our men. The men you called together at New River last spring."

"The men you trained, Bill."

"We trained them together, sir."

"That we did, Bill. And they are the finest damn Marine division in the world. The finest damn Marine division in history."

Rupertus smiled again. "Tell you what, sir. When I knock this fever out, I'll drink to that."

"Count on it," Vandegrift said. "Get well. I need you for the rest of the war."

"Aye, sir. Semper Fi."

"Semper Fi."

The fighting on Guadalcanal did not end with the Battle for Henderson Field, but it did end, once and for all, Japan's concerted efforts to take the airfield by a ground invasion. Along with the Battle of the Tenaru and the Battle of Edson's Ridge, this battle became the third and final major land offensive launched by the Japanese.

For his heroic actions, John Basilone was awarded the Medal of Honor and became a national hero. As the sun rose over Guadalcanal on Sunday, October 25, only Basilone and Private First Class Nash W. Phillips of Fayetteville, North Carolina, were left alive. Every other Marine under Basilone's command in the machine gun encampment was killed. Rupertus had never met a Marine like Basilone.

After the battle, the Marines and then the army continued to pursue the Japanese throughout the island and would battle them at Koi Point the following month, a battle Rupertus again commanded. But in the end, nearly three thousand Japanese died at the Battle for Henderson Field, marking Japan's largest defeat on Guadalcanal. As fate would have it, because General Vandegrift had taken a three-day trip to Nouméa as part of his military duties, General Rupertus commanded Guadalcanal's final and largest major land battle campaign. Even though the Sendai Division retreated on the early morning of October 25, the Imperial Japanese Air Force continued to bomb Henderson Field all day as the Cactus Air Force dueled the Zeros in the skies above Guadalcanal. This activity forced the Marines into their dugouts, and October 25 became known as "Dugout Sunday."

Rupertus noted that at least seventeen Japanese Zeros and five Japanese bombers were shot down over Cactus.

Diary, Sunday, October 25
10:50AM 3 Jap DDs entered the channel, fired on Seminole YP (Timid) and sank some—opened fire on them, and got three hits. Trevor and Zeus escaped from Tulagi eastward. Many Jap planes over Cactus this day—shot down 17 Zeros, five bombers, plus one X recovered. Sporadic firing at Matanikau and the south flank during night.

Diary, October 26
0630 Archer returned—1:30 PM. Captain Greenman, Captain Compton, Captain B.H. Smith and Captain Bradshaw and I left Cactus for Ringbolt—5PM arrival.

The Battle for Henderson Field, as it turned out, was the decisive battle that broke the backs of the Japanese in the Solomon Islands, and history records that Rupertus was in command.

Chapter 56

Six Weeks Later
Assistant Division Commander Headquarters
Near the Tenaru River
Guadalcanal
December 9, 1942
Late Afternoon
From outside his command post, two hundred yards west of the Tenaru River and only seventy-five yards from the beach, Bill Rupertus inhaled on his cigarette and, with a long exhale, looked out to the sea.

The reassuring sight before him seemed like something that would never come to pass.

Under warm sunshine and bright blue skies, the USS *President Jackson*, USS *President Adams*, USS *Crescent City*, and other beautiful gray warships were anchored off Lunga Point. The ships, which left in a rush after the disastrous first Battle of Savo Island, had returned. Their purpose: to transport the 1st Marine Division the hell out of Guadalcanal and Tulagi. Destination: Australia.

Earlier in the day, at 1100 hours, General Vandegrift had turned Guadalcanal over to Major General Alexander Patch, commander of the US Army's XIV Corps.

Already it had been an emotional day visiting the cemetery of fallen Marines and soldiers.

"Beautiful sight, isn't it, sir?"

Rupertus recognized the voice of his former chief of staff, Colonel Bill Enright.

"That it is, Bill." Another draw from his cigarette. "Would you like one?"

"Thank you, sir."

"Here you go." Rupertus gave Enright the cigarette and then offered a light. "Happy for our boys. Australia might be the perfect medicine. These boys have earned some rest, and then some."

"Well, sir, if I may, I believe that the general has also earned some relaxation."

266

"I agree, Bill. General Vandegrift has worked hard. There's not a finer Marine out there to lead Marines. He's been like a big brother to me for many years."

Enright smiled. "With respect, sir, while I agree with your comments about General Vandegrift, I was speaking of you, sir. You have earned and deserve some rest and relaxation yourself before we go back into battle."

Rupertus chuckled. "R&R? What's that?"

"I'm serious, sir. All the senior officers believe that you'll be taking command of the division soon, assuming that General Vandegrift becomes commandant.

"The Battle for Henderson Field, which you commanded, was the largest land offensive launched by the Japanese in the whole Guadalcanal campaign. And it was their final attempt to take our airfield. Now they're on the run. I think history will record this battle as one of the greatest of this war. And then, after that, you led the expedition to rescue Colonel Hanneken when he and his men were trapped and pinned down."

Rupertus smiled. "I appreciate your kindness, Bill. But I took command only by fate, because General Vandegrift happened to be off Guadalcanal at the time. And our Marines won this battle, not any one man.

"Besides, Lieutenant Colonel Hanneken is a national hero—Medal of Honor winner in Haiti. He killed the rebel leader Charlemagne Peralte. Any Marine would go into harm's way to save that guy. Fortunately, I shook the dengue fever and could stay over here to run that mission."

"True, sir," Enright said. "Any decent Marine would have gone after Colonel Hanneken. But not every commander could have pulled off that rescue mission like you did. Hanneken was fully surrounded at Koli Point. It took a hell of an effort from leadership to get him out of there."

Rupertus smiled. "You're too kind, Bill."

After the great victory at the Battle for Henderson Field on October 25, Rupertus had returned to his former headquarters on Tulagi Island to battle dengue fever. Under the supervision of his medical officer, Lieutenant McLarney, he recovered to the point that by November 4, Vandegrift brought him back to Guadalcanal to assume command over the entire eastern sector of the island.

When Rupertus returned to Guadalcanal, a crisis erupted: the rescue of Colonel Hanneken and his men.

General Vandegrift's new strategy was to wipe any remaining Japanese off Guadalcanal proactively. He ordered Lieutenant Colonel Henry Hanneken to march with his 2nd Battalion thirteen miles east from the Lunga perimeter to the Metopana River. That evening, they witnessed, in the dark, driving rain, a Japanese cruiser and transport arriving with at least fifteen hundred soldiers unloading weapons.

The Japs quickly discovered Hanneken's Marines and suddenly outnumbered and surrounded them as a bloody firefight erupted.

Hanneken radioed division headquarters for help but had connection problems and could not break through for several hours, so he ordered his Marines to withdraw over the river to Koli Point to wait for support.

By the next morning, Colonel Hanneken reached division headquarters on the radio and reported their dilemma to Vandegrift, who ordered Rupertus to personally lead the force into the battle zone to extricate Hanneken and his men.

Rupertus took three battalions of infantry, including Puller's 1/7, artillery, and tanks. He also took the 2nd and 3rd Battalions of the army's 164th Infantry Regiment. Their goal was to surround the enemy from the east, west, and south and either kill them or drive them north into the sea.

Rupertus moved his forward post from the area around the Ilu River to Koli Point. The units he commanded pressed forward. Puller's battalion was initially in boats on the sea while Moore's 164th Infantry marched in from the south. Puller's battalion joined Hanneken at the Nalimbio River, where they came ashore and began to push from the west, east, and south.

Puller himself was blown to the ground by flying metal, which lodged in his legs and lower body. Badly bleeding, he went to call for help but saw the telephone wires for the radio were severed. When he tried to stand to fix the wires, he ended up getting shot twice in his arm.

Puller was evacuated from the battle space.

Rupertus personally moved into the front lines as his troops advanced. The Japanese forces dug in. As he reached the front lines, a Jap soldier tossed a live grenade toward Rupertus. The grenade missed Rupertus but exploded near Captain Powell, Rupertus's assistant D-2. The grenade wounded Powell, and, like Colonel Puller, he was immediately evacuated off the front lines.

Rupertus responded by blowing the hell out of the Japanese with heavy artillery barrages, which proved effective. The Japs retreated, and Rupertus and his men reached Hanneken's men and brought them back to safety before finishing off the enemy.

"You know, sir," Enright said, "if they'd killed or captured a Medal of Honor winner, that would've been a major propaganda coup for the Japs, especially this early in the war. And a public relations disaster back home, too. You took decisive action and stopped that nightmare from happening."

Rupertus smiled. "My men made it happen, Bill. And that includes you. We'll leave it to the army to take a broom and dustpan to sweep the rest of the Japs off Guadalcanal. But this has been a team effort, our victory."

"True, sir. We've had great leadership and were fortunate to have men on Guadalcanal like Basilone, Twining, and Puller. The right men at the right time."

"Damn right. We also have to give credit to the navy. They had to pull out prematurely, but they came back and fought like hell out in that channel, fighting battle after battle against the Jap navy to keep the Japs off our asses."

"We've got the finest navy in the world," Enright said. "And we've lost way too many sailors out there in that sound."

Rupertus looks at a bomb labeled for Tojo.

"Yes." Rupertus swigged from a cup of coffee and looked out to the channel. Already, landing craft, jammed full of Marines, churned across the water toward the large gray navy transport ships that had brought them to Guadalcanal a little over four months ago.

"It's a beautiful sight, isn't it, Bill? Seeing these guys finally get off this island? They'll be in Australia in a few days, hoping to recover from malaria, soak up some sunshine, and enjoy the air of freedom."

Rupertus watched the landing craft pull alongside the ships and Marines beginning to board. His thoughts wandered to family. Christmas was coming soon, and how he wished he could be there to hold Sleepy in his arms and watch Patrick open presents under the tree.

"How about you, sir?"

"Excuse me?"

"When do you get to leave this hellhole, sir?"

Rupertus chuckled, "Me?"

"Yes, sir."

"Well, Vandegrift will be flying out for Australia in a couple of days. We're having a big soiree for him tonight at my command post, complete with the Marine Band playing. And I want you there, Bill."

Enright smiled. "Wouldn't miss it, sir. Thank you. But with due respect, the general did not answer my question, which is the general's prerogative. But will you be leaving the island with General Vandegrift?"

"I wish. But no. I'll be here on Guadalcanal for a few more weeks to take care of a few things and help the army and General Patch in any way needed. I'll be heading to Australia in early January. There, I will be assigned to the army as an adviser as I continue as ADC of the 1st."

"Excuse me, General."

Rupertus turned and saw one of the captains on his staff.

"Yes, Captain."

"General Vandegrift and Colonel Thomas have arrived, sir. The general has asked that I convey to you his desire to have a drink of whiskey to celebrate our victory on Guadalcanal before the night's festivities."

Rupertus chuckled. "Tell the general I will be right with him."

The captain saluted. "Aye, sir."

Rupertus turned to Enright. "Well, Bill, I guess that's my cue. I hope to see you there tonight. But if I don't get to tell you then, I'll tell you now. You've been a hell of a chief of staff, especially after Killy left, and one of the

General Rupertus and Colonel Simms make coffee while watching Higgins boats come in. (USMC PHOTO)

General Rupertus and Colonel Clifton Cates. (USMC PHOTO)

General Rupertus and staff on Guadalcanal. (USMC PHOTO)

General Rupertus. (USMC PHOTO)

best damn Marines on my staff. We could not have done this without you. I see some medals."

Enright smiled. "And likewise, sir, if I may?"

"Certainly."

"Sir, you've been the finest leader for whom I've ever served."

"Thank you, Bill."

"Sir, Semper Fi."

"Semper Fi."

"Leaving Guadalcanal!" (Rupertus quote). (USMC PHOTO)

Chapter 57

Headquarters
Assistant Division Commander
Mount Martha, Australia
Six Months Later

Arriving in Australia six months after their great victory at Guadalcanal was the best thing that could happen to the 1st Marine Division, aside from returning home to the United States.

On December 13, 1942, one year and six days after the Japanese bombed Pearl Harbor, the first echelon of the 1st Marine Division arrived in Brisbane, Australia, where General MacArthur's headquarters was; his army troops were dispersed to various camps several miles outside Brisbane. Upon the Marine Corps' arrival, the division was loaded onto trains and shipped to Camp Cable, twenty-six miles to the south. Camp Cable was an army training base in Queensland, recently vacated by the army's 32nd Infantry Division.

Camp Cable proved to be a mosquito-infested swamp ground for malaria, the very last thing that these Marines needed. They came to Australia in part to recover from mass malaria infections. Over 75 percent of the division was infected.

When General Vandegrift learned that Camp Cable would be detrimental to his men's recovery, he contacted Admiral Halsey to protest the dire situation. After about three weeks, Halsey made arrangements to ship the division from Brisbane to the south, to cooler, dryer Melbourne.

Rupertus and the 1st Marine Division's second echelon arrived in Melbourne on January 12, 1943, on board the USS *West Point*, USS *President Hayes*, USS *President Adams*, and USS *President Jackson*, which carried Rupertus and his staff. The division spread out to various locations all over Melbourne's metropolitan area, including several hospitals equipped to treat infected and wounded Marines.

A total of 18,200 Marines had arrived, and the locals joked that an "invasion" had come to their shores.

The Marines had multiple housing arrangements throughout the Melbourne metropolitan area. Aside from the Marines hospitalized with malaria and war wounds, the most extensive accommodation were in the city cricket clubs in central Melbourne, or the "MCG," as the locals knew it.

The clubs provided stadium-like shelters, which were enormous in size and had ample bathroom and shower facilities. Almost two-thirds of the Marines billeted among two cricket clubs.

The 7th Marine Regiment, including Lieutenant Colonel Puller's 1st Battalion and Lieutenant Colonel Hanneken's 2nd Battalion, found quarters about twenty miles to the southeast of Melbourne, in the Bayside suburbs of Balcombe, Frankston, and Mount Martha.

For this short time in Australia, General Vandegrift set up his headquarters in a home on the ocean provided by a wealthy Australian family, closer to the center of Melbourne.

Rupertus set up his headquarters in an equally gorgeous house overlooking the ocean in Mount Martha, another thirty miles or so to the southeast. Rupertus was okay with this arrangement, as it placed him closer to Puller and Hanneken, both proven valiant warriors, whom Rupertus would call on with confidence once his Marines received their next battle assignment.

General Rupertus's house in Mount Martha.

General Rupertus and Colonel Selden overlooking the harbor.

Soon after Rupertus and the second echelon had arrived in Melbourne, Vandegrift and his chief of staff, Colonel Thomas, left Australia to return to the United States for meetings with the Marine Corps commandant in Washington, DC. Vandegrift would be away from Australia from January through the middle of March, once again leaving Rupertus solely in charge of the entire division. Colonel Twining became Rupertus's chief of staff.

First, the weary Marines needed to recover. Southern Australia, with its cool ocean air and social opportunities around Melbourne, provided the perfect respite for his Marines to begin to rest and heal.

During Vandegrift's absence, Rupertus's concern also became public relations. His Marines were having a jolly good time, enjoying libations and nighttime activities in and around the numerous pubs of Melbourne and Mount Martha. They had gotten into multiple fistfights with returning Aussie soldiers, who were jealous that the leathernecks had better luck with the Aussie girls than the Aussie soldiers were having.

The Marines' victory on Guadalcanal gave them revered hero status in Melbourne and throughout the country. The Japanese had bombed Darwin in the northern part of the country, and the fierce Japanese army and navy remained a constant concern to every Australian.

But these Marines had beaten the Japanese off Guadalcanal and Tulagi. Millions of Aussies felt relieved the US Marine Corps had landed on their soil and dubbed the Marines "the heroes of Guadalcanal."

Even if the Aussie armed forces could not beat the Japanese on their own, these Marines could, and they'd proven it. There was an aura about the boys of the Old Breed, making them instantly popular with single Aussie women.

Rupertus helped smooth things over, using his adroit diplomatic skills with local political leaders. Working closely with the lord mayor of Melbourne, they struck up a friendship. They arranged several major public events to help shore up public relations and goodwill between the Marines and the locals, planning joint mingling and social opportunities between the Marines and the Aussie troops outside the confines of an Aussie bar.

They were, after all, ultimately fighting the same enemy. Rupertus figured they might need each other's back one day, in some jungle-infested hellhole.

Rupertus talking with Vice Admiral Carpenter (USN); Colonel Simms on right. Australia, April 19, 1943. (USMC PHOTO)

Admiral Helfrich (Royal Dutch Navy), Brigadier General Rupertus (USMC), Lord Mayor Nettefold, General Blamey (commander-in-chief of the Australian Military Forces). Melbourne, Victoria, Australia, February 2, 1943.

Sir Dugan, governor of Victoria, and Brigadier General Bill Rupertus. Melbourne, Victoria, Australia, February 22, 1943.

Colonel Buckley, Brigadier General Bill Rupertus, Major Murray, and a civilian at a camp show. Melbourne, Victoria, Australia, February 1943.

As he thought about the things his Marines had done together with the Aussies, a smile crossed his face. One of the significant events was the parade on George Washington's birthday, February 22. Thousands of Melburnians turned out in force to cheer "the saviors of Australia" as his Marines marched from the Shrine of Remembrance, the great memorial honoring Australians who served in World War I, to Parliament House and past Flinders Street Station and the Town Hall.

One of the big hits with the Australian people came just three weeks later, on March 14, when

General Rupertus saluting as the US Marines pass by in the parade. Melbourne, Victoria, Australia. (USMC PHOTO)

Peking veterans. (USMC PHOTO)

Rupertus proposed having his Marines host a beer party for the Australians on the cricket grounds, with the alcohol provided by Uncle Sam. One reason for the tensions between the Marines and the Aussie troops was a shortage of beer.

So Rupertus proposed the occasion as an opportunity for goodwill, though he accepted a suggestion from Captain Leon Brusiloff, commander of the 1st Division band, to serve the beer in paper cups so nobody could throw bottles if things got rowdy.

To help publicize the event, the Melbourne newspaper, the *Argus*, published an announcement a week before the event, inviting all Melburnians to attend and announcing that the Americans would serve libations from 1900 until 2200 hours.

The party on the cricket grounds was a popular smash with the Aussie troops and went miles toward mending fences. It became the most memorable event at the MCG, with nine thousand men drinking beer in paper cups without any fights.

By the time Vandegrift arrived back in Australia from Washington in mid-March, Rupertus had completed working his diplomatic magic, and the

Major General Bill Rupertus advises Marines to find their target and shoot! Mount Martha, Australia, July 1943. (USMC PHOTO)

General Rupertus places award on Colonel Edson. (USMC PHOTO)

Left: Major General Bill Rupertus with Lieutenant Colonel Weber and Sergeant John Basilone (pointing). Mount Martha, Australia, July 7, 1943. (USMC PHOTO)

Below: Major General Bill Rupertus and Lieutenant Colonel William Enright watch South Pacific maneuvers from Mornington Peninsula. Mount Martha, Australia, July 15, 1943. (USMC PHOTO)

Rosy (Rosecrans), Edelman, Krueger, Edson, Rupertus, an Aussie, Cresswell, and Hanneken. Mount Martha, Australia, March 19, 1943. (USMC PHOTO)

Colonel Selden and General Rupertus. (USMC PHOTO)

General Vandegrift and General Rupertus.
Mount Martha, Australia, April 1943.
(USMC PHOTO)

General Rupertus greets Cresswell.
(USMC PHOTO)

Rupertus pins a medal on the 5th Marines as Colonel Edson looks on.
(USMC PHOTO)

General Walter Krueger of the 6th Army inspects the training of Marines at Mount Martha, Australia. Here his aide talks with Major General William Rupertus and Colonel Merritt "Red Mike" Edson. (COURTESY OF JOHN S. DAY, SR. COLLECTION (COLL/2927), MARINE CORPS ARCHIVES & SPECIAL COLLECTIONS)

1st Marine Division, with many of his Marines recovering from their wounds and sickness, had fallen into more of a routine, and relations with the Aussie troops had gotten much better. Training could begin.

As the end of June rolled around, chilly winter temperatures arrived in South Australia. The change of seasons from the Australian fall to winter also brought changes in the division.

Rupertus's friend and mentor, Alexander Vandegrift, back from Washington for less than ninety days, was about to leave for good.

Today, Vandegrift was on his way to Rupertus's headquarters to give him a briefing. Rupertus suspected that he might be given full command of the division, with Vandegrift becoming commandant. But that had not been finalized.

"Excuse me, sir." Rupertus looked up and saw one of the junior officers on his staff.

"Is General Vandegrift here?"

"Not yet, sir," the captain replied, with a smile on his face.

"Something amusing, Captain?"

"No, sir. My apologies. It's just that something arrived in the mail today that I thought the general might be happy to see. Would you like me to leave it on your desk, sir?"

"No. You can hand it to me."

"Aye, sir." The captain handed Rupertus the envelope and stepped back.

Rupertus took the envelope and looked down at the return address: "Alice Hill Rupertus, 3732 Van Ness Street, Washington, DC 20016."

Rupertus smiled. "Thank you, Captain. Let me know when General Vandegrift arrives. That will be all."

"Aye, sir."

Rupertus ripped open the letter Sleepy had written more than ninety days ago as the captain stepped out. The post office was way behind because more letters were being sent to Marines in the Pacific than were sent in the continental United States.

Vandegrift was lucky. He had the opportunity to return to Washington and, of course, got to see Mildred. But for the time being, Rupertus would cherish this letter from Sleepy and hope another one would come soon.

Rupertus folded the letter and put it back in the envelope after hearing a hard knock on the door.

"Enter."

"Sir, General Vandegrift is here."

"On my way."

He rose and quickly walked out to the foyer, where he saw Vandegrift, wearing his winter service uniform, with a drab green jacket and khaki shirt and tie.

"Archer!"

"Bill! Gerry Thomas drove me, but I asked him to give us a few minutes alone. He should be back shortly."

"That's great," Rupertus said. "Please, come into my office, Archer."

Rupertus led Vandegrift into his main study, where the two men took seats in wingback chairs across from a coffee table.

"Cigarette, Archer?"

"Thank you," Vandegrift said, as Rupertus offered a cigarette from his pack of Camels and then offered a light.

"How about coffee?"

"No thanks, Bill."

Rupertus sat back and examined his old friend. "Something tells me you may be getting ready to leave town again, my friend."

Vandegrift smiled. "Bill, your military instincts are always on the mark. One of the many reasons you're a great general."

"I learned from the master, sir."

"You surpassed the master, Bill." Vandegrift chuckled.

"Respectfully disagree, General."

"Well, first off," Vandegrift said, "I just heard from the commandant, and I wanted you to hear it firsthand. You're going to be formally promoted to commander of the 1st Marine Division at some point within the next week. Until then, and effective tomorrow, you are active commander.

"It's more than well deserved. Between your victory at Tulagi, the way you took control of the Battle for Henderson Field when I was in New Caledonia, and then the way you commanded the rescue of Lieutenant Colonel Hanneken, the choice was obvious, and General Holcomb agrees.

"Plus, the way you've managed these liquor-swilling Marines in my absence, as the whole division has recovered from malaria, has been masterful. Congratulations, Bill."

Rupertus nodded. He had expected this for some time, but now, with General Vandegrift delivering the news, it seemed surreal.

"Anyway," Vandegrift continued, "congratulations, Bill. I'm delighted more than you know. The division is in great hands."

"Thank you, sir," Rupertus said. "But likewise, sir, I hope that I'm able to reciprocate the congratulations upon your appointment as commandant of the Marine Corps."

Vandegrift nodded. "Well, not quite yet."

"I don't understand, sir."

"Well, as it turns out, Roosevelt likes Holcomb and is not quite ready for him to retire yet. And I don't blame the president. Holcomb's been serving on active duty for forty-three years, and FDR has confidence in him. So do I."

"You're not retiring, are you, General?"

"You know me better than that, Bill." Vandegrift chuckled. "Hell would freeze over before I retire in the middle of this war before we won it for good."

"Then what's next?"

"Well," Vandegrift said, "the president wants Holcomb to stay until January 1. Meanwhile, they're going to pin another star on me and send me over to command the 1st Marine Amphibious Corps. Then, depending on how I perform there, Roosevelt will consider me a possible successor to Holcomb for commandant. But no guarantees."

"The president has seen enough of your record to know that you're more than ready for the job, especially after awarding you the Medal of Honor. Of course, I am rather biased and in your camp, sir."

"Thanks. I know you are. But I'm good with it, Bill. I'm a Marine, and we do our duty. Holcomb is ready to retire and wants to retire. He's told me so. Forty-three years is a long time in any organization, and war or no war, it will wear you down. The president has a comfort level with Holcomb and wanted to squeeze another six months out of him. Holcomb agreed as a favor to the president, and here we are."

"Well, I'm sure you'll do a kick-ass job at the Amphib Corps. I had heard through the scuttlebutt that the commandant and the Joint Chiefs were not satisfied with General Vogel as commander of the Amphib Corps."

"Yep. Hold it here. But that's my understanding also," Vandegrift said. "Anyway, if Vogel had satisfied his superiors, he'd probably be in line to succeed Holcomb. Plus I think Roosevelt wants to see if I can do a better job taking command of the Amphibious Corps before he makes a final decision."

"I'm sure you will be his final decision, General."

"Thank you, Bill. And if so, I hope that you succeed me, just like you're succeeding me as commander of the 1st Marine Division."

Rupertus laughed. "Well, I can say that my young wife would like that because it would at least get me closer to home and in the same bed every night."

"How are Sleepy and Patrick?"

"Doing great, best I can tell. Sleepy and her sister Jo are getting ready to move into another house there in Washington. I just got a letter from her in the mail, although she wrote it in March."

"Hell, if I'd known, I'd have hand-delivered it to you when I came back here in the middle of March. At least I would have been good for something during that time."

"Not necessary, sir."

"Anyway," Vandegrift continued, "if and when I do become commandant, I will try and bring you back to Washington in between the fighting, just like Holcomb brought me back. We're going to need you in Washington for war bonds, PR, and other matters."

"When do you officially take command of the Amphib Corps, General?"

"July 1. Effective tomorrow, Bill. The same day you become active commanding general of the 1st Marine Division."

"Aye, sir."

"There is one thing I wanted to cover with you."

"Yes, sir?"

"It's about MacArthur," Vandegrift said.

"Aah. MacArthur. The Great White Father."

Vandegrift laughed. "Remember that name?"

"My recollection, sir, is that you invented it."

Vandegrift laughed some more. "For the record, Bill, I'm not letting you pin authorship of that name on me. Especially if he finds out, if General Holcomb asks, I'll blame it on you." Vandegrift snickered.

"Feel free to pull rank if you would like, sir." Rupertus chuckled. "So what's the latest with the dear general?"

"Bill, now that the 1st Marine Division has been here in Australia for six months, and with all the positive publicity we got back home for our victories at Tulagi and Guadalcanal, MacArthur wants to bring the division under control of the army. It will not be under the control of the navy anymore."

"The army?"

"Yes," Vandegrift said. "The army. In other words, he wants the division under his overall command rather than Nimitz's command."

"Man." Rupertus took a sip of lukewarm, black coffee. "The man does have the biggest ego to walk the planet since Napoleon."

"That's an understatement, Bill. MacArthur is a hell of a general. But his ego is bigger than Napoleon's and Genghis Khan's combined."

"I'll bet this idea has gone over well with Admiral Nimitz," Rupertus said.

"Like a lead balloon," Vandegrift said. "Nimitz and Halsey are not happy about it. General Holcomb doesn't like it either."

"Out of curiosity, what's MacArthur's reasoning?"

"His reasoning is we're now in Australia, right in his backyard, and operating in the southwest oceans area, over which he is in command of all forces."

"Is this going to happen, sir?"

"Roosevelt's kicking it around. You know Roosevelt. He's somewhat like Lincoln was. He can be vague and ambiguous when it comes to delineating lines of authority among his senior officers. He often plays one off against the other. It would not surprise me if FDR approves this for your next mission, which I'm sure will be somewhere closer to Japan. And as you know,

MacArthur is arguing for New Britain because the Japs are already there, at Rabaul.

"But right now, whether they move the division under MacArthur or keep it under Nimitz, that decision is beyond our pay grade. We will have to keep an eye on it."

"Aye, sir."

A knock on the door.

"Enter."

"Generals, I have been asked to inform you that Colonel Thomas has arrived."

"Thank you, Captain."

"Well," Vandegrift said, "that's my ride back to the cricket grounds."

"I appreciate your visit, Archer. On a personal level, I'm going to miss having you around."

"I'll miss being around. But we'll be together again soon. In the meantime, just keep kicking ass."

"Aye, sir."

After the generals exchanged a brief salute, a handshake, and a backslap, Archer Vandegrift walked out the door, leaving Bill Rupertus in sole command of the 1st Marine Division.

Soon he would move on to dealing with Douglas MacArthur and preparing his Marines for the next battle. Rupertus had a feeling that it would all happen sooner rather than later. Meanwhile, the more training time he could buy for his men, the better.

*****

Melbourne Airport
Melbourne, Australia
September 8, 1943
0700 Hours

The twin-engine DC-3 flew over the airfield, banked, looped around, and began its descent on final approach.

A sizable crowd had assembled outside the small terminal area, and just watching the plane fly once over the airfield got the crowd excited.

This morning Rupertus, decked out in his service dress green uniform, found himself on the tarmac, along with members of the press and various other local and provincial dignitaries, including the governor of Victoria, Sir Winston Dugan, and his wife, Lady Dugan; and the lord mayor of Melbourne, the Right Honorable Sir Thomas Sydney Nettlefold, with his wife.

Rupertus had gotten to know Nettlefold well and liked him. They developed a good working relationship in sponsoring several joint events between his Marines and the local community—the parade on February 22, 1943, honoring the Marines and featuring the fabulous Marine Band of the 1st Marine Division, and, on March 14, the massive party on the Melbourne Cricket Grounds promoting fun and camaraderie between the Marines and Australian soldiers.

The governor, Lord Dugan, a career British army officer who fought in the Boer Wars in the First World War, rising to the rank of major general, had previously been governor of South Australia before being appointed governor of Victoria. Rupertus has also met Dugan but did not know him as well as he knew Lord Mayor Nettlefold. Still, Rupertus had great respect for Dugan's distinguished military service and considered him a brother in arms.

As the DC-3 touched down on the runway, not only did the crowd get more excited, but so did the greeting party. A string of photographers and reporters moved into the ready position, surrounding the outside rear of the greeting party in a human horseshoe. Several Aussie soldiers stood by to push an airplane stairwell into place.

Rupertus reflected that he would rather be training with his Marines this morning, and getting ready for the next mission, most likely another jungle island environment, closer to Japan, with the objective soon finalized.

Standing here for this particular ceremony made him think about Sleepy—not that he did not think of her every day anyway. He wished Sleepy could be here to relish the pomp and circumstance and take over in the conversation, where she would flourish and excel with her bubbly personality, natural conversational skills, and diplomatic chatter.

With its twin engines roaring and rotors blowing wind and dust, the pilot taxied the airplane onto the tarmac and then cut the engines. Three Aussie soldiers raced out to push the mobile stairway up against the plane.

A moment later, as flashbulbs began to explode, the main cabin door of the plane opened. A woman appeared from inside the plane, stood at the open doorway, and began to smile and wave. She was tall, perhaps in her early sixties, and neither particularly attractive nor unattractive. She was rather plain looking in appearance and wore a drab, light blue suit dress. Except for the pale blue color, her suit could almost pass for a woman officer's uniform in the US Army or Marine Corps. She wore on her head what looked like a soldier's cap—also light in color.

But the woman was not US military, that was for sure. And her pedestrian looks did not stop the crowd from clapping while oohing and aahing.

The woman began to descend the stairway as the Victoria governor and the Melbourne lord mayor and their wives inched closer to the base of the stairwell. Rupertus waited behind them, content to let the political dignitaries have the first bite. He would get plenty of facetime later with the guest of honor.

When the woman descended the stairs and stepped on the tarmac, a series of smiles, handshakes, and exchanges of pleasantries unfolded with the dignitaries. As she chatted with the lord mayor, Rupertus saw that the uniform she wore was that of the American Red Cross. And she had a Red Cross pin on the front center of her cap. The woman oozed with a charisma that made one forget her very plain looks, a charm that almost seemed to rival that of his dear Sleepy.

A moment later, she stepped away from the circle of political dignitaries and walked toward him. "Ah, my dear General Rupertus. I have heard so many wonderful things about you—a great warrior to lead our Marines in this part of the world. Franklin is so pleased with your leadership," the First Lady of the United States said.

"Thank you, ma'am. And likewise, Mrs. Roosevelt, if I may, I've heard wonderful things about you, too. The Marine Corps, especially, appreciates your work with the Red Cross. And may I also add that it is an honor to meet you finally."

A broad smile broke across Eleanor Roosevelt's face. "I understand that you will be my Marine escort here in Melbourne."

"Yes, ma'am," Rupertus said as he bowed. "The honor and privilege will be mine."

"Well, as I'm sure you have seen, we have a jam-packed itinerary. I hope to visit the Red Cross and as many hospitals and children's facilities as possible. Do you think you can keep up with me, General?"

Rupertus chuckled. "That may be a challenge, ma'am, but I will do my very best."

"Excellent. Shall we get on with it, then?"

"Yes, ma'am, our squad car is parked right over here, with the driver in place and ready to go. We have cars for your staff and entourage right behind the lead car."

"And I hope and assume you will be accompanying me in the lead car, dear General?"

"If you will have me, yes, ma'am."

"I would not have it any other way."

"Very well. If you would come with me, please."

The announcement from the White House that Eleanor Roosevelt wanted to tour Australia and various other military encampments in the South Pacific had set off multiple alarm bells within the higher echelons of the military. The president, Commandant Holcomb, and Vandegrift knew Rupertus had to be her escort in Melbourne.

Eleanor, Rupertus, and the entourage set off together to accomplish her mission. They visited Marine camps, hospitals, YMCA huts, and a children's hospital overlooking the sea. At that hospital, Rupertus had the Marine Band play for the children and staff. A young girl with cholera they visited so touched him that he had his aide get a stuffed koala from the car that he was saving for his son Pat and gave it to the girl.

Eleanor Roosevelt and General Rupertus. Melbourne, Victoria, Australia, September 9, 1943.
(USMC PHOTO)

Later, they enjoyed a dinner at the Red Cross Club, where Rupertus enthralled the first lady with stories of the Pacific, training the Marines at Mount Martha, working with the army, and what might lay ahead.

That night, when she returned to Sydney, Eleanor Roosevelt penned a personal note to Rupertus, which was delivered to him by courier the next day.

> *The Australia Hotel*
> *Sydney, N.S.W*
> *September 8, 1943*
> *My Dear General,*
> *I want to thank you for all the time you had to spend going about with me & for your kind hospitality which I greatly appreciated. I hated to wake you each time but realize it is perhaps necessary. Your staff was a wonderful-looking group, and everyone around you was so kind that I hope you will convey my thanks to them. If any of your group of officers wants me to contact their families upon my return, will you tell them to send me a line with the address?*
> *With thanks to you.*
> *Very Sincerely Yours,*
> *Eleanor Roosevelt*

Chapter 58

Goodenough Island

Now under the overall operational command of the US Army's General Douglas MacArthur, the division left Australia in September 1943 to train in New Guinea. Their next mission was Cape Gloucester on the western end of New Britain, a 350-mile-long volcanic island in the Bismarck Archipelago of the Southwest Pacific.

MacArthur wanted to use the amphibious 1st Marine Division to put a noose around the Japs' necks at Rabaul, the huge Japanese navy base sitting on the far eastern tip of New Britain. If Rupertus and his 1st Marines could take the two airfields on Cape Gloucester, on the same island as Rabaul, they would neutralize the enemy and tighten their grip.

Colonel W. C. Lattimore (USA), Major General Rupertus, and Captain McLeod check out amphibious training on Goodenough Island. (USMC PHOTO)

They called the Cape Gloucester plan "Operation Dexterity." Under the plan, Rupertus would report to General MacArthur through Lieutenant General Walter Krueger of the 6th Army.

Rupertus wasn't crazy about being under the army. None of the senior US Navy or Marine Corps officers liked it. But Roosevelt had approved it. Thus, Rupertus's orders were to secure the beachhead and then capture the airports and eliminate the enemy presence on Cape Gloucester.

After eight months of R&R in Australia, followed by intensive training, morale was high, and the division was ready for action.

On November 14, Rupertus's birthday, his staff threw a party to celebrate.

Rupertus slices a turkey for his birthday party. Seated, smiling, is Colonel William Whaling. (USMC PHOTO)

Major General Bill Rupertus with Father Fitzgerald "Padre," Goodenough Island.
(USMC PHOTO)

The large division split between Cape Sudest, Goodenough Island, and Finschhafen, all part of Papua New Guinea in the Solomon Sea. The plan was for the division to regroup on Goodenough Island by December 15 in preparation for D-Day on December 26, 1943.

Intelligence estimated over 10,500 Japanese were in Cape Gloucester and more than 90,000 in Rabaul under Lieutenant General Sakia's command with the Japanese Imperial Army's 17th Division.

Photographs and relief maps of Cape Gloucester showed narrow beaches, a sizable coastal plain, soaring mountains, and dense, wet jungle. The natives in New Guinea warned Rupertus about the heat, humidity, malaria-breeding insects, snakes, and monsoons that would dump torrential rain on the Marines.

Rupertus took note, as he and his staff were thick into battle planning. He realized the island's deep jungle terrain would require unique air support. One day, while viewing the army's artillery air spotting exercises, a possible solution emerged.

Why not use the army's small Piper Cub planes for transport, reconnaissance, artillery spotting, and other vital missions on Cape Gloucester? As a pilot himself, Rupertus liked this idea and cut through the red tape to form a mini squadron to assist the men of his division.

General MacArthur promised to give Rupertus twelve vintage L-4 Piper Cubs from the army by the next operation. Rupertus needed pilots to fly the aircraft and mechanics to fix and service them. The "Air Liaison Unit" was in full start-up mode. He tasked his pilot, naval aviator Captain Theodore A. Petras, to oversee it.

Petras sent an advertisement throughout the division. Four pilots and twenty-two Marines, of varying piloting and mechanical skills, responded.

The Air Liaison Unit included an ex–bush pilot, two graduates from the Civilian Pilot Training Program, two men owning personal planes back home, an artillery officer, a tank officer, two privates first class from special weapons, truck mechanics, drivers, and a bulldozer maintenance man.

Captain Petras and his co-pilot, Second Lieutenant Bob Murphy, began testing the flight skills of the Marine Corps volunteers. Their goal was to narrow the field down to a limited group of seven pilots to fly the planes and a few more-mechanical Marines to service them.

General Rupertus was in command of the overall ground operation and capturing the airports. He selected the landing beaches and solved the

Rupertus greets an officer with plans. (USMC PHOTO)

logistical problem of the shallow and narrow waters around New Britain by using smaller ships, no larger than an LST (Landing Ship, Tank), to transport troops onto the beach.

Less cargo room on the boat meant carrying minimal equipment. Rupertus ordered his officers to tell their men, "Only bring the equipment you need to live or fight."

The naval and air 7th Fleet support for the operation was a combination of American and Australian ships under Vice Admiral Kinkaid. Seven task forces made up the fleet responsible for the Cape Gloucester landing. However, Task Force 74 (cruisers and destroyers) under British Rear Admiral Crutchley, RN, Task Force 76 (amphibious force) under the command of Rear Admiral Barbey, and Task Force 70.01 (PT boats used to cover the left flank of amphibious force by patrolling Vitaz and Dampier Straits) were of primary importance to the Marine Corps landing.

On the overnight voyage to Cape Gloucester, Rupertus would join Rear Admiral Barbey on his flagship USS *Conyngham*. Brigadier General Lemuel

Major General Chamberlain, Lieutenant General Krueger, General MacArthur, Vice Admiral Kincaid, Brigadier General Whitehead (5th Air Corps), Major General Rupertus. Cape Gloucester, 1943. (USMC PHOTO)

General MacArthur and General Rupertus walking with officers and staff.
(USMC PHOTO)

"Lem" C. Shepherd Jr., as assistant division commander, would command the logistics on the beachhead and expand the Marines' perimeter to the south and into Borgen Bay. He would arrive by LST.

On December 14, 1943, General MacArthur and General Krueger visited Rupertus at the 1st Marine Division command post on Goodenough Island in Papua New Guinea to discuss the division's proposed plan for the upcoming Cape Gloucester invasion.

Sweat covered their faces and drenched their clothes as Colonel Pollack displayed the maps on a large table in the hot, humid CP, and discussion began.

General MacArthur presented his thoughts and then looked up and asked, "Does the 1st Marine Division like this plan?"

Pollack clenched his teeth, inhaled deeply, and looked at Rupertus and then MacArthur. "We don't like it. Including paratroops in the plan makes it too risky."

Major General Rupertus, commanding general of a Marine division (right), points out a spot on the map for General Douglas MacArthur, supreme commander of Allied Forces in the Southwest Pacific, as Major General Chamberlin (left) and Lieutenant General Walter Krueger look on during a conference at which plans for an offensive against the Japanese were discussed.
(USMC PHOTO BY SERGEANT ROBERT HOWARD)

The outburst seemed to surprise MacArthur, who made a few remarks and left. But MacArthur conceded most of the points the Marines wanted and eliminated paratroops from the operation.

The Japanese were already anticipating the invasion. Soon after MacArthur's visit, Radio Tokyo reported, "The 1st Marine Division, assorted cutthroats' degenerates, and jailbirds have been chased out of Melbourne and are now in camp in New Guinea and will try to invade Cape Gloucester. I am pleased to add that our soldiers are fully prepared to repulse these insolent attempts. The jungles will run red with the blood of Guadalcanal butchers."

Christmas card from officers and men to Rupertus (December 1943).

The Japanese threats did not deter Rupertus in the least. Yes, he knew that some of his Marines would shed blood at Cape Gloucester. But as far as he was concerned, the Japanese had better worry about shedding their own blood. The general would do everything in his power to ensure that more Japanese blood was shed than American blood.

D-Day would come the day after Christmas, and the Marines did what they could to remember the holy season while preparing for battle at the same time. Three days before Christmas Eve, December 21, the division celebrated with dinner and religious services. They dined on steak, turkey, potatoes, green beans, and Rupertus's favorite—ice cream. The regimental

Merry Christmas
and a New Year that
will bring Hers back
permanently to you and
the "chillun". Keep smiling
and your chin up —
We're strong because
you all back there are
holding us up with
your love and cheer.
— Bill

Peace on Earth
Good Will
Toward Men.

1st Marine Division Christmas card.

chaplain offered to hold a midnight Christmas Eve service for all and a special midnight mass for the Catholic men.

Hours before midnight, the skies opened and rain flooded the camp. Yet the Marines and their commanding general, Rupertus, came out for the service. As they knelt together side by side on the wet, muddy ground, Rupertus prayed for his Marines and the crucial battle ahead.

The following day, Rupertus sent a letter to all officers.

Confidential US forces, APO 320, December 22, 1943
Message to all Officers
As it is physically impossible for me to address each of you, I take this method to impart the following:
1. Leadership is of primary importance and extends down to the echelons of command. Every officer must lead his men. The leadership displayed by the officers of the force means the difference between a clear-out victory and a shoddy one, which will be open to criticism. You have the tools, by your leadership, to do the job!
2. Conserve water, food, and ammunition so there will be enough for all. Waste of either is considered criminal and an aid to your enemy. Do not permit men to fire promiscuously to create noise and build up false security. Make every shot count. Be sure of your target then give 'em hell.
3. The world, other folks back home, other Marines will watch anxiously the reports of the progress of this course. You have once scored an acknowledged unparalleled victory over the Japs. Another such victory is in the making. Any man of this for us is a better fighter than any Jap of any force.
God be with you,
W.H. Rupertus, Major General, US Marine Corps

Chapter 59

USS *Conyngham*
Bismarck Sea
D-Day Cape Gloucester
December 26, 1943

On the predawn morning of December 26, 1943, the morning after Christmas, with stars above and a slight fog over the water, the fleet raced in the dark toward Cape Gloucester, on the northwest corner of New Britain. As the sun crusted the horizon at 0600 hours, from the bridge of the USS *Conyngham* Rupertus watched across the waters as the US and Australian Navies, and B-24 Liberator bombers finished bombing the hell out of the eastern tip of New Britain Island, shattering the dawn's quiet ascent for a full ninety minutes. It was an exciting yet chilling show for the Marines waiting, again, for battle.

The US Navy had already shelled Cape Gloucester for twenty-six days to soften the resistance at the beachhead. However, the shelling and pounding made it easy for the Japanese to figure out the Americans' next target.

"This is a night scene of our anti-aircraft fire against a Jap plane—isn't it pretty? Tojo would have a small chance to survive this—which he didn't!" (Rupertus quote). Cape Gloucester, December 1943. (USMC PHOTO)

The smoke cleared, and the massive and ominous target, known as "Target Hill," became visible.

When they hit the beaches, the Marines would face the robust Japanese Matsuda Force, commanded by transportation expert Major General Iwao Matsuda. The Matsuda Force included the 65th Brigade (which took part in Bataan), the 4th Shipping Command, and elements of the 27th and 51st Divisions. Their mission: to protect Cape Gloucester and keep the Japanese supply lines moving to New Guinea.

Rupertus made his battle plans clear. His Marines would first capture the "Yellow Beaches" on the east coast of the large peninsula closest to the two strategic airports, six miles inland from the beachhead. Much like Henderson Field on Guadalcanal, the airports were valuable for launching air attacks on the Japanese stronghold at Rabaul, three hundred miles away, at the opposite end of the island.

Rupertus organized the division's attack force into three combat teams: The 7th Marine Regiment, commanded by Colonel Julian Frisbee, would attack and then hold the beachhead at "Target Hill." The 1st Marine Regiment, commanded by Colonel Bill Whaling, would also attack the beachhead and then move inland to seize the airfields. Colonel John Selden's 5th Marine Regiment would serve as Division Reserve, and the 11th Marines Artillery, commanded by Colonels Robert Pepper and William Harrison, would provide ground fire support.

At the exact time the 7th and 1st Regiments hit Yellow Beach, the 2nd Battalion, 1st Marines, led by Rupertus's friend from Washington, James Masters, would land on the designated "Green Beach," seven miles southwest of Cape Gloucester, to block, defend, and patrol the coastal trail from enemy movement.

Naval fire support enabled the Marines to disembark from the ship at 0746 hours, a few hundred yards offshore. They slid into their landing barges, jumped out into three feet of water, and stormed the island, encountering little resistance.

That first wave of the attack force included two battalions of the 7th Marine Regiment, commanded by Julian Frisbee. The 3rd Battalion, commanded by Lieutenant Colonel William K. Williams, landed on "Yellow Beach 1." The 1st Battalion, commanded by Lieutenant Colonel John E. Weber, landed on the nearby "Yellow Beach 2."

Unlike the wide white beach with palm trees and coconuts at Guadalcanal, the Cape Gloucester beach was black sand and narrow, with tree branches arching over the sand into the water. As the Marines moved ashore in the waves, they hoisted their nine-and-a-half-pound M1 rifles above their heads to avoid drenching them.

Once they hit the beach, only seven hundred yards of slim shoreline separated the two battalions. The second wave of Marines, Battalion Landing Team 21, part of 2nd Battalion, 1st Marines, was called "Stoneface Group." Commanded by Rupertus's friend Lieutenant Colonel James Masters, Stoneface Group landed on Green Beach at 0748 hours, carving out a beachhead fifteen hundred feet long and five hundred feet deep. Their mission—defend the coastal trail west of 6,600-foot-high Mount Talawe to prevent any Japanese reinforcements from entering or escaping. They soon found themselves wrestling through the deep jungle of the tropical rainforest.

By 0815 hours, more Marine battalions hit Yellow Beach 1. Moments later the 3rd Battalion, 1st Marines, led by Lieutenant Colonel Joseph F.

Hankins, passed through the 3rd Battalion, 7th Marines, veering north toward the airport. By 0845 hours, the 2nd Battalion, 7th Marines, commanded by Lieutenant Colonel Odell M. Conolly, arrived to join the 7th's 1st and 3rd Battalions on the beachhead.

The 1st Battalion, 1st Marines, arrived on Yellow Beach 1 and joined Hankins's 3rd Battalion to march to the airports in the north. Then the 11th Marines Artillery came ashore to set up their amphibian tractors and supporting weapons.

With no initial enemy gunfire, an arduous journey to the coastal trail began as they hacked through the mangrove swamps, in water that was waist and shoulder high, rifles held high in one hand, with knives and machetes in the other.

The enemy commander, General Matsuda, knew this tropical sludge would challenge the Americans. As the Marines headed inland to find the trail to the airfields, they saw a few enemy guns aimed at the water, but no enemy in sight, other than the dreadful terrain.

At 1015 hours, General Rupertus and his staff arrived on the beach. Rupertus's assistant division commander, Brigadier General Lem Shepherd, and his staff also came ashore on D-Day.

Navy supply boats delivered heavy equipment, food, and supplies. Army trucks arrived with more supplies and acted as a mobile supply dump.

By 1440 hours D-Day, Marines had secured the beachhead, with the 1st Marines marching toward the airfields.

But as the battalions hunkered down on their objectives, the Japanese arrived to attack the fleet by air, with sixty fighter jets and twenty dive bombers. The battle for Cape Gloucester was on.

As the Marines pushed inland, the Japanese attacked Borgen Bay, south of the Yellow Beaches. Their bombers hit and sank the destroyer USS *Brownson*, killing 108, and severely damaged another. During the sudden flurry and chaos of so many enemy planes in the air, friendly fire downed four American bombers, causing fifteen Marine casualties.

As darkness settled in and rain dumped on the island, an entire battalion of Japanese ground troops, embedded in camouflaged bunkers in the deep roots of the massively tall trees, and snipers lying low in the Kunai grass, appeared out of nowhere and opened fire.

The Marines had excellent fire discipline, as Rupertus had trained them before the battle. Remembering their commander's training, they stayed

Marines wade through deep water at Battle of Cape Gloucester on D-Day,
December 26, 1943. (USMC PHOTO)

cautious and held their own firepower until the right moment, at which point they unleashed with a fury. The 7th Marines decimated the Japanese, killing virtually all the enemy in the beach area.

*****

Cape Gloucester
Command Post
December 27, 1943

The following morning, as rough waves found the black beaches of Cape Gloucester, Rupertus considered his options.

The first Jap ambush had been fierce. Rupertus knew in his gut that more ambushes were coming, and he wanted more firepower. He contacted General Krueger and called up the Division Reserve (5th Marines) waiting on Goodenough Island. The 5th Marines, known as Combat Team A, were led by Colonel Selden, whom Rupertus had known since their days in Haiti and Peking.

The 5th Marines landed on Beach Blue, three miles to the right of the Yellow Beaches, to join the 1st Marines, led by Whaling, in capturing the airfields.

They quickly learned the Japs weren't their only enemy. The weather was awful, far worse than on Guadalcanal.

As a monsoon descended on them, the 5th Marines marched inland to assist the 1st, initially finding little enemy resistance. But the heavier rainfall bogged them down. Then a maze of enemy defenses and trenches sucked them into a bloody battle they would term "Hell's Point."

The bloody fight in the rain, which lasted over an hour, left nine Marines dead and thirty-six wounded, along with 260 dead Japs. With the battle over, two battalions of Marines led by Colonel Selden pressed on toward the airport through deep jungle swampland.

By December 29, the Marines arrived at the airfields, which appeared abandoned, and created a perimeter to defend Airfield 2.

But on a peak diagonally across from the airfields, looking down at the Marines, 1,400 men of the Jap 53rd Infantry, commanded by Colonel Kouki Sumiya were waiting to attack. His orders were to destroy the Marines defending the airports at all cost.

After a savage fight that raged for nearly twenty-four hours, the airports fell to the Marines on December 30, four days after they took the Cape Gloucester beachhead. Rupertus's instincts to call in reinforcements had been correct.

Rupertus called for a brief ceremony at Airfield 2 to celebrate their success. They hoisted the American flag high on a pole located in front of a burned Japanese bomber. They knelt around the flagpole, with Rupertus leading them in prayer to honor the lives lost. After praying, he circled men around him to read a radio telegram dispatched to General Walter Krueger for delivery to General MacArthur:

> *The 1st Marine Division Presents to you an early New Year Gift, the complete airdrome [sic] of Cape Gloucester. Situation well in hand due to the fighting spirit of our troops, the usual Marine luck, and the help of God. By noon both strips were occupied. Consolidating perimeter defense around drome.*

And then he read the response from General MacArthur:

> *I extend my heartiest congratulations to your officers and men. I am filled with pride and gratitude for their resourceful determination in capturing Cape Gloucester. Your gallant Division has maintained the immortal record of the Marine Corps and covered itself with glory.*

General Rupertus reads a radio telegram from President Roosevelt. (USMC PHOTO)

Marines in prayer. (USMC PHOTO)

Near the front lines of attack: Colonel Frisbee, General Rupertus, Colonel Pollack, and war correspondent J. L. Shafer.

The badly bombed airfield needed the army aviation engineers to whip it back in shape to be operable for large planes. However, it was in perfect condition for Rupertus's Air Liaison Unit's small Piper Cubs.

The airports were secure, but on New Year's Day, the Japs launched a series of attacks that would harass the Marines for weeks to come.

Once the Marines had captured the airfield and created a perimeter, General Shepherd took two battalions with tank support to clear Borgen Bay.

The next day, the Japanese attacked a small group of 7th Marines defending their observation point on Target Hill and hit a machine gun nest, killing two Marines and severely wounding the gunner. The injured Marine gunner continued firing on them with more than five thousand rounds until someone could take over, fending off the attack. Gaining intelligence from a dead Japanese officer on Target Hill, Shepherd learned of a Japanese encampment near a creek and sent Sherman tanks ahead to clear the road.

The stream was named "Suicide Creek" after the fierce battle that ensued, which ended when the Seabees arrived to build a corduroy road through the wet, flat ground for the tanks and troops to pass over so they could destroy the enemy. It ended January 5 with the help of the Seabees, but not without loss of American lives: 41 Marines were killed and 218 wounded or missing. Hundreds of Japanese died.

Native helping wounded man along trail from Aragalpua to Agulupella, New Britain, February 5, 1944.
(USMC PHOTO BY PRIVATE ROSENBURG)

"This is jungle warfare!" (Rupertus quote). (USMC PHOTO)

"Blood transfusion in the jungle just behind the front lines!" (Rupertus quote).
(USMC PHOTO)

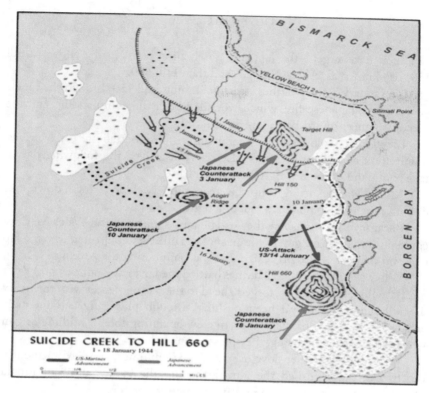

SUICIDE CREEK TO HILL 660
1 – 18 January 1944

"Razorback Hill that was taken by Whaling's Regt. overlooking the airfield" (Rupertus quote). (USMC PHOTO)

Their next target—the Japanese observation point in the cliffs on Hill 150, also known as "Aogiri Ridge." And then Hill 660.

On January 7, the Marines started climbing Hill 150 through the muck, facing heavy Japanese fire, which wounded both the commanding and the executive officer of 3rd Battalion, 5th Marines.

Lieutenant Colonel Puller, commanding 3rd Battalion, 7th Marines, briefly took charge until Colonel Lewis Walt arrived the following day to take command of the 3rd Battalion on Hill 150.

As the Marines trudged up the steep, slippery slope facing a downpour of both rain and Jap bullets, a hell of a fight followed.

Because of the monsoon, they had no tank support. But if Walt's Marines could push their heavy gun to the crest of the hill, they could eradicate the Jap observation post on Aogiri Ridge that was hammering the Marines.

While the 11th and 7th Marines battled the Japanese on the ridge, Walt's 3rd Battalion, 7th Marines, forged ahead to the narrow center with the heavy 37-millimeter gun they'd been pushing. Though physically and mentally exhausted, with four of the nine-man crew operating the 37-millimeter gun wounded and morale diving, they pressed on.

Walt and his gunner dove over to the 37-millimeter gun. Miraculously, the two of them pushed the gun farther up the incline until additional Marines arrived to propel the massive weapon to the top.

The Marines battled the worst weather and terrain conditions they had faced in the Pacific. New Britain was one of the many Pacific islands not claimed by any European power, and for good reason. Nearly everybody caught malaria, dysentery, fungus infection, dengue fever, or scrub typhus.

Falling trees killed twenty Marines and lightning struck at least three others. A corporal found a nine-foot python in his foxhole during an air raid, and an alligator chewed off the arm of an army officer. Nine inches of rain fell in a single night, causing one stream to shift its course two hundred yards, washing out two regimental command posts and depositing an eel in Rupertus's spare field shoes.

Yet, despite fighting the vicious elements along with the Japanese, the Marines continued to battle for Hill 150, as the Japanese had entrenched themselves on the top. The Japanese made a few suicidal stands on the day the hill fell. A savage Jap counterattack on the following night was believed to have been a mass suicide by units that had decided not to survive if it involved the hill's capture. Perhaps the Marines' tenacity was the last straw that broke the Japanese defenders' morale.

When Rupertus learned of Walt's courage, he recommended that Aogori Ridge be named "Walt's Ridge." Walt also received the Navy Cross for his leadership.

By January 11, Master's Stoneface Group had fought the Japanese in a violent battle, killing 256 Japs while losing six Marines on a patrol inland, with another thirteen Marines wounded. As the Stoneface Group arrived to assist in the airfields' defense, they also had five POWs tagging along.

Meanwhile, General Shepherd and his Marines continued attacking the Japanese post on Hill 660. The challenge of climbing 660 feet to meet the enemy was given to the 3rd Battalion, 7th Marines, commanded by Lieutenant Henry Buse Jr.

On January 13, 1944, the battalion trudged to the top, climbing through deep ravines and tangling vines as the rain and enemy firepower pummeled them.

As combat correspondent Vincent Tubbs said to another reporter the next morning as they raced to the scene and talked to a Marine at the communications post:

> It turned out to be the meanest fighting the Marines have ever experienced—even worse than Guadalcanal. Jap casualties exceeding three thousand. Ours were not meager. Men climbing the hill had to crawl along on all fours in the sludge, their muddy hands grasping vines and feet digging into the earth where the heel of the preceding Marine had left a dent. All the time, the enemy fought back from caves, gun nests, and pillboxes. The Marines fought for almost every inch of ground.

By almost completely surrounding the enemy hiding in pillboxes and machine gun nests, they created a pocket to envelope the Japanese with all they had left in grit and ammo. Using 105-millimeter guns, 75-millimeter howitzers, 50-caliber machine guns, Sherman tanks, and the mortar platoon, the final objective of the assault phase, Hill 660, was captured on January 16.

The assault phase was over, and rooting out the remaining enemy became top priority. Tubbs caught a ride back on a tank, and as they rolled down the hill, they saw a group of men trudging through the muck.

The tank operator slowed the tank and said, "Hey, that's General Rupertus!"

"Sir, would you like a ride?"

Rupertus replied with a wry smile, "Walk in four feet of this muck or plow through with a tank? I'd love a ride. Thanks. Drop me off at the CP."

Kunai grass on Cape Gloucester. (USMC PHOTO)

Rupertus hopped in, greeted Tubbs, chatted a bit, and then jumped out when they arrived at his command post. "Thanks again, Marines. See you out there."

On January 21, General Sakia ordered Mastuda to evacuate Cape Gloucester and withdraw his forces to a rendezvous point nine miles to the east. Disregarding the order for fear of his troops' safety, Matsuda left his command post, and his Matsuda Force marched 170 miles to Cape Hoskins instead.

Throughout this battle, the Air Liaison Unit's primary mission was artillery spotting. But requests for food, supplies, and medical equipment flooded in, and the pilots worked overtime to deliver. If there was a call from infantry, however, some pilots had to return to ground duty, leaving only four pilots flying seven days a week, often for eight to ten hours a day.

General Rupertus cooling his dawgs, Cape Gloucester. (USMC PHOTO)

When Rupertus found out about the aviation staffing problem, he borrowed pilots from the Seabees and the 12th Defense Battalion. Even the general's pilot began to fly missions.

To get the job done, warriors flew double duty as pilots.

For example, the Air Liaison Unit's Lieutenant Colonel Charles Nees commanded the 5th Battalion, 11th Marines, and Captain Petras, Rupertus's pilot, and Captain Murphy began flying missions in their spare time when not needed on the ground. Paul Perkins, machinist first class, came from the Seabee battalion attached to the 17th Engineers to fly missions, as did PFC Woodrow Witherspoon from the 12th Battalion.

Lieutenant Colonel Nees wanted to get a better idea of the terrain on the Cape. Like Guadalcanal, their tattered, old maps were often wrong. With Rupertus's approval, Nees used the Air Liaison Unit to begin correcting the maps for future use.

To accomplish this task, the planes positioned themselves over the targets shown on the map. Then air observers on the ground called in to mark the proper position, confirming or enhancing the old charts, allowing for incredible accuracy.

By February 1944, in full control of Cape Gloucester, Rupertus still needed to mop up and wipe out the remnants of Japanese in the area. He assigned that job to his go-to ground officer, Lieutenant Colonel Chesty Puller.

Puller led the "Uncle Patrol," which consisted of over five hundred men, to cross the island of New Britain and mop up any Japanese in the deep jungle near the airstrip. But just as a patrol headed out on its mission, it started raining like hell.

Torrential flooding made it impossible to get supplies or food in to the 5th; no jeeps, trucks, or tanks could get through the deep mud. Puller's Marines tirelessly looked above for the never-ending battle with enemy snipers, either tied to low trees or hiding high up in trees.

When the Army Air Corps dropped cases of K-rations so large and over such a vast area, the Marines on the ground in the jungle had to run for cover or dig a foxhole to hide so they were not pummeled or killed by the K boxes.

Frustrated by multiple challenges, including lack of food and supplies, and their slow progress, Puller called headquarters for assistance. Rupertus responded by sending the small Air Liaison Unit to the rescue, which supported Puller's 5th by air for more than twenty days.

The small planes held only two boxes of K-rations, so they were safer sky deliveries for the Marines on the ground. To do this effectively, the pilots flew to the drop zone and then radioed for clearance. A few Marines on the ground ran ahead, cleared and marked an area for the boxes to be dropped, and then ran the hell away to take cover. The small planes skimmed the trees, and once the pilot spotted the marking, he tossed out the boxes and headed back to the airfield to reload.

The pilots logged multiple trips a day to and from the 5th Marines' base camp, delivering supplies, including food, barbed wire, mail, tools, plasma for the injured, and anything else the troops needed, even sunscreen.

As the Japanese retreated, Colonel Puller and his regiment raided Japanese commander Major General Iwao Matsuda's abandoned headquarters, located inland on Cape Gloucester, and were stunned to find an elaborate command post.

The Japanese general's domicile was a three-story dwelling built of imported red spruce, with hardwood stairs and floors inlaid with Japanese designs. On the second floor was an imported four-poster bed with a mattress eight inches thick.

Puller grabbed a wicker chair that had belonged to Matsuda and found a gold mine of intelligence, including documents the Japanese had buried versus burned. Puller sent the chair to his superior, General Rupertus, for his use in the division's new headquarters.

On February 4, Rupertus wrote a five-page letter to General Vandegrift to summarize the status of the 1st Marine Division after taking his own Beechcraft to a conference with General Krueger in Finschhafen on February 2, where they discussed the plan for the division under MacArthur.

Krueger thought the Marines could stay in place and get comfortable in the jungle for several months, with their next job in a group of islands, under the command of COMSOWESPAC (Commander Southwest Pacific Area—General MacArthur). In this letter, Rupertus wrote, "We have learned much, especially from the errors of Guadalcanal, and I feel sure that we've profited from them in this operation. It has been one of the smoothest, most coordinated operations that's been my experience to participate in, even including our peacetime exercises."

On February 10, General Krueger declared that Operation Dexterity was completed.

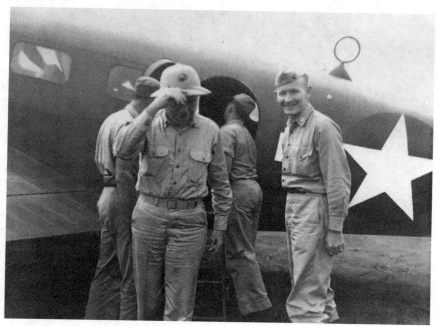

General Rupertus tips his hat and smiles at Captain McLeod. (USMC PHOTO)

Rupertus in front of a plane with happy Marines on Goodenough Island. (USMC PHOTO)

Rupertus and officers at Cape Gloucester. (USMC PHOTO)

Rupertus points at a map with Colonels Simms and Selden to right. (USMC PHOTO)

*****

Cape Gloucester, New Britain
Command Post
March 4, 1944

By month three of the intense combat in challenging terrain, the goals had been achieved. The Japanese were forced to the western part of the island, and praise for the Marines was widespread.

Back in the command post on March 4, 1944, in the quiet of the night, Rupertus sat down in his new wicker chair to write to Sleepy's parents in response to their February letter to him.

March 4, 1944
The Commanding General
First Marine Division
Dear Dixie and Paddy,
I just received your friendly letter, which I enjoyed very much. At the same, I feel helpless about my beloved Sleepy girl. I love her so much and our precious son

"Outside German house on New Britain" (Rupertus quote). (USMC PHOTO)

Pat. It makes me, at times, so lonesome for them. I've told Sleepy that I thought she was overdoing it, keeping her thin figure. Maybe it's the strain of waiting and hoping for me to come back—it's hard when you care for someone and that someone is out of reach.

Thanks for the newspaper clippings—what kind of general washes his own feet in mud! Sleepy wrote to me about the newsreel where I walked right toward them. That must have been uncanny! Glad I had a smile. Steve has all the luck, darn it. But I'm happy one of the three of us can be with their family during war.

I don't know where Bev is. Do you? Your news about Sleepy and Eleanor Roosevelt having tea together is news. I am eager to hear all about it! I hope she doesn't have any competition in rank—she won't win looks, I know. I am all OK and having fun with that dirty rat Tojo who won't stand still long enough for me to sock him good.

Tell Paddy the PT boats last night sunk up a Jap barge sneaking out and later found it contained some geisha girls! The navy's sold on us. They will back us up in anything, which makes it double for us as a team.

You know I will be tickled to see Pat. He is a handsome smiling boy and loves his mother so much that it is the best part of him I love. Keep the mint bed growing. I'll bring the "wherewith," you supply the mint!
Lots of love to you both,
Sincerely, Bill

Chapter 60

Operation Appease
March 6, 1944

Rupertus learned that the next Allied mission, "Operation Appease," was to halt retreating Japanese on the northern coast of New Britain's Willaumez Peninsula and capture the airport on Talasea.

MacArthur's logistics were never straightforward, and Rupertus communicated this issue in a February 18 letter to Vandegrift, now commandant of the Marine Corps.

Commandant Vandegrift wanted Rupertus to return to Marine Corps headquarters in March 1944 to assess the troops, talk with the secretary of the navy, recruit, and do the same public relations tour Vandegrift himself had done under Commandant Holcomb after Guadalcanal.

Rupertus made tentative plans to return to the states by mid-March. But MacArthur heard about Vandegrift's plans and threw a fit. MacArthur wanted the division under his control and not returned to the navy's control under Admiral Nimitz. He quickly planned more attacks for the division beyond the Cape Gloucester objective. A political tug-of-war seemed to be erupting between McArthur and the US Navy over future control of the 1st Marine Division.

As part of the MacArthur versus Nimitz competition for the division (at least from Rupertus's perspective), General Krueger, MacArthur's operations officer, ordered Rupertus to transfer the 1st Marine Division's shore party battalion, medium line tank company, and the entire Marine amphibious tractor battalion to the army's 1st Cavalry Division for the Manus operation the army was conducting. Then Rupertus received another order by radio from Krueger to turn over all of his buffaloes—armored LVTs (Landing Vehicles Tracked) for carrying troops.

Rupertus had followed Krueger's previous orders but resisted this last one. His Marines would not get the cover they needed in unarmored alligators in an assault on fortified positions. He recalled in the back of his mind MacArthur's remark that he would fight this division to its destruction.

General Rupertus chats with Lieutenant Colonel Charles G. Meints. (USMC PHOTO)

In the letter to Vandegrift, Rupertus wrote about MacArthur's demands to pluck assets from the 1st Division:

> *I can assure you that we are not afraid to do any damn job the Army presented to this Division, and we will do it well and efficiently. My men and officers are at the peak of morale and fighting efficiency, and I know that we can go through these Japs like tissue paper. But that means the loss of fine American Marines to kill several thousand bastardly Japs, which will not materially affect the entire war with the Japanese in the Pacific. Why not just have the entire Division do the job together, so all the men had the coverage they needed? Better yet, let the Army do it and find an Army Division they could use.*

Nonetheless, MacArthur's planned attack on Talasea, "Operation Appease," was moving forward. Rupertus ordered Brigadier General O. P. Smith and his 1st Battalion, 5th Marines, to land at Volupai Plantation on the western shore of the Willaumez Peninsula and then trek through the jungle toward Talasea to destroy the estimated 430 Japanese of the 1st Battalion, 54th Infantry, commanded by Captain Kiyomatsu Terenuma, at Talasea.

The 1st Battalion arrived on March 6, facing no significant enemy firepower other than mortar and sporadic rifle fire. They captured the Talasea airfield on March 8.

Then all hell broke loose. The Japanese counterattacked, killing 17 Marines and wounding another 114. The fighting raged for several days before the Marines got the upper hand, killing 150 Japanese.

Once they secured the airstrip at Talasea, Rupertus flew in to monitor the battle from the front. He flew into a hornet's nest. During the next few days, the Japs attacked the 5th Marines by gunfire and mortar fire. The 5th Marines began to suffer losses.

The continued Jap attacks angered Rupertus so much that soon after he landed on the island, Rupertus called one of his pilots, Technical Sergeant

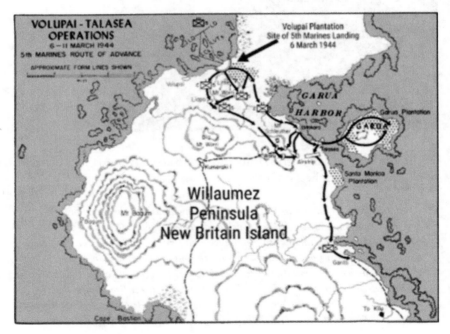

Lowell Schrepfer, into his command post. "Schrepfer, tomorrow morning, at the break of dawn, I want you to fly me out beyond the front, to look for pockets of Japs."

It was a dangerous notion for the division commander to fly in a small plane over enemy territory. But Rupertus feared nothing and no one and wanted to increase the attacks against the Japs.

Next morning, as Schrepfer revved his plane in the dark, Rupertus walked out with something bulging under his shirt and pants and carrying a lumpy sack. Seeing Schrepfer's confusion about what the hell he was carrying, Rupertus looked at the sergeant and grinned. "Grenades."

They took off at sunrise, searching for Jap hideouts under the coconut palms in the jungle. When they spotted the Jap positions, Rupertus ordered Schrepfer to fly in low; then he tossed live grenades out the door and shouted expletives at the Japs below. The enemy did not return fire, lest they expose their position for massive bombing by B-24s.

Every morning, until the division left Talasea, Rupertus took off at sunrise to drop live grenades across the enemy's jungle hideouts.

On one grenade-dropping mission, Rupertus noticed a plane down in the water off Cape Gloucester and a struggling swimmer nearby. Rupertus dropped a life belt to the downed pilot.

Then he ordered his regular pilot, Captain Petras, to "flap the plane's wings, so we attract the attention of friendly natives."

A native saw the alert from Rupertus's plane and swam out to the stranded pilot, identified as Corporal Alvin Jay Hoffman Jr. The native pulled Hoffman into shore. Rupertus had Petras fly low to give the native a salute and shouted, "Well done!"

Because of the torrential rains, Cape Gloucester was one of the worst battles Rupertus had ever fought. Wetness, oppressive humidity, and the jungle's natural scent magnified the sickening, putrid smell and overpowering fumes of decaying Japanese bodies.

By March, the Marines' uniforms were soaked, muddy, and smelly. The enemy's ongoing night attacks added to the stress.

Before resting, the tired Marines laid barbed wire on the perimeter to hear if the Japanese came too close. To sleep in these conditions, they had to find a tree to lean on, or else a dugout on a hill to keep the water level in their "bed" to a minimum. Leaving their foxholes to take a leak or a dump was not an option.

Fortunately, their operations against Talasea ended on March 11, 1943, in complete victory.

Vandegrift, during the Battle of Talasea, still wanted Bill to come back temporarily to Washington, DC, to assess the division, talk about the war in the Pacific, and recruit. Vandegrift wrote asking when Rupertus might be available.

Rupertus replied, saying he could not leave until at least March 20, after mop-up operations following the Battle of Talasea.

On March 20, Bill got a radiogram that Krueger wanted to see him at his headquarters across the strait at MacArthur's headquarters, to discuss releasing Rupertus and the division. Rupertus explained that Vandegrift wanted him in Washington, and MacArthur, incredibly, relented.

After a harrowing flight, Rupertus stopped on Guadalcanal to refuel and visited with General Geiger, General Halsey, and Vice Admiral Wilkinson.

On March 22, Rupertus arrived at Pearl Harbor. While waiting for the plane to refuel, he got an urgent radiogram from Krueger calling him back to MacArthur's headquarters in the Pacific. General MacArthur had changed his mind and overruled General Vandegrift's request for Rupertus.

As a result, Rupertus's plane turned back to the Pacific. He arrived on Cape Gloucester on March 23.

General MacArthur protested that Rupertus and the division had not completed its mission, and it should stay under his control. In a telegram to General Krueger, commander of the US 6th Army, MacArthur wrote:

> *To HQ Alamo Force*
> *From GHQ SWPA*
> *General Rupertus services cannot now be spared as he is commanding his Division in combat in New Britain. He will be made available as soon as his services can be spared and alert withdrawal of the Division from combat. Since I have advised MARCORPS as above, delay execution.*
> *SJD MacArthur*

Rupertus wrote General Vandegrift detailing what had transpired with MacArthur. Frustrated, Vandegrift shared Rupertus's letter with Admiral Ernest J. King. Admiral King had previously told MacArthur the 1st Marine Division was on loan to the Southwest Pacific only for operational control in amphibious landings (which did not include shore-to-shore operations if MacArthur was planning to use it to attack Rabaul).

Further, when Admiral Nimitz discovered MacArthur's plans for the Marines, Nimitz said the Marines had completed their mission, and he had already slated the 1st Division for another operation.

This time, Roosevelt sided with Nimitz over MacArthur, and the 1st Division returned to naval control. Their next mission was to return to the South Pacific to capture the airport on Peleliu. General MacArthur finally accepted this strategy, attacking the Palaus. Taking control of the airports and communication lines in this vital strait was the key to his drive to the Philippines.

But MacArthur was sore about losing the division and said, "You know, in the Central Pacific, the 1st Marine Division will be another one of six Marine divisions. If it stayed here, it would be my Marine division."

As April arrived and they waited to be relieved by the army, word spread that General MacArthur planned a congratulatory visit to the division.

On the afternoon of April 17, the USS *Nashville* arrived off the Cape Gloucester coast, from which MacArthur appeared, complete with photographers and journalists. He came ashore, walked toward Rupertus, shook hands, posed for photos, and made clear he would keep the visit short.

General MacArthur wanted to stretch his legs on the island with Rupertus. Several officers, including his new assistant division commander, Brigadier General O. P. Smith, Rupertus's staff, and photographers followed them as they walked and talked about Rupertus's operation on Cape Gloucester.

"General," MacArthur said to Rupertus, "I was so impressed with your effective strategy on this island that I wanted to come ashore and personally thank you and the men of your division for your courage during this challenging campaign."

After more handshakes, a few more complimentary words, and a final salute, General MacArthur and his entourage prepared to leave. In honor of the great general, Rupertus ordered the division band to send MacArthur off to "Semper Fidelis," "The Marines Hymn," and "Onward Christian Soldiers." MacArthur returned to USS *Nashville*, paving the way for complete control of the division to revert to the navy.

After a year of risky yet vital service, Rupertus disbanded the air unit that had served them so well in New Britain. New Marine air squadrons had arrived in the Pacific with fresh pilots, new planes, and a more extensive maintenance team joining the division. Rupertus's makeshift air force had suffered no casualties and only lost one plane to mechanical failure.

General Rupertus walks with General MacArthur. (USMC PHOTO)

Rupertus congratulated and thanked the members, recommending them all for the Air Medal. He shook each pilot's hand, lamenting, "This is like disowning one's own children!"

None of the Air Liaison Unit pilots officially had wings of an aviator, and yet their additional service to the 1st Marine Division was awarded an Air Medal.

Rupertus with Marines in front of his plane, *Sleepy*. (USMC PHOTO)

As the division prepared to leave Cape Gloucester, congratulations flooded in.

Melbourne's Lord Mayor Nettlefold cabled Rupertus on behalf of Melbourne's citizens:

> *We recall the visit to the city of you and your men with great pleasure and would be glad if you would convey to them our heartiest congratulations on their magnificent achievement at Cape Gloucester. We look forward to the return here of your men after further successes for recuperation. They have already done a great job. Happy landings and good hunting.*

General Rupertus replied to their Aussie friends:

> *I assure you that Melbourne has been in the minds and hearts of each and every one of us since we left your beautiful city. There's never been such a warm-hearted friendliness shown to us Americans by any community, and we shall carry with us always the gratitude and love of the people of Melbourne. Please extend to them from the whole division, a heartfelt thanks for your inspired words. I assure*

you that should we not have the good fortune to return to our US homes, we will someday, in lieu thereof, return to our foster home: The city of Melbourne.

On May 2, 1944, General MacArthur pulled a shocker. He boarded a ship and steamed through a tropical storm to return to Cape Gloucester, unannounced, to personally thank Rupertus.

New York News reporter Jack Turcott described the scene:

MacArthur got off his cruiser and climbed into a tiny landing barge, five miles offshore. The barge tossed like a cork as a coxswain maneuvered it to escape the reefs on Borgen Bay. As the barge scraped ashore, MacArthur's party stepped off into the stinking black New Britain mud. A few soldiers in nearby tents looked up indifferently, curious why anyone would come ashore in a small boat and such vile weather.

A moment later, one soldier said, "Hey, they're officers."

A corporal jumped forward and exclaimed, "Jeepers, it's MacArthur," as Marine Virgil March pulled up in a jeep.

MacArthur and his party piled into the jeep and made the 12-mile ride to General Rupertus's headquarters, bouncing over rocks and ditches, slithering from one side to the other, skidding in mud.

When they arrived, a stunned Rupertus came out of his C.P., shook MacArthur's hand, then MacArthur thanked Rupertus and the Division, once again, for achieving the mission. He read the Army's citation and gallantly pinned the Army's distinguished service medal upon Rupertus.

According to Turcott, "MacArthur returned to the beach and waved his hand at the crowd which had gathered at the beach and called out, 'Nasty night, boys.'"

That night, Rupertus sent a short v-mail to Sleepy to describe the event and give her a heads up of what she might read in the paper:

My Darling,
I'm taking the last leg tomorrow early, and when I arrive, I'll write you a real letter. I'm sending you a package containing a silk nightie and some linens that I bought in town today at the P.B. Today, General MacArthur presented me with the Army Distinguished Service medal for the job we just did. Quite a surprise. The photos and one of my DSM will be released in the V.J. tonight. All my love to you and Pat, Darling. I'll be coming home someday. That's what we are always fighting for.
Always Yours, Bill

Rupertus dreamed of being home in Washington with Sleepy and Pat but sensed he was staying in the Pacific. He knew the Japanese soldiers' dogged tenacity and their fanatical willingness to fight to the death against all odds, which would keep both him and the Marines occupied.

Though the tension between the Marine Corps and the US Navy and US Army proved to be frustrating at times, the collaboration paid off in the end. In a closing ceremony before finally leaving Cape Gloucester, General Krueger, like his boss MacArthur, commended the 1st Division: "I wish to state that the 1st Marine Division did a grand job in the western New Britain operation, one that it has every right to be proud of. My relations with General Rupertus and his staff were always most pleasant and cordial and many close friendships have stemmed therefrom."

On a tactical level, in New Britain the 1st Marine Division achieved perfection never equaled at that time in jungle operations. From the surprise attacks to selecting landing beaches, perfecting amphibious techniques and overall planning and collaboration helped enable patrols to trek 130 miles through the jungle along New Britain's northern coast Additionally, this campaign taught that experience matters.

On May 4, two days after MacArthur's surprise visit, the torch passed to the US Army and the 1st Division left New Britain. The decision was made for the exhausted 1st Marine Division to be relieved rather quickly. General Roy Geiger was to have overall command of the next Marine-Army joint operation.

Rupertus and the Marines dreamed of returning to Australia—a perfect spot to recover. They knew what to expect, plus they had hospitals, retail, bars, and good relations with the Australians.

But MacArthur and Nimitz had competing plans that would change the trajectory for Rupertus and his Marines, launching them into difficult, bloody battles.

Chapter 61

The Division Heads to Pavuvu
Washington, DC
May 1944

After two years of bloody jungle fighting at Guadalcanal, Tulagi, Gavutu, and Cape Gloucester, the worn-out division needed another respite.

While Rupertus and his staff thought the division would return to Australia, General Geiger, his superior, ordered them to an island called Pavuvu, the largest island in the Russell's within the Solomon Islands. One of Geiger's staffers had flown over it and thought it a suitable location with a pretty white sand beach, and he told this to Geiger, who quickly approved the site. Australia was too far, and Geiger assumed Pavuvu had a base camp.

Like most of the Marines, Rupertus had never heard of Pavuvu, though it was just sixty miles from Guadalcanal. Geiger knew they could have gone back to Guadalcanal because the Marines had a solid base there. But he thought it best for the 1st Marine Division to avoid Guadalcanal, as the 3rd Marines were already there, conducting daily work parties. They would undoubtedly pressure the exhausted 1st to join them.

The Marines felt the ship slow and were dreaming of Melbourne when word blasted over the ship's intercom: "Prepare to disembark on the island of Pavuvu."

"Pavuvu?"

As they approached Pavuvu harbor, they could see this was no Australia, but it looked inviting. Rupertus and the Marines saw palm trees, docks, beach sheds, plantains, coconut trees, and a white sand beach beyond the shallow blue-green water. The tropical island had a deserted six-hundred-acre coconut plantation on it. All and all, it might be paradise.

They landed and disembarked the ship. To Rupertus's surprise, not only was there no camp they could move into, as Geiger had incorrectly assumed, but the weary Marines would have no mess hall to eat in and no roads on which to train. Pavuvu was an intelligence failure. They would have to fend for themselves until the Seabees arrived.

Marines pitched their tents and hammocks among the coconut trees, figuring out how to build the camp on top of thousands of rotten and decaying coconuts. And then the rain started falling, bringing mosquitoes, huge rats, and land crabs, which ran rampant, drawn to the millions of sweet coconuts rotting on the ground.

The first night's morale was pretty bad. Melbourne was great for R&R. Pavuvu? But when the sun rose and the Navy Seabees eventually arrived, morale picked up.

Rupertus had been ordered back temporarily to Marine headquarters in Washington, DC, as soon as possible after his men were on the island. Following the commandant's orders, Rupertus and his chief of staff, Colonel Selden, started the long flight back to Washington. They would return in a few weeks.

*****

Washington, DC
Marine Headquarters
May–June 1944

Rupertus spent one night in his command post on Pavuvu with staff. The next day, the general and Colonel Selden left for Washington for a conference at the Marine Corps headquarters with Vandegrift and the new secretary of the navy, James V. Forrestal.

Vandegrift had wanted Rupertus to do this in March, but MacArthur blocked it, delaying Rupertus until early May 1944. He and Selden first flew to the West Coast and then to Marine Corps HQ in Washington.

Rupertus and Selden, back in Washington, reported on the condition of the 1st Marine Division and argued that Marines away from home more than twenty-four months should be sent home.

Marine headquarters agreed, for the most part. They approved 260 officers and 4,600 veterans who'd been in the Pacific for twenty-four months to return home to the United States. But 264 officers and 5,750 men, many of whom had not quite completed twenty-four months, could not be spared. They had to remain for at least the next campaign.

Headquarters needed more work from Rupertus while he was in Washington. General Vandegrift wrote to General Roy Geiger, who had overall command of the Peleliu operation, to tell him he wanted Rupertus in DC longer.

Office of the Commandant, US Marine Corps, Washington, DC
May 16, 1944
Dear Roy:
Thanks for your letter, which came several days ago. Rupertus got in the day before yesterday, and I have had several long talks with him about his Division and things in general. I'm dropping you this note to state that I intend to keep him here until June 15 unless you radio in that you need him before that time. That will give him a good blow here in the states and get him back to your area in ample time for things to come.
Most Sincerely,
Archer

In Washington, on May 17, 1944, Rupertus and Vandegrift first met with Secretary James Forrestal and the media to talk about the war in the Pacific. The *New York Times*'s Sidney Shalett reported this on Thursday, May 18, 1944.

On Thursday, May 19, at 10:30 p.m., *NBC News* interviewed Rupertus about the New Britain campaign for the "March of Time" on the NBC network broadcast from Washington, DC, sponsored by *Time*.

He remained in Washington for nearly a month on stateside duty. The best part above all was spending time with Sleepy and Pat. On June 15, he kissed and hugged them on the front porch of their home in Washington and walked out to his waiting staff car. It was time to go back to war, to finish the job with his men. Sitting in the back of the staff car, Rupertus looked out the window, smiled, and waved as his car pulled away.

By the grace of God, he would see them again.
******

Pavuvu, Russell Islands
June–August 1944

Rupertus and Colonel John Selden returned to Pavuvu on June 20, 1944. Rupertus moved into a large old plantation house, surrounded by tropical flowers and overlooking Macquitti Bay, which he shared with his assistant division commander, O. P. Smith, and staff.

Rupertus was appalled after returning to his Marines and hearing about the continued mess on Pavuvu. He wrote General Vandegrift on June 22 to inform him of the problems.

Meanwhile, many of his Marines on Pavuvu had fought in three battles—Tulagi, Guadalcanal, and Cape Gloucester—and desperately needed a

Rupertus's office, Pavuvu.

Rupertus/assistant division commander house on Pavuvu.

break. Wild rumors spread quickly among the division. Some officers told a group of veterans that they would have to stay and "stick it out" for the next engagement. Word spread that no Marines of the 1st Division could go home.

A false rumor spread that General Rupertus had gone home to Washington to see his "new bride," even though he was married eleven years, and his "infant son," even though Pat was five years old. But the biggest whopper was that Rupertus "went on vacation with MacArthur."

If Rupertus were to go on a vacation, it would not be with MacArthur—although he did appreciate MacArthur's two visits toward the end of their time at Cape Gloucester to express his appreciation for their sacrifice and victory on the island.

When the sun finally came out, morale improved a bit. The Marines got to enjoy the beach, jumping in the water—buck naked and tan—like a scene right out of Hollywood, California.

By late June, the Seabees arrived in full force and did their magic, building out the camp, a decent mess hall, and a movie theater. They sprayed for mosquitoes and built roads out of the coral so training could commence.

During one field maneuver on an isolated island, the Marines raced to the beach in cold, eye-stinging rain as dawn was breaking, and when they jumped out, there stood their division commander, General Rupertus, waiting for them on the beach. He had surprised them by traveling 150 miles from headquarters to witness this small maneuver by a single battalion to ensure it went smoothly. Rupertus was proud of his Marines and wanted them to know that.

On July 1, Rupertus watched 1st Division maneuvers on another nearby island, taking his boat to meet an LVT (Landing Vehicle Tracked) that took him to the beach. After viewing the exercises, he headed back to the LVT to return to his boat. As he stepped into the LVT with one foot, he grabbed onto a tattered canvas handle for balance, and it instantly broke. Rupertus slipped and fell backward, landing on the ground as the skin-piercing coral dug into his ankle.

"Shit!" He reached for his ankle. "Argh!"

A corpsman raced over to Rupertus with first aid and wrapped his foot. "It could be a sprain or break, sir. Either way, for it to heal, you'll need crutches to keep pressure off the ankle."

Rupertus could have died of Bright's disease, scarlet fever, bouts of malaria, dysentery, and dengue fever over his lifetime. They had never slowed him down as much as this damn ankle injury might. Rupertus returned to Pavuvu and was taken to the hospital. The doctor cleaned and wrapped his ankle and told Rupertus to stay off it.

After a painful night's sleep, Rupertus returned to sickbay in the morning for a follow-up. There, the division doctor dropped the bomb.

"It's broken, General. You'll need crutches and will have to limit your mobility for several weeks."

"This is the last damn thing I needed to hear." But Rupertus knew if he ignored the doc's orders, it could impact his ability to join his men on the beach on D-Day as in the past.

That wasn't going to happen. Hell would freeze before he would abandon his men, broken foot or not.

In early August, General Vandegrift visited Rupertus and the 1st Marine Division on Pavuvu. Rupertus came out of the command post on his crutches and greeted his friend with a huge smile. They shook hands and slapped backs; then they went inside and talked for over an hour about Marine headquarters and the mission ahead. Later, Vandegrift gave a speech on the porch,

Left to right seated: Captain Bozart (USN), Captain Lough (USN), Colonel Fenton, Colonel Harrison, General Rupertus, Colonel Selden, Colonel Kaluf, Colonel Harris, Lieutenant Colonel Tschirgi. Left to right standing: Major Gober, Major Myers, unknown Marine, Lieutenant Colonel Deakin, Lieutenant Colonel Fields, Lieutenant Colonel Ramsey, unknown Marine, unknown Marine. (USMC PHOTO)

Left to right seated: Major Meyers, Lieutenant Colonel Tschirgi, Captain Lough (USN), General Rupertus, Colonel Selden, Colonel Harris, Lieutenant Colonel Fields. Left to right standing: Captain Bueard (aide), First Lieutenant Beecher (pilot). (USMC PHOTO)

Left to right: Colonel Puller, Colonel Harrison, General Rupertus, Colonel Hanneken, Colonel Fellers. (USMC PHOTO)

posed for some photos, and walked around camp to visit with Marines before jumping on his Guadalcanal flight.

Both Vandegrift and Rupertus had a special place in their hearts for the 1st Marine Division they brought to life at New River, North Carolina.

The division now faced another savagely brutal campaign, but there was no doubt in either of their minds that they would prevail, as they had at Tulagi, Guadalcanal, and Cape Gloucester.

In mid-August 1944, the USO and Bob Hope toured the South Pacific to perform for the troops and stopped at Banika. It was a roaring success, but thousands of Marines on nearby Pavuvu missed out, so Rupertus sent the division's recreation officer to Banika to ask Bob Hope whether the USO would visit the 1st Marine Division back on rural Pavuvu.

Hope did not hesitate. Within an hour, he and the division's recreation director flew in one of the Piper Cubs from the Banika dirt airfield, landing on the crushed coral airfield at Pavuvu, while his USO team followed in transport boats. Rupertus, Marines, and sailors were already waiting for them.

Bob Hope and the USO team boosted the Marines' spirits. Hope sat next to Rupertus in the first row before the stage and, in talking with Rupertus,

USO performers Joe Corona, guitarist (left), and Tony Romano (right). (USMC PHOTO)

Rupertus watches USO show on Pavuvu with Bob Hope on his left and Admiral Forte on his right. (USMC PHOTO)

Rupertus with USO performers and Gary Cooper; Colonels Whaling and Simms behind him. (USMC PHOTO)

Rupertus and staff examine map, Pavuvu, 1944. (PHOTO FROM USMC FILM)

learned that most of the Marines had been in the Pacific for over twenty-five months. Veterans were training with the new Marines who had just arrived for an upcoming mission on the island of Peleliu.

Hope asked Rupertus, "How does the upcoming battle look?"

"It's going to be a tough operation; we're hoping and praying it will be fast."

On August 26, 1944, Rupertus embarked aboard the USS *Dupage*. The division sailed to Guadalcanal and participated in amphibious landing exercises from August 27 to September 7, 1944. From there they returned to Pavuvu September 9 to 14.

The American ships in the Pacific had strict orders for blackout conditions at night. No personal lights were allowed, including cigarettes, cigars, or butts thrown over the deck, which could reveal their position to the enemy. Any butts or trash in the water could leave a hot trail to their course or previous location.

345

With all lights out, sailing on a clear night revealed an expansive blanket of the moon and thousands of twinkling stars above. Marines loved this view from the deck of their ships, as did Rupertus, who used the quiet time to write and read reports and letters. Like most Marines at war, Rupertus enjoyed mail, especially from Sleepy. Pat was two and a half years old when Rupertus had left to join the division at New River in March 1942. Now Pat was five. God, he missed them.

But mail was often delivered sixty, ninety, or even more than one hundred days after the fact.

On the night of September 9, as the division steamed from Guadalcanal back to Pavuvu, Rupertus opened Sleepy's letter, which she had written more than a month earlier.

August 7, 1944
Dear Bill,
Always remember I love you more than life itself. You are my very life. I'm proud of you, and I respect and admire you more than anyone in the world. I know you'll do the best possible job no matter what it is. Keep your chin up and keep that wonderful cheerful spirit of yours. You are bound to win out there, and I expect you to mow the Japs down, and I know you will. But above all come home to us. We can be cheerful and happy and carry on as long as we have that to look forward to. The officers and men in your command are fortunate to have such a fine leader. I know they will do their best for you and you will do your best for them.

God bless you, my darling, and everybody in your command. Good luck and happy landings when the time comes to sit under the apple tree.
All my love,
Sleepy
PS. Alger says Pat has one speed, "full speed ahead!"

Chapter 62

The Japanese Plan to Defeat America at Peleliu
The "Attack, Delay, and Bleed" Strategy

With the Japanese getting whipped in battle after battle against the Marines, they had to change strategies or risk destruction. Plus they needed to draw a line across the water to stop the Marine Corps' island-hopping advance toward Tokyo.

They would draw that line at the Palau Islands, particularly on Peleliu and Anguar, located five hundred miles west of the Philippines. If Peleliu fell, the Americans would face less resistance and firepower if they tried retaking the Philippines, as MacArthur had promised when he left in disgrace in 1942. Like at Guadalcanal in Cape Gloucester, the Japanese military airfields at Peleliu were crucial to the war effort.

Word came down from the high command in Tokyo to Japanese commanders General Sadae Inoue and Colonel Kunio Nakagawa: "The Palau Islands will be firmly secured as the final position against the enemies' Pacific penetration operations. Defend Peleliu and Anguar and the airfields on Peleliu—at all costs."

But to win, the Japanese needed to radically change their battle tactics in response to Marines' amphibious invasions. Previously, they had employed a "retreat and ambush" strategy, allowing the Marines to come ashore unopposed and move deep into enemy territory, at which time they would ambush the Americans from hiding places in the jungle by surprise attack.

Except for Tanambogo, which was so small that "retreat and ambush" could not be used, and Tulagi, where Rupertus's men had slipped in from the backside of the island undetected, the Japanese used the strategy at major amphibious landings, like Guadalcanal and Cape Gloucester. The Marines came ashore without direct opposition and then faced surprise-attack ambushes by the Japanese either hours or days after the fact.

But the Japanese "retreat and ambush" strategy had failed. Without a radical change in tactics, the US Marine Corps would soon be landing in Tokyo. In response, the Japanese devised a new strategy: "attack, delay, and bleed."

Rather than hiding deep in the jungles and attacking at night, they would attack the Marines at the water's edge from fortified structures built into the island. When the remaining Marines raced toward the firepower coming from the hidden fortifications, the Japs would fire at close proximity to create mass casualties and deaths.

This surprise strategy change would present a fundamental problem for Rupertus and the Marines, eliminating any chance of a tough but quick campaign that the division leadership or the Joint Chiefs of Staff had planned.

The Marines' amphibious doctrine was to land on the beach, move quickly to secure the island's airports, and then clear the enemy from the island. For the Marines, speed saved lives and material. It also helped the navy. The longer the supporting naval ships stayed offshore, the more vulnerable they became to Japanese kamikaze attacks and naval assaults.

So while the US Army mopped up at Cape Gloucester, and the 1st Marine Division was on Pavuvu to rest, rebuild, and train, the Japanese dug in and reinforced.

Peleliu consisted of sharp pinnacles, deep crevices, caverns, and honeycombed caves, and the Japanese took full advantage. Using the natural caves, rock formations, and vegetation, they built deep, hidden, strong defenses that could be neither detected from reconnaissance planes nor destroyed by naval bombers.

Before the Marines descended on Peleliu on September 15, 1944, seven thousand Korean laborers and the Japanese military constructed a vast network of well-fortified tunnels and hideouts in over five hundred caves and cliffs. Some tunnels were reinforced concrete, with entry shafts four to five feet straight down, and additional tunnels branching off at the bottom. A few tunnels and caves were six stories deep. In some places the concrete was four feet thick.

They wired the bunkers with electricity and wireless communication. The fortifications contained barracks, kitchens, medics, command centers, ammunition, and more—all designed to withstand enemy bombing.

The dense, crushing coral surrounding Peleliu would slow Marines' amphibious landings and ferrying troops and supplies. To further obstruct the landing, the Japanese planted five hundred connected sea mines in the water to booby-trap the Marines.

At thirty inches wide, the mines' sensors would activate by contact with a dense force, such as an Amtrac, creating an explosion, or Japanese soldiers could detonate the mines by shooting them.

They scattered mines along shipping lanes around Peleliu, posing a constant threat to American warships.

The US Navy had conducted multiple bombing missions from March 30 up to D-Day on September 15, 1944. The naval campaign had blown up what was aboveground, including buildings, Japanese planes, and the airstrip. The Japanese hiding deep in the underground of Peleliu were harassed but survived, their embedded defensive fortifications unscathed.

By August 1944, the Japanese fortifications were complete, the mines were in place, and the Japanese war plan was ready. They had drawn their line in the sea, awaiting Rupertus and his Marines.

On September 3, 1944, General Inoue of the Japanese forces learned the Americans were coming and alerted his commanders on the ground, proclaiming:

This battle may have a part in the decisive turn of the tide in breaking the deadlock of the "Great Asiatic War." The entire Army and people of Japan are expecting us to win this battle. There will never be another chance as these few existing days for the people living in the empire to repay the Emperor's benevolence again. Rouse yourselves for the sake of your country! Officers and men, you will devote your life to winning this battle and attaining your long-cherished desire of annihilating the enemy.

Chapter 63

The American Plan for Peleliu

Taking the Palau Islands was a cornerstone of General MacArthur's plan to protect his advance on the Philippines, and the 1st Marine Division and US Army's 81st Infantry were slated for the job. MacArthur wanted his western flank watched when he sloshed onto the beach at Leyte Gulf.

Planning for Peleliu started at the highest echelons during the Casablanca Conference between FDR and Churchill in January 1943. Peleliu's planning continued at the Cairo Conference in November 1943, with FDR, Churchill, and Chiang Kai-shek.

On March 10, 1944, the Joint Chiefs of Staff directed Admiral Nimitz to "speed up the plan" against the Japanese with specific instructions: "Occupy the Mariana-Palau line."

Thus, "Operation Stalemate" was born. Nimitz set D-Day at Peleliu for September 8, 1944.

The Americans would take Peleliu, Ngesebus, Yap, and Ulithi to flank MacArthur's advance and use the airstrips, bays for ships, and secure lines of communication.

US intelligence discovered that Peleliu was fortified with enemy installations and occupied by over ten thousand Japanese. More than twenty-five thousand Japanese soldiers were placed strategically across the Palau Islands, on call to kill US troops.

The Joint Chiefs of Staff plan for invading the Palaus was copied and sent out to the commanders and staff of the Pacific, many stationed at Pacific headquarters at Pearl Harbor. Rupertus sent his intelligence officer (D-3), Lieutenant Colonel L. J. Fields, to Pearl to participate in the planning with the navy.

On June 2, with Rupertus and Selden in Washington, he sent his assistant division commander, Brigadier General O. P. Smith, to Guadalcanal to get the plan.

Rupertus returned to Pavuvu on June 21 and began studying the plan in detail with General Smith, Colonel Selden, and Lieutenant Colonel Fields.

The intelligence team had provided a basic map of Peleliu from old maps with limited surveillance. On the map they saw the airfield, power plants, and administration buildings, as well as a radio station, water cisterns, and roads.

The terrain looked flat, and the hill (or spine) on the center of the island appeared tiny, maybe two hundred feet high. The planners knew the Marines would receive fire from the hill, but they would not see the intensity of that fire until D-Day.

One significant difference between the Palaus operation and the other operations executed by the 1st Marine Division involved the army. With the war winding down in Europe, the US Army had begun to devote more resources to the Pacific. In this case, the 1st Marine Division at Peleliu would be joined by the army's 81st Infantry Division back in Pearl Harbor, initially held in reserve to back up the Marines. Because this was a joint Marine Corps–Army operation, and because other, smaller islands in the Palaus were targets along with Peleliu, Marine Major General Roy Geiger had overall command.

Under the plan as presented, the 1st Marine Division had the major tasks to take Peleliu and Ngesebus, and the 81st Infantry Division would take Anguar and Ulithi.

The 1st Marine Division would land on Peleliu, a six-mile-long and two-mile-wide island, and leave one battalion in reserve. Their objective—to capture the airfield quickly and then push north along the line across the width of the western part of the island to clear out the enemy. They would have to attack and move fast to achieve the mission and avoid higher casualties.

The plans called for extensive pre-invasion bombing on critical targets by US Navy planes, in theory to "soften the beachhead" for a safer landing for the Marines during D-Day. The pre-suppression naval gunfire was essential to the division for tactical planning and maneuvers.

Shortly before D-Day, Rupertus learned that his Marines would be more short-handed than planned. At the last minute, some units were redesignated for another operation in the Marianas. Additional troops had been reassigned to join MacArthur on his return to the Philippines. Rupertus wasn't happy about these force reductions. He raised concerns up the chain of command, to no avail.

With the reductions, the Marines would have nine infantry battalions against the ten thousand Japanese thought to be on the island. The army's 81st Infantry Division would have six infantry battalions against fifteen hundred Japanese on Anguar.

The plan called for landing on Peleliu first before taking Anguar. However, Major General Paul J. Mueller, the commanding general of the 81st Division, and his naval task unit commander, Rear Admiral H. P. Blandy, wanted to land on Anguar by September 17.

While he thought it would be a quick campaign, Rupertus and his staff were concerned that if the army attacked Anguar when they assaulted Peleliu, there would not be backup to support the Marines on Peleliu. Vice Admiral Theodore S. Wilkinson ignored Rupertus's concern. The army would go forward on Anguar.

Rupertus wanted as many Marines onshore at Peleliu as quickly as possible. "We need 4,500 Marines ashore in the first nineteen minutes," Rupertus told his staff, "to take advantage of the heaviest of naval bombing before and during landing." He took a swig of water from his canteen. "The Amtracs will carry the troops in, stop about two thousand feet from the shoreline, and the men will transfer into smaller boats to reach the island."

The Marines felt confident. Combined with the success of previous battles, the months of air surveillance, strategy, planning, scheduling, bombing, and practical simulation helped cement this feeling.

On August 2, 1944, Rear Admiral George Fort, the attack force commander, came to Pavuvu to work out Marine and navy cooperation for Peleliu. Rupertus and his planners knew it would be a vicious assault, potentially with moderate casualties because of the terrain and enemy.

Because of the navy's intensive pre-suppression fire and months of strafing, the planners thought Peleliu would be a quick operation.

Rupertus shared his optimism with the division, after a movie on Pavuvu four days before D-Day. "We'll have some casualties, but let me tell you, it's going to be a short one. It will be tough but fast. We will be there for three days. It may only take two."

Optimism prevailed, though not every officer shared Rupertus's confidence. Yet nobody knew that ten thousand Japanese soldiers on Peleliu were alive, hiding in caves, even after the massive naval bombing campaign.

Two days before D-Day on Peleliu, the Joint Chiefs were assembling in Quebec when Admiral Halsey sent an urgent telegram to Admiral Nimitz. Admiral Halsey suggested to Admiral Nimitz and the Joint Chiefs that they cancel the Peleliu operation.

Halsey wanted the ground forces turned over to MacArthur for the invasion of Leyte. Invading Peleliu, Yap, and Anguar, Halsey argued, might bog them down.

MacArthur wanted to invade Leyte just days after the Marines landed on Peleliu. However, Halsey wanted the 1st Marine Division's help in Leyte to secure bases and remove threats in the right flank of MacArthur's charge to the Philippines, which was five hundred miles away from the Palaus.

Admiral Nimitz was willing to bypass Yap but insisted on the capture of Peleliu. The Joint Chiefs and President Roosevelt intervened. They sided with Nimitz, rejecting Halsey's idea to stop the invasion on Peleliu and send the 1st Marines to Leyte. They saw Peleliu and its coves, strategic airfield, barracks, and administration buildings, and the small airstrip at Ngesebus, as necessary on their march toward Japan.

The Joint Chiefs offered a compromise, ordering MacArthur and Nimitz to combine forces for an invasion of Leyte for October 20, 1944, two months ahead of time. If the operation went quickly on Leyte, the remaining force of five Marine infantry battalions would then go to Peleliu to assist the 1st Marine Division should they get bogged down in October. Likewise, if it went quickly on Peleliu, the 1st Marine Division would head to Leyte.

Admiral Nimitz ordered the Eastern Attack Force to report to General MacArthur in the Southwest Pacific in preparation. Meanwhile, the Western Attack Force would continue under Nimitz onward to Peleliu.

Part of this decision was driven by the fact that there had surprisingly been no Japanese response during the navy's fire on the islands in March 1944—pre-D-Day.

Before the invasion, a Balao-class submarine made a combined effort to put reconnaissance photography and a demolition team off Peleliu and Yap. As another harbinger of what was to come, three of the men who swam ashore at Yap disappeared.

Halsey continued scouting Peleliu and the region from the ocean, with four boats watching important straits, and nine forming a double scouting line between the Philippines and Palaus. Two submarines from each of the three wolf packs began the first line of six, and the third line boats of each pack formed the second line in the safety position.

During this time, the American submarines never made contact with the Japanese and never saw the Japanese navy. By all accounts, it appeared that the Japanese had abandoned all efforts to put up stiff resistance at Peleliu.

As he had done before Cape Gloucester, Rupertus penned a motivational letter to the division and gave it to officers to distribute two days before the battle.

D-Day.

Headquarters First Marine Division
Fleet Marine Force
Care of Fleet Post Office, San Francisco, California
Memorandum to all officers and men of the First Marine Division
Men of the First Division:
Once again, the eyes of the Marine Corps will be focused on you. In a few days, you will prove that your selection to spearhead another and deeper thrust into enemy territory is an honor that you richly deserve. At Guadalcanal, Cape Gloucester, and Talasea, you demonstrated you were superior to the best troops the enemy can place in the field. YOU ARE STILL SUPERIOR.

You will land after the intensive naval bombardment and air bombing to meet the enemy with one idea uppermost in your minds—to carry out the mission entrusted with you.

Within forty-eight hours from the time that the first Marine puts foot on enemy soil, our country should have still another base from which to continue the march to Tokyo. That each and every one will do his duty is well known. I am proud to command such a body of men and to be with you in your victory.
Good luck and God be with you.
William H. Rupertus
Major General, US Marine Corps
Commanding

After writing the letter, Rupertus had one last staff meeting and reviewed the plan. Privately, Rupertus had his reservations. The invasion plan was finalized only three weeks before by the powers above him in the chain of command. The battle could be more difficult than envisioned. But the general would carry out his orders and organized his division in the following manner:

Task Organization—1st Marine Division
MajGen William H. Rupertus, Commanding
Three Combat Teams (with supporting units) will land on the western beaches of Peleliu.

Combat Team 1 ("Spitfire")—Colonel Lewis B. Puller and the 1st Marines land on the beaches to the left, designated White 1 and White 2, then advance to the northern tip of Peleliu.

Combat Team 5 ("Lone Wolf")—Colonel Harold D. Harris and the 5th Marines land in the center on Orange Beaches 1 and 2 with a mission to secure the airfield then move north.

Combat Team 7 ("Mustang")—Colonel Herman H. Hanneken and the 7th Marines (less 2nd Battalion) land on Orange Beach 3, then move in to secure the southern tip of Peleliu.

11th Marine Regiment, Artillery—Colonel William Harrison will land after the infantry.

The US forces included the 1st Marine Division's nine thousand infantrymen, eleven regiments, division artillery, war dog platoons, and nonfighting support personnel. Peleliu's attack force included the Montford Point Marines (the first African American recruits in the Marine Corps trained at Montford Point) and Native American Navajo Code Talkers. They had served with them throughout the Pacific. Even with this, they did not have the number of Marine units in reserve Rupertus wanted.

American and Japanese warriors were about to meet, both with missions to achieve on Peleliu—no questions, no diversions, no retreat.

The fleet made their way to Peleliu, and the night before the invasion, Rupertus sat down in his ship's quarters to write a letter to Sleepy, which he knew might be his last communication with her.

Thursday, September 14, 1944
My darling,

It's 9 p.m. the night before we land. There is no moon out there—plenty of stars, it's fairly dark out, but you can see the shadowy lines of the ships around us now plowing forward. Everyone's all set, and we land tomorrow at 8 a.m. preceded by intense air and naval bombardment.

Halsey has been giving Peleliu full hell the past four days, and we have received some good photos of the results as well as enemy defenders. This will be a sort of Tarawa on a large scale—naturally in an atoll like this, the enemy can do but anything—defend all around and stick.

He hasn't any place to escape or run to if he could or wanted to. There's no fear of the outcome, but it may be a tougher job than I first visualized, and we may have moderate casualties, although at mass today, I prayed we would not. OP Smith goes in first with an advance echelon from H.Q. Then Selden and several others of the staff at 11 a.m.

And then when he sends me a radio that the command post is set up onshore & is in contact with the regts, I come in with the rest of the H.Q. and take over the command ashore. This will be at about 12:30 p.m.

My ankle is OK with only a slight tenderness, but I'll take my cane. I forgot to tell you, but while we were up at Roy's place, a blue jacket came up to me (about 24 years old) and said he had come over from another ship to say hello to me and said his name was Rupertus! It turned out that he was my third cousin, a carpenter's mate, first-class, and was in the Navy for two years! Small world. Also, there is 1st Lt. Stavers aboard here used to go with Ella's daughter Matilda. Again, a small world.

Selden just came in and told me he could see our battleships & cruisers firing at the Palau's on the horizon. So, it looks as if we will keep Tojo's boys awake all night long. By the time you get this, you will know more about our doings & will know of my welfare. Please don't worry too much, my darling, about me. We've done all we can on planning, training, etc., and now it's all in God's hands.

I am hoping it won't take too long to do the job so I can come home to you and Pat. You're the dearest wife and mother any man could ever wish for—I know Pat wouldn't have anyone other than you for his Mommy—and I guess me for his Daddy too. All I can think of tonight is you and Pat and how dearly I want to be with you both to make you happy and satisfied— my happiness will come from that, and your sweet love. I'll mail this aboard here, but it will be delayed some days—but it will be sure to get to you this way. Goodnight my beloved—all my heartfelt love for you and Pat—see you over the beach.
God bless you and keep you both from all harm. I love you.
Always Your Bill

Rupertus kissed the letter, turned off the light, and went out on the deck for some air. As he gazed up at the sky full of stars, he prayed to God for his men.

Chapter 64

Bridge, USS *DuPage*
Off the Coast of Peleliu
The Western Pacific
D-Day, September 15, 1944
0730 Hours

From the bridge of his command ship, the USS *DuPage*, Rupertus gazed out at the six-mile-long, almost mountainous contour of the mysterious island called Peleliu. Now, after all the sketchy intelligence reports, here it was, in front of his eyes. Already, what he was seeing with his own eyes differed somewhat from the intelligence reports delivered by high command. Most believed that Peleliu was low and flat. But this hilly contour was anything but that.

With all the bombing the navy had conducted over the past few months, hardly a tree or any other vegetation stood in place. The island looked like it could be the surface of the moon. Whatever challenges his Marines were about to face, at least they weren't going to be battling through a jungle swampland reeking with malaria and tropic fever, like Guadalcanal or New Britain.

But mosquitoes and snakes were not the only environmental problem in the Pacific. Already out here on the command ship, it was hot as hell. Heat could be a factor for his boys on the island, which is why he hoped for a quick and successful operation.

Off to the periphery of *DuPage*, his fellow commanders in this joint Army–Marine Corps operation were also spread out on separate ships: General Geiger and General Julian Smith, commander of Expeditionary Troops 3rd Fleet, joined Admiral Fort on board USS *Mount McKinley*, and his assistant division commander, Brigadier General O. P. Smith, was on the USS *Ellmore*.

But right now the general's only focus was on the seventeen thousand men in his division, and issuing the order to launch the invasion. They had steamed over 2,100 miles across the Pacific from Pavuvu for this moment, and now they were ready.

The ankle injury he had suffered back on Pavuvu had largely healed, thankfully, and he was now able to move unencumbered. Thank God he had listened to the doctor's orders, as much as he had wanted to resist, because he would not miss being with his men on this day for anything.

Shortly after sunrise the 1st Marine Division's three infantry combat battalions, the 1st, 5th, and 7th Marines, aboard Higgins boats and Amtracs, off-loaded and circled in the water to their rendezvous positions, awaiting the final "go" command.

Naval gunfire continued for a few minutes. Then, at Rupertus's command, they embarked from the sea, across the fringing coral reef toward the three planned landing sites on the southwestern beaches of Peleliu, barreling through the water and smashing into the shore. Justifiable fear was calmed by prayer, jokes, smokes, and camaraderie.

Then all hell broke loose. Boats blew up around them. Amtracs caught fire. The enemy unleashed machine gun fire in waves. Men stepping out of the boats to try to charge the beach got their heads blown up.

The enemy had met them en masse at the shore.

On Peleliu, over ten thousand Japanese soldiers and high-ranking veteran officer Colonel Nakagawa, who had fought in China, and his 2nd Infantry (Reinforced) hid among honeycombed caves and fortified tunnels, waiting.

The plan was to land on the beaches across from the airfield on the southwest tip of the island. As they got closer, their amphibious LVTs (Landing Vehicles Tracked) and Higgins boats faced cutting volcanic coral reefs as they dropped the Marines off to bolt ashore. The Japanese fired at them, as mines and drums of gas they had planted in the water exploded or burst into flames. Navy bombers hit the Japs on the beaches, causing massive shell-shocking explosions in the water all around the invading Marines.

The LVTs crossed the coral, but the Higgins boats struggled. Marines jumped from the boats and waded ashore with their gear and rifles held high, many mowed down by Jap machine gun fire as they stepped from the boats.

Bogged down by Jap fire, the Marines needed to move faster. The navy had their back with firepower, but friendly fire posed a danger.

With Jap bullets raining down and drawing blood, NCOs yelled at their men, "Get the hell off the beach! Fast."

Rupertus had ordered Puller's 1st Battalion to land on White Beach on the far north and take the high ground. Davis's 5th would land in the center of Orange Beach, and Hanneken's 7th would land south and flank the 5th. When the 5th and 7th finished their mission the first day, they would assist the 1st. Two combat teams would surround the high ground to support the 1st and 7th.

The battalions carried a new, improved flamethrower that projected burning flame and napalm over 150 yards. They also had an additional sixty new amphibious trailers to move equipment.

Going into D-Day, the Marines had two full-scale rehearsals in August and training on Pavuvu and Guadalcanal. They were as ready as they could be.

Beach on Peleliu. (USMC PHOTO)

Marines on and around a tank. (USMC PHOTO)

At the division command post aboard the *DuPage*, Rupertus braced himself as the ship swayed in choppy waters due to the explosions. He jotted a note on top of his letter to Sleepy: *"September 15. D-Day. The Naval gunfire has started. Terrific. No enemy air reactions as yet. Halsey radioed, 'The gate is wide open!' 8:30 am. Pullers unit is ashore OK—5th ashore OK—7th ashore."* As Rupertus sat in a chair in the command post, all around him, radios covered every piece of activity in the landing operation.

His intelligence officer called out status reports in rapid flow, jotting in the logbook:

0832 Troops landed on White beach number 1 & 2.
0833 Troops landed on Orange number 1.
0834 Some gunfire enemy coming from shore.
0836 Troops have landed on all beaches. Encountering difficulty. Cannot tell what the trouble is.
0840 Troops on Orange #2 are pinned down!
0843 Meeting considerable opposition on all beaches!
0847 Troops on White # 2 are 150 yards inland and troops evidently meeting heavy opposition, apparently pinned down!
0850 Troops moving forward inland on Orange #1!
0851 Troops on Orange #1 are receiving artillery and heavy mortar fire!
0853 Troops receiving heavy fire on Orange #3. One LVT believed knocked out.
0900 Three LVTs knocked out at this time.
0924 Friendly troops inland appr. 200 yards on beaches White, Orange #1, #2, #3. Four small submarines sighted.
0929 Concrete pillbox spotted.
0930 White Beach #2 about 20 LVTs & LVTAs knocked out early.
0930 Friendly troops 400–500 yards inland at Beaches Whte #2 and Orange #1.
0936 Enemy shelling seems to have slacked out on beaches.
0932 Obstacles negligible on beaches White 1 & 2.
0940 Enemy gun positions on unnamed island.
0955 Enemy fire from ship.
1010 Enemy tanks approaching the airfield.
1018 Enemy using carrier pigeons.
1012 18 LVTs knocked out on Orange Beach #3.12, 13, 14 wave delayed.
1025 Tanks will be fired on by ships. (NGF)
1040 Left flank stopped by pillboxes.
1055 LVT out on Orange #3. Due to heavy barrage on right can only land on left through the gap. Wave 1 delayed 45 mins. 5 Japs seen wearing gas masks.
1100 Shotgun landing successful. Opposition heavy (7th Mar).

1115 On beach Orange 3 heavy casualties. Need ammo.
1140 Due to lack of LVTs slow going and situation onshore obscure on proceeding to the beach. Mortar and artly. fire falling among troops. 14 wave going in now.
1140 Report LT 1-5 am 50 yard short of 1x. Few landmines and very light resistance on front. No signs of gas or biological warfare.
1145 Located 15 mines on the beach. All have been marked.
1146 Adv. CP proceeding to shore.
1155 Many rounds exploding on Beach Orange.

Braswell Dean of K-3-1 Company later described the hell the assault team faced that morning while approaching the beaches.

It was about 0730 hours, and we were to hit the beach at 0830 hours. For about an hour, the many boats circled and lined up for the final move forward. As we moved in, we saw some of our planes shot down. A tractor or boat on each side of us blew up, and the bodies of Marines were thrown about. Salvos were endlessly and automatically unleashed. As our tractor crawled over the coral reef and toward the shore, shells were dropping like rain, machine gun fire was rattling all around us; mortar fire and phosphorous smell and smoke, and the stench of burning fumes were present. The remnants of half-burned coconut trees caught our attention.

As we exited our tractor, we were in a crossfire from the Japanese on the hill, the ridge in our front, and the enemy at the point to our north enfilading all of K Company as we landed.

When the phosphorus smoke they had used to cover the landings had cleared with the wind, Rupertus saw the grave situation his division faced. To Rupertus and staff listening to the radio and the Marines experiencing it on the beach, it became clear this was a different enemy strategy.

Burning Amtracs sat on the beach. Ground communications were sketchy. Marines were progressing but at a slow rate due to the rough landing, enemy firepower, and surmounting a ridge one hundred yards inland not shown on the map.

Observation planes overhead radioed, "Things are bad on the reef—it looks like up to twenty Amtracs burning on the beach."

Rupertus paced the command post as tensions rose. He radioed his assistant division commander, Brigadier General O. P. Smith, on the USS *Elmore*. "Go ahead ashore as planned to set up a command post."

By 1130 hours D-Day, Smith and a small staff got ashore, set up the command post in an anti-tank ditch the Japanese had dug, and got the telephone line (shore party line) set up so he could reach division command and the 1st, 5th, and 7th command posts.

Smith repeatedly attempted to establish communications with the 5th and 7th Battalions. But by mid-afternoon, still no luck.

With the pandemonium on landing and the brief update from Smith, Rupertus wanted to go ashore himself to see what the hell was happening. Loss of momentum in the face of this fierce opposition would add to the Marines' loss of life.

*****

1st Marine Division Command Post
USS *DuPage*
D-Day, September 15, 1944
1330 Hours

Growing increasingly anxious about the lack of communication with his three division commanders, at approximately 1330 in the afternoon, Rupertus radioed Smith, who had been on shore a little over an hour, "What do you hear from Puller and the location of his 1st Marines?"

Smith replied, "No contact made yet, sir."

"Is it a good time to come ashore?"

Smith radioed back, "The situation appears favorable."

With that, Rupertus prepared to go ashore, but his chief of staff, Colonel John Selden, disagreed with Smith. "I don't want the commanding general to go ashore on D-Day. There's enough division staff already on the ground. To put you ashore now is far too dangerous."

"That's bullshit," Rupertus shot back. "I need to be on shore with my men. I'm their commander." The discussion got more heated.

"General, if you go ashore, you'll know no more than you know now. General Smith is already onshore, and reports are scarce even from him!"

Selden persuaded Rupertus, reluctantly, to hang tight. "Well, then, if I'm not going, let's send a runner for a better picture of what the hell is going on."

Selden sent the runner in a boat to the beach to assess the situation, but he raced back to the *DuPage* in a panic, unable to reach the beach, freaked out by massive Japanese firepower that almost killed him. The runner made no sense in his reporting and had to calm down before Rupertus or the staff got any intelligence.

Rupertus's Marines were facing violent opposition unmatched in any previous engagement so far. Brigadier General Smith radioed in. Smith had finally reached Colonel Hanneken, who requested immediate support and reinforcement.

After discussing options with his staff, Rupertus radioed Smith, "What about sending the Division Reconnaissance Company to reinforce Colonel Hanneken's 7th Division?"

Smith radioed back, "General, there is simply no room on the beach for them."

Colonel Selden then radioed, relaying General Smith's message.

Hanneken immediately radioed back to the *DuPage*, "The 7th Division would be happy to make room for them on the beach as necessary."

Colonel Selden was convinced the entire command leadership might be wiped out if the commanding general went ashore, so he volunteered to go after the runner's attempt failed. Selden left the *DuPage* with a group of eager Marines from the HQ to see what was going on.

Along the way, they passed the Division Reserve waiting in the water on transport. Things were moving slowly because of the number of Amtracs that had burned upon landing, which were now blocking the beaches.

When Selden and his team hit the shore, after dodging dozens of Japanese bullets, he found the beaches packed with men and equipment. Initial reports claimed that Chesty Puller's 3rd Battalion had suffered forty casualties, but when Selden got ashore, he learned the real story: Many Marines had perished, and five of the Amtracs were hit on the way in and burned. They estimated 250 casualties on landing. In actuality, there were 500.

Colonel Selden realized there would not be enough room for his large group, two LCVPs, and the additional Reserve Division.

While assessing the situation and what to do, the day wore on. Right around dusk, Japanese fire descended upon them. Selden got on the shore party line, notifying Rupertus, "We're returning to the *DuPage* with our people for their safety. I can go back in the evening to better clarify the situation and make room for the Division Reserve to move in more quickly to assist the 7th."

Rupertus agreed. "Okay, come back to the ship. But be careful."

When Selden got back to the *DuPage* that evening, he immediately briefed Rupertus. "The situation is bad, sir. The Japs have changed their tactics, and there is a hell of a lot more of them than we realized. It appears that they dug themselves deep into caves and the naval bombing did no good at all. It may be a slow trudge, General."

"Damn it!" Rupertus paused. "Anything else from Hanneken and anything from Puller?"

"Yes, sir. Hanneken feels that the situation has stabilized enough that he does not need the Reserve Division anymore. So we can hold them back unless you direct us otherwise, sir."

"About damn time we got some good news." Rupertus lit a cigarette. "What about Chesty?"

"General Smith finally heard from Chesty. His radio had blown up when they hit the beach, and it took awhile to get through the initial fighting and rewire the radio. His casualties are much heavier than we thought. But he has regrouped and is moving inland."

Rupertus lit a cigarette. "Okay, John. You talked me out of going ashore once. What are your thoughts on that now, because you know I'm ready to go."

"I think we try again in the morning, sir."

Rupertus smiled and nodded. "Roger that. That's exactly what we'll do."

At the end of the first day, all five battalions had gotten ashore, and the 1st Marine Division held the beachhead. The division would have to continue its forward progress to get to the airport.

Though Marine losses were grim, by this time the Japanese had already lost an entire battalion.

*****

Peleliu

D-Day + 1

September 16, 1944

Rupertus returned Smith's salute. "What do we know, O. P.? And what's the damn temperature? We're gonna need water for our men, and fast."

"Good morning, sir. It's brutal. Maybe 115 in the shade. Come into the command post so I can tell you what I know."

Rupertus sat down in the anti-tank-ditch-turned-command post as Smith updated him on the tactical situation.

"Fresh water's scarce on Peleliu, sir. Our Marines arrived with only two canteens. Hydration will be an ongoing issue until we get access to the Japanese water cisterns. Until then, we can take halazone tablets to purify any brown groundwater the engineers uncovered by digging shallow wells. We have salt tablets to battle dehydration."

Rupertus marches ashore and greets Smith at the command post at 2150 hours.
(USMC PHOTO)

"It's mosquitoes, alligators, or heat," Rupertus said. "Pass the word. Resupply all our platoons with extra salt tablets and halazone."

"Aye, sir."

Rupertus spent the rest of the day monitoring the positions of his troops on the ground and issuing orders to his commanders. Later that night, hell broke out.

"Take cover!"

Rupertus, Smith, and staff were suddenly under enemy fire. Enemy bullets flew into the command post like heavy rain, whizzing by their heads.

A staff member later described the attack:

That night was a frightening experience. Shortly after dark, we discovered that a sniper had infiltrated between us and the beach. We were in a tank ditch that the Japanese had built. Major General Rupertus was there with us. I recall the commanding general as I was bedded on the ground right next to his aide.

A sniper was firing into the tank trench, so we had to keep our heads down. And there was firing all night. It was very close to us. Later, reports reached us that the 1st Regiment was having a rough time. Perhaps without the push by Colonel "Chesty" Puller, they might have folded.

They pushed on in a rather shut up condition and made some good gains perhaps, but at a considerable expense to the personnel of the regiment. Some said that Colonel Puller had a thorn in his side. By the time we landed on Peleliu, his brother Sam Puller died on Guam. As a result, Colonel Puller was very bitter toward all Japanese.

*****

Peleliu
September 17 (D+2) and 18 (D+3), 1944

On D+2, Rupertus and his staff moved his division command post to an old administration building and got settled in for the fight. Geiger came ashore to check in and stopped by the command post to relay his concern over Puller's Spitfire regiment. He also proposed bringing in the army's 81st Wildcat Division as soon as they were available to reenforce Puller's 1st Marines. As of September 16, the army was still in battle.

"I think our Marines can handle it while the army is occupied, Roy," Rupertus said. Geiger then wanted to see the airfield, located about two hundred yards from the command post. When he headed out into the open air for a look, a Japanese 150-millimeter shell shot by his head and exploded off to the side.

"Damn, that was a close call," Geiger said.

"You okay, Roy?" Rupertus asked.

"I'm fine, Bill. Another day at the office."

Geiger quickly returned to his ship.

Geiger's proposal was academic, as the army remained bogged down on Anguar, against Rupertus's recommendation that they first be in reserve to support the Marines at Peleliu. Most Marine reserves were transferred to MacArthur for his triumphant march to the Philippines, over Rupertus's objections.

The Marines had advanced only three hundred yards in three days from the shoreline toward the airport. Hundreds were evacuated with stomach problems from the gas-tinged water. Rumors flew that the navy would pull out, like at Guadalcanal, leaving the Marines without fire support or supplies.

Colonel Clifford West, who joined the division at Pavuvu as a regimental forward air controller with the 1st Battalion under Puller, later discussed the first three days: "We were pinned down, but Puller walked around telling people to do this or move here, sometimes hollering at them if a person was cowering or not pulling his load. He was severe with them. Just seeing Puller as fearless helped out a lot."

Some compared Puller to a bull in a china shop. Like his boss Rupertus, Puller embraced the Marine doctrine to push hard and fast on a full-frontal attack, taking heavier casualties up front rather than go slow and have more later on.

On September 18, D+3, Puller radioed Selden, "I need the Division Reserve."

"Not yet, Chesty," Selden said.

"Then send in some replacements from division headquarters."

Selden shot back, "No chance, they aren't trained to fight. They're cooks, bakers, and mess staff."

Puller exploded, "Send them the hell to me! I'll teach 'em to fight overnight!"

Selden acquiesced, releasing one hundred volunteers from the shore party. Selden updated Rupertus on Puller's situation and discussed the option to release the Division Reserve 2/7 to reinforce Puller's torn-up regiment.

The decision was risky, totally depleting reserves. Rupertus called Puller to relay that the 2/7 was available to assist his 1st Marines. Chesty listened and agreed to accept and lead the 2/7, which became attached to the 1st.

Rupertus turned to Selden. "All right, Johnny. Go ahead, but I've shot my bow when they go in. But that's it. We've got no other reserves while the army's tied up in Anguar."

That same day, September 18, as the intense fighting continued, Rupertus received a letter from General Vandegrift, back home in Washington.

It was surreal considering the brutal conditions Rupertus and his Marines currently were in. He congratulated Rupertus and the men on their difficult work and discussed next steps after the mission was complete.

Washington, DC
September 18, 1944
My Dear Bill:
First, let me congratulate you and the Division on the perfectly splendid work that you are doing and your present operation. Of course, it is nothing new for the first to do excellent work because they have done so right along, but this is one of the hardest jobs that they have had handed them, and I want you and them to know that we back here appreciate it. Of course, I will say this officially a little later on when the action is over, but I want to say personally to you at this time.

With reference to your duty, when I knew that I was going to bring you home, I had thought at that time of sending you down to take over the Schools but did not do it because I was afraid that you would not understand my motive in doing so, that perhaps you would not feel such a job commensurate with what you've done. I think it is now a good idea.

I think you should take your Division back to the rehabilitation area and then if you will let me know by Airmail when you feel the proper time for you to come, I will get out the necessary order.

Things here are moving along in their usual routine way and nothing much to write about. I talked so Sleepy over the phone the other night after the landing. She seemed in fine spirits and not worrying. Please give my best regards to the boys out there.
Most Sincerely,
Archer

*****

Peleliu
September 19–20, 1944

By September 19, D+4, the airport was secure. But Puller's 1st Battalion had suffered fifteen hundred casualties. The heat and the steep, rocky terrain had slowed their progress. The Japanese remained embedded in fortified pillboxes and caves, a tactic the Marines had not yet seen.

By September 20, D+5, Navy Seabees had repaired the airfield, and Marine pilots started nonstop bombing runs, dropping napalm on Jap positions and caves. Napalm ignited widespread flames, setting the enemy ablaze, as flames and smoke proved more lethal against enemy caves than bombs.

Despite high casualties, the Marines made slow, forward progress on the mission. Still, Puller's decimated battalion needed help. The decision to have

Rupertus checks on wounded Marines, Peleliu, 1944. (USMC PHOTO)

Minister offers communion and prayers for the Marines, Peleliu. (USMC PHOTO)

the army attack Anguar, and to give most of Rupertus's reserves to MacArthur, was putting the operation in a pinch.

The following day, General Geiger was coming back ashore to discuss relief options, and ahead of that, Rupertus had called together his top two assistants, Brigadier General Smith and Colonel Selden, to discuss the battle situation.

Rupertus first looked at his assistant division commander. "O. P.?"

"Yes, sir," Smith nodded. "Nearly seven days after landing, we controlled all the southern end of Peleliu, as well as the high ground immediately dominating the airfield. All beaches are in use and under our control. There's room for deployment of all the artillery, including the Corps Artillery. We have unhampered unloading capabilities and can get anything on the island we need. We control the airfield, and essential base development work is under way.

"Furthermore, unlike Guadalcanal, we've destroyed, early on, the Japs' ability to launch a major counteroffensive, sir. We've clipped their wings early on."

General Rupertus and Colonel Selden talk with General Julian Smith (on left).
(USMC PHOTO)

Rupertus nodded. "True. They can't push us off the island. But there's a bunch of those bastards holed up in those hills, shooting at us with rockets and machine gun fire." He looked at his chief of staff. "Johnny? Your thoughts?"

"Agree with General Smith's and your assessment, sir. On the one hand, it's been hard as hell. Our stretcher-bearers and navy corpsmen have worked triple-time to save many severely wounded and dehydrated men and return them to action or send the very injured home.

"Not only that," Selden continued, "but our pre-invasion intelligence largely failed us this time. Hills showing on our maps marked as a hundred feet turn out to be six hundred feet. With the massive naval bombardment that we saw, nobody believed that any Japs could have survived. And then the Japs changed their battle tactics, something nobody anticipated.

"On the other hand, we've achieved our major military objectives of taking control of the island and the airstrip. The Japs no longer control the island and can no longer use Peleliu to hit MacArthur's flank when he marches triumphantly into the Philippines. So, like at Cape Gloucester, we've done the Supreme Commander a huge favor."

Rupertus chuckled when he saw Selden grinning. "I like your description of MacArthur, Johnny. Anything else?"

"Yes, sir. Even though we now control the operational base of the island and have clipped the Japs' wings so they can't use Peleliu to hit MacArthur, it's gonna take a hell of a lot of work and manpower to root those bastards and their machine guns out of those hills."

Rupertus took a drag from his cigarette. "I agree with you both."

On September 21, 1944, General Geiger arrived at the 1st Marine Division command post with Colonel Harold D. "Bucky" Harris, the 5th Marines commander.

Earlier, on September 19, Harris had taken off from the airfield to fly over the area on the island's spine called the "Umurbrogal Pocket." In doing so, he better understood the terrain and danger they would face attacking the devilish pocket. Harris proposed the Marines approach it just from the north versus approaching from the north and south. The map Harris sketched looked as though the Umurbrogal Pocket had a flatter area on the north side. The Marines could more easily navigate this safer option versus blazing up the enormous slopes on both sides. The map showed more exact details of the pocket. The hill was almost six hundred feet high in places—much higher than pre-invasion intelligence showed—and full of crevices, caves, and ridges.

Rupertus, Colonel Harris, and an unknown Marine walk on Peleliu. (USMC PHOTO)

General Geiger, Colonel Harris (center), and General Rupertus as Harris explains his plan for taking northern Peleliu.
(USMC PHOTO)

Rupertus and Geiger were initially reluctant to alter their battle plans. But after reviewing the pros and cons, they agreed with Harris's suggestion.

For Rupertus, Harris's reconnaissance again underscored the pre-invasion intelligence failure for Peleliu. In fairness, the pre-invasion reconnaissance team could not get on the island, so the division relied on old maps and aerial photos. Now they knew the spine was brimming with deadly Japs who had to be rooted out. Based on this new intel, Rupertus authorized Harris's new plan.

*****

USS *Mount McKinley*
Off Peleliu
September 21, 1944

Following his conference with Rupertus, Geiger returned to his ship, USS *Mount McKinley*, safely anchored off Peleliu. Rupertus and his men had fought their asses off and taken control of the operational sections of Peleliu. But they were worn out and needed reinforcements to finish the job.

Geiger radioed the army's 81st's commander, General Paul Mueller, to see whether the 81st was available yet to help on Peleliu.

"We're ready, General," Mueller said. "But I need more time to organize a regimental combat team."

He's ready, but he needs more time? What the hell?

Unsatisfied with Mueller's answer, General Geiger, General Julian Smith, and Admiral Fort all visited General Mueller at his headquarters on Anguar to persuade him to move things faster.

"Remember, Paul, "Geiger said, "your army units were part of the reserve for the Marines. Rupertus is in a buzzsaw on Peleliu, and they need backup."

"We are moving as fast as we can, Roy," Mueller replied.

Later that day, Geiger came ashore again and went to the front lines with O. P. Smith to see Chesty Puller. He found Puller without a shirt and limping around due to the injury he suffered on Guadalcanal.

When Puller saw Geiger, he hung up his phone and turned to Geiger. "What can I do for you, General?"

"I thought I'd drop in and see how things are going," Geiger said.

"We're still advancing, but some of our companies are damn small."

"Do you need more reinforcements, Chesty?"

"I'm doing all right with what we have, sir."

General Geiger, commander of 3rd Marine Amphibious Force, talks to Colonel Puller, commander of 1st Marine Regiment on Peleliu. (USMC PHOTO)

Geiger pulled closer to Puller. They had an uncomfortable and heated discussion to get an accurate view of the situation. Geiger sensed Puller was exhausted but would not admit it, nor ask for help.

After that visit, General Geiger walked with Smith to the division command post to tell Rupertus what he had seen and to discuss the next steps.

Colonel Selden, Colonel Jeff Fields, Rupertus's assistant chief of staff, and Colonel Deakin were present and in thoughtful conversation with Rupertus when Geiger arrived.

Geiger greeted them and said he wanted to see Puller's casualty report and talk about bringing in the army.

"Bill," Geiger said, "Puller seemed unable to give a clear picture of his situation. His unit is spent. Just look at these casualty reports. They need to be relieved by the army."

"It's a hellhole," Rupertus responded, "but we've made good progress and feel the division could finish the job soon." He looked at his assistant. "O. P.?"

General Geiger and General Rupertus, Peleliu. (USMC PHOTO)

"Sir, I agree that Puller and his 1st Marines are worn out. But if Mueller needs more time, maybe Puller can be relieved by the newly freed 5th Marines."

"Good point, O. P." Rupertus turned to Geiger, "Is the army ready, Roy? They're fairly green in this situation and we don't have time to train them."

"Understand your concern, Bill. Mueller himself said that he needed more time, which is why we paid him a visit. He declared Anguar secure on September 20 but says he needs more time. I don't buy that.

"So if I can speed them the hell up, I will. Right now, I don't see many options. He was supposed to be our reserve unit anyway before they went off and decided to invade Anguar earlier than we had hoped. I have my reservations about the army, too, but I don't see that we have a choice right now."

A moment of silence followed. Then Geiger turned to Rupertus. "Bill, we've got to take the army. Puller's regiment is finished."

Rupertus and the exhausted staff stood in silence. "Aye, General," Rupertus said as he turned to his staff with red eyes. "Gentlemen, General Geiger is right. Let's figure this out."

He turned back to Geiger. "Roy, my staff and I will make plans to relieve Puller's 1st Marine Battalion and move forward with the army reserve unit. This will be tough on Chesty. He's a proud bastard, and, frankly, my best field commander, and doesn't want to admit that he needs help from anybody else but a US Marine. If Chesty takes help, he'd rather take help from a Marine Corps mail clerk than an army infantryman."

Rupertus took a drag from his cigarette. "But you're right, Roy. The army did a hell of a job supporting us at Guadalcanal, and Chesty, of all people, should remember that. If General Mueller can get the army's shit together, then the 81st Infantry Division is in Chesty's best interest and in the best interest of his men, whether he wants to admit it or not. But I'm frustrated they took my reserves and gave them to MacArthur to march into the Philippines. If they hadn't done that, we wouldn't be in this manpower pinch."

"I agree, Bill. You are a good man and a great general," Geiger said. "I'm going to order the army's 81st Infantry Division to reinforce our Marines here at Peleliu."

*****

Colonel Lewis J. Fields, General Rupertus, and General Geiger on Peleliu.
(USMC PHOTO)

Peleliu
The Army Arrives
September 23, 1944

By September 23, two days after Geiger issued the order to reinforce, the 321st Regiment Combat Team of the US Army's 81st Infantry Division finally stepped onto the beaches of Peleliu. They landed at the northern end of Umurbrogal Mountain, nine days after Rupertus and the 1st Marine Division had landed.

As it turned out, Colonel Hanneken's 7th Marines wound up relieving Chesty Puller's 1st Marines, a move probably more palatable to Colonel Puller's stomach.

The 321st's first mission was to support Hanneken's 7th Marines advance on the Umurbrogal Pocket to carry out the new mission Rupertus had ordered, to attack from the north, after Colonel Harris had spotted flatter ground atop the "pocket," at the island's spine. By the following day, both the 7th Marines and the 321st had encircled the pocket, literally placing an American military noose around the necks of the stubborn Japs embedded on top.

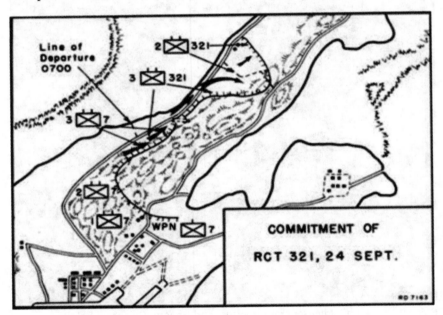

As the Marines gained more control on the ground in the coastal regions, on September 24, Rupertus and his staff moved into a Japanese administration building. The Marines had taken over the building, which had space to assess the progress casualties in full.

Rupertus called Colonel Bucky Harris, his regimental commander, to check how things were going with having the army on board for the assault on the pocket.

"I'll tell you, General," Harris said. "At one point, I got so annoyed with those army guys that I made a point to lose radio communication with them. But I've got to give credit where credit's due. They hit the Jap caves with everything they could blast them with: bazookas, demolition charges, and tank-mounted long-range flamethrowers."

"Great to hear," Rupertus said. "Helps me sleep a little better."

Despite the Marines' high casualty rate, the Japanese lost far more men, and the holdout Japs remained isolated in the devilish "pocket."

By D+12, September 27, Colonel Harris and the 5th Marines reached the island's northern end. Three hundred yards away from the high ground, they conducted a flag-raising ceremony.

As assistant division commander O. P. Smith later recounted, "Things were looking up, and seeing the American flag gave the Marines a jolt of much-needed optimism."

But as they celebrated the flag-raising, the air exploded with the sound of gunfire. The Japanese also saw the American flag raised, and it angered them. Blood splattered everywhere, and several Marines fell over. Colonel Harris called Rupertus and requested naval gunfire against the target. Rupertus responded immediately, and the navy's quick response was accurate on the target, and overwhelming, suppressing the sudden Japanese ambush.

Harris later credited Rupertus for acting swiftly to coordinate naval gunfire support. "Only by the echelons of command repeatedly displaying the same high degree of skill in coordinating fire and maneuver was the complex enemy defense system in northern Peleliu cracked and destroyed."

As they moved north, the Marines came under gunfire from the neighboring island of Ngesebus, about seven hundred yards away. The Japanese snipers were firing from a phosphorus mine that the Japanese had turned into a cement blockhouse.

Rupertus and Smith drove in a jeep to the northern side of Peleliu to observe the situation from a distance. They'd have to attack Ngesebus to stop the harassment. Also, the higher command wanted access to Ngesebus's tiny airstrip. Rupertus ordered the 5th Marines to dispatch one of its battalions to attack Ngesebus and the small islet of Kongauru to destroy the Japanese.

Colonel Harris complied, ordering his 3rd Battalion, along with supporting tanks, amphibian tractors, and the entire panoply of naval gunfire and air support, to launch a shore-to-shore operation to seize Ngesebus and Kongauru, six hundred yards north of Peleliu.

After a spectacular naval assault on September 28, the 3rd Battalion hit the beaches at both Ngesebus and Kongauru, supported by Marine Aviation flying off Peleliu. Thirty-five hours later the island fell, ending all Japanese harassment fire against the Marines, and now the army, encircling the "pocket" on Peleliu. The Ngesebus landing marked the first time in the Pacific War when Marine Aviation provided the full air support of a landing, rather than US Navy aviation. Back on Peleliu, the remaining Japanese had to be dug out cave by cave.

Eventually they had to change tactics. Corsairs dropped infused belly tanks filled with napalm followed by white phosphorus mortar that ignited the napalm.

One Marine later recounted the difficulty in rooting them out:

They were in trees. They would be sniping at you from trees. It was hard to locate them. I guess the first one [sniper] I saw was at the regimental CPA, and he was in a tree probably as close as the house next door. People were getting killed, but you couldn't tell from where it was coming. It was half or three-quarters of an hour before they finally got them. The hills were fortified, and they were honeycombed.

The Japanese would come out, fire, and withdraw, so no way you can get at them. They had it well fortified. We were never able to pull back. There was no reserve to bring in.

Even one hundred pounds of dynamite failed to close the tunnels. The only way to blast this system was bulldozer tanks with low-to-earth blades in front of the tank and flamethrowers to burn the enemy out.

As Lieutenant Jim Hunter said, "Everywhere on the island were Japs. You would turn and turn and see yet another Jap or cave of Japs! Puller was trying to push our division on to keep going, but why? How could we? We had lost more than half of our battalion. Most of the officers and leaders had all died, so the younger Marines with little to no experience had to take charge."

Brave stretcher-bearers evacuated the wounded Marines to field first-aid stations. Hospital ships anchored offshore treated the severely sick and wounded. Following Rupertus's orders, the Marines did everything possible to leave no man behind, dead or alive. That proved sometimes challenging on Peleliu, given the high casualty rate of 53 percent. The Marines had taken the airport in three days as Rupertus planned. But the enemy had dug in deep, and the fighting raged on.

US Army tank (1st Platoon, A Company) follows Marines on Peleliu. (USMC PHOTO)

By late September, the troops were exhausted and hungry. Many members of the 1st Marine Division had fought through three major bloody campaigns.

At one point, only four days of rations remained, which meant these Marines needing energy and water could only have two rations a day. Rupertus called Guam requesting more food and supplies, which were promptly delivered by the Marine Air Group 11. They provided forty-two thousand 10/1 rations.

He then requested more clothing because the Marines' blood-stained clothes had gotten soaked in the rain and then mildewed and dried rough around the edges in the hot sun, making it difficult to maneuver through the brush and sharp coral and up and down the deep ravines. At Rupertus's request, the Marine Air Group brought in one thousand dungarees, five thousand pairs of socks, and one thousand pairs of boondockers.

When the army arrived, the 1st Marines prepared to leave on October 1 for Pavuvu. But not before a burial at the new cemetery on Orange Beach 2.

Burial at gravesite on Peleliu. (USMC PHOTO)

Colonel Puller and General Rupertus at burial. (USMC PHOTO)

They had no choice but to prevail.

A sad day for Rupertus and the division came on October 12, 1944, when the assault phase was declared officially over. A beloved Marine, Captain Andy Haldane, an expert rifleman, went sniper hunting to find the Japanese sniper who was killing off his men on Hill 140. Haldane took a shot to the head by one of the snipers he was hunting, dying instantly.

With only days to go before the Marines handed off Peleliu to the army, Haldane's loss stung Rupertus and the men who knew him. Haldane had served with the division with gallantry and bravery from Guadalcanal to this final day on Peleliu. When Rupertus learned about Haldane's death, he called in firepower to pound the hell out of the enemy snipers and their friends.

Rupertus was privately grieving the loss of so many when the Red Cross brought news from home that his beloved mother, Augustina, had died on September 5.

He shook off his grief and wrote a letter to be distributed to the officers and men the next day. They had to fight on.

October 13, 1944
OFFICERS AND MEN OF THE FIRST DIVISION:
Twenty-nine days ago, we landed on Peleliu. Since that memorable day, you have pushed the enemy from every position that he could conceive. You now have him in one small Pocket where he is fighting for his last fanatical and dying gasp. You are tired. You have accomplished what to many would have been impossible, but one Pocket remains to be cleared of the enemy and revenge our colors—they will be killed or captured, to the last man!

This Division has never been defeated in battle and has never left a job before his mission was accomplished. We came here to take the airfield and kill or capture the enemy.

We have taken the airfield, and from it, planes are operating against the enemy. But we still have a few strongly entrenched enemy to kill.

Tomorrow, battalions from both the 5th and 7th Regiments, after two or more days rest, will drive forward to break the last hold the enemy has on the island of Peleliu. When this has been accomplished, you will be returned to your staging area for a much-needed rest and many of you to your homes.

This Division has never failed—and it will not fail now. We will complete our mission.
W. H. RUPERTUS
Major General, US Marine Corps Commanding

By mid-October the army brought more reinforcements, relieving the beleaguered Marines, and by November thoroughly routed the last few Japanese.

Time's Robert "Pepper" Martin wrote his view as a reporter embedded with the Marines:

Peleliu is a horrible place. The heat is stifling, and rain falls intermittently—the muggy rain that brings no relief, only greater misery. The coral rocks soak up the heat during the day, and it is only slightly cooler at night. Marines are in the finest possible physical condition, but they wilted on Peleliu. By the fourth day, there were as many casualties from heat prostration as from wounds. Peleliu is incomparably worse than Guam in its bloodiness, terror, climate, and the incomprehensible tenacity of the Japs. For sheer brutality and fatigue, I think it surpasses anything yet seen in the Pacific, certainly from the standpoint of numbers of troops involved and the time taken to secure the island.

The officers and men on Peleliu all agreed. They had faced unbelievable odds and yet prevailed on the mission given to them—one of the most brutal campaigns in history.

Rupertus with Pedro "Pete" DeValle. (USMC PHOTO)

General Rupertus (center) with staff, Peleliu. (USMC PHOTO)

*****

Farewell to Peleliu
October 20, 1944

After proper burial services and with the establishment of the US Army's 81st Division command post on October 20, the top Marine echelons departed at once by air: General Geiger and the Corps staff that morning; General Rupertus and the division staff would fly out at 2300 hours.

The night before at a party put on by the army, Rupertus, as the commanding general of the 1st Marine Division, paid tribute to the army unit that had fought with him and so well in the battle.

The day he left, Rupertus sat by the window of his staff plane, a DC4 nicknamed "Sleepy," as they lifted off the airstrip his Marines had captured. He looked down, making out the lights from the army's command post as the plane lifted into the sky. Stars and a waxing moon provided enough light for him to make out the whitecaps crashing the shoreline of Peleliu, and the moonlit sky provided a strained view of the island's outline.

His Marines had just won the bloodiest battle of the Pacific War, and the moment left him awash in thought. Thoughts of commanding the first American victory on the ground at Tulagi, of the young Marines he had buried there, of Gavutu, of the Battle for Henderson Field, of John Basilone and his heroics.

Then he thought of Melbourne, his relationship with Vandegrift, and finally becoming commander of the division. Then came MacArthur, wanting to keep the division under his command after their victory at Cape Gloucester. And then there was death, always too much death.

He had lost his mother, Augustina. He could not attend her funeral, just as he could not attend the funerals of Marguerite, William Jr., and Ann Rodney. Then he thought of the rawest death, Captain Andy Haldane, a young officer for whom he had developed a great affection.

But when his thoughts turned to Sleepy and Pat, he smiled, and the pain eased, knowing that he would be with them soon.

The lulling roar of the airplane's twin engines and the cooler air reminded him that he was on the first leg of his journey home. The outline of Peleliu disappeared below, giving way to nothing but the dark Pacific. Nearly eleven thousand Japs had been killed on Peleliu, and their commanders had committed ritual suicide. But over a thousand Marines had been killed, and another five thousand wounded, though some of the wounded had returned to battle. Either way, Peleliu had some of the highest American casualty rates of the war, to date.

He looked out the window of the plane and saw a million stars filling the sky and said a prayer.

All was well, and all would be well. He closed his eyes and tried to get some sleep.

Chapter 65

Back on Pavuvu
October 21, 1944

In the afternoon of October 21, Rupertus and the remainder of the 1st Marine Division arrived on Pavuvu to recover and rebuild. A few days after Rupertus cleaned up, had some drinks with his officers, and slept, he settled down at his desk at his command post overlooking the water to write some crucial accolades and then write to Sleepy.

First, he formally commended the army, and the 7th Marine Ammunition Company, the African American unit out of Montford Point, North Carolina, who carried ammo to the front lines and on return were vital stretcher-bearers. Many took up guns in tough situations to support the fight. "I wish to convey to the command these sentiments and inform them that in the eyes of the entire 1st Marine Division, they have earned a sincere 'well done.'"

Over a week, Rupertus wrote more commendations, including one for the war dog platoon tragically killed on Peleliu. And he sent letters to Vandegrift and Sleepy.

Base Camp
23 October '44
US Marine Corps
My Darling,
Here I am back again in what appears to us all, a Garden of Paradise, after that hellhole of Peleliu. I, with my staff and HQ force, in four transport planes arrived here on the 21st at about 4 PM. After cleanup, each one of us just was talking just like a quartet of old Civil War veterans returning from their battles.

They all asked me if they could celebrate, and I said sure. I wrote to AV to thank him for my job. All I need is the four days travel—time delay—that's my orders from DC to HQ. We can visit the Dressler's in New York later in the winter, maybe around New Years' time.

Our first Christmas though should be at our house, for now, you, Pat and me. I estimate I'll leave here on 3 November arriving in San Francisco either the 4th or 5th—more like the latter—then take the plane and arrive in DC about the 6th.

I will have to fly the southern route instead via Chicago on account of weather, but it will make a little difference in time. I won't try to buy presents for everyone this time darling—maybe a box of candy for Pat? Tell Paddy to be in shape for a rear bout.

Oh, I love you so, darling and I'm wildly excited to be with you and Pat. Always yours,
Bill

23 October, 1944
My Dear General:
I have just received your letter upon my return here to the basecamp. I deeply appreciate your kindness in giving me this fine assignment, and I assure you that I will do all I can to warrant your confidence. Pete DeValle is here close by, and I have requested III Corps that he confer with me for several days during the next few days. I want to give him a complete picture on the personnel and materiel problem, as well as to permit him to make his assignment of staff, regimental, and two battalion commanders.

I left Peleliu at 11 p.m. on the 20th and arrived the next day here. I turned over the defenses to the 81st CG upon orders from the Corps, whose Headquarters left that same date at 8:15 a.m. I left O.P. Smith with the junior staff at Peleliu as CG of the remainder of the Division (CT 5, Reinforced, which included the Corps' artillery). Upon the sailing of CT 5, O. P. Smith, with his command staff, will return here by air, and I expect him to be here on or about the 1st of November.

A large number of our men demonstrated beyond question their ability to be non-commission officers and also NCO's to be advanced in rank. They demonstrated this upon the death or wounding of their commanding officers, and in my opinion testified what one would expect of a leader.

We have asked FMF, Pac, for authority to make these meritorious promotions from these men, but so far have received no answer. These are the men I feel are deserving of this reward as well as acknowledgment of their ability, and they will then be available as leaders in the next show.

I consider it highly desirable that all of the officers and men who have been out here for over two years be returned at the earliest practicable time, for it is not at all desirable to have men feel that they will remain here indefinitely or until returned as a battle casualty.

Relative to the detachment of Selden, Lt. Col. Fields, Puller, Hanneken, Gober, Ballance, Lt. Col. Smith (Engineer Bn.), Nees and Woods (artillery), I recommend that upon the reporting of their reliefs they be detached to the United States: I feel sure that the detachment of our officers can take place prior to the arrival of their reliefs. We have the necessary executives remaining here who can carry on the work until the arrival of their chiefs.

The food is wonderful here, and everything has been done to welcome these men, including the gratuitous issue of beer and Coca-Cola. The first I knew of it being sent to us was when I received a letter from Sleepy when she informed me that Mrs. Vandegrift told her.

To return here to this beautiful basecamp after being on the God-Forsaken-Island of Peleliu was like returning to the Garden of Paradise.

I noticed that you mentioned you would give me a brief leave upon my return. If I have the necessary four days in my travel orders, that will be quite sufficient for me to pack up and move. You were extremely kind in granting me that leave last June, and I feel that I have had all the leave that I really rate. Again, thanking you for your very kind letter, I am
Very Sincerely,
Bill

Chapter 66

Coming Home
Washington, DC
November 2, 1944

Rupertus read the orders, and re-read them, just to be sure. Finally, after over twenty-four months at war, he was relieved of duty in the Pacific and passed the baton of command of his beloved 1st Marine Division to his good friend, General Pete DeValle.

The orders, which he expected, brought a smile to his face. Yet at the same time, a moment of bittersweetness overcame him. The 1st Marine Division was his baby. They were family.

He and Archer Vandegrift, through blood, sweat and tears, had worked together to bring the division to life at New River in 1942. And now the division would be under a new commander, someone other than the two men who were there from the beginning. But he was going home to his first family, to Sleepy and Pat. He couldn't wait to see the look on little Pat's face when he walked through the door. Back home, he would assume his new role as commandant of the Marine Corps Schools at Quantico, and Pat and Sleepy would be with him.

He touched down in San Francisco on November 5, after a long flight over the ocean and a planned layover at Pearl Harbor. He stepped off the plane and breathed in the satisfying air of freedom.

He reported to the Department of the Pacific in San Francisco and on November 6 made it back to Washington to crispy, cool weather in the low forties, just a little over two weeks before Thanksgiving Day. The fallish weather might have been chilly, but his reception was warm.

Between Rupertus, Sleepy, and Pat, dozens of hugs, kisses, and presents were exchanged. Thanksgiving began that day in the Rupertus household and would last until Christmas. It was great to be home!

Sleepy had already packed up to move the family to officers' quarters at Quantico on November 9. General Vandegrift immediately ordered Rupertus to get on the Marine Corps PR train, to remind America that the war wasn't over. Rupertus's first national interview came with CBS radio reporter

Don Pryor, perhaps appropriately, on Armistice Day, on the thirty-fourth anniversary of the end of World War I.

Major General Rupertus
WJSV-CBS
November 11, 1944
2:30–3:00 p.m., E.W.T.

Pryor: *General Rupertus, with three major campaigns in the Pacific to your credit, you are an authority on the war against the Japanese. You were assistant division commander of the 1st Marine Division at Guadalcanal, in charge of the landing operations at Tulagi, Gavutu, and Tanambogo. You commanded the 1st Marine Division at Cape Gloucester. And you just returned from leading the 1st Division in the assault on Peleliu. Which were your toughest operations?*

Rupertus: *I don't believe there's any measure of comparison. Each campaign was against the same fanatically determined enemy. Each had its own problems of weather, terrain, and distribution of enemy strength. All the campaigns against the Japanese were hard, bitterly contested operations that demanded the utmost of every man engaged in them. I know that every man in every branch of the military service fighting the Pacific is willingly giving everything he has to achieve a common goal—the complete defeat of the Japanese enemy. If that aim is to be reached, the people back home—each related in blood to a fighting man—must contribute in the same measure.*

The war against the Japanese is a very personal war. Every bomb and every bullet sounds as though it is meant for you in person. Much of the fighting is at the closest quarters. You are the man that the saki-crazed warrior is charging at as he runs screaming toward your lines. You are the man that gleaming samurai sword is going to cut through if you don't strike first. That's just what we've been doing out there—striking first and striking hard.

Pryor: *That policy has worked very well. We've gone a long way in the Pacific in the past two years. Do you think we're close to the goal of the complete defeat of Japan?*

Rupertus: *The hardest part of the war lies ahead. As we get closer to the Japanese homeland, Japanese determination and fanaticism becomes even greater. Their military strength also increases as we get closer to its source. This is no time to sit back and contemplate our past successes. Rather we should consider the tremendous task that lies ahead, and mentally resolve to match in willing personal contribution, inspired by the love of country, the fanatic devotion to the Emperor that spurs the Japanese.*

Pryor: *Friday was the 169th anniversary of the founding of the US Marine Corps, General. What do you think that the 170th year holds for your organization?*

Rupertus: *I think it will be one of the fightingest years in our fighting history. We Marines are proud of our past achievements, and as a Marine, I can assure the people of the United States that every man in the Corps will do everything he can do to sustain our record and justify the motto of the Marine Corps—Semper Fidelis—always faithful!*
Pryor: *Thank you, General Rupertus!*

On November 21, 1944, two days before Thanksgiving, Rupertus assumed command of the Marine Corps Schools in Quantico. Mrs. Vandegrift welcomed Rupertus and Geiger home with a celebratory dinner party in their honor at the commandant's house.

On December 11–13, Rupertus traveled to Chicago as a guest speaker with General George C. Marshall, for two thousand influential business executives at the Illinois Manufacturers Association's 51st Annual Dinner Meeting. After dinner, Rupertus gave a fascinating talk called "Behind the Pacific." Soon after, Christmas was in the air, and being his first Christmas with Sleepy and Pat since he had left to join the division at New River in 1942, Rupertus wanted to spend it at home to cherish their time as a family.

On January 29, 1945, Rupertus was scheduled to be awarded the US Navy Distinguished Service Medal in a ceremony with a parade at Quantico and review of the troops. It was a cold, windy day, with a high of only thirty-five degrees. But after the hot hellhole that was the South Pacific, frankly Rupertus relished the colder weather.

Sleepy's family came up early for the celebration, and everybody took pictures to capture the moments with Pat and his cousins. Rupertus chatted with Sleepy's parents, tiny Dixie, and a jovial Lieutenant Commander Hill. Sporting a white suit, he laughed so hard at Patrick and his cousins playing war that tears flowed from his eyes.

After the brunch, the clouds set in. The group changed into formal clothes and bundled up. The family and many of Rupertus's US Marine and Navy friends and their wives dressed in their finest furs, hats, and pearls.

Rupertus donned his uniform slowly, ensuring it was just right, remembering all he and the Marines fought through with each button. The family gathered at the reviewing stand as they watched the Marines parade by in spit-and-polish precision, unmatched by any branch of the American armed forces.

Rupertus received the Distinguished Service Medal at Lyman Field from Major General Phillip Torrey, commanding general, who read the citation by Admiral Nimitz and then pinned the medal on Rupertus's chest.

General Torrey pins the Distinguished Service Medal on General Rupertus, Quantico, Virginia. (USMC PHOTO)

Both General Torrey and Rupertus wore Marine-issued wool overcoats for officers and black leather gloves. As General Torrey pinned the DSM award on Rupertus's lapel and smiled, Rupertus stood tall with honor and humility, thinking of his men lost and those still fighting in the Pacific. Along with this award and the stars on his left shoulder sleeve, he wore the Guadalcanal patch of the 1st Marine Division.

Rupertus was cited for meritorious service "while serving as Commanding General of the 1st Marine Division during operations against Peleliu Island from September 15 to October 14, 1944," signed by Secretary of the Navy James Forrestal.

Admiral Nimitz lauded the general's courage and determination and established him as an "outstanding leader." A grand party followed the ceremony to celebrate the occasion. It was good to be home with Marine friends.

Patrick Hill Rupertus, age five, with his dad, General Rupertus, Quantico, Virginia. (USMC PHOTO)

The Rupertus family enjoyed their time in Quantico, and Pat was happy to have his daddy home, get his hugs, and hear his tales about war. Pat rode on ponies with his dad and played in tanks and airplanes. Watching it all, Sleepy felt at peace, realizing a dream she thought might never come true.

Rupertus remained the confident husband she knew and loved, but the war had aged him. His brown hair and mustache were now gray, and at times when she looked into his blue eyes, he seemed a thousand miles away.

Chapter 67

A Farewell to Arms
Washington, DC
March 25, 1945

It was the beginning of Holy Week, Sunday, March 25, 1945, one week before Easter Sunday. After a cooler snap with temperatures only reaching the high forties, the last couple of days saw a return to springtime in the Washington area, with the daytime highs reaching the seventies.

Rupertus, Sleepy, and Pat were headed to Washington for the weekend to attend a party at the Navy Yard in Washington, DC, hosted by Rupertus's old friend and former chief of staff of the 1st Marine Division, Colonel Robert J. Kilmartin, and his wife, Alice. They had arrived in Washington on Saturday, March 24, in time for Sleepy to take in the cherry blossoms in bloom around the Tidal Basin, which, ironically, had been a gift to the United States from the Japanese government back in 1912, before all hell broke loose. They spent Saturday night at the Marine Barracks with their dear friends, Edythe and Tom Hill.

Sunday would bring a fabulous reunion. Colonel Kilmartin, now commanding officer of the six-acre Marine Barracks, would be there. So would General Vandegrift and many officers and wives they knew and loved.

Rupertus, wearing his spiffily tailored dress blue uniform, resplendent with rows of shining medals, and Sleepy, wearing a long, flowing, dark red dress, looked glamorous as the happy couple departed for the dinner party at the Navy Yard, just a half mile south of the entrance to the Marine Barracks.

When they arrived, Kilmartin greeted Rupertus at the door with a salute, huge smile, and strong handshake. "Sir, it's great having you back."

"Thanks, Killy. I missed you," Rupertus said. "Lots to catch up on, so let's get this party started."

The event started at six, and after dinner and dessert, the cocktails were flowing, and the party roared with conversation and scuttlebutt about the war, the economy, the Marine Corps, and more. At about 9:00 p.m., Rupertus walked outside to join his friends on the porch to chat. He looked up at the stars in the clear night sky and decided to have a cigarette.

After finishing the cigarette, something seemed wrong. He coughed and turned to his buddy Tom Hill. "I am going inside to get some water."

Rupertus walked back inside Kilmartin's house, got a drink of water, and visited with friends a little longer. "I need to go back outside to get some air."

He waved to Sleepy, deep in conversation, and then stepped outside. Still, something didn't feel right.

He sat down on the steps, loosened his jacket buttons, and rubbed his forehead. He felt sweaty, tight chested, and tingly in his left arm. Dread set in.

At 9:35 p.m., his heart suddenly jerked and went into a chaotic rhythm. Within a minute, his breathing slowed.

Kilmartin raced inside to call sickbay and tell Sleepy, who dropped her drink on the floor and bolted out the door. She found Rupertus unconscious on his side.

"No, no, no!" Sleepy cried. She wrapped her arms around Rupertus. "Bill! Bill! Wake up! Please!"

A moment later, he took his final breath and died in her arms. Tears streamed down her face as she held him tight. "No, no, my love, my Bill."

Disbelief, shock, and anguish engulfed the party with a sudden hushed silence as Sleepy held her hero, her one and only beloved husband, in her arms. When the medics took Rupertus out of her arms to take his body to sickbay, Sleepy went into shock.

Edythe Hill, also in tears, came out and hugged Sleepy. Sleepy did not want to leave the Kilmartins' house or tell Pat, her sisters, and her parents the horrible news.

Rupertus had returned from the Pacific in November 1944. Four months later, he was dead at age fifty-five.

Rupertus died of a heart attack the same day his beloved 1st Marine Division landed on Okinawa. Like his commander-in-chief, Franklin Roosevelt, Rupertus would never see the end of the war, would never see justice for his Marines, or see his son grow up to be a Marine aviator, and his great-grandson a naval aviator.

The following morning, Sleepy's sister Dixie Hill Brodie sent a telegram to sister Jo and her husband Bev, stationed in Hastings, Nebraska.

WESTERN UNION
WASHINGTON DC MAR 26 (814 AM)
CMDR B.E. CARTER
RUPERTUS DIED SUDDENLY OF HEART ATTACK SUNDAY
NIGHT. HE WAS RELEASED FROM THE HOSPITAL THURSDAY
AND FELT ALLRIGHT. HE WAS TO BE RETIRED FOR PHYSICAL
DUE TO HIS HEART CONDITION. SLEEPY IS WITH MOTHER
AND DADDY = DIXIE

Chapter 68

Final Salute
Arlington National Cemetery
March 27, 1945

At 1000 hours on Tuesday, March 27, 1945, the military funeral took place at Fort Myer Chapel. Rupertus would be buried in Arlington National Cemetery with full military honors.

The honorary pallbearers, all wearing their resplendent Marine Corps dress blues with white gloves, included Lieutenant General Alexander A. Vandegrift, commandant of the Marine Corps; Major General P. H. Torrey, USMC, commanding general of the Marine Barracks, Quantico; Brigadier General Alphonse DeCarre, USMC; Brigadier General Samuel C. Cumming, USMC; and General Gerald C. Thomas and Colonel R. C. Kilmartin Jr., USMC.

They slowly brought the flag-draped casket from the chapel, and minutes later a thirteen-gun salute, lasting one minute, fired volleys as the military escort entered the cemetery.

In a black dress with a matching hat and veil, Sleepy was escorted by Brigadier General W. P. T. Hill, their longtime friend. She was brave and gracious, but she cried deep inside as she gently wiped tears away with a cotton handkerchief.

Some of the mourners paying their last respects were the honorable Secretary of the Navy James Forrestal; Admiral E. J. King, US Navy, admiral of the US fleet; Vice Admiral F. J. Horn, USN, vice chair of naval operations; Major General Deepak, USMC, assistant commandant of the Marine Corps; several military representatives from the British Embassy, the Netherlands Embassy, and the China Embassy; and a host of ranking US Navy and Marine Corps officers and enlisted and civilian personnel.

After the chaplain's remarks, a Marine Honor Guard, in service dress blues, lifted the American flag off the casket and, in crisp precision, unmatched by anyone other than the Marine Corps, carefully folded the flag, step by step, into a tight triangle. The captain overseeing the honor guard slowly turned and handed the flag to Brigadier General Hill.

General Hill took the flag, stepped over to Sleepy, and came down on one knee. "Ma'am, the president of the United States presents this flag to you on behalf of a grateful nation."

Sleepy accepted the flag with a smile and whispered, "Thank you." Another thirteen-gun salute cracked the air, this one lasting five seconds, as they lowered the casket into the grave. Sleepy dropped her head as a stirring rendition of "Taps" sounded in the distance against the soft breeze.

For the great commander of the 1st Marine Division, the war had ended.

He died undefeated in battle, unmatched in his love of family, and unflinching in his duty to country.

Postlogue

FATHER O'NEIL AND CHAPLAIN HINDMAN HAD LED RUPERTUS'S FUNERAL service. A few days later Hindman sent a letter to Sleepy:

> *I pass on to you an observation that I made, which indicates the high regard that men of all ranks and warrants held for your husband. After most people had left the grave, I noticed a Marine Corporal standing some 5 or 10 yards away from the grave leaning against a tree, his whole body wracked with sobs of mourning for a lost friend. Then slowly, the Corporal composed himself and joined the crowd.*

Sleepy received hundreds of sympathy letters from friends and family, which she saved for her and Pat to treasure. She returned to Quantico on April 3 to pack up and sift through Rupertus's belongings. She kept one khaki uniform, Rupertus's brown aviator jacket, two USMC caps, and the American flag from his casket, along with wooden trunks full of photos and military memorabilia. On April 12, Sleepy and Pat moved back to Washington, DC, to a small apartment.

On May 8, 1945, two months after Rupertus's death and one month after President Roosevelt died, the Allies accepted Germany's unconditional surrender, igniting a worldwide celebration. Japan's leaders, however, held out and refused to surrender.

While millions cheered the victory in Europe, the US Marines, Navy, and Army remained engaged at Okinawa, with no end in sight should the war go on to Japan.

On May 30, 1945, Sleepy read about Rupertus's 1st Marine Division on Okinawa:

> *AP NEWS: First Marines Fulfill a Pledge to Rupertus*
> *By S. Sergt Walter N. Wood and Sergt. Leo T. Batt*
> *Marine combat correspondents*
> *A promise made to late Major General William H. Rupertus when he gave up command of the 1st Marine Division has been kept—the American flag, which his men planted at Cape Gloucester and Peleliu, now flies over Shuri Castle.*

The American flag being rasied at Shuri Castle on Okinawa. (USMC PHOTO)

Marine Lieutenant Colonel R. P. Ross Jr. planted the flag on the highest rampart standing in the shell-plastered castle. Rifle bullets whined past the officer as he climbed to raise Old Glory.

In June 1944, Sleepy received a letter from Secretary of the Navy James Forrestal announcing that a new US naval destroyer would be named in honor of her late husband.

On August 15, 1945, Japan offered an unconditional surrender to the United States.

On September 21, 1945, Sleepy traveled to Quincy, Massachusetts, to see the USS *Rupertus* launch. Looking elegant in dress, hat, and mink stole around her neck, she valiantly christened the USS *Rupertus*, DD-851, by smashing a champagne bottle against the new ship's bow to give her the spark of life.

Her sister Jo sent a telegram:

We're thinking of you today and sending you all our love. May the USS Rupertus's officers and crew carry on the finest traditions of the naval service and always be a credit to the memory of your Rupertus.

Sleepy Rupertus about to christen the USS *Rupertus*. (US NAVY PHOTO)

Sleepy Rupertus smashes champagne bottle on USS *Rupertus*. (US NAVY PHOTO)

USS *Rupertus* launches. (US NAVY PHOTO)

Acknowledgments

In 2017, my friend Don Brown, who was working on another book at the time, discovered that William H. Rupertus was my grandfather. He reached out to confirm our connection and then promptly gave me a challenge that altered the course of my life for the next five years.

This book would not be before you without the unyielding support and encouragement of my dear sisters, Heather Rupertus Bates and Kimberly Rupertus Robinson, as well as Don.

When I accepted Don's challenge to write my grandfather's story, I did not fully realize the level of research and work that was ahead of me. As I labored away for the next four years to create an accurate and complete historical record of my grandfather's incredible life, I became even more fascinated by this time in history and the astounding times in which my grandfather lived.

Kimberly and Heather joined me in visiting the Marine Corps History Division at Quantico, Virginia, for research, and they also came to Charlotte, North Carolina, to help organize the massive amount of family and military material that lay in the wooden trunks that our grandmother, Alice Hill Rupertus (aka "Sleepy"), saved after our grandfather, William Henry Rupertus, died unexpectedly in 1945.

Kimberly devoted countless hours to conducting in-depth research at various archives and connected with various historians, scholars, and veterans. She collected hundreds of primary-source materials while organizing and cataloging that research along with our family collections. She also took time to read drafts, offering suggestions. Her persistence, attention to detail, intelligence, and encouragement made her an invaluable contributor to the entire project.

I also completed the military writers' "On Point Workshop," led by former Marine officer Tracy Crow. As my developmental editor, she provided honest feedback and gave me ongoing support to keep me moving forward. As a civilian, she and a peer reviewer suggested that I should partner with someone with military experience to make this important story the best it could be. I took their advice and reached back out to Don Brown, a former

US Navy JAG officer, to join me as my coauthor and get this book to the finish line. I am thankful he accepted the challenge. It has been a wise collaboration and a lot of fun.

Thanks to Dave Sharrett, my former English teacher and dear friend, who reviewed the first "rather cathartic" essay I wrote about my late father, former USMC Captain Pat Rupertus.

Thanks to our agent, Chip MacGregor, president of MacGregor and Luedeke Literary, for his tireless work on our behalf and guidance in helping us work effectively as coauthors.

Thanks to Scott Syfert for his early support and for reading my first "Hail Mary" manuscript, as well as his guidance with edits to add color to my work.

Thanks to historian Annette Ammerman and archivist Alisa Whitley for their support and for quickly responding to our multiple requests for USMC and US Navy files and oral histories over the years.

Thanks also to Dominic Amaral and the stellar team at the USMC History Division.

Thanks to our friend Commander John Blackwelder (USN Ret.) for reading the second draft and supporting this story since the beginning. We are grateful for the service and historical input of World War II Marine veterans Jim Hunter, Woody Williams, Braswell Deen Jr., William Finnegan, and William White.

Thanks also to US Army veteran Jack Miller of La Mesa, California; Maria Faber of Evergreen, Colorado; Marie Prys of Salem, Oregon; and Rob Suggs of Atlanta, Georgia—for their excellent editorial feedback.

Thanks to Senior Editor Dave Reisch, Senior Production Editor Patricia Stevenson, Editorial Assistant Stephanie Otto, and our book team at Rowman & Littlefield for their interest, patience, and work on our behalf to get this book out to the world.

A bundle of gratitude, love, and thanks goes to my family, including my husband Edwin, for hours of conversation with me about the book and history. I'm ever grateful to our children, Bruton and Avery, for supporting and encouraging their mom during these pivotal years in their lives.

This book was a team effort. Thank you, Old Breed General Team!

Bibliography

Roots

Evening Star editors. "Because of Ill Health, Cadet Rupertus Resigns from the Revenue Cutters Service." *Evening Star* (Washington, DC), June 22, 1913.

"Everywhere You Look: German Roots in Washington." Goethe Institute. https://www.goethe.de/ins/us/en/kul/sup/deu/was.html.

Hunt, Virginia. Rupertus/Rubertus Genealogy: Gottlieb Rupertus of Washington, DC, and Henry Rupertus of Montevideo, Minnesota. 1980.

Major General Rupertus Marine Corps File, Marine Corps History Division.

Meranski, Sophie Ruth. "Red-Headed Stepchild (The Barrett Family Memoir of Navy Life)." http://www.barrettfamilymemoir.com/redheadedstepchild-revisedhomepage.html. Accessed online January 17, 2020.

Smith, Horatio David. "Early History of the United States Revenue Marine Service or (United States Revenue Cutter Service) 1789–1849, Washington, DC." 1989. https://media.defense.gov/2017/Jul/02/2001772348/-1/-1/0/USRCS1789-1849.PDF. Accessed online January 8, 2020.

William H. Rupertus US National Archives P.E.P. File.

Wolverton, W. H. Letter of Reference (June 1906). William H. Rupertus National Archives File.

The Making of a Marine Officer

Barde, Robert E. *The History of Marine Corps Competitive Marksmanship.* Marine Corps Library, 1961. https://archive.org/stream/historyofmarinec00bard/historyof-marinec00bard_djvu.txt. Accessed online February 11, 2020.

Jacobs, W. E. Letter to William H. Rupertus (June 17, 1913). William H. Rupertus National Archives File.

Lejeune, John Archer. Letter of Commendation. William H. Rupertus National Archives File.

Rupertus, William H., National Archives File. 1914 Marine Corps Rifle Team Orders. History of USMC Rifle Team.

Cemeteries and Graves

Ashurst, William Wallace. https://www.findagrave.com/memorial/49002657/william-wallace-ashurst. Accessed online August 19, 2019.

Holcomb, Thomas. http://www.arlingtoncemetery.net/tholcomb.htm. Accessed online February 11, 2020.

Larsen, Henry. http://www.arlingtoncemetery.net/hllarsen.htm. Accessed online February 11, 2020.
Masters, James. http://www.arlingtoncemetery.net/jmmasterssr.htm. Accessed online February 11, 2020.
Rupertus, Patrick Hill. http://www.arlingtoncemetery.net/patrick-hill.htm. Accessed online February 11, 2020.
Rupertus, William Henry. http://www.arlingtoncemetery.net/whruper.htm. Accessed online February 11, 2020.
Rupertus Family. http://www.prospecthillcemetery.org. Accessed online February 11, 2020.

Civil War
American Battlefield Trust. Civil War Facts. https://www.civilwar.org/learn/articles/civil-war-facts. Accessed online February 11, 2020.

World War I
Andrews, Evans. The Zimmerman Telegram. National Archives. August 31, 2018. https://www.archives.gov/education/lessons/zimmermann. Accessed online February 11, 2020.
History.com editors. *World War 1: Summary, Causes, and Facts*. http://www.history.com/topics/world-war-i/world-war-i-history. Accessed online January 31, 2020.
McClellan, E. N. "American Marines in the British Grand Fleet." *Marine Corps Gazette* (pre-1994) 7, no. 2 (1922): 147–64.
Page, Walter. Telegram from United States Ambassador to President Woodrow Wilson Conveying a Translation of the Zimmermann Telegram. 862.20212 / 57 through 862.20212 / 311; Central Decimal Files, 1910–1963; General Records of the Department of State, Record Group 59; National Archives at College Park, College Park, MD. https://www.docsteach.org/documents/document/translation-zimmermann-telegram. Accessed online January 15, 2020.
Rupertus, William H. Diary, USS *Florida*, 1913.

Haiti
Belton, F. "Police Department, Port au Prince, Haiti." *Leatherneck* (pre-1998), 14, no. 6 (1931): 7–8, 48–49.
Borno, Louis. Letter to General McDougal, Port-au-Prince. March 20, 1923.
Davis, Elizabeth. "Brigadier General Herman Hanneken." https://marines.togetherweserved.com/usmc/servlet/tws.webapp.WebApp?cmd=ShadowBoxProfile&type=Person&ID=50447. Accessed online January 9, 2020.
Davis, R. B., Jr. "Letter from Secretary of the Legation Davis to the Secretary of State." Washington, DC, January 12, 1916. https://history.state.gov/historicaldocuments/frus1916/d352. Accessed online January 10, 2020.
Glueck, Meredith. "Haiti, Caco Revolts." *Encyclopedia of Latin American History and Culture*. https://www.encyclopedia.com/humanities/

encyclopedias-almanacs-transcripts-and-maps/haiti-caco-revolts. Accessed online on January 16, 2020.

"National Rifle Association Shoots." *Marine Corps Gazette* (pre-1994) 19, no. 1 (1935): 39–62.

Naval History and Heritage Command. "US Occupation of Haiti, 1915–1934." April 28, 2015. https://www.history.navy.mil/research/library/online-reading-room/title-list-alphabetically/u/us-occupation-of-haiti-1915-1934.html. Accessed online January 10, 2020.

Plummer, Brenda Gayle. "The Metropolitan Connection: Foreign and Semiforeign Elites in Haiti, 1900–1915." *Latin American Research Review* 19, no. 2 (1984): 119–42. www.jstor.org/stable/2503341. Accessed January 16, 2020.

Schmidt, Hans. *The United States Occupation of Haiti, 1915–1934.* New Brunswick, NJ: Rutgers University Press, 1995.

Waller, Captain. Radiogram dated November 13, 1917. William H. Rupertus National Archives File.

Peking

Brain, Jessica. "The Battle of Peking, Historic U.K." The History and Heritage Accommodation Guide. https://www.historic-uk.com/HistoryUK/HistoryofBritain/Battle-of-Peking/. Accessed January 15, 2020.

Brown, Walter. "Japanese Bombard Civilians in Shanghai's Chapei." February 2, 1932. UPI Archives. https://www.upi.com/Archives/1932/02/02/Japanese-bombard-civilians-in-Shanghais-Chapei/1703141119892. Accessed online January 22, 2022.

China Marines editor. "Peking." http://chinamarine.org/Peking.aspx. Accessed online January 8, 2020.

History.com editors. *Boxer Rebellion.* A&E Television Networks, November 9, 2009. https://www.history.com/topics/china/boxer-rebellion. Accessed online January 16, 2020.

Japanese Monograph. http://www.ibiblio.org/hyperwar/Japan/Monos/pdfs/JM-160_OutlineOfNavalArmament/JM-160.htm. Accessed online June 19, 2019.

King, Thomas F., PhD. "The Islands of the Japanese Mandate in 1937." https://tighar.org/Projects/Earhart/Archives/Research/ResearchPapers/mandates.html#h4. Accessed online June 19, 2019.

Larsen, Henry L. Letter to Mr. Terrance Gorman (February 27, 1930). William H. Rupertus National Archives File.

Maddox, H. "Annual Rifle and Pistol Matches in China Split with US Army." *Leatherneck* (pre-1998) 12, no. 12 (1929): 41.

Madrolle's Guidebooks. "Detailed Map of Peking Legation Quarter. From: Northern China, The Valley of the Blue River, Korea." Hachette & Company, 1912. Perry–Castañeda Library, University of Texas at Austin. https://legacy.lib.utexas.edu/maps/historical/peking_legation_quarter.jpg. Accessed online January 22, 2020.

"Marine Detachment Peking China." *Leatherneck* (February 1929).

Neville, Wendell C. Dispatch to William H. Rupertus (December 29, 1929). William H. Rupertus National Archives File.

"North China Marines." http://www.northchinamarines.com/index.htm. Accessed online August 18, 2019.

Rupertus, William H. Dispatch to Marine Corps Headquarters (February 26, 1929). William H. Rupertus National Archives File.

Rupertus, William H. Telegram to Marine Corps Headquarters (December 27, 1929). William H. Rupertus National Archives File.

Russell, Clem D. "The China Marine." November 1930.

Santore, Holly E. Bushido. "The Valor of Deceit." ISME Convention, January 1, 2010.

Wilfred, Teo Weijie. "Empire in Asia: A New Global History." National University of Singapore. https://www.fas.nus.edu.sg/hist/eia/documents_archive/nanking-treaty%20v2.php. Accessed online January 15, 2020.

Home

"Major Rupertus and Alice Hill Marry." *Washington Star*, 1933.

Rupertus, William H. "Some Interesting Lines about the Navy's New West Coast Air Station." *Marine Corps Gazette* (May 1934).

Shanghai

American Presidents Line History. https://en.wikipedia.org/wiki/APL_(shipping_company).

Camp, R. D., Jr. "The Powder Keg: US Marine Defense of the International Settlements, Peiping and Shanghai, 1937." *Marine Corps Gazette* 82, no. 10 (October 1999).

China Rhyming editors. "Black Saturday—August 14, 1937." August 14, 2015. http://www.chinarhyming.com/2015/08/14/black-saturday-august-14-1937. Accessed online June 19, 2019.

Facing History editors. "Atrocities." Nanking learning guides. https://www.facinghistory.org/nanjing-atrocities/atrocities. Accessed online June 19, 2019.

Facing History editors. "The Nanjing Atrocities Timeline." https://www.facinghistory.org/nanjing-atrocities/educator-resources/timelines?__hstc=46213176.3b61cd0363 2bc1e49b5f62302c80a968.1478731782829.1478731782829.1478737288849.2&__hssc=46213176.2.1478737288849&__hsfp=3090435354. Accessed online June 19, 2019.

Flanagan, Damian. "Bushido: The Samurai Code Goes to War." *Japan Times*, July 23, 2016. https://www.japantimes.co.jp/culture/2016/07/23/books/bushido-samurai-code-goes-war/#.XTYWXy3MyCc. Accessed online July 22, 2019.

Headquarters, 4th Marines. Evacuation orders. Shanghai, August 18, 1937.

Henriot, Christian. "August 1937: War and the Death en Masse of Civilians." Paper presented at "War in History and Memory: An International Conference on the Seventieth Anniversary of China's Victory for the War against Japan," Academia Historica (Taipei), July 7–9, 2015. http://www.virtualshanghai.net/Texts/Articles?ID=130. Accessed online August 18, 2019.

Kuhn, Irene Corbally. "Shanghai: The Way It Was: A Glance Back at a Short but Extraordinary Era." *Los Angeles Times*, October 19, 1986. https://www.latimes.com/

archives/la-xpm-1986-10-19-tm-5888-story.html. Accessed online on February 3, 2020.

Masters, James. 1937 China Marines, Walla Walla.

Metcalf, G. H. "Marines in China." *Marine Corps Gazette* (September 1938).

National Library of Australia digitized copy. "Refugees Evacuated." *The Mercury Newspaper*, August 18, 1937. https://trove.nla.gov.au/newspaper/article/25421287 Accessed online June 19, 2019.

Newsweek staff. "Exposing the Rape of Nanking." November 30, 1997. http://www.newsweek.com/exposing-rape-nanking-170890. Accessed online June 19, 2019.

Pacific War Online editors. "An Attempt to Explain Japanese War Crimes." http://www.pacificwar.org.au/JapWarCrimes/Explaining_JapWarCrimes.html. Accessed online July 22, 2019.

Price, Dolly. Diary, August–September 1937.

Rothwell, Richard. "Shanghai Emergency." *Marine Corps Gazette* 56, no. 11 (November 1972).

"Shanghai 50 Years Ago." *Marine Corps Gazette* 70, no. 11 (November 1987). https://www.mca-marines.org/leatherneck/1987/11/shanghai-50-years-ago.

Thacker, Joel D. "The Marines in China and the Philippines." *Marine Corps Gazette* 28, no. 8 (December 1943). http://www.jewsofchina.org/shanghai. Accessed June 19, 2019.

Versaw, Donald LeRoy. "Last China Band." 2000. http://lastchinaband.com/photos_band.htm. Accessed online February 8, 2020.

World War II

Antill, P., and T. Kane. "Operating Far from Home: American Logistic Support in the Pacific War." In D. Moore and P. Antill, eds., *Case Studies in Defence Procurement and Logistics, Volume II: From Ancient Rome to the Astute Class Submarine*, 125–62. Cambridge: Cambridge Academic Press, 2014.

Antill, Peter. "Pearl Harbor: The Day of Infamy, December 7, 1941." October 28, 2001. http://www.historyofwar.org/articles/battles_pearl_harbor.html. Accessed online June 19, 2019.

Bartlett, Tom. "Vignettes of War." *Marine Corps Gazette* 74, no. 12 (December 1991).

Champie, Elmore A. "A Brief History of the Marine Corps Base and Recruit Depot, San Diego, California, 1914–1962." USMC Historical Branch, Washington, DC, 1962.

Dugdale-Pointon, T. D. P. "Battle of Midway, June 1942." August 3, 2000. http://www.historyofwar.org/articles/battles_midway.html. Accessed online June 19, 2019.

Hirohito. Japanese Declaration of War against the US, December 8, 1941. http://tmc-daniel.palmerseminary.edu/Rescript-English.pdf. Accessed online February 29, 2020.

History.com editors. "Hirohito." https://www.history.com/topics/world-war-ii/hirohito-1. Accessed online June 19, 2019.

History.com editors. "Tōjō Hideki." https://www.history.com/topics/world-war-ii/tojo-hideki. Accessed online June 19, 2019.

Lend-Lease Act. https://www.history.com/topics/world-war-ii/lend-lease-act. Accessed online June 19, 2019.

MCRD San Diego, Public Affairs Office, and Museum Historical Society. "Recruit Training Mission Expands with Growth of Depot in the 40s." Published in the *Leatherneck* forum, story identification number: 2003912142241, September 12, 2003.

Office of the Historian, US Dept. of State. "1937–1945: Diplomacy and the Road to Another War." https://history.state.gov/milestones/1937-1945/foreword. Accessed online June 19, 2019.

Rickard, J. "Vice-Admiral Robert Lee Ghormley, 1883–1958." May 5, 2008. http://www.historyofwar.org/articles/people_ghormley_robert.html. Accessed online June 19, 2019.

Roosevelt, Franklin. "Day of Infamy Speech, December 8, 1941." http://docs.fdrlibrary.marist.edu/tmirhdee.html. Accessed online June 19, 2019.

Rupertus, William H. "My Rifle: The Creed of a United States Marine." *Marine Corps Chevron* (San Diego, CA), March 14, 1942.

"Text of Roosevelt Address Calling for Sacrifices to Win Long, Hard War Against Japan." *Times-Herald* (Washington, DC), December 10, 1941.

The USMC Code Talkers and Montford Marines

Jevec, Adam. "Semper Fidelis Code Talkers." *Prologue* 33, no. 4 (Winter 2001). https://www.archives.gov/publications/prologue/2001/winter/navajo-code-talkers.html. Accessed online June 19, 2019.

Ministry for Culture and Heritage. "US Forces in New Zealand." Updated August 5, 2014. https://nzhistory.govt.nz/war/us-forces-in-new-zealand. Accessed online February 16, 2020.

Montford Point Marines. https://library.uncw.edu/web/montford/index.html. Accessed online June 19, 2020.

Reports of General MacArthur: The Campaigns of MacArthur in the Pacific, Volume 1. Prepared by his general staff, re-released in 1994. https://history.army.mil/books/wwii/MacArthur%20Reports/MacArthur%20V1/index.htm. Accessed online June 19, 2019.

Rickard, J. "Vice-Admiral Robert Lee Ghormley, 1883–1958." May 5, 2008. http://www.historyofwar.org/articles/people_ghormley_robert.html. Accessed online June 19, 2019.

Operation Watchtower: The Battle of Guadalcanal/Tulagi

1st Marine Division Record of Events Journal, 23 April–6 December 1942. National Archives and Records Administration (NARA).

1st Marine Division Record of Events, Tulagi, 21 July–27 September 1942. NARA.

1st Marine Division Record of Events, Tulagi, 28 September 1942–5 January 1943. NARA.

Antill, P. "Operation Watchtower: The Battle for Guadalcanal (August 1942–February 1943)." November 11, 2001. http://www.historyofwar.org/articles/battles_guadalcanal .html. Accessed online June 19, 2019.

Associated Press. "Nimitz Decorates Guadalcanal Fighters" (photo), n.d.

Cooke, F. O. "Solomons Spearhead!" *Leatherneck* (pre-1998) 25, no. 10 (1942): 13–18, 61–69.

Division Intelligence Section, Headquarters, First Marine Division, Fleet Marine Force. Prisoner Report of Fukuzuni Hiroshima Interview, November 13, 1942.

Division Intelligence Section, Headquarters, First Marine Division, Fleet Marine Force. Prisoner Report of Fushimi Shoji Interview, November 12, 1942.

Division Intelligence Section, Headquarters, First Marine Division, Fleet Marine Force. Report compiled by Major R. A. Evans, following an interview with Seaman First Class Dale Emory and MM1/c Harold Taylor, December 6, 1942.

Division Intelligence Section, Headquarters, First Marine Division, Fleet Marine Force. Translation of captured Japanese address of instruction by commander of the Second Division, Lt. Gen. Masao Maruyama, November 3, 1942.

Division Intelligence Section, Headquarters, First Marine Division, Fleet Marine Force. Translation of captured Japanese address of instruction by commander of the 29th Infantry Regiment, Seijiro Furumiya, October 2, 1942.

Donigan, H. J. "Peleliu: The Forgotten Battle." *Marine Corps Gazette* 78, no. 9 (1994): 96–103.

Dunn, William. "New Britain Landings Escape Jap Aerial Attack for 7 Hours." Associated Press, December 27, 1944. Rupertus Family Collection.

Frank, B. M. "Vandegrift's Guadalcanal Command." *Marine Corps Gazette* (pre-1994) 71, no. 8 (1987): 56–58.

Gehring, Father Fred P. "Remembering Guadalcanal." *Florida Catholic*, May 26, 1989.

"Giants of the Corps." *Leatherneck* (pre-1998) 58, no. 12 (1975): 46–49.

Hargrove, Marion. "The Magnificent Amphibian." *Yank: The Army Newspaper*, September 14, 1942.

Harmon, M. F. "The Army in the South Pacific." June 6, 1944. NARA.

Hough, Frank O. "The Cape Gloucester Campaign." *Marine Corps Gazette* (pre-1994) 28, no. 4 (1944): 7–16.

Hurlbut, James. "USMC Generals in Front Lines." December 8, 1942.

Langille, Vernon A. "General Vandegrift." *Leatherneck* (pre-1998) 31(2) (1948): 24–29.

Merillat, H. L. "How Marines Landed and Won: Officer Reporter Tells the Story." *New York Herald Tribune*, August 21, 1942.

Miller, Robert C., 1st Marine Division. "Writer at Scene Tells of Battle for Solomons." August 9, 1942.

No author or date. "Entire First Division of Marines Cited for Gallantry in Solomons" (article).

The Old Breed News. First Marine Division Association Incorporated, No. 10, November 19, 1973. "The 'George' Medal," also known as the Faciat Georgius Commemorative Medal. http://www.omsa.org/files/jomsa_arch/Splits/1974/14991_JOMSA_ Vol25_2_28.pdf. Accessed online June 19, 2019.

Piatek, Tony, and 1st Marine Division. Hand-drawn and signed Christmas card to General Rupertus, December 24, 1942.

Rupertus, William H. Diary, September–November 1942. USMC Archives.

Smith, Major John, VMF 223, Guadalcanal Island in Bureau of Aeronautics. Interview. November 10, 1942. NARA.

Thompson, P. L. "Birth of a Patch." *Leatherneck* (pre-1998) 65, no. 8 (1982): 22–23.

United States Fleet. Message Traffic, 1942–1943.

USS *Neville*. War Diary, August 1, 1942–August 31, 1942. Office of Naval Records.

Vandergrift, Archer. Letters 1942–1945. Marine Corps Archives, Quantico, Virginia.

Operation Backhander: The Battle of Cape Gloucester

Anonymous. "Air Force Liaison Unit: The Dauntless Piper Cub at Cape Gloucester." *Marine Corps Gazette* (March 1985).

Associated Press. "Flamethrowers Cut through Jap Lines on New Britain Front." *Evening Star* (Washington, DC), December 30, 1943.

Baird, Joseph H. "Washington General Has Opened a Highway to Tokyo over Which Marines Hope He Will Lead Them." *Sunday Star* (Washington, DC), March 12, 1944.

CG Alamo. Congratulations telegram to C. G. Backhander for General Rupertus, S. G. D. Krueger, n.d.

CG Alamo Forces. Congratulations telegram from Admiral Barbey to General Rupertus, January 1944.

Christie, J. J. Division bulletin from Major General Rupertus, April 19, 1944.

"The Dauntless Piper Cub at Cape Gloucester." *Marine Corps Gazette* (pre-1994) 69, no. 3 (1985): 43–45.

First Marine Division Special Action Report, Cape Gloucester, 1943–1944. National Archives.

Frank, Richard B. "Raging War in the Rainforest." *Naval History Magazine* 24, no. 2 (April 2010).

Halsey, Bill. Congratulations telegram to commander, 1st Marine Division, n.d.

Hough, Frank O., and John A. Crown. *The Campaign on New Britain*. Washington, DC: Historical Branch, Headquarters, US Marine Corps, 1952.

Hunt, Richard M. "General Rupertus Improvised Air Force." *Marine Corps Gazette* 33, no. 6 (June 1949).

Krueger, S. G. D. Congratulations telegram to C. G. Backhander, CMDR 7th Fleet, CMDR TF 76, CG ADV ON5, n.d.

MacArthur, Douglas. Congratulations telegram to Major General William H. Rupertus, December 31, 1943.

Nalty, Bernard C. *Cape Gloucester: The Green Inferno*. World War II Commemorative Series. Washington, DC: Marine Corps Historical Center, 1994.

No author (told by Master Sergeant John W. Black). "Flier Saved by Rupertus." n.d.

No author (told by Lansing Hatfield). "How Gen. Rupertus Won Mouth Organ." *Evening Star* (Washington, DC), n.d.

No name given. Congratulations telegram to Major General William H. Rupertus, C. G. Backhander, S. G. D. Krueger [most likely from Vandegrift], n.d.

O'Brien, C. J. "Those Pesky Little Grasshoppers of World War II." *Leatherneck* 84, no. 5 (2001): 14–21.

O'Leary, Jeremiah A. "Reporter Decides Gen. Rupertus Is Ace Hitchhiker." *Evening Star* (Washington, DC), n.d.

Rickard, J. "Battle of Cape Gloucester, December 26, 1943–April 1944." April 24, 2015. http://www.historyofwar.org/articles/battles_cape_gloucester.html. Accessed online June 19, 2019.

Rickard, J. "Operation Dexterity—New Britain Campaign, December 16, 1943–March 9, 1944." April 15, 2015. http://www.historyofwar.org/articles/operation_dexterity_new_britain.html. Accessed online July 23, 2019.

Rupertus, William H. Telegram to Lieutenant General Krueger, n.d.

Rupertus, William H. Telegram to General Walter Krueger, December 30, 1943.

Spencer, Murlin. "Rupertus Credits Marine Luck in Cape Gloucester Landing." *Evening Star* (Washington, DC), December 28, 1943.

Turcott, Jack. "M'Arthur Gives Rupertus D.S.M., Braves Squall." *New York Daily News*, May 2, 1944.

Whitehead, Ennis. Congratulations telegram from Air Force to C. G. Backhander, December 31, 1943.

Operation Galvanic: The Battle of Tarawa and Apamama

Antill, Peter. January 22, 2002. "Operation Galvanic (1): The Battle for Tarawa November 1943." http://www.historyofwar.org/articles/battles_tarawa.html. Accessed online June 19, 2019.

Operation Stalemate: The Battle of Peleliu

Antill, Peter. "Peleliu, Battle for (Operation Stalemate II): The Pacific War's Forgotten Battle, September–November 1944." http://www.historyofwar.org/articles/battles_peleliu. Accessed online July 16, 2016.

Associated Press. "Marines Land on Palau's in Bitter Battle." September 15, 1944.

Associated Press. "Japs Reported Shacking Men to Assure 'Stand' on Peleliu." By telephone to *New York Times*, September 19, 1944.

Caporale, L. G. "The Pacific War: 1941–45." *Marine Corps Gazette* (pre-1994) 69, no. 11 (1985): 46–50, 54–57.

Commander Task Force 31. "Report on Peleliu Operation." November 1944. National Archives.

Evans, E. J. "Men from Montford Point." *Leatherneck* (pre-1998) 30, no. 11 (1947): 32–36.

Fields, Lewis J. "Historical Tactical Study, Palau Operations September 15, 1944–October 20, 1944: A Study by the Commanding General of the First Marine Division in the Landing of Peleliu Island." Amphibious Marine School, Marine Corps Schools, 1947–1948.

First Marine Division D2—Journal Peleliu, September 15, 1944–October 20, 1944. National Archives.

First Marine Division (Ref), Palau Operations, Pal. "Special Action Report Palau Operation." Marine Corps Archives, Quantico, Virginia, September 13, 1944.

Gayle, Brigadier General Gordon D. *Bloody Beaches: The Marines at Peleliu.* Marines in World War II Commemorative Series, 1996.

Gypton, Jeremy. "Bloody Peleliu: Unavoidable yet Unnecessary." http://ww2f.com/ threads/bloody-peleliu-unavoidable-yet-unnecessary.13824/.

Hough, Major F. O. *The Assault on Peleliu.* Washington, DC: USMC Historical Branch, G-3 Division, Headquarters, US Marine Corps, 1950.

Johnson, Mac R. "Marines, Japs in Bitter Fight on Peleliu." September 22, 1944.

Marine Corps Chevron. "Peleliu Stories." October 7, 1944.

O'Leary, Jeremiah. "Hell in the Umurbrogal." Distributed to *Washington Evening Star, Leatherneck,* October 10, 1944.

Owsley, Roy. Letter to General Geiger. Marine Corps Archives, December 16, 1945.

"The Palau Operation: Japanese Studies in World War II." Monograph Office of the Chief of Military History, US Army. Compiled by the First Demobilization Bureau in 1946. http://www.ibiblio.org/hyperwar/Japan/Monos/pdfs/JM-49/JM-49. Accessed online July 22, 2018.

Patch, Nathaniel. "Bakuhatai: The Reconnaissance Mission of the USS *Burrfish* and the Fate of Three American POWs." US National Archives, Winter 2015. https://www.archives.gov/files/publications/prologue/2015/winter/bakuhatai .pdf?fbclid=IwAR2iI5txVdNpCzob-LktbjC6uZJ4wR9fCinZ01H4fPAYpBWWzPa N3SaYgEY. Accessed online September 4, 2019.

Phelan, W. C., for Headquarters Island Command. "Japanese Military Caves on Peleliu." May 25, 1945.

Rosenberg, Zach. "D.I.Y. Ice Cream in Wartime." *Air & Space Magazine* (August 2018). https://www.airspacemag.com/as-next/cool-side-tropical-warfare-180969515. Accessed online June 19, 2019.

Rupertus, William H. Letter to Julian Smith (July 19, 1944). Marine Corps Archives.

Schmuck, D. M. "Battle for Peleliu." *Marine Corps Gazette* (pre-1994) 28, no. 12 (1944): 2–8.

Smith, Julian. Letter to William H. Rupertus (July 26, 1944). Marine Corps Archives.

Staff writer. "Tarawa and Saipan Were Never Like Peleliu." *Sunday World-Herald* (Omaha, NE), September 24, 1944.

Staff writer. "Yanks 26 Miles from Cologne, Aachen's Fall Near; Marines Seize Main Palau Airport, Kill 1400 Japs." *Washington Post,* September 17, 1942.

Staff writer embedded with Marines. "The Lesson of Peleliu," n.d.

Tasmania, Hobart. "Battle Scenes from Italian Front and Marines' D-Day in Pacific." *The Mercury,* October 14, 1944.

A Tribute to Michael Lazaro and Peleliu Veterans. http://www.thomas5.com/tribute/ Vets1.html. Accessed online June 19, 2019.

Trumbull, Robert. "Landing on Peleliu. Marines Win Beachhead and Close in on Main Airdrome." September 15, 1944.

UPI, Pearl Harbor. "Marines, Army Inching Ahead on Isles, Smash Counterattacks." September 18, 1944.

"US Forces Now Control 9 Islands." *Los Angeles Examiner*, October 2, 1944.

US Pacific Fleet Headquarters (AP). "10,000 Japs Slain in Palaus. 4 Armies Repel Nazis, Push On."

US Pacific Fleet Headquarters (AP). "Enemy Stalls Marine Drive on Peleliu," n.d.

US Pacific Fleet Headquarters (AP). "Fierce Battle Rages on Peleliu Despite Killing of 7,045 Japs." September 21, 1944.

US Pacific Fleet Headquarters (AP). "Marines Bypass Hills and Drive to within Mile of Peleliu's Tip." September 26, 1944.

US Pacific Fleet Headquarters (AP). "Marines Gain Mile and Half in Palau Landing." September 16, 1944.

US Pacific Fleet Headquarters (AP). "Nimitz Says Control of Peleliu, 8 Other Islands Is Secure." October 2, 1944.

US Pacific Fleet Headquarters (UPI). "Palaus Provide Front Air Bases." October 2, 1944.

US Pacific Fleet Headquarters (AP). "Yanks Seize 3 More Palau Islands." September 29, 1944.

Wilkinson, T. S. Memorandum to Admiral Fort. "Unscrambling of Stalemate." Marine Corps Archives, Quantico, Virginia, September 19, 1944.

Quantico and Washington, DC

Connery, George. "Casualty Totals Near-Total Strength. Marines Blaze Bloody Pacific Trail." N.d.

"Defense Point Changed to Rupertus Point." *The Indian* 6, no. 26 (1954), US Naval Base, Guantanamo Bay, Cuba.

Petit, Don. "Gen. Rupertus Assumes M.C.S. Staff School." November 23, 1944.

Pryor, Admiral. *World News.* Transcript of Major General Rupertus interview. WJSV-CBS. November 11, 1944.

Quantico Sentry. "Sudden Heart Attack Fatal to Gen. Rupertus." Marine Barracks, Quantico, Virginia, March 29, 1945.

Quantico Sentry. "Taps for a Fighting General: Maj. Gen. William H. Rupertus." Article by editor and drawing by Sergeant Geo Ward. Marine Barracks, Quantico, Virginia, March 29, 1945.

Staff writer. "D.S.M. to Schools Director." *Quantico Sentry*, January 29, 1945.

Staff writer. "Gen. Rupertus, Solomons Hero, Drops Dead Here." *Evening Star* (Washington, DC), March 26, 1945.

Staff writer. "General Marshal Addresses 51st Annual Dinner Meeting of Illinois Manufacturer's Association." *Industrial Review*, January 1945.

Staff writer. "Marine Gen. William H. Rupertus, Hero of Pacific Isles, Dies Here." *Washington Post*, March 27, 1945.

Staff writer. "Marine Heroes Are Honored." *Quantico Sentry*, n.d.

Staff writer. "Military Rites Tomorrow for Gen. Rupertus." *Times-Herald* (Washington, DC), March 27, 1945.

The Battle of Iwo Jima
Interview, Woody Williams, September 2018.

The Battle of Okinawa
Hammel, Eric. "Battle of Okinawa: Summary, Facts, Pictures, and Casualties." Initially
published in *World War II* magazine, June 2005. http://www.historynet.com/battle-of-
okinawa-operation-iceberg.htm. Accessed online June 19, 2019.

World War II Military Casualties
Bender, Jeremy. "This Chart Shows the Astounding Devastation of World War II." *Business Insider*, May 29, 2014.
Hamby, Alonzo L. "The Decision to Use the Atomic Bomb." *Britannica*, August 5, 2010.
https://www.britannica.com/topic/Trumans-decision-to-use-the-bomb-712569.
Accessed online June 17, 2019.
Townsend, Susan. "Japan's Quest for Empire 1931–1945." *BBC History*, March 3, 2011.
http://www.bbc.co.uk/history/worldwars/wwtwo/japan_quest_empire_01.shtml.
Accessed online June 19, 2019.

Marine Corps History Division Oral History Transcripts and Related Interviews
Cates, General Clifton, by Benis Frank, 1973.
Chapman, General Leonard F., Jr., by Benis Frank, January 17, 1979.
Davis, Raymond G., USMC, by Benis Frank, February 1977.
Deakin, Brigadier General Harold O., USMC, by Benis M. Frank, 1972.
Deen, Braswell, Jr., by Amy Rupertus Peacock, August 2019.
DeValle, Lieutenant General Pedro A., by Mr. Condit, October 7, 1957.
Felds, Lieutenant General Lewis J., by Thomas E. Donnelly, 1976.
Finnegan, Bill, USMC, by Amy Rupertus Peacock, September 2020.
Haig, Dirk, by Amy Rupertus Peacock, June 2018.
Harris, Brigadier General Harold D. ("Bucky"), transcript. USMC History Division. No date.
Hill, Edith, by Amy Rupertus Peacock, Washington, DC, 1995.
Hunter, Lieutenant Jim, by Amy Rupertus Peacock, Charlotte, North Carolina, June 2017.
Kilmartin, Brigadier General Robert C., USMC, by Benis Frank, May 9, 1973.
Krulak, Lieutenant General Victor H., USMC, by Benis Frank, 1973.
Masters, Lieutenant General James, by Benis Frank, August 1981.
Merrill, Dr. John E., January 31 and February 7, 1980.
Platt, Major General Jonas M., USMC, by Benis Frank, 1984.
Pope, Major Everett Parker, USMC, by Benis Frank, 1996.
Puller, Lewis B., and William A. Lee, by John H. Magruder III, September 1961.
Rupertus, John, USN, by Amy Rupertus Peacock, September 2016.
Selden, General Gerald, USMC, letter to Major Frank Hough, USMCR, October 26, 1949.

Shepard, Lemuel C., by Benis Frank, 1966.
Silverthorne, Lieutenant General Merwin H., USMC, by Benis Frank, 1973.
Simmons, Edwin H., by Gary Solis, February 2002.
Smith, General Oliver P., USMC, by Benis Frank, 1973.
Thomas, Gerald, by Benis Frank, September 1966.
Toth, Margaret, by Amy Rupertus Peacock, 1984.
Twining, General Merrill B., USMC, by Benis Frank, 1967.
West, Major General, USMC, by Benis Frank, no date.
White, William by Kimberly Rupertus Robinson, November 2020.
Williams, Woody H., by Amy Rupertus Peacock, July 2018.

Marine Corps History Division Personal Papers in Archival Files
Colonel Joseph Alexander
General Breckenridge
General Clifton Cates
General Harold O. Deakin
General Pedro A. DeValle
General Lewis J. Fields
General Roy Geiger
General Harold D. Harris
General W. P. T. Hill
General Thomas Holcomb
General James Keating
General Robert C. Kilmartin
General Charles Price
General Lewis B. Puller
General John C. Russell
General Lemuel C. Shepherd
General Merwin H. Silverthorne
General Holland Smith
General Julian Smith
General O. P. Smith
General Merrill B. Twining
General Alexander Archer Vandegrift
Sledge, Eugene; Papers, R.G. 96 Auburn University Libraries

Books
Batchelder, Alf. *Melbourne's Marines: The First Division at the M.C.G. 1943*. East Melbourne: MCC Library, 2002.
Braswell, Judge Deen. *Trial by Combat*. Atlanta, GA: Deen Books, 2000.
Cameron, Diane. *Never Leave Your Dead*. Las Vegas: Central Recovery Press, 2016.
Camp, Dick. *Last Man Standing: The 1st Marine Regiment on Peleliu, September 15–21, 1944*, 1st ed. Minneapolis, MN: Zenith Press, 2011.

Camp, Dick. *Shadow Warriors: The Untold Stories of American Special Operations during WWII*. Minneapolis, MN: Zenith Press, 2013.

Chang, Iris. *The Rape of Nanking: The Forgotten Holocaust of World War II*. New York: Basic Books, 2012.

Clark, George B. *Treading Softly: U.S. Marines in China, 1819–1949*. Westport, CT: Praeger, 2001.

Davis, Burke. *Marine! The Life of Lt. Gen. Lewis B. (Chesty) Puller, USMC Ret*. Boston: Little, Brown, 1962.

Grasso, Joseph A. *Manila John: The Life and Combat Actions of Marine Gunnery Sergeant John Basilone, Hero of Guadalcanal and Iwo Jima*. Pittsburgh: RoseDog Books, 2010.

Hallas, James H. *The Devil's Anvil: The Assault on Peleliu*. Westport, CT: Praeger, 1944.

Hammel, Eric. *Guadalcanal: Starvation Island*. Pacifica, CA: Pacifica Military History, 2009.

Hoffman, Jon T. *Chesty: The Story of Lieutenant General Lewis B. Puller, USMC*. New York: Random House, 2001.

Hough, Frank O., and John A. Crown. *The Campaign on New Britain*. Washington, DC: Historical Branch, Headquarters, US Marine Corps, 1952.

Hough, Frank O., Verle E. Ludwig, Henry I. Shaw Jr., Douglas T. Kane, Bernard C. Nalty, Edwin T. Turnbladh, George W. Garand, Truman R. Strobridge, and Benis M. Frank. *History of U.S. Marine Corps Operations in World War II. Vol. 1: Pearl Harbor to Guadalcanal*. Washington, DC: Historical Branch, G-3 Division, Headquarters, US Marine Corps.

Hunt, Captain George P. *Coral Comes High: US Marines and the Battle for the Point on Peleliu*. New York: Harper and Brothers, 1946.

Jeans, Roger B., and Katie Lechter Lyle. *Good-bye Old Peking: The Wartime Letters of US Marine Captain John Seymour Lechter, 1937–1939*. Athens: Ohio University Press, 1988.

Jersey, Stanley C. *Hell's Islands: The Untold Story of Guadalcanal*. College Station: Texas A&M University Press, 2005.

La Bree, Clifton. *Gentle Warrior: General Oliver Prince Smith, USMC*. Kent, OH: Kent State University Press, 2001.

Leckie, Robert. *Helmet for My Pillow from Parris Island to the Pacific*. New York: Random House, 1957.

LIFE Books. *Pearl Harbor: 75 Years Later*. New York: Time Inc. Books, 2016.

Manchester, William. *Goodbye Darkness*. Boston: Little, Brown, 1978.

Margaritis, Peter. *Landing in Hell: The Pyrrhic Victory of the First Marine Division on Peleliu*. Havertown, PA: Casemate Publishers, 2018.

McMillen, George. *The Old Breed: A History of the First Marine Division in WWII*. Washington, DC: Infantry Journal Press, 1949.

Nez, Chester, and Avila Judith Schless. *Code Talker: The First and Only Memoir by One of the Original Navajo Code Talkers of WWII*. New York: Dutton Caliber, reprint edition 2012.

O'Reilly, Bill, and Martin Dugard. *Killing the Rising Sun: How America Vanquished WWII Japan*. New York: Henry Holt & Co., 2016.

Office of Naval Intelligence. *The Landing in the Solomons 7–8 August 1942*. Publications Branch, 1943. Reprint published by Naval History and Heritage Command, Washington, DC, 2017.

Office of Naval Intelligence. *Solomon Island Campaign 1: The Landing in the Solomons*. Publications Branch, 1943.

Patton, Benjamin. *Growing Up Patton*. New York: Dutton Caliber, 2012.

Potter, E. B. *Nimitz*. Annapolis, MD: Naval Institute Press, 1976.

Potter, E. B., and Chester W. Nimitz. *Sea Power*. Englewood Cliffs, NJ: Prentice-Hall, 1960.

Roberts, Andrew. *The Storm of War: A New History of the Second World War*. New York: Harper Perennial, 2012.

Ross, Bill D. *Peleliu, Tragic Triumph: The Untold Story of the Pacific War's Forgotten Battle*. New York: Random House 1991.

Russell, Clem D. *The China Marine*. Self-published autobiography, November 1930.

Shaw, Henry. *The First Offensive: The Marine Campaign for Guadalcanal*. Darby, PA: Diane Publishing, June 1992.

Shisler, Gail B. *For Country and Corps: The Life of General Oliver P. Smith*. Annapolis, MD: Naval Institute Press, 2009.

Sledge, E. B. *With the Old Breed at Peleliu and Okinawa*. Annapolis, MD: Naval Institute Press, 1996.

Sloan, Bill. *Brotherhood of Heroes: The Marines at Peleliu 1944*. New York: Simon & Schuster, 2005.

Thayer, Soule. *Shooting the Pacific: Marine Corps Combat Photography in WWII*. Lexington: University of Kentucky Press, 2000.

Toll, Ian W. *The Conquering Tide*. New York: W.W. Norton, 2015.

Tregaskis, Richard. *Guadalcanal Diary*. 1st ed. New York: Random House, 1943.

Twining, Merrill B., USMC. *No Bended Knee: The Battle for Guadalcanal*. Novato, CA: Presidio Press, 1994.

Vandegrift, A. A., and Robert Osprey. *Once a Marine: The Memoirs of General A.A. Vandegrift, Commandant of the Marines in WWII*. New York: Ballantine Books, 1964.

Ward, John. *Ships of World War II*. Osceola, WI: M.B.I. Publishing Company, 2000.

Wellons, Major James B. *General Roy S. Geiger, USMC Marine Aviator, Joint Force Commander*. CreateSpace Independent Publishing Platform, 2014.

Zimmerman, John L. *The Guadalcanal Campaign*. Washington, DC: USMCR Historical Section, Division of Public Information, 1949.

Photos, Films, Additional Online

"Amazing Pictures of Washington DC in the Early 1900s." http://www.businessinsider.com/history-of-washington-dc-life-2011-11?op=1. Accessed online August 18, 2019.

"American History in Pictures: Washington DC 1900s–1930." Sky Warrior Studio. http://www.youtube.com/watch?v=rJzeVRKf3hE. Accessed online August 18, 2019.

Amos, John. Montford Marine Association. Montford Point Marines Vignettes on Soundcloud. https://soundcloud.com/user-230339744-508005496. Accessed online August 27, 2019.

Baseball in Washington DC. http://blogs.weta.org/boundarystones/2014/05/19/sunday-baseball-comes-dc-1918. Accessed online August 18, 2019.

Basilone, John. "The Story of Gunnery Sergeant John Basilone." http://www.raritan-online.com/jb-online-menu.htm.

Chambers, Major Justice. https://en.wikipedia.org/wiki/Justice_M._Chambers.

Coulson, William R. "Traveling to Tulagi, the Site of a Deadly World War II Offensive." https://www.historynet.com/tulagis-idyllic-shores-were-once-home-to-a-deadly-1942-battle.htm. Accessed online April 2020.

Garand, George W., and Truman R. Strobridge. *History of the US Marine Corps in WWII. Vol IV: Western Pacific Operations.* https://www.marines.mil/Portals/1/Publications/History%20of%20the%20U.S.%20Marine%20Corps%20in%20WWII%20Vol%20IV%20-%20Western%20Pacific%20Operations%20%20PCN%2019000262700_1.pdf.

Guadalcanal: Walking a Battlefield. "Coffin Corner—Battle of Henderson Field." You-Tube. https://www.youtube.com/watch?v=yTWWSoILsfs&t=377s.

Hill, General William P. T. http://www.usmilitariaforum.com/forums/index.php?/topic/32876-majgen-william-pt-hill-usmc-5-decades-of-service. Accessed online August 29, 2019.

Hope, Bob. The National WWII Museum. August 27, 2017. Bob Hope and USO on Pavuvu video.

Jersey, Stanley C. "Our Time in Hell." History.net. https://www.historynet.com/our-time-in-hell.htm.

Key, Lieutenant Eugene. https://en.wikipedia.org/wiki/Eugene_Morland_Key.

Larsen, Lieutenant Harold H. US Navy, CO VT-8, USS *Saratoga.* https://www.findagrave.com/memorial/85504880/harold-henry-larsen.

Miles, Navy Lieutenant J. G. Samuel. https://www.findagrave.com/memorial/56125686/samuel-stockton-miles.

Montford Point Marines. https://montfordpointmarines.org/Museum.

Nalty, Bernard C. *The Right to Fight: African American Marines in World War.* https://www.nps.gov/parkhistory/online_books/npswapa/extcontent/usmc/pcn-190-003132-00/sec10.htm.

National World War II Museum. 2019 International Symposium. Participated online November 29–December 1, 2018.

Nickel, Private Thomas F. https://marineraiderassociation.org/nickel-thomas-f/.

Pearl Harbor Stories. Ray Suarez. http://www.sandiegouniontribune.com/lifestyle/people/sdut-ray-chavez-pearl-harbor-veteran-104-2016mar08-story.html. http://fox5sandiego.com/2018/03/11/pearl-harbors-oldest-surviving-veteran-turns-106/. Accessed August 18, 2019.

Rendezvous at Gavutu. https://www.nps.gov/parkhistory/online_books/npswapa/extcontent/usmc/pcn-190-003147-00/sec4a.htm.

Santelmann, William F. "From Eagle to Star." A tribute to Marine Corps General Rupertus on occasion of Rupertus's promotion to brigadier general, 1942.

Shands, Admiral. https://www.fold3.com/page/628636515-courtney-shands.

Smithsonian on Flicker: How Cities Change Photos DC Early. https://www.flickr.com/photos/smithsonian/sets/72157624790639858. Accessed online August 18, 2019.

USS *Rupertus*. http://www.navsource.org/archives/05/851.htm. Accessed online June 1, 2019.

Wikipedia. "Battle of Tulagi." https://en.wikipedia.org/wiki/Battle_of_Tulagi_and_Gavutu%E2%80%93Tanambogo.

Wikipedia. "O. K. Pressley." https://en.wikipedia.org/wiki/O._K._Pressley.

Wikipedia. "Robert H. Williams (soldier)." https://en.wikipedia.org/wiki/Robert_H._Williams_(soldier).

Yokohama Air Group. https://en.wikipedia.org/wiki/Yokohama_Air_Group.

Rupertus Family Collection: Original Articles, Letters, Telegrams

Christmas card, birthday card, and command post drawings by 1st Marine Division.

Handwritten letter from a native chief on Tulagi.

Letter from the Chinese embassy.

Photos and condolence letters from family, friends, fellow Marines, and military friends.

Photos and thank-you note from Eleanor Roosevelt.

Photos from USS *Florida*, Peking, Shanghai, California, Tulagi, Cape Gloucester, Peleliu, Arlington Cemetery.

Photos of USO stars and autograph from Gary Cooper.

Red Tape Cutters Award designed by Dr. Seuss.

Sketched award for "Grenade Dropping General."

Taped interview by Amy Rupertus Peacock with Margaret Toth, June 1996.

Telegram from MacArthur to General Vandergrift.

USS *Rupertus* File.

William H. Rupertus diaries from the USS *Florida* and Tulagi.

Letters and Correspondence

Altmann, Stella. September 1943. Letter to William H. Rupertus.

Eichelberger, R. I. September 1943. Letter to William H. Rupertus.

Geiger, Roy S. October 14, 1944. Commendation to the Commanding General, 1st Marine Division.

Harry (?). March 23, 1943. Headquarters USMC letter to William H. Rupertus.

Helms, Edith. January 23, 1944. Invitation to White House to Mrs. W. H. Rupertus.

Hill, Pete. April 25, 1943. Letter to William H. Rupertus.

Hope, Bob. August 1944. "Bob Hope's Communique." King Features Syndicate, Inc.

MacArthur, Douglas. March 1944. Telegram to MARCOM.

Maesiedi, J. David. September 27, 1942. Letter to "The Right Honorable, the General at Tulagi."

Nettlefold, Lord Mayor. 1944. Letter to William H. Rupertus.

Roosevelt, Eleanor. September 8, 1943. Letter to William H. Rupertus.

Rupertus, Alice Hill. June 30, 1938. Letter from Shanghai, China, to Mrs. Dixie Hill.

Rupertus, Alice Hill. April 1943. Letter to William H. Rupertus.

Rupertus, Alice Hill. August 7, 1944. Letter to William H. Rupertus.

Rupertus, William H. November 23, 1942. A letter with enclosure of Society of Red Tape Cutters Award and letter to Mrs. W. H. Rupertus.

Rupertus, William H. August 7–November 1942. Tulagi Diary.

Rupertus, William H. August 19, 1943. Letter to Cmdr. and Mrs. Robert Brodie.

Rupertus, William H. October 22, 1943. Letter to Mrs. W. H. Rupertus.

Rupertus, William H. October 23, 1943. Letter to Mrs. W. H. Rupertus.

Rupertus, William H. October 27, 1943. Letter to Mrs. W. H. Rupertus.

Rupertus, William H. December 22, 1943. Message to all officers of the First Division.

Rupertus, William H. December 24, 1943. Letter to Mrs. W. H. Rupertus.

Rupertus, William H. December 27, 1943. Letter to Mrs. W. H. Rupertus.

Rupertus, William H. February 2, 1944. Letter to Mrs. Dixie Hill.

Rupertus, William H. April 24, 1944. Letter to Archer Vandegrift.

Rupertus, William H. May 1944. V-Mail to Mrs. W. H. Rupertus.

Rupertus, William H. May 10, 1944. Letter to Archer Vandegrift.

Rupertus, William H. June 15, 1944. Telegram to Mrs. W. H. Rupertus.

Rupertus, William H. June 16, 1944. Telegram to Mrs. W. H. Rupertus.

Rupertus, William H. July 31, 1944. Letter to Mrs. W. H. Rupertus.

Rupertus, William H. August 13, 1944. Letter to Mrs. W. H. Rupertus.

Rupertus, William H. August 15, 1944. Letter to Lord Mayor Nettlefold of Melbourne.

Rupertus, William H. August 15, 1944. Letter to Mrs. W. H. Rupertus.

Rupertus, William H. August 18, 1944. Letter to Mrs. W. H. Rupertus.

Rupertus, William H. August 22, 1944. Letter to Mrs. W. H. Rupertus.

Rupertus, William H. August 25, 1944. Letter to Mrs. W. H. Rupertus.

Rupertus, William H. August 27, 1944. Letter to Mrs. W. H. Rupertus.

Rupertus, William H. August 30, 1944. Letter to Mrs. W. H. Rupertus.

Rupertus, William H. September 2, 1944. Letter to Mrs. W. H. Rupertus.

Rupertus, William H. September 3, 1944. Letter to Mrs. W. H. Rupertus.

Rupertus, William H. September 4, 1944. Letter to Mrs. W. H. Rupertus.

Rupertus, William H. September 5, 1944. Letter to Lt. Cmdr. Patrick Hill, USN (Ret.).

Rupertus, William H. September 5, 1944. Letter to Mrs. W. H. Rupertus.

Rupertus, William H. September 6, 1944. Letter to Mrs. W. H. Rupertus.

Rupertus, William H. September 8, 1944. Letter to Mrs. W. H. Rupertus.

Rupertus, William H. September 13, 1944, Letter to officers and men of the First Division.

Rupertus, William H. September 14, 1944. Letter to Mrs. W. H. Rupertus.

Smith, Julian. July 10, 1944. Letter to Roy S. Geiger.

Stella. August 8, 1944. Letter to William H. Rupertus.

Vandegrift, Archer. May 16, 1944. Letter to Roy S. Geiger.

Vandegrift, Archer. July 24, 1944. Letter to William H. Rupertus.

Vandegrift, Archer. September 18, 1944. Letter to William H. Rupertus.

Funeral/Condolence Letters to Sleepy (Mrs. William H. Rupertus)

Banyon, Lt. and Mrs. H. H. March 27, 1945. Long Beach, California.

Bolton, Fred. March 30, 1945. Arlington, Virginia.

Brodie, Dixie. March 25, 1945. Telegram to Cmdr. B. E. Carter. Hastings, Nebraska.

Brodie, Robert, Jr. April 9, 1945. USS *Grayson*. F.P.O. San Francisco, California.

Carter, B. E. March 27, 1945. Naval Ammunition Depot, Hastings, Nebraska.

Cates, Clifton. April 9, 1945. Fourth Marine Division, FMF PAC, F.P.O. San Francisco, California.

Cates, Jane. April 2. Chestnut Hill, Pennsylvania.

Coen, Ha-Hsiung. March 27, 1945. Chinese Military Mission in the United States.

De Bruyne, M. R. March 27, 1945. Royal Netherlands Marine Corps. Washington, DC.

DeValle, Pete. March 28, 1945. Hq. 1st Marine Division ⊠ F.P.O. San Francisco, California (Okinawa).

Fellers, William. March 27, 1945. Headquarters US Marine Corps, Washington, DC.

Halsey, Fannie. March 25, 1945. Telegram.

Harrison, Ross R. March 27, 1945. Hope Club, Providence, Rhode Island.

Hindman, Lloyd S. April 5, 1945. The Chaplains Office, Marine Barracks, Quantico, Virginia.

Johnston, D. H. April 2, 1945. L.S.T. Flotilla 35, F.P.O San Francisco, California.

Kriendler, Jack. April 1, 1945. New York City, New York.

Krulak, Brute. April 1, 1945. 6th Marine Division, "In the Field."

Krueger, Walter. April 1, 1945. Headquarters, 6th Army.

Logue, J. B. March 27, 1945. US Naval Hospital, Key West, Florida.

Luther, Mrs. Karl K. April 8, 1945. Washington, DC.

Marshall, George C. March 25, 1945. Letter to General Vandegrift.

Nettlefold, Lord Mayor. May 30, 1943. Town Hall, Melbourne, Australia.

Pelzman, Helen C. (Mrs. Frederick). March 26, 1945.

Phillips, Sal. March 26, 1945.

Powell, Ralph. April 1, 1945. Berkeley, California.

Rosecrans, H. H. May 6, 1945. 7th Field Depot. FMF PAC, F.P.O. San Francisco, California (Okinawa).

Rupertus, Alice H. April 19, 1945. Letter to Gretchen Campbell (husband of RA Robert Campbell, USN).

Selden, John T. June 24, 1945. La Jolla, California.

Sister Emmanuel. April 21, 1945. Carmelite Monastery, San Diego, California.

Smith, Seymour P. March 28, 1945. District Med. Office, Twelfth Naval District, San Francisco, California.

Turnage, Hal. April 7, 1945. Alexandria, Virginia.

Underhill, J. L. April 15, 1945. Headquarters FMF PAC, F.P.O. San Francisco, California.

Vandegrift, Archer. March 27, 1945. Letter to General Marshall. Headquarters, US Marine Corps.

Vandegrift, Mildred. March 27, 1945. Commandant's house, Marine Barracks.

VanSant, K. F. April 23, 1945. USS *Wisconsin*. FMF, F.P.O San Francisco, California.

Virden, Kay (Mrs. Frank). March 26, 1945. Evanston, Illinois.

Whaley, Louis. April 9, 1945. F.P.O. New York, New York.

USS Rupertus

Forrestal, James. June 11, 1945. Letter to Mrs. William H. Rupertus designating her sponsor of the USS *Rupertus* (DD-851).